X

QUEEN *of* VAUDEVILLE

Q̶UEEN of V̶AUDEVILLE

The Story of EVA TANGUAY

ANDREW L. ERDMAN

CORNELL UNIVERSITY PRESS • ITHACA AND LONDON

First published 2012 by Cornell University Press

Printed in the United States of America

Library of Congress Cataloging-in-Publication Data

Erdman, Andrew L., 1965–
  Queen of vaudeville : the story of Eva Tanguay / Andrew L. Erdman.
    p. cm.
  Includes bibliographical references and index.
  ISBN 978-0-8014-4970-3 (cloth : alk. paper)
  1. Tanguay, Eva, 1878–1947. 2. Women entertainers—United States—Biography.
3. Vaudeville—United States—History—20th century. I. Title.
  PN2287.T164E73 2012
  791.092—dc23   [B] 2012011311

Cornell University Press strives to use environmentally responsible suppliers and materials to the fullest extent possible in the publishing of its books. Such materials include vegetable-based, low-VOC inks and acid-free papers that are recycled, totally chlorine-free, or partly composed of nonwood fibers. For further information, visit our website at www.cornellpress.cornell.edu.

Cloth printing   10 9 8 7 6 5 4 3 2 1

For Mary B.

Contents
⌇

Acknowledgments

THERE ARE a great many people whose useful and generous help made this book a reality. First I'd like to thank Dan Johansson and his mother, Barbara Johnson. As the surviving members of Eva Tanguay's immediate family, they were immensely helpful in supplying pictures, letters, and anecdotes about their famed relative's life in and out of vaudeville. Elaine Dufresne, Barbara Johnson's sister-in-law, also helped by first putting me in touch with Dan, "the family historian," and his mother.

Archivists, both professional and amateur, and librarians aided me greatly in my research. In particular, I want to acknowledge Susy Doolittle of the Essex County Historical Society; Devon Dawson, formerly of the Holyoke History Room, and its present administrator, Michael Baron; Nancy Gray Garvin of the Ashfield Historical Society; the entire staff of the Benson Ford Research Center; Sylvia Wang of the Shubert Archive; Michael Kirley of the Los Angeles Public Library; Dace Taube and Ned Comstock of the University of Southern California libraries; Julie Graham of the UCLA library; Bob Britton and Céline Wojtala of the Time Inc. Archive; and Carol Booker, Grace Lesure, Roger Howes, Lt. Col. (Ret.) Robert A. Howes, and Kimball Howes for their genealogical assistance. Also helpful in supplying ancestry information were Ron Allen and Art Corbeil.

I was fortunate to receive input and assistance from individuals in and around the Eastern Townships of Quebec, many of whom supplied information and impressions about the Tanguays and their French-Canadian forebears. In this regard, the help of Jacques Robert, Manon Vaillancourt, Lorraine Lemelin, Helene Liard, Sophie Morell, Nancy Duchesne, Sara Line Laroche of the Association touristique et culturelle de dudswell, and Regent Tanguay of the Tanguay Family Association was indispensable.

Other individuals I'd like to thank include Beth Touchton, relative of Al Parado (at one time Eva's love interest and musical director), who kindly supplied me with photographs; Mark Berger, creator of a website devoted to Julian Eltinge (who was one of Eva's more bizarre dalliances); Frank Cullen of *The Vaudeville Times;* Daniel Uytiepo of the Hollywood Forever Cemetery, where Eva is entombed; Judith Taylor, MD, whose knowledge of medicine and medical history was an aid to this effort; and both Jim Wilson and Marion Wilson (no relation), former classmates of mine in the PhD Program in Theatre at the City University of New York Graduate Center. I would also like to acknowledge the input of Yfat Reiss Gendell of the Foundry Literary + Media agency in New York. I am further indebted to Professor Kathleen Golden of Edinboro University in Pennsylvania, who produced and directed the documentary film *Three Vaudeville Women,* as well as Professor Robert W. Snyder of Rutgers University's Newark campus for his invaluable insights and assistance in developing my manuscript. Finally, I would like to thank my editor at Cornell University Press, Michael J. McGandy, for all of his many efforts.

On a personal note, I'd like to acknowledge the support and wisdom of the actress Mary Birdsong, without which this book would not be what it is. I am also grateful for the suggestions, guidance, and input of the songwriter and composer Mary Brett Lorson.

Introduction

༄

The Most Famous Performer
in America

IN 1905, Eva Tanguay was appearing at a vaudeville theater in the small city of Vincennes, Indiana. She played before a "fashionable" crowd, according to a journalist who was there, trotting out songs from her recent hit Broadway musical, *The Sambo Girl*. Vincennes, a municipality of some 10,250 souls, lay on the banks of the Wabash River by the Illinois border. It had a proud history stretching back to the eighteenth century when it was a fur trading post and fort in the French Louisiana Territory. The French-Canadian nobleman for whom the city was named was unfortunately burned at the stake in 1735 by an army of angry Chickasaw Indians against whom he had waged war. Forty-four years later, during the American Revolution, the Colonial military commander George Rogers Clark put Vincennes on the historical map when he defeated a much larger British force at nearby Fort Sackville through cunning, trickery, and unusually good shooting. Vincennes remained a fairly peaceful place for the next 116 years.[1]

Then Eva showed up.

The people of Vincennes had long enjoyed theatrical entertainments, having erected their first playhouse in 1806. Recently, they favored "the lighter vaudeville plays," according to a history of Vincennes published in 1902. More important, the venue was a natural stop on the way from Indianapolis to Saint Louis. And since performers like Eva made their living by playing circuits that stretched around the country, a place like Vincennes was as solid a gig as any.[2]

As Eva took the stage, the crowd broke into applause. She had recently gained notoriety in New York and was on her way to national stardom. After saying her hellos, she launched into a set of upbeat, off-kilter songs accompanied by jerky movements that in some people's eyes may, or may not, have passed for dance. A little boy sat among the well-dressed throng. Eva began a rendition of "I Don't Care," her signature number, and other tunes from *Sambo*. The little boy whistled. He liked this crazy Eva lady; something about her was full of childlike vigor, even if her songs made some of the grownups blush.

But when Eva heard the boy whistle, she stopped in her tracks, ceased her warbling, and trained a suspicious eye on the entire crowd. In a heartbeat she went from devil-may-care frivolity to crotchety anger. The throng was stunned. The curly-haired entertainer stepped toward the footlights at the edge of the stage and roasted the audience, giving them a stern lesson in how to express themselves and when to simply be quiet and listen. The little boy was probably terrified. He had meant only to show his appreciation. But somehow he had made the funny lady really mad.[3]

In the years to follow, Eva Tanguay became famous for inexplicable, often outrageous mood shifts, usually backstage and offstage but sometimes right there in the limelight. It never seemed to put audiences off. In fact, Eva's temperament, ever a challenge to her colleagues, became a source of fascination to her devoted followers. Who knew what she might do at her next show? Scream and run off the stage? Take a dozen encores? Throw money at the crowd? With Eva Tanguay, soon to be the reigning queen of vaudeville, anything was possible.

If Eva's moods were inscrutable, so too was her popularity. In her peak decade, approximately 1908–1918, nobody quite knew why she had become the most famous and popular live entertainer of her day. To many, it did not matter. Somehow, she was what the theatergoing masses wanted. She was the jewel in the crown of a mass-market brand of entertainment whose size and scope had never been seen before. Embracing scandal, flouting conventional morality, and luxuriating in an abundance of furs, diamonds, and automobiles, she became an early-twentieth-century megacelebrity. From the stage, she ruled a popular culture that bristled with opportunity, seduction, and the kind of chaos that was both glamorous and sordid. She delivered frenzied performances that at once sated audiences and left them thirsting for more. They did not come to Eva looking for an astounding vocal range, gifted dancing, or impressive acting; if they had, they would have been sorely disappointed.

Her fans came for something else, something vital and unique. They came for *Eva*. And she always gave it to them.

Like "I Don't Care" and other hits, including "I Want Someone to Go Wild with Me," Eva's songs were topical, suggestive, and lively, though rarely tuneful. They were a marked departure from the sentimental parlor music of the 1890s. Her costumes were equally lively—and then some. One was made of then-new Lincoln pennies, which she yanked off one at a time and tossed into the audience, marking perhaps the only time in modern memory when a leering crowd collected the tips at a striptease.

A little later in her career, Eva let the press take photos of her playing with two young but formidable-looking lion cubs. "In all the months that my lions have been in pictures, none of them ever bit a lady more than once!" she gaily explained to a theater full of fans. "Well—*once* was *enough*." The crowd broke into hysterics. "Why, this lioness wouldn't *hurt* you—she's so old she lost one of her teeth last week!" Eva continued. "She's got plenty [of] teeth left for *me*, right *now*…she'll probably lose another tooth *next* week [but] she won't lose that tooth in *me*, you can bet on *that*!" Merely looking at the words, it is hard to appreciate their humor. But it was never lost on her thousands of followers. Eva talked about predatory wildcats in a way that made fans fear for the animals' well-being.[4]

At other times, Eva employed puns that could hardly be described as timeless comedy. But coming from her, they killed, as comics like to say when the audience dies with laughter. "Why, that lioness won't kill *any* one. She's *ten* years old and I call her '*Lizzie*,'" declared Eva. "Yeah? I know a man who's got a *Ford* that's *twenty* years old, and he calls her 'Lizzie' too, but *she's* killed forty-two human *beings*, and three traffic cops, and she's *still* going strong," joked the comedienne, referencing the perils of the new Ford Model T motorcar, popularly known as the Tin Lizzie. "I'm a good *Christian*," quipped Eva, "a *martyr* to my art, and I get around to the theater early, but I'm not an early *Christian* martyr, and I'm *not* going to be thrown to *any* lions!" Her gag lines shot out of her mouth with all the harmony of machine-gun rounds. The folks in the seats were happily slain.[5]

It is nearly impossible to convey the rapid-fire cadence and mirthful lunacy with which Eva delivered her patter. Coming from another performer or simply read on a page, they fall flat. But coming from Eva Tanguay they were box-office gold. The eccentric songs, outrageous costumes, freakish dancing, and untranslatable jokes made one thing clear: her shows were more than the sum of their parts. "About the time I first began to go to vaudeville shows Miss Tanguay was the most famous

Figure 1. Eva flies the flags.
Eva in a typical getup: timely, eccentric, popular . . .
and just a little bit outrageous.
(From the Collections of The Henry Ford.)

· · · · · · · · ·

performer in America," remembered a *Time* columnist in 1931. Not surprisingly, the legendary Mae West consciously modeled herself on Eva.[6]

To many, she personified the popular theater of her day more than any of her contemporaries. "To her generation, Eva Tanguay *was* American vaudeville, and for almost its entire existence, she *was* the medium's greatest female star," wrote Anthony Slide in *The Encyclopedia of Vaudeville*. Douglas

Gilbert, a chronicler of the popular stage, had this to say back in 1940: "It is virtually impossible to overestimate Tanguay's personality, or her influence in vaudeville. In the years she was tops, this woman alone jolted the maudlin period of the 1900's away from its eye-dabbing with the vigor of unashamed sex." In today's terms, it is possible to compare her to Madonna (as others have done) or perhaps Lady Gaga (as others will likely do). Though Eva did not have the dancing skills of the Material Girl or the songwriting gifts of Gaga, she nonetheless turned being outrageous into a desirable talent. It is also possible to see a touch of Eva's spirit in the self-promoting antics of Kim Kardashian, a media personality with little talent other than extending her fifteen minutes in the spotlight. Rarely have a performer and her art form been so perfectly matched. Eva's impact, creativity, and effect on audiences all live on in U.S. entertainment. The outsized personalities of today's stage, screen, and Web all keep alive the glittery, fast-paced spirit of vaudeville's wild girl, even if they are unaware that they carry on her legacy.[7]

To understand Eva Tanguay—pronounced "TANG-way"—it is crucial to know the world in which she prospered. Eva's realm was the city. Some of the cities she lived and worked in were vast, like New York or Chicago, and some were more modest, like Iowa City, Louisville, Kentucky, or even Vincennes, Indiana. But no matter the locale, Eva's success and growth ran parallel with the flourishing North American urban scene. Her fans came from the swelling ranks of the white-collar workforce along with a healthy scattering of blue-collar working men and women. In Eva's audience were bank clerks and salesgirls, production-line machine minders from the larger factories and social workers from settlement houses where immigrants and the city's working poor sought better lives. Some in attendance were mothers looking for diversion from the worries of home life, while others were young singles whose chief mission, at the moment anyway, was the pursuit of amusement. They were the new urban masses, and each day it seemed their ranks grew larger and more influential.

Between 1900 and 1920, the demographic makeup of the United States was rapidly shifting. In these two decades, the population of cities and large towns rose 80 percent, to 54 million, while the corresponding rural number inched up a mere 11 percent, to 51 million; in this period urbanites came to outnumber their rural counterparts for the first time in the history of the republic. In the cities, work hours were down and wages were up. The simpler, family- and community-oriented values of small-town existence, the way of life for most in generations past, were quickly becoming antiquated. In their place a new culture rose up, one based on

Figure 2. Never shy.
Eva opened herself up to audiences—emotionally, sensually,
aesthetically—in a way few performers ever had before.
She would be the last great performer of the unmediated, live-only era.
(Private collection, courtesy of Beth Touchton.)

· · · · · · · · ·

commerce, the drudgery of labor, and escape via mass leisure. The city, in the words of the historian David Nasaw, was "becoming as much a place of play as a place of work," a milieu focused on the ethos of pleasure.[8]

Work yielded something called "disposable income," which could be spent on things other than housing, food, and education. Consumer products abounded—useful but not essential objects like fashionable, mass-produced clothing and inexpensive jewelry. It could also buy fun in a city full of diversions.[9] There were dance halls and eateries, baseball games and amusement parks. There were things called dime museums that were not so much repositories of high art as storefronts full of semiconvincing oddities and freaks, a stationary version of the traveling carnival and famously embellished by showman P. T. Barnum. For the thicker-skinned, there were pubs and concert saloons, "haunts" of "juvenile delinquents"

6

and "libertines" among others, where the booze flowed and some of the women were not just waitresses. For the less daring, there were parks, beaches, and zoos. Increasingly, of course, there were movies, though in its early period, the cinema was largely a gaudy, shabby affair. Once lured in by the showy facade, pleasure-seekers were led to a darkened back room that had only a small screen and maybe a piano accompanist. They were known as nickelodeons, though the true price may have actually been a dime.[10]

For a few crucial decades, however, the premier amusement of city folks was vaudeville theater. Taking its name from a concoction of French musical and theatrical terms that stretched back centuries, and its content from pretty much every form of popular entertainment that existed in the United States, vaudeville ruled from the late 1890s through about 1920. Vaudeville shows were a few hours' worth of diverse entertainments, a kind of theatrical hodgepodge with one routine following another onto the stage: fiddle players, barbershop quartets, Levantine acrobats, stand-up comedians (known back then as "monologists"), trained animals, lecturers, strongmen, eccentric dancers, ballet dancers, belly dancers, actors in short plays, and sundry other entertainments. The acts were all situated on a single bill around a headliner, the big-name star who filled the seats and got perhaps twenty minutes of stage time in comparison to the five or ten minutes allotted the supporting troupers. Whatever your taste, there was "something for everybody" in vaudeville, it was said, but the headliner drove the show and kept the theater packed.[11]

The behind-the-scenes power brokers who controlled vaudeville, a class of businessmen who enjoyed a level of wealth and respect unthinkable to their predecessors, valued Eva above all the other headliners in their industry. Even if they sometimes scratched their heads trying to figure out *why* their customers loved her, they had to admit that the eccentric comedienne was a surefire moneymaker and cultural icon. Of this they were regularly reminded.

It was 1908, the year that saw pioneering transmissions of long-distance radio waves, the construction of the first true skyscraper (the forty-seven-story Singer Building in Manhattan), and the introduction of the toaster by General Electric. Communications, skylines, and sunny-side-up eggs would never be the same. In the last week of February, despite the cold weather, Eva was heating up Keith & Proctor's 125th Street vaudeville theater, one of the top "big-time" houses in New York City. The theater's stone facade capped by an ornate pediment looked like a castle of fun amid retail stores brimmed by striped awnings. The name "Keith & Proctor's"

7

rose high above the theater, hoisted on a metal latticework. Inside, with Eva headlining, it was no surprise that every seat had been sold; in fact, extra chairs had to be set up in the boxes. There were also four rows of standees. The queen of vaudeville, as she was sometimes called, came on and sang seven songs to the throng. The audience demanded six bows and three speeches before letting her leave. With all that shouting, clapping, and carrying-on, many poor folks in the nosebleed seats couldn't have heard very much. (Of course, they only paid a dollar.) After the show was over, the theater manager wrote a memo about Eva to the bigwigs in the head office in which he declared, "This woman is the greatest artist in the profession today." Hyperbolic as that statement may sound, exaggeration was not in his interest. His success was carefully measured by the executives who ran the theater chain in which his concert hall was but a link. He knew he had to keep booking Eva to stay on top; puffing up a sagging performer would only result in his failure. That night Eva showed herself to be the greatest artist of the vaudeville stage. The manager counted on her to do the same the next night and the night after that.

Eva was a particularly valuable element in the vaudeville formula where acts, though disparate, were nonetheless carefully arranged into a program that sought optimal pacing, tone, and buildup (and, toward the end of the show, build-down). With just the opening words, "Hello, everybody!" she could turn around crowds that had grown restive sitting through some clunker acts. More than turning them around, she drove crowds crazy and kept them coming back. In Boston, she caused a "riot." In Philadelphia, the fans simply "would not let her go." Her unbroken, fourteen-month run in New York, spanning the 1908–1909 season, clocked a record, according to the sporting and theatrical newspaper the *New York Clipper*. "She was like nothing else that ever happened on a stage," remembered Edward Marks in *They All Sang,* a history of U.S. entertainment written in the early 1930s.[12]

While Eva packed the theaters wherever she went—and in so doing, drove her salary to $3,500 a week, said to be the highest in vaudeville—she never tried to deny her lack of recognizable talent, happily admitting that she could neither carry a tune nor move her body with anything approaching elegance or style. "As a matter of fact," said this most famous of vaudevillians, "I am not beautiful, I can't sing, I do not know how to dance. I am not even graceful." While some might argue that using self-deprecation helped female comedians like Eva deflect sexist rhetoric, those who saw her perform confirmed that Eva was not being modest. Caroline Caffin, a writer who saw Eva around 1913, described her as "A Song and

Dance Artist who does not dance, cannot sing, is not beautiful, witty or graceful, but who dominates her audience more entirely than anyone on the Vaudeville stage." Still, Caffin attested just as surely to Eva's ability to hypnotize a crowd. When Eva went on, she wrote, "we suddenly find that every one is sitting up, straight and eager," full of "breathless intensity." The orchestra is "playing with new vim," the horns and piano sounding "sharper and louder." Even the "very lights appear to burn brighter, so tense is the atmosphere of expectancy." Then Eva spoke and broke her own spell—or cast a new one. Her "loud chattering voice" pierced the air while the comedienne stretched out her arms, as if embracing the entire audience. Eva was not merely playing up her inability to sing and dance nor was she simply mocking herself. That would have grown stale long before Eva herself ever did.[13]

Ultimately what appealed to theatergoers again and again was Eva's commanding and unique self-presentation. She was able to project individuality and personality in a way few had ever done and at a time when her audiences longed for something striking and highly individualistic. A Chicago journalist who saw Eva in 1907 felt she was a "unique figure in the mimic world of today" with "no counterpart, no imitators and is herself so original, so temperamental that there is not the slightest similarity between her work and that of any other performer on the stage." Another newspaperman concluded, "This exceptional woman is sui generis." She possessed the uncanny ability to lay bare and expose her special personality before crowds in a way that seemed both intimate and yet larger-than-life. She was one of "you," yet she flouted social norms with abandon. Doing so allowed Eva to wrench apart the concept of "talent" from that of "skill" more successfully than any performer before her. In place of adept singing, dancing, and acting, she offered truckloads of charisma and emotion.

Her stage strategy fit the needs of her city-dwelling fan base particularly well. Leisure was now more than just the time between shifts at work. Urban wage earners asserted their independence and identity by the *choices* they made in the amusement realm. If being at the factory, office, or warehouse meant having one's individuality drowned out by a machine, actual or metaphorical, when the five-o'clock whistle sounded, it was time to take things back. Increasingly, urban amusement-seekers hungered for an individual star. They sought someone whose value was based on *who* they were as much as *what* they did—or perhaps more so. Eva showed her fans, who pushed their way onto packed subways and trolley cars and fought to clear a path on bustling sidewalks, that you could be unique without being elite or exceptional. And that was enough. She offered a rousing model of human visibility.[14]

It helped that Eva's own story paralleled the personal history of many in her fan base: they could see themselves in her. She was born on August 1, 1878, into a homogeneous, tight-knit rural community in Quebec. When she was just a young girl, her family moved to the bustling, modern industrial city of Holyoke, Massachusetts. There, she was encouraged by cultural and economic conditions, family needs—and dysfunctions—and ambition to pursue a career onstage. No one knew better than Eva that what once had been provided by ties to clan, community, and posterity, from material needs to emotional solace, now had to be bartered, bargained for, and bought. Whereas tradition once offered structure and meaning, in the new marketplace of the city, it was your ability to convince others of your worth that mattered most.

SOME ENTERTAINERS, both in Eva's day and our own, have managed to turn amusing gimmicks into flash-in-the-pan careers. We all know the stand-up comic who spoke in a weird, foreign accent or the rock band that dressed as robots. Even if Eva's bag of tricks were regarded as a shtick, it was one that nonetheless remained vital and profitable for a long time—a near eternity, actually, in the world of showbiz. In 1915, nearly a decade since she had first started out as a solo act in vaudeville, the *New York Dramatic Mirror* argued that only two other entertainment "artists" boasted followings as large as Eva's: Sarah Bernhardt and Mary Pickford. Not bad company, considering Bernhardt was the most celebrated and influential dramatic actress of her era, while a journalist of the day rightly labeled silent-screen siren Pickford "the most popular motion picture star in the world."[15]

Still more remarkable was the fact that Eva managed to stay on top even when buffeted by scandals that might well have toppled her peers. Her resilience was in part the happy result of her impressive PR skills—her use of the growing news media to present a fascinating personality, as so many modern celebrities now try to do. Eva had no problem conveying what seemed to be contrasting images of herself: erotic yet prudish, argumentative yet coquettish, self-centered yet bighearted. The more one gets to know Eva, the more such paradoxes seem not just part of a brilliant strategy but also a genuine reflection of all the complicated urges that drove her from both within and without. She consorted with many men (including those outside her race and class), decried marriage, and never really sought to be part of a conventional couple, either economically or sexually. Eva managed all this while never suffering the sort of moral outrage that landed Mae West in jail during that sashaying blonde's rise to stardom in the late 1920s.

In some ways, Eva created a persona that both took from the past and looked to the future. She resembled the iconic "Gibson girl," an active, new, freewheeling archetype of womanhood created by the artist Charles Dana Gibson in the popular press of the 1890s, and yet she departed noticeably from Gibson's wholesome aesthetic. In her influential book, *American Beauty,* the historian Lois Banner identified Eva as a "flapper," the playful, boyish symbol of a new kind of femininity that emerged in the 1920s. While Banner rightly credited Eva with opening up new frontiers for women, Eva was not quite a flapper. Nor was she a true Gibson girl. She was part voluptuous icon, part self-defined celebrity, and part lone woman trying to package herself into a winner while struggling with the demons and defects that always threatened to take her down, and eventually did.[16]

While Eva borrowed elements of an emergent, modern female identity, she also synthesized the work of actors and actresses who had come before her. In fact, to get an accurate view of Eva's contribution to the world of entertainment and celebrity, it is crucial to briefly understand her in historical context. Those who labored before Eva, in their own ways, cleared a path for the creative choices she made. Similarly, Eva cleared a broad path in the wilderness over which many of the twentieth and twenty-first century's biggest names have happily bounded. A look at Eva's artistic forebears shows us the way in which she embodied their collective accomplishments and yet transformed them all into something new.

As far as women onstage are concerned, the heritage of performers that led up to Eva can be said to begin with the Jacksonian-era superstar Fanny Kemble (1809–1893). Kemble first bowed before audiences in 1832 at New York City's prestigious Park Theatre. Through her various roles and by means of the plaudits she earned, Kemble demonstrated how a woman could succeed in the world outside the home. She also accomplished something else quite impressive by putting distance between the ideas of actress and prostitute, two professions that since Shakespeare's time had been intertwined in public opinion. Kemble's virtue remained undiminished as she treaded the boards. Now a woman could see the possibility of selling her talents in public, as it were, rather than languishing—and laboring—in domestic doldrums as a wife and mother. It was a distant but important first step toward a world in which

Eva could be sexually alluring without being thought a whore, and where she did not have to fake a desire to marry and have children.[17]

Charlotte Cushman followed hot on Fanny Kemble's heels. The remarkable Cushman (1816–1876) did not slip by chance into the role of actress, but, like Eva, strove consciously from an early age to achieve stardom. She mastered a variety of roles and not only ascended higher than many of her famous male peers but did so without resorting to sensational displays of her body. Nor did she rely on conventional notions of prettiness. She also became financially comfortable without any man's help. Cushman dared to portray grotesque characters, such as the wraithlike gypsy Meg Merrilies in the stage adaptation of *Guy Mannering* (1837), and she famously—and convincingly—played Romeo, opposite her sister in the role of Juliet. When asked who he thought was the greatest living performer, Edwin Booth, perhaps the most celebrated American actor of the 1800s—and the brother of Lincoln's assassin, John Wilkes Booth—unhesitatingly named Charlotte Cushman. Toward the end of her career, Cushman gained notoriety for chronically announcing her retirement, not unlike a modern-day sports or pop-music icon. Between the late 1850s and early 1860s, she orchestrated no fewer than three farewell tours, generating what we might today call buzz.[18]

Kemble and Cushman established new paradigms for what a woman could do onstage. But Anna Cora Mowatt (1819–1870) was not content to leave it at that. In addition to acting, Mowatt muscled her way into the decidedly male world of playwriting, gaining renown for her hugely popular 1845 comedy, *Fashion*. As an actress, she broke free of prevailing norms of feminine decorum by turning herself into a theatrical athlete. To prepare for one role, she not only mastered the art of fencing but also pumped iron with dumbbells to, as she put it, "overcome the constitutional weakness of my arms and chest." Eva, in her own day, was to become known for her displays of energy and endurance under the lights by "wriggling her hips, waggling her breasts, kicking her legs wildly, and shaking her derriere," in the words of the theater scholar Jane B. Westerfield. One observer who saw Eva perform compared her to a prizefighter "who depends entirely on jumping, rushing, and slugging." It was sometimes alleged that Eva covered four miles during a typical show! Others reported that Eva's muscles were so tight after her high-speed stage antics that she had to have her calves flogged with wooden planks to loosen them up. Eva was clearly willing to suffer for her art.[19]

While actresses were boldly striking out in new directions, breaking social taboos and pushing cultural boundaries, men too were laying the groundwork for new notions of artistry, celebrity, and success. Specifically, male performers were starting to play dramatic roles in ways that reflected their own distinctive personalities as individuals. This let their supposedly authentic selves shine through even the most famous characters they portrayed. Notable in this regard was the Englishman William Macready (1793–1873), the so-called eminent tragedian, who made numerous U.S. tours in the 1820s and 1840s. Macready considered his acting to reflect his genuine self in a way that previous generations might have found alien or distasteful. Though now commonplace in the acting world, his psychological identification with the characters he played was considered groundbreaking at the time. In the title role in James Sheridan Knowles's *Virginius,* Macready said of the scene in which he gave his daughter away to be married, "I spoke from my soul—the tears came from my heart." Like other actors of his day, Macready was trying to introduce a new, more natural style of acting, one that moved away from the bombast and hysterics so popular in the early nineteenth century. To that end, Macready would do things like turn his back to the audience and, when penning letters and notes onstage, actually write out their full contents. Such attempts at realism were revolutionary.[20]

Macready and his brethren not only brought their own personalities to their roles, they further blurred the lines between their onstage and offstage personas by suggesting that they were above the common fray of humanity—and also by flinging copious mud at their peers. Women, relative newcomers to the world of theatrical celebrity, were not yet known for such haughtiness and slander, though Eva would become no stranger to these tactics. Macready most famously came into conflict with the popular U.S. actor Edwin Forrest (1806–1872), whom he saw as unartistic and fake. (He also sneered at Fanny Kemble, deeming her "ignorant of the very first rudiments of her art.") It won Macready few friends in the profession. But it kept him in the headlines, and made him popular with ticket buyers for a long time[21]

Needless to say, Edwin Forrest did not take kindly to Macready's jabs. He was a formidable, barrel-chested man given to highly physical displays of bluster and bravado in his portrayal of the title character in *Metamora; or, The Last of the Wampanoags,* a popular play about a Native American chief that debuted in 1829, or as the barking-mad King Lear. Described as a "man of powerful physique and great vocal strength," Forrest grew to hate Macready, a sentiment only amplified by Forrest's paranoia. Animosity between the actors exploded when mobs of their fans clashed on the night of May 10, 1849, as each squared off in interpretations of *Macbeth* in lower

Manhattan. Armed state militiamen attempting to quell the violence ended up killing twenty-five civilians and injuring a hundred others. The influence and power of popular actors had reached a new peak. But the most dominant actor of the period was the legendary Edwin Booth (1833–1893). Born illegitimately to the well-known British actor Junius Brutus Booth and Mary Ann Holmes, U.S.-born Edwin grew so powerful (and haughty) thorough his memorable portrayals of Shakespeare's heroes, evincing a nuanced, "natural" quality that was considered uniquely American, that his career suffered hardly a blow after his brother John Wilkes assassinated President Abraham Lincoln.[22]

In modern terms, it might be said that Macready, Forrest, and Booth were "branding" themselves as actors: promoting their image with a slew of identifiable and appealing traits. But no figure in U.S. entertainment was more successful and influential in this effort than P. T. Barnum. Phineas Taylor Barnum (1810–1891) was born to a humble shopkeeper and his wife in Bethel, Connecticut. Though not explicitly a performer, Barnum became more famous than any other show-business personality of the pre-Eva age by exhibiting and publicizing attractions ranging from sideshow freaks to acclaimed international singers. His first big success came in 1835 when he put on display a woman named Joice Heth who Barnum claimed was 161 years old and had worked as George Washington's nurse. From there, he promoted a seven-year-old boy named Charles Stratton who, owing to a pituitary disorder, weighed about fifteen pounds and stood only twenty-five inches tall. Perfectly proportioned, articulate, and talented in mimicry, Stratton became "General Tom Thumb." On tour and at Barnum's American Museum—an oddity hall rather than a temple of high art, located on lower Broadway in New York City—Thumb became a smashing success, "the perfect man-child, the perpetual boy, appealing to all ages and conditions," in the words of the biographer and historian Neil Harris. P. T. Barnum went on to even greater success backing the Swedish singing prodigy Jenny Lind, as well as producing popular circus shows and writing the best-selling autobiography, *The Life of P. T. Barnum,* published in 1855.

In a sense, Barnum made the United States resemble a vast stage; his magic involved training a spotlight on the playful and eccentric personalities who populated that stage, then growing rich off the masses eager to pay for a glimpse. The most successful entertainers learned Barnum's lessons well, especially famed escape artist Harry Houdini, who would one day become a vaudeville contemporary of Eva's. Houdini, born Ehrich Weiss (1874–1926), was celebrated as the "King of Handcuffs." One of his favorite ploys involved walking into police stations and challenging the cops to put him in manacles, from which he would inevitably escape. In so doing, Houdini turned the urban world around him into a sort of impromptu vaudeville sketch.[23]

The work of Macready, Forrest, Barnum, and Edwin Booth helped build the U.S. theater into a vastly popular and successful enterprise during the nineteenth century. Its growth was also aided by the rise of transcontinental railroads and modern corporate management, which together supported systematized, large-scale tours. These men were stars and impresarios who could command princely salaries, earn vast sums for powerful theater owners and producers, play by their own social rules, and take artistic risks by, for example, demanding to do marathon runs of their favorite plays. While their cultural, artistic, and financial freedoms only grew as the age wore on, the same was not true for their female peers. By dint of certain cultural and economic conditions, not to mention a few significantly timed historical accidents, women performers increasingly found their freedoms diminished in a patriarchal industry. The bravado and dignity won by Fanny Kemble, Charlotte Cushman, and Anna Cora Mowatt did not translate so readily to the women coming after them in the years during and after the American Civil War. A theater business run by powerful men began to prize women's bodily allure and sexuality over their personality and acting talent. In this climate, actresses and other stage women of the later nineteenth century struggled to balance their more sophisticated abilities with their appeal as sex objects.

Perhaps the first lady thespian to attempt this balancing act was Adah Isaacs Menken (1835–1868). Known as a striking beauty with a mysterious past, Menken was most famous for playing the title role of the 1861 drama *Mazeppa* in which she shed her clothes. It raised eyebrows and titillated many audience members. But somehow, by virtue of Menken's artistry and talent at advertising, neither she nor the show lost the mantle of middle-class respectability.

Though Adah Isaacs Menken made a name by showing off her body, she never saw herself as a hapless victim. Indeed, she managed to make her charismatic personality into an object of public fascination as well. With the help of a growing newspaper and magazine industry, she built a storied, scandalous, larger-than-life persona that was hard to separate from an underlying "real" individual. In the words of the historian Renée M. Sentilles, "Once famous, Menken did not sell tickets to plays but rather to see the Menken." In due time, Eva would crystallize such efforts into a high art.[24]

In Menken's wake, conditions continued to worsen for actresses who were unable or unwilling to pose, at least in part, as sexual objects. In 1866, a troupe of comely British dancers arrived in New York. But when the venue they were to play burned down, they suddenly found themselves transplanted to a theater called Niblo's Garden, putting on a send-up of the Faust legend called *The Black Crook*. It ran for 475 performances (an unheard-of run in those days) largely because of some abbreviated costumes, the occasional hint of cleavage, and scenery and costuming schemes that were glittery, diaphanous, and designed to entice the senses. Though restrained by the standards of today, and of Eva's day, *The Black Crook* not only excited urban theatergoers, it drew moral outrage from clergy and social do-gooders.

Shortly after *Crook* reached the end of its first run—it was to be revived at least eight times between 1868 and 1892—the English actress Lydia Thompson brought a group of "British Blondes" to New York to capitalize on the hunger for views of the female leg onstage. Her most famous production, *Ixion; or, The Man at the Wheel,* was made up of song parodies and topical references stitched together with puns, high-kicking ladies, and plenty of costumes cut to reveal the thighs of dancers. The Blondes, who really invented modern burlesque as we know it, were also buxom and curvy, a departure from earlier ideals of feminine beauty in U.S. culture.[25]

Like Adah Isaacs Menken, Lydia Thompson tried to sell her personality as much as her pretty face and form, even while her Blondes remained veritable bodies without brains. But she could not attempt Charlotte Cushman's artistic grotesquery or Anna Cora Mowatt's mannish (for the age) athleticism. Rather, she had to be charming and effervescent, charismatic but decorous. Fortunately, Thompson's skilled dancing rarely went unnoticed.[26]

The decades following Adah Isaacs Menken and Lydia Thompson saw women's roles constrained further in the large-scale U.S. industry that was popular theater. Powerful syndicates packaged elaborate tours that swung from one hub city to another and delighted audiences in smaller locales along the way. Major stars linked up with stock companies whose veteran troupers were versed in a vast number of popular plays, for runs of varying lengths. More and more money rode on each production as backers, usually based in New York, laid out growing capital on competing productions. With a few exceptions, women became exotic showpieces who could reliably appeal to (heterosexual, male) theatergoers, while megastars such as Edwin Booth and Joseph Jefferson III (1829–1905), famous for playing the lead in a stage adaptation of *Rip Van Winkle,* set the standards of stage artistry. To break this unfortunate pattern would require a woman from a different culture, one with a less-disrupted chain of female prodigies. If she were talented enough, as well as uniquely charismatic and iconoclastic, so much the better. Luckily for Eva and female performers to follow, Sarah Bernhardt arrived just in time. Though French, Bernhardt's influence on both sides of the Atlantic was incalculable and exceeded that of any actress before her.[27]

Sarah Bernhardt (1844–1923), the most storied dramatic actress of her day, was the daughter of a Jewish courtesan living in Paris. She trained at the esteemed Comédie-Française, France's legendary theater and guardian of its dramatic canon. There, she honed her skills in oratory, dramatic interpretation, and stage movement. Before she was twenty years old, and despite some notable run-ins with those in charge of the Comédie, Bernhardt had become recognized as a leading "classic tragedienne," eventually known for playing an array of roles from Shakespeare and the French neoclassical dramatist Racine, to the "well-made" plays of the late nineteenth century, most famously *La dame aux camélias* (sometimes mistakenly referred to as *Camille*), by Alexandre Dumas, *fils.* As her career grew, Sarah Bernhardt, like Adah Isaacs Menken, made it clear that it was she *herself,* rather than the vaunted roles she played, that accounted for her star power. Her trademark gestures and attitudes were easily recognizable from one role to the next, be it a contemporary melodrama or something from the classical stock. Her dramatic abilities were unmatched, yet her unique persona was never lost in the parts she assumed. Theatergoers, critics, and the gossip-hungry public loved her. She even made a tour of vaudeville.[28]

By the time Eva began her career in 1890s, directly in the wake of Bernhardt, who remained tremendously successful onstage and on the silent screen, a woman who wanted to make it big in show business had therefore to master related, if distinct, demands. First, she had to possess a tantalizing personality, one that stretched from the stage to her personal life. So she had to be comfortable with, if not able to actively manipulate, the emerging mass media's coverage of that "personal" life. Indeed, from the 1830s onward, but particularly by Eva's time, cheap, mass-circulation newspapers (and the magazines that were influenced by them) devoted a great deal of space to revealing the "real" person behind the famous facade, thereby molding our modern concept of celebrity. Second, an actress had somehow to deploy sex appeal in a way that would not offend middle-class theatergoers (especially women) but would draw the eyes of men accustomed both to leg shows and at least the artifice of the female figure. Finally, a woman aspiring to fame in the entertainment world had to challenge male primacy while remaining feminine enough, in the

Figure 3. Eva and her amazing, cyclonic legs.
Eva claimed she tried to cover up her legs for fear of moral censure—but she
winked knowingly while making such a statement. In vaudeville,
a performer's legs could make or break her career.
(From the Collections of The Henry Ford.)

· · · · · · · · ·

conventional sense, not to repel prospective fans and society's established
critics. It was a worthy challenge.[29]

As we have seen, appreciating Eva in her historical context means
understanding the ways in which stage celebrities before her, both women
and men, had changed the profession and won success on a mass scale. Yet
it would be a grave error to see Eva as merely the culmination of work that
began with Fanny Kemble and continued through Sarah Bernhardt. Eva was

so much more. She took the allure of personality, which players like Lydia Thompson had leavened with sex appeal, and made it the very centerpiece of her art. Such were personal magnetism and idiosyncrasy in Eva's hands that she no longer had to pretend they were justified by a prodigious skill in, say, dancing or joke-writing. She was popular in every sense of the word, reminding fans of the glory they possessed simply by being themselves. With Eva, the age of individual-as-entertainment had begun.[30]

In our day, the shadow of Eva Tanguay may be seen in Madonna videos, Lady Gaga concerts, Sarah Silverman comedy routines, and, in years gone by, the work of Bette Midler, Cher, and Janis Joplin. Her legacy permeates the work of talented, iconoclastic women (and some men) of the entertainment world whether they are aware of possessing Eva's artistic DNA or not. But if you wish to see more obvious evidence of "the girl who made vaudeville famous," as she was known, it is there too. You just have to know where to look.

Check out the 1948 William Dieterle film, *Portrait of Jennie,* starring Jennifer Jones and Joseph Cotten, the next time they show it on after-hours TV or a classic-movie cable channel. Jennie is a girl out of an artist's imagination, a petite, alluring specter from the vaudeville era. Cotten's character, Eben, and his taxi-hack pal, Gus, discover an old newspaper from 1910 that Jennie has left behind. Opening it, they see an ad for Hammerstein's Victoria, one of the country's most famous vaudeville theaters until its closing in 1915. Appearing at the Victoria are Will Rogers, "expert lariat thrower," the Appletons, "Novelty High Wire Act," and, above all, "Eva Tanguay, the American Comedienne"—mangled as "co-me-dee-ANNIE" in Gus's Hollywood-imagined, working-class patois. Eva was never known as "the American Comedienne." In a movie released a year after her death, she was already misremembered. But the point is clear enough: Eva was vaudeville, and vaudeville was Eva.

You may also spy Eva's ghost by riding mass transit in New York City. On the tiled wall of the subway station at Twenty-third Street and Broadway, there is a clever display of what has come to be known as subway art.[31] Depictions of hats and bonnets worn by New York's legends of yesteryear are rendered in colorful mosaic, floating at about eye level. There are plaques too, telling you whose headwear you are looking at. Sophie Tucker's is here, as is Lillian Russell's. A little further down, see the lid worn by Jimmy Walker, New York's mayor in the late 1920s, a singing, dancing dandy who was forced out of office on corruption charges. Houdini's red-banded, straw boater is upside down, as though he were in the middle of an escape act.

Then, near the Twenty-third Street station sign itself, is a cute straw affair with a shallow crown, wide brim, bluish band, and embellishment resembling butterfly wings. The plaque below it reads: "Eva Tanguay. Entertainer." As trains roll into the station, bouncing noise and light off the shiny, tiled walls, it is possible for a moment to imagine Eva Tanguay bolting onstage at Keith & Proctor's Twenty-third Street theater to waves of thunderous applause that subsided only because the queen of vaudeville was now ready to start her show.

1

♋

Freak Baby and the Paper City

EVA TANGUAY once claimed that her father was a Parisian doctor who had set out for the New World from the Old, conquering
the rigors of frontier life and thereby reinventing himself. But like
other assertions she made, this one appears largely false. She may have
fabricated such a tale about her father in part to distance herself psycho-
logically from him. Or she may have been employing a tactic popular
with other actresses of the day, who revised their true backstories to make
themselves appear more interesting. Adah Isaacs Menken long claimed
that her father had been a Jewish merchant (mildly interesting, given the
era), while Anna Held, wife of the legendary showman Florenz Ziegfeld,
boasted of highbrow Parisian lineage despite the fact that she was half
Polish.[1]

What was beyond dispute is that Eva Tanguay's father, Joseph Octave
Tanguay, came from French-Canadian stock going back at least six
generations. The father of Eva's father was also named Joseph and worked
as a farmer, according to a local register. His predecessors had also worked
the land, but farming life, it would seem, was not for Joseph Octave
Tanguay. In May 1860, before he was twenty-two, he received what
passed back then for a degree in medicine. Dr. Tanguay likely learned
his trade within an antiquated apprenticeship system, though he may also
have briefly attended Montreal's l'École de médecine et de chirurgie. By
1847, the provincial College of Physicians and Surgeons would require
licensure and standardized training, and it was this body that formally
recognized him as a doctor on July 7, 1877. In those first days of his

medical practice, there was little to hold young Dr. Tanguay back. He and cousin Charles Tanguay struck out for the town of Weedon, Quebec, and set up shop.[2]

Joseph Octave Tanguay, *fils,* not only took his medical degree in 1860, he also took a wife. On December 1, 1860, having thrice declared in church their intention of so doing (as tradition required), Joseph Tanguay married Adèle Pajeau with the blessings of both their fathers and a witness named A. Malhiot. Adèle Pajeau was the daughter of a shoemaker, Marcellin Pajeau (sometimes spelled "Pageau"), the husband of Adele Allard. The Pajeaus, while Francophone, were American born. They hailed from the town of Keeseville in upstate New York, across majestic Lake Champlain from Burlington, Vermont.[3]

Newlyweds Dr. and Mrs. Tanguay moved to the Eastern Township of Marbleton, under ten miles from Weedon, where they occupied a number of residences, often sharing the cramped quarters of boarding houses and simple wood-framed structures. It was said that Dr. Tanguay was "well known and loved" by the local peoples, a "well-remembered...country doctor" who made the rounds, traveling, at times even relocating, to the villages of Coaticook, Sherbrooke, and Robinson. He plied his trade wherever patients needed attention and had cash to pay.[4]

On November 1, 1861, Joseph Octave and Adèle Pajeau Tanguay had their first child, a son. The infant was promptly baptized, perhaps because he was sickly and it was feared he might die. The boy was also named Joseph Octave, and his godmother, Matilde Lafrance, signed the birth certificate. Seven years passed before the appearance of the next Tanguay child. Adolphe Étienne Tanguay was born July 4, 1868. Sometime in his youth—it is not known exactly when—Adolphe Étienne became "Mark." Six years after Mark was born, the Tanguays welcomed their first female child, Blanche, born Agnès Blanche Tanguay, on July 7, 1874, in the town of Coaticook near the U.S. border. She was baptized there as well, eleven days hence.[5]

By 1878, the Tanguays and their three children had returned to the hamlet of Marbleton. And it was here, in this microscopic metropolis, not far from the United States and yet somehow worlds away, on the plowshare's edge between the rural past and industrial modernity, that their fourth and final child, a baby girl, was born. Hélène Eva Tanguay arrived in the world the first day of August 1878. She weighed but five pounds and later claimed to have been as many inches long. For three days she barely moved. Her parents, despite her father's medical efforts, feared the worst. The infant Eva was placed in a sewing basket "improvised as an incubator" and set beneath the kitchen stove so that the heat might revive the tiny girl.

When she had later become a star, Eva looked back on the circumstances of her infancy and cast them in Barnum-esque terms. For nearly a year, she said, she barely grew or put on weight. She once eagerly told a reporter that people came from all over to see "Dr. Tanguay's freak baby," now appearing in the Tanguays' new home at Harding Corner, a cluster of modest dwellings and simple shops that passed for the business district of the Lime Ridge mining region.[6]

According to Eva, her diminutive size and birth weight led a nursemaid to remark that the baby girl was only "as big as a pin." The nickname stuck; friends and intimates called her "Pins" well into adulthood. (Eva never indicated whether they called her the French word for pin, épingle). Beyond that, however, it is unclear just how sickly or in need of cookstove incubation she really was. For she was not baptized until some twenty months after her birth, suggesting that whatever shape Eva Tanguay entered the world in, her parents were not worried about her making a hasty exit. Eva's godparents were present at the baptism, held at Saint-Michel church in Sherbrooke and presided over by Father Chalifoux. Absent from the occasion, either because of the demands of his schedule, as an omen of things to come, or perhaps both, was her father, Dr. Joseph Octave Tanguay.[7]

Beyond the fact that she was supposedly a freakish, pin-sized baby, the details of Eva's early life in Canada are few. She and a playmate named Mabel Barker, neighbor and daughter of James Hugh Barker, a manager at the Dominion Lime mining concern, quarreled often owing to the personality of the "little lioness," though they just as readily mended fences and moved on as children do. Mrs. F. H. Bradley, who grew up in Sherbrooke, remembered Eva as "a lovable but mildly erratic child. She and I had many a squabble but always made up and were good friends again." Throughout her life, Eva tried to downplay her erratic and combative nature. But nearly everywhere one looks, those who knew her characterized their relations with Eva Tanguay, both as a child and an adult, as a mix of conflict and closeness.[8]

In time, bigger problems loomed. Eva had been born five years into what was to become known in Canadian history (and Western history generally) as the Great Depression, which lasted from 1873 until 1896 (after the Great Depression of the 1930s, the earlier period was designated the Long Depression). The doldrums were the result of disastrous economic policy, but more directly of the so-called Panic of 1873, a domino effect of dropping silver prices, industrial overexpansion, and crashing investments both in Europe and the United States. Partially because things may have seemed especially bleak in Canada at the time, and maybe because of a simple wanderlust, in 1883 Dr. Tanguay and his family did what many of their countrymen had done. They made their way south to New England.

Dr. Tanguay chose Holyoke, Massachusetts to put down stakes. Occupying a jutting elbow of land on the west bank of the Connecticut River, about fifteen miles north of the Connecticut state border, Holyoke was in many ways a logical destination for the Tanguays. At the time they arrived, it had one of largest populations of French-Canadian émigrés in the United States. The town even counted a few other Tanguay families, likely cousins or distant relations. A scandal rippled through Holyoke in 1884 when the newly elected truant officer, Wilfred Tanguay, himself committed a grievous act of marital truancy by taking his son and running out on his wife who lay dying of consumption. Officer Tanguay had already induced "a healthy young woman to represent his wife at the medical examinations," thus obtaining a $15,000 insurance claim for her life.[9]

Though they were definitely in a new land with novel values, the presence of so many ethnic, cultural, and linguistic brethren also reminded them of a long, ancestral road that led from the Old World to the New. The Tanguays of North America, both those in Holyoke and their relatives back in Quebec, in fact reached back to 1692, when Jean Tanguy, born thirty years earlier in Ploudiry (east of Brest near France's Brittany peninsula), arrived in the colony of New France. He came to Quebec as a soldier, but Jean Tanguy somehow earned the nickname of *La Navette,* meaning "the Shuttle," perhaps referring to his noncombat duties. Tanguy also found an extra a added to his surname—hence, Tangu*a*y—likely the result of how his thick Bretagne accent made it sound to an immigration or military official. Once in Quebec, La Navette married Marie Brochu.[10]

The Tanguay generations that followed Jean and Marie knew lives of hardscrabble existence. Despite the rigors of frontier life, they and their fellow countrymen grew in number—while the region's Native Huron inhabitants suffered grievous losses due to war and the diseases of the white man. Blossoming trade in furs also spurred the growing French population; by 1672, there were 6,230 men and 770 women of European descent living in the region. About half of the first wave of immigrants came from a Parisian orphanage, l'Hôpital Général, while one-third hailed from western regions of France, mainly Normandy and Poitou, near La Rochelle. The millions some made in the fur business further attracted more Frenchmen; by the 1780s, there were over one hundred thousand people of European descent living in Quebec. New France had matured into an alluring destination for hearty and ambitious French settlers.[11]

Most inhabitants of colonial Quebec were granted land under a system known as seigneury, which was little more than a feudal holdover from the Middle Ages. Under seigneury, tenants known as *censitaires* were given small, rectangular strips of land fronting a river. Charged an annual rent and any number of arbitrary levies by their seigneur overlord, *censitaires* lived in houses on their lots that together formed a *côte*. Jean Tanguy and his wife Marie lived on a *côte* situated on the Saint Lawrence waterway in Saint-Vallier-de-Bellechasse. They had lucked out, though, as the land was given them outright as a kind of wedding gift by the owner, Marie's father, Jean Brochu.[12] Life was surely hard since the growing season was short and about five such seasons were needed for a farming family to achieve self-sufficiency. But hard did not mean impoverished, and Jean and Marie Tanguay were owners, not renters.

The hardships of the land were small compared to the difficulties that came after the British conquest of Quebec and the Treaty of Paris in 1763. With it, the province of Quebec fell under British rule. With the ascendency of the British and the English language, the French speakers of Quebec were officially marginalized.[13] It did not help that the Tanguay clan descended from Jean and Marie had by now settled in a region known as the Eastern Townships, a place whose very name suggests an Anglophone majority amid otherwise Francophone Quebecois. The Townships, a loose scattering of villages east of Montreal near the spot where New Hampshire's northern border meets the sloping Maine frontier, were perhaps the one locale in Quebec where speaking French as the Tanguays did could actually put you in the minority.[14]

BY COMING from Canada to the United States, the Tanguay clan enacted a cultural narrative that was at once unique and universal. They had suffered economic and political hardship but had survived and even prospered. Working the land led to owning the land. Successive generations of farmers eventually turned out a doctor. And that doctor made his way to an immigrant enclave in a foreign city that in many ways could not have been more different from the traditional, homogeneous, agrarian world the Tanguays had known in the sylvan Eastern Townships of Quebec. For Holyoke, despite the insularity of its French Canadians, was most certainly a hectic, diverse city on the rise, percolating and shuddering with industrial growth. Where the Tanguays' neck of Canada had been rural, its economy based on farming, fishing, hunting, trapping, and timber, Holyoke's soul was the factory. Paternalistic family mores and Catholicism gave meaning and structure to small-town life in New France. Holyoke, though it had a sizable Catholic population, was governed by large-scale investment and business capital, a strong, individualistic Protestant work ethic, the sometimes queasy admixture of different cultural and ethnic groups, and the many faces of excitement, commerce, and strife that were and still are the hallmarks of urban North America. "Here was a new community with no tradition of its own. Some of its many problems were inherent in the industrial development of the town; some were born of the rapidity of the shift from an agrarian to an industrial community; and most of the rest were brought by the influx of foreigners." So wrote Constance McLaughlin Green in her definitive 1939 book, *Holyoke Massachusetts: A Case History of the Industrial Revolution in America*. It may not have been as big as New York or as old as Boston, but in everything that made a nineteenth-century city both good and bad, Holyoke wanted for little.[15]

From a relative backwater on the Connecticut River, Holyoke, between the 1850s and the time of the Tanguays' arrival in 1883, had emerged as the undisputed paper-milling capital of North America. The first paper plant went up in 1853, and dozens of others followed. By 1890, the city boasted twenty-five factories employing thirty-five hundred people, with the combined enterprises capitalized at some $11 million. Holyoke was duly nicknamed "Paper City."[16]

Holyoke was like many other centers of industry: merchant bankers looking for investment growth plowed heady sums into the hardware, physical plant, and labor of private enterprise. But in another way, Holyoke was different. If industry took root in other, already-established urban milieus, in Holyoke it was pumped in so quickly and frenetically that what had been a marginal, postagrarian community bloated into a factory-floor city at fantastic and dreadful speed. "The city of Holyoke is a unique one among similar mill towns of the area," wrote the historian Therese Bilodeau. "Unlike other towns, [in Holyoke] industry came first, then community." Labor shortages were one immediate result. Beginning in 1859, French-Canadian economic émigrés fled south to towns such as Holyoke, seeking work in the growing factories and their environs in industrializing New England.[17]

By 1870, three years after Holyoke officially became a city, there were 1,731 French Canadians among 10,733 total inhabitants. A decade later, there were 4,902 Canadians in a city of 21,915 people. By 1903, survey evidence suggested that as many as half of all Holyoke residents were of French-Canadian descent. Like many immigrant groups, the French Canadians of Holyoke tended to cluster together in tight-knit enclaves. "Canada Hill" was their initial precinct. In time, the city's First and Second wards near the industrial canals and mills would become heavily French-Canadian. And by the early twentieth century, Ward 2 was known simply as "the French Ward."[18]

In coming to Holyoke, then, Dr. Tanguay and his family were arriving in a young city strewn with their own countrymen and ripe with opportunity. Hardships and challenges loomed, to be sure; life in any nineteenth-century mill town had them, and an outsider's life anywhere is rarely easy. But from the Tanguays' perspective, here was a robust community of linguistic and cultural brethren.

On his arrival in Holyoke, Dr. Tanguay set up both home and office at 321 Main Street and promptly took out a sizable listing in the *Holyoke City Directory*. "Dr. J. O. Tanguay, Licensed 1860, College of Physicians and Surgeons, Canada," was ready to receive patients. He even had a phone.[19]

The location at 321 Main was bustling and unglamorous to say the least. Set on a commercial strip of working-class shops huddled beneath tenement flats, it was smack in the heart of Holyoke's main French-Canadian enclave. While the Tanguays probably lived a little better than many of their countrymen, conditions were far from ideal. Main Street ran roughly east–west, stretching beyond Holyoke's industrial canals. Though not quite as bad as the low-lying "flats" to the south on the banks of the Connecticut River, Main Street was still a confusion of tenements where thousands of French-Canadian mill workers and their families lived cheaply, if not hygienically, within walking distance of their factory jobs.[20]

Dr. Tanguay's medical practice at first succeeded well enough that by 1884, a year after his arrival, he could move his family to 60 Race Street. A short, historical item on the Tanguays in the *Holyoke Daily Transcript* from 1981 refers to Race Street as having been "fashionable" back then. While probably an improvement over the racket of Main Street, Race was nonetheless next to one of the factory's gushing channels. For true respectability one had to ascend the slope up to High Street and the inviting greenery of the common, or further uphill yet to Pleasant Street where stately houses bloomed on a crest far away from the squalor of the canals.[21]

And yet for all the disease, want, and overcrowding that many of its inhabitants faced, Holyoke also offered its people something tantalizing: the myriad diversions of modern urban life. For in scrambling to make a living, the people of Holyoke, worker and professional, French, Irish, and German, up the hill or down by the canals, also carved out niches for recreation, escape, and self-enrichment. They did so to find enjoyment and meaning beyond the grinding factory and the dreary home.

By the time the Tanguays arrived, Holyokers had a number of options for public leisure. The well-heeled could enjoy "a select private musicale" on the evening of January 11, 1887. Invitees—it was an invitation-only affair—could savor the works of Haydn, Schubert, Schumann, and Wagner played by members of New York's Philharmonic corps. The city was also fond of throwing masquerade balls with a prince and princess of the carnival presiding over the festivities. In 1892, townsfolk at the twentieth annual masquerade fest, sponsored by a local German-American group, dressed up as Little Lord Fauntleroy—one of the era's favorite pop-culture figures—the devil, the devil's daughter, Spanish cavaliers and sundry tambourine girls, jockeys, ballet dancers, Japanese ladies, peasants, clowns, and fairy-tale characters. Other attractions of urban life included the so-called Lyceum at the local Masonic Lodge, "where debaters assailed each other with rhetoric." There were fire musters, music-school recitals, sleigh rides, picnics, and a yearly fair to round out the offerings. For the more sedate, literary associations and reading rooms came into existence during the 1880s.[22]

"Because of drunkenness," it was said in 1868, a preacher named Harkins formed the St. Jerome's Temperance Society as an "instrument in his war upon saloon culture." St. Jerome's was among the first and certainly the most prominent of Holyoke's many ethnic or religious groups that fostered a sense of community via civic, creative, and mutual-aid projects. In addition to crusading against vice, the St. Jerome organization also gave amateur thespians a shot at the stage and many citizens their first taste of proper or "legitimate" theater (as opposed to musical revues and variety acts). They put on a drama called *Hidden Hand* in March 1884. On St. Patrick's Day night three years later, theatergoers filled every seat to see the St. Jerome Temperance Society Dramatic Club render *O'Neal the Great*, a paean to the organization's Irish heritage.[23]

Those favoring professional theater had the Holyoke Opera House, one of many "opera houses" that sprang up in smaller cities and towns across the United States in the 1800s. These opera houses brought troupes of blackface minstrels, low variety acts, short farces, lectures, "magic lantern" slideshows, and just about every other form of entertainment—except, for the most part, opera—to the masses. Holyoke's edition specialized in "third-rate burlesques," according to Constance McLaughlin Green. Opening night, March 25, 1878, the stolid, Romanesque playhouse featured a farce titled *A Quiet Family,* followed by the historical drama *Louis XI.* The building itself was a kind of huge stone monument with a monolithic facade. It fairly shouted that Holyoke was to be taken seriously in the cultural realm, no matter that its offerings included *Our College Boys; or, Medical Students on a Lark,* a supposedly "side-splitting" comedy penned by one Preston Sweet, MD—which is exactly what patrons paid to see the last week of August 1881.[24]

On occasion, finer fare made its way to Holyoke. Edwin Booth, that mightiest of nineteenth-century actors, starred in *Macbeth* opposite the renowned Madame Modjeska as his Lady Macbeth. The large crowd marveled at Booth's acting, but felt that Modjeska, despite her reputation, could not quite keep up.[25]

Parsons Hall, where Eva would later make her debut, offered variety entertainment to enthusiastic audiences, which included many middle-class women, a mark of bourgeois respectability. By the early 1890s, vaudeville and minstrelsy could be seen at other venues, especially the Empire. To meet the growing demand for all things dramatic, the *Holyoke Daily Transcript* added a "Theatre Tidbits" column, later renamed "Stageland Gossip," with news from Broadway.[26]

In the 1890s, Holyoke's theatrical offerings were widened further when a builder named Frank H. Dibble had the Mountain Park Casino put up. The casino was a partially open-air theater in Holyoke's Mountain Park. Band concerts, vaudeville, and on one occasion a show starring trained goats took the stage. There was even a short-lived stock company at the casino. Along with the Mountain Park venue, Holyoke's Pavilion, Eden Musee, and Bijou theaters eventually brought Wild West shows, jugglers, singers, dancers, and sporting demonstrations—in other words, the prime ingredients of vaudeville—to the city.[27]

Holyoke also offered an increasingly modern understanding of women's place in society. Its main newspaper, the *Transcript,* was full of editorials on the subject of women's lives, rights, and desires. An editorial, "How Do Holyoke Women Kill Time?" presented the argument that women's labor in the home was just that—legitimate work. Another essay, "Why Women Marry," held that the "motives for which women marry are as numerous as the sands of the sea." It acknowledged that love was not always the main reason—in fact rarely so—and that in the end, a mix of social, economic, and psychological factors coaxed women toward nuptial union. In addition, there were schools and libraries open to everyone in the city, and there had been at least two generations of women and girls working in the cotton and paper mills. There was a rich tapestry of entertainment

Figure 4. The circus comes to Holyoke.
Life was hard for immigrants in a bustling, sometimes chaotic, nineteenth-
century mill town like Holyoke, Massachusetts. But it gave Eva and others their
first taste of popular urban amusements, such as variety shows and the circus,
shown here parading down High Street, Holyoke's main thoroughfare.
(Courtesy of the Holyoke Public Library History Room.)

· · · · · · · · · ·

and culture where women starred, sang, and recited. In short, Holyoke
was a fine place for a young girl to get the idea that earning her own way,
perhaps even succeeding mightily in the world, was possible.[28]

It was in this realm that eight-year-old Hélène Eva Tanguay tried her luck
at a local amateur night. With her mother's help, Eva first mounted the stage
at Parsons Hall. On other days it was where the Unitarians met. Tonight it
was where anyone from town could take to the boards and sing, dance, or
offer whatever they had in the way of talent in exchange for a cash prize.

Eva trembled as she climbed onstage. As she did so, the crowd burst into
derisive laughter. What was happening? Had she made a mistake before
even starting? As the uproar faded, the emcee asked, "Dear child, would
you kindly tell me where you found this outfit?" Eva now saw that it was
her costume that had triggered the audience's laughter. It is possible that
Eva Tanguay considered abandoning the stage at this fragile moment; what
frightened child wouldn't? She was, after all, dressed in a very curious getup.
For a dress, she wore the fabric of an old black umbrella with a hole cut in
the top permitting her head to poke through. Ribbons and bows were sewn

Figure 5. Young Eva in her amateur-night debut costume.
When she was just a girl of perhaps eight, Eva made her first stage appearance
at a local amateur night. "We are very poor. I didn't have money" to buy a
costume, she told an audience that wondered why
she was dressed in an old umbrella. "I want to become a famous actress,"
she said. That night, Eva took first place.
(From the Collections of The Henry Ford.)

· · · · · · · ·

onto the hem like a grotesque ballerina's tutu. Napkins, sections of lace doily, knit chair-throws, and the occasional tissue paper rounded out the affair.

Rather than run in shame, however, Eva chose to speak. "I made it myself," she told the throng. "We are very poor. I didn't have money to buy myself one. At our home, I found what was necessary. I want to become a famous actress and earn a lot of money to help my mother." And that was it—she had them. It was the first of many times Eva Tanguay would win the day with her ability to read a crowd and react with vulnerable emotional pluck. (Of course, on occasion she would misread a crowd, though her responses were just as convincing.) She went on to sing "The Fisherman and His Child Are Drowned" and to dance a hornpipe. She secured first prize: one dollar.

Encouraged, Eva began singing and dancing at other social halls and clubhouses around town. There were many to choose from. There was Temperance Hall, the Alsace-Lorraine, the auditorium used by the Bridge Street Turners gymnasts, and more. All became Eva's theatrical playground. She became nineteenth-century Holyoke's version of the modern child star. Her days were devoted to developing her career, and she would often be called in from playing with friends "to study whatever part or song I was to attempt," she later wrote, only to find herself staring longingly out the window at her frolicking mates. "To me, *that* was a most trying sacrifice," she said. Eva's reminiscences, such as this one, are hard to interpret. Was this true? Or was she trying to make her unconventional childhood, one that prepared her for the theatrical profession rather than domesticity, sound more acceptable by linking it to the Yankee work ethic? Either way, following amateur night at Parson's, Eva's life was to change forever.[29]

The Tanguay family had undergone an important change even before Eva's amateur night success. On September 6, 1886, her father died. According to the childhood narrative that Eva later propagated, her father's death sent the family tumbling into poverty. Her mother, Adèle, now rented a room at 348 High Street and took to cleaning and housekeeping for other families. Once a doctor's wife, she now toiled with broom and bucket to stave off destitution.[30]

But first, there is evidence to suggest that the Tanguays may not have been so financially comfortable even when Dr. Tanguay was alive, for it is unclear just how much success he ever enjoyed in his medical practice, either back in Canada or in Holyoke. Indeed, a failing practice up north could have been one of the reasons he took his family and fled to the States. In 1903, the performer Ullie Akerstrom delivered a lecture in Holyoke titled "A Glimpse of the Real Eva Tanguay." In it, she stated without qualification that "as time passed, financial embarrassments gathered thick and fast about doctor Tanguay." Mismanagement of money was also one of Eva's lifelong problems, dogging her until the end.[31]

The Tanguays might not, then, have had very far to fall after the death of the family breadwinner. At the same time, it does not appear that they plummeted into abject poverty. The family's name does not appear on the rolls of Holyoke's paupers in the years following Dr. Tanguay's death. And although various family members lived at times in cheap flats on Bond Street, the French-Canadian community was close-knit and had organized a number of mutual aid societies that may have offered support to the widow Adèle (who by now was also referred to in both public and private sources as "Marie," a nickname that eclipsed her given name) and her children. Furthermore, by this time, sons Adolphe Étienne, now known as Mark, and Joseph were old enough to work and contribute. Joseph was a machinist, though he would soon move to Lee, Massachusetts, forty miles west of Holyoke. Mark held a post at Holyoke's Henry Seymour Cutlery concern.[32]

Dr. Tanguay was forever an ambivalent figure in Eva's life. When she was younger, she recalled him as a kind of dashing romantic figure, a "Parisian" doctor who had bravely set out for the New World. As we have seen, that was not the case. As she aged, though, Eva's family reminiscences are remarkable for their exclusion of her father, as well as her two brothers. Within this void, Eva Tanguay constructed an adoring mythos of her mother. "She worshipped the memory of her own mother," wrote Wes Eichenwald in a 2001 magazine article. In 1915, she debuted a paean to her mother, a song called "M-O-T-H-E-R: A Word That Means the World to Me" (lyrics by Howard Johnson, music by Theodore Morse). Its chorus began, "'M' is for the million things she gave me," and followed with lines such as "'T' is for the tears that were shed to save me." In 1909, she told a journalist that she had written a book called *A Hundred Loves* that she hoped to publish. Though it sounded like a racy love résumé, it was in fact a novel. "It starts with a happy love—a mother's love for her child," she told journalist Charles Darnton. It was never published.[33]

The circumstances surrounding Dr. Tanguay's demise may also shed light on Eva's ambivalence toward him, as well as his questionable ability to provide. On Joseph O. Tanguay's certificate of death, issued by the Commonwealth of Massachusetts on October 1, 1886, twenty-five days after he passed away, the cause of death was listed as "abdomina dropsy."

Figure 6. In her mother's arms.
The picture is shadowy but the sentiment is clear: Eva Tanguay adored her
mother. Her relationship with her father was more ambiguous.
(Courtesy of the Holyoke Public Library History Room.)

· · · · · · · · · ·

Reading this as either an attempt at Latin or, more likely, a typo, Dr. Tanguay died of *abdominal dropsy,* eleven days after his forty-eighth birthday.

These days, medical professionals no longer use the term *dropsy,* much less *abdominal dropsy.* But in the annals of nineteenth-century medicine it was commonly employed to identify a class of life-threatening disorders. According to a medical dictionary of the day, dropsy was the "accumulation of watery fluid in the tissues or cavities of the body"—in other words, an obstruction of some duct or vein causing liquid to back up and fill the nearest anterior reservoir. In modern parlance, dropsy is called edema. The term *dropsy* on its own referred to an edema of the heart, known today as congestive heart failure. But Dr. Tanguay did not die of dropsy. He died of "abdominal dropsy." Such an edema does not indicate congestive heart failure at all but an obstruction in the middle of the body causing the peritoneum—the sac that lines the abdominal cavity and contains the organs—to fill up like a water balloon. Abdominal dropsy or edema is now known medically as ascites. It may be "chylous," meaning the fluid contains suspended fat, or "hemorrhagic," meaning it contains blood. In contemporary medical terms, it was ascites that claimed Dr. Tanguay's life, or, more precisely, the underlying dysfunction that led to it.[34]

Liver disease was most likely what caused the fatal ascites that killed Dr. Tanguay. The link between liver failure and ascites was common scientific knowledge back then, no matter that some of the terminology was different, as it had been for hundreds if not thousands of years. Among liver disorders, cirrhosis was the most likely culprit. And to be sure, cirrhosis was most commonly brought on by excessive drink. Both points are made clear in the medical literature of Dr. Tanguay's time, as they continue to be.[35]

Was Dr. Tanguay an alcoholic? The evidence is circumstantial. He died at forty-eight of a disease most commonly, if indirectly, linked to excessive alcohol consumption. He also appears to have died insolvent, suggesting he was unable to attend to his work for some reason. Throughout her life, Eva inveighed almost maniacally against the evils of drink. She was described by at least one personal and business relation as a "perfectionist" who never imbibed and rarely went out to nightclubs. This was at a time when staying out late at swanky, freewheeling cabarets and lobster palaces after your last curtain call was de rigueur for many stage folks. "I do not drink and I do not smoke," Eva told a journalist in 1927. "I can not and will not have drunkards around me. Drinking is the kill thought, you know." The kill thought. Had her father's drinking killed him? Had it killed the possibility of having anything like a happy family existence?

Furthermore, would it lead Eva to later unwittingly choose romantic partners who drank, used drugs, and abused her?[36]

A local culture of alcoholism may also have influenced Dr. Tanguay's intemperate behavior, for if there was a New England town that suffered from the social ill of drunkenness it was Holyoke. "It may well be understood," wrote one citizen, "that Holyoke is one of the Rumest places in the Rum County of Hampden." Locals had organized a temperance society as early as 1857 (predating St. Jerome's by a decade). In 1870, Holyoke had no fewer than eighty-nine liquor shops, approximately one for every 120 citizens. Compare that to the present-day figure of a dozen retail liquor stores in Holyoke, or less than one for every 3,100 citizens. The bulk of criminal proceedings in town arose from drunkenness or the illegal sale of liquor. In 1884, the year after Dr. Tanguay and his family moved to town, Holyoke saw 999 arrests, 597 of which—by far the most of any category—were for inebriation.[37]

The problem of drunkenness was especially grave among Holyoke's French Canadians. A visitor in 1885 observed that for "amusements...so far as the males are concerned, drinking, smoking and lounging constitutes the sum of these." Though this observation may reflect ethnic and cultural bias, it is undeniable that drinking was a chief pastime for Holyoke's French-Canadian population. Many among them knew little other than hardship and struggle. So, according to Constance McLaughlin Green, their chief comfort "was their church on the one hand or the saloon on the other." Not surprisingly, many French Canadians and Irish in Holyoke long opposed efforts at Prohibition.[38]

WHILE EVA HAD her heart set on making money as a performer, her sister followed the more conventional path for women, settling down at age seventeen and soon after starting a family. At seventeen, Blanche married Alfred Skelding, son of Jesse and Maria Skelding, in Holyoke. Skelding was not a local boy, but a musical director with a touring company out of Pennsylvania, the Redding Stanton stock players, which was to play a pivotal role in launching Eva's career. The two were married on February 8, 1892, in Holyoke shortly after the Redding Stanton company had arrived in town. With Skelding, Blanche had a daughter, Lillian Mary, born December 13, 1894.[39]

Eva's theatrical career was by this time beginning to take shape. Still a teenager, she began traveling with the Redding Stanton players, who had come to Holyoke with a stage adaptation of one of the most popular works of fiction of the day, *Little Lord Fauntleroy* by Frances Hodgson Burnett.[40]

Little Lord Fauntleroy, which took Burnett six weeks to write, first appeared in serialized short-story form in 1885. When eventually novelized, it went on to sell hundreds of thousands of copies and enjoyed translations in French, Italian, and German. The story concerns a boy named Cedric Errol who discovers he is in fact British nobility. Whisked off to England, Cedric finds his way in and out of one tribulation after another, his angelic, somewhat effeminate demeanor adding color to tales that were sugar-frosted in sentiment. Something of a *Harry-Potter*-meets-*The-Princess-Diaries* of its day, the *Fauntleroy* stories made their creator very rich indeed. Capitalizing on it success, Burnett herself promptly adapted it to the stage. It debuted in New York at the Broadway Theatre, at Forty-first Street and Seventh Avenue, on the night of December 3, 1888, directed by the author-playwright herself, and ran for four years.[41]

It is said that Frances Hodgson Burnett based her title character on both her son, Vivian, and the playwright and poet Oscar Wilde. Vivian Burnett never lived down his reputation as the model for perhaps the most sissified literary character of his era, enduring chants of "Fauntleroy— mama's boy" while running track meets at Harvard. "I try to get away from it, but I can't," he later admitted in anguish. Nor, for a time, could countless boys escape Fauntleroy-ification at the hands of mothers who thought it cute to dress their sons in ruffled suits and plush trousers. As for Oscar Wilde, whom Frances Hodgson Burnett had met in 1882, he was a complicated and brilliant figure, known for many things. But an uncomplicated, hetero-macho look was not one of them.[42]

It was thus culturally fitting that the symbolically castrated lead role in *Fauntleroy* was most often played by a girl to make it palatable to mainstream audiences. Indeed, the role of Cedric was famously played first by the actress Elsie Leslie (sometimes known as Elsie Leslie Lyde). It was not until Ray Maskell took over the role at Niblo's—the same venue where the racy *Black Crook* made a smash in 1866—that a male enacted it. The character was perfect for a young girl who needed not so much to be tomboyish as presexual, enthusiastic yet composed. The name of the girl who played Cedric Errol in the Redding Stanton touring production of *Little Lord Fauntleroy* when it ambled into Holyoke in the late 1880s has been lost to history. What is known about her, however, is that she fell ill, necessitating a hasty replacement. Eva Tanguay, Holyoke's favorite child performer, had in fact already endeared herself to the troupe by going backstage after a performance and showing off her flair for dancing. She was hired to fill in for the lead and earned eight dollars a week.[43]

Figure 7. The child actress plays Fauntleroy.
At age ten, Eva Tanguay became a theatrical orphan touring with a stock
company in the popular role of Little Lord Fauntleroy.
(From the Collections of The Henry Ford.)

· · · · · · · · ·

Some accounts of Eva's life say she was eight when Redding Stanton snapped her up. But that would have been 1886, two years before the play's debut. It seems more likely that Eva Tanguay was ten when the Redding players recruited her. Eva was to stay with the company for five years. During that time, though still a child, her increasing popularity allowed her to send at least some money back to her family in Holyoke. In addition to Fauntleroy, Eva assumed soubrette roles in any number of hackneyed but popular nineteenth-century melodramas. The soubrette, a standard character type derived from French farce, was usually a canny servant whose liveliness and penchant for playing the tomboy set her in stark contrast to the passive ingenue heroines whom they served. When Eva first took to the boards, the most famous soubrette actress in the United States was probably Lotta Crabtree (1874–1924). In such parts, according to Eva many years later, "I dashed night after night to save the heroine from being sawed in two by the vile villain." When needed, she could also be bound and unsexed back into juvenile parts such as that of a starving child in *The Face on the Barroom Floor*.[44]

Life on the road with the Redding Stanton crew involved hardship and loneliness, especially for a child. But it also provided Eva with a unique and resourceful role model in the person of Francesca Redding, the troupe's coleader.

Francesca Redding was born in Boston and, like Charlotte Cushman and other stage women before her, determined early on to make it as an actress. Redding had a leg up, however, as she hailed from a theatrical family. Not only was Redding known for possessing formidable acting talent, she was also a showbiz entrepreneur. She pioneered the idea of taking legitimate plays and telescoping them down to one-act entertainments that would fit nicely into a vaudeville program.[45]

In many ways, Francesca Redding as both an actress and a manager worked in the tradition of Fanny Kemble, Laura Keene, and other women of the nineteenth-century who demonstrated that the theater could be as much their dominion as a man's.[46] The possibility of becoming a competent, self-reliant show-business professional must have appealed greatly to a girl who had grown up with instability, an alcoholic father, and financial uncertainty. A journalist in the 1930s would memorialize Redding as "the first to exploit Eva Tanguay."[47]

Early in 1892, the Redding Stanton company came back through Holyoke, now boasting hometown favorite Eva Tanguay. But Eva was no longer just a local girl with talent; she hovered somewhere on the outskirts of national recognition. The troupe served up a variety of delights during its weeklong stint at the Holyoke Opera House, including *Maritana,* an "operatic romance." When she came onstage, Eva Tanguay, barely thirteen years old, faced "a storm of applause," thanks not only to fans but to personal friends and admirers as well, "who had not forgotten her work in the past when she used to appear here in local entertainments," according to a newspaper account. The local drama critic saw her as unfinished, a work in progress. But he sensed she was headed for bigger things, much bigger, driving toward "the front rank of what seems to be her natural profession." Her compulsory performance of *Fauntleroy* during her engagement convinced observers of the same thing: Eva was bound for greatness.[48]

At this early point in her career, Eva was already trying to maintain a facade of being properly trained and skilled while playfully reaching out to the crowd from deep within herself. Portraying a singing, dancing newsboy in something called *The Fool's Idol,* Eva held under her arm what was clearly a stack of *Holyoke Daily Transcript* newspapers. The crowd loved it. They loved *her.* By the following year, Eva was big enough to merit a week on her own at the Pavilion Theatre and had earned the title of "Holyoke's favorite daughter." In April 1894, the Holyoke Opera House counted itself lucky that Eva had "consented" to appear for a short engagement. She was not yet sixteen, nor was she a full-blown star. But her years with Francesca Redding had helped her on her way to grander possibilities.[49]

Eva would spend some four years with the Redding players. It is unclear how her relationship with the troupe ended, but there is nothing to suggest enmity or a bad-faith split. In fact, little is known about Eva's career in the latter half of the 1890s. It was said that she briefly joined a traveling medicine show called the Kickapoo Indians, but Eva later denied it emphatically. "I might willingly own up to scrubbing kitchen floors, but never to a medicine show engagement. That's the limit." Eva was unpredictable. But in the cultural economy of U.S. entertainment she had learned which associations made her more interesting and which ones threatened her reputation.[50]

It seems possible that Eva also spent time in Holyoke during the latter 1890s tending to her mother and perhaps taking refuge from the rigors of the road. She was later to say, "I long for the contentment that I knew there, just as a poor little girl longs for a rag dolly." But that was a decade and a half after she had last kept a home of any kind in Holyoke. The town seems by that time to have become an emotional symbol to Eva, mutating in her mind from something to be fled into a refuge of lost simplicity. Talking nostalgically about life in her adoptive hometown also permitted

Figure 8. The teenage actress plays the dude.
In her barnstorming youth, Eva not only played the saucy soubrette, she also
donned trousers and a top hat when the part called for them. It gave Eva some
distinctly modern—and playful—notions about gender roles.
(Courtesy of the Holyoke Public Library History Room.)

· · · · · · · ·

Eva to indulge in a kind of sentimental retrospective cleansing to which public women of the era often had to resort.[51]

The 1890s saw further changes and complications in Eva's life. She was increasingly on the road, making a name for herself as a musical-comedy trouper and sending home her paycheck when she could. While Eva may not have resided in Holyoke for great lengths of time, the evidence strongly suggests that she was there enough to have had at least one romance that led to a pregnancy—and a child she could never admit was hers.

Officially, Florence Tanguay was Eva Tanguay's niece. Florence had grown up believing her date of birth was June 1, 1898. But in October 1952, Florence's daughter Barbara was visiting Massachusetts with her husband, Helge Johnson. Barbara urged her mother to procure a copy of her birth certificate from the Holyoke City Clerk's office. Florence did so, and what she discovered unsettled her. (Suspicion of the truth may have been one reason why she had never before sought a copy of her birth certificate.) The official document indicated that her true date of birth had been September 25, 1897, while the certificate itself had been drawn in "Feb. 1898," at least four months after the event. Delayed registry of births, or failure to register them at all, was so common in Holyoke in the late nineteenth century that even doctors were eventually hit with punitive measures for consistently failing to produce accurate records. "Births Must Be Reported," read a headline from a *Holyoke Daily Transcript* article, which told of a $25 fine levied on physicians and others who could not be bothered to fill out the proper paperwork.[52]

Florence Tanguay's true birth date grew even hazier after her passing, on December 29, 1976. At the time of her death, she was in Plainsfield, Florida, visiting one of her sons at nearby Tyndall Air Force Base. (She was by now Florence Tanguay Dufresne, often called "Flossie.") The death record, issued January 22, 1977, put her age at death at 80 years, 6 months, and 28 days. This would have meant her birth date was June 1, *1896,* not 1898. Florence, who had died of "cardiac arrest, bacteremia & cerebrovascular accident," was laid to rest at Hilltop Cemetery in Plainfield, Massachusetts, upriver from Holyoke.[53]

If it was unclear *when,* exactly, Florence Tanguay Dufresne was born, it was also unclear to *whom* she was born. "We all grew up believing that [Eva] was my mother's mother," wrote Barbara Johnson, adding, "I have always felt Aunt Eva was my mother's mother, my brothers' too. But I guess she could not admit having a child." Elaine Dufresne, widow of Florence's son Larry, concurred. Her late husband and his two brothers, Doug and Dick, "seemed to think [Barbara] did not want to talk about

Figure 9. Photo portrait of Florence "Tanquay."
The name "Tanguay" is misspelled on the original photo, inadvertently
reflecting the cloudy parentage of the girl who many believed to be Eva
Tanguay's illegitimate daughter. One thing is certain: Florence was not the child
of Eva's brother Mark as the family tried to claim when Florence was born.
(Original from the archives of the Ashfield Historical Society.)

. . . .

it too much at the time, [but] she has changed her mind considerably,
and seems to believe more now that her mom was Eva's daughter." The
rumors that Flossie was Eva Tanguay's illegitimate daughter were not
confined solely to the Tanguay family. "I went to school with Florence
Tanguay who said she was the niece of Eva Tanguay[,] but the rumor
was she was her daughter." So wrote Doris Luce in a note to Ella Merkel
DiCarlo, an indefatigable researcher, local historian, and columnist for the
Holyoke Transcript-Telegram, who tried to get to the bottom of it all in the
1980s but never did.[54]

There is nothing that clearly proves Eva Tanguay was Florence's mother. Yet circumstantial evidence and common-sense reasoning shout otherwise. Eva would have been eighteen or nineteen years old when she gave birth to Florence. She was not yet a nationally known figure and could not afford the potential stain to her reputation or the emotional and financial encumbrance that acknowledging motherhood would have brought. It is true that Sarah Bernhardt never acknowledged the paternity of her one child, Maurice, born in 1864 when Sarah was twenty-one. But Eva Tanguay was not yet in Sarah Bernhardt's league and had not yet earned that kind of star capital. Though Eva would later be renowned for "sexual adventure" and "urban sophistication," according to the historian Kathryn J. Oberdeck, the social mores of the time, combined with her own personal misgivings about motherhood made it far too risky for Eva to confess having been an unwed teenage mother.[55]

Pointing the finger more clearly in Eva's direction is the fact that the people who were officially recognized as Florence's birth parents simply could not have been. These people took awkward measures to try and cover up the fact, making it stand out all the more. On her birth certificate, Florence's father was listed as "Mark M.," and her mother, "Margaret Grundy." Mark M. is presumably Mark McPherson Tanguay, otherwise known as Adolphe Étienne Tanguay, Eva's brother. Mark appears to have married an Irish immigrant named Katie Costello on July 1, 1891. Allegedly, they had a son, but no further information on him exists. In 1896, Mark is said to have married Margaret Grundy, an Englishwoman, and to have had two girls with her: Beatrice and our Florence. But what genealogical "evidence" there is suggests the two girls would have been born *three and a half months apart* in 1897. If the dates are correct, they clearly could not both have belonged to Margaret Grundy and Mark Tanguay, at least not biologically. That is probably why Florence had been raised to believe she was born on June 1, 1896, or June 1, 1898. Those dates were, conveniently, precisely one year before and one year after the birth of Beatrice Tanguay. "This is very confusing and I doubt if true," wrote Barbara Johnson in a personal letter to the *Holyoke Transcript-Telegram*'s Ella Merkel DiCarlo.

There is also the matter of Florence's name. Quite simply, there is no mention whatsoever of "Florence" on her birth certificate. Rather, her given name was "Eva Adela Tanguay," linking Florence not only to her famous "aunt" but to Eva's mother Adèle "Marie" Tanguay. "I had forgotten her name was Eva Adela Tanguay," wrote Florence's daughter Barbara Johnson. "Where did Florence come from?" she wondered, referring to the girl's name, but also her provenance.

Mark M. Tanguay died in 1930. According to Ella Merkel DiCarlo, his obituary contained "no mention of children surviving him." Elaine Dufresne, Florence's daughter-in-law, says that all of Florence's children called Mark Tanguay granddad but knew "[Florence's] dad was someone else, another Mark." It is unclear who that other "Mark" was, and further investigation into the matter of Eva Adela "Florence" Tanguay's parentage renders things only more shadowy. "What is not really known is who Florence Dufresne's parents are." So wrote Ella Merkel DiCarlo in a letter to Barbara Johnson. "I wonder when your mother started using the name Florence," she wrote to Barbara Johnson on another occasion, but never got a response. In any case, Florence seems to have lived with Mark Tanguay and his wife only a short time before Eva made other, better accommodations. Florence, in fact, had "no love" for Mark Tanguay. She claimed he took from her the jewelry and other special gifts, including a gold-chained watch, that Eva had given her. This was Eva's characteristic largesse. Though unable to be physically or emotionally very present in the girl's life, her wealth and generosity allowed her to show up *writ large,* if only by proxy.[56]

One thing Mark never took from Florence, though, was a lovely doll she treasured throughout her girlhood. She called that prized dolly "Eva Elizabeth."[57]

IN 1899, Eva's mother passed away and was laid to rest in her hometown of Keeseville, New York. Eva rarely talked about her mother's death, but the loss must have been monumental, perhaps like losing both parents rather than just one. It is unclear just how much material comfort Eva had been able to provide for her aging, widowed mother. Throughout the 1890s, Adèle "Marie" Tanguay lived in modest boarding houses in Holyoke and nearby towns sometimes with her son Mark, sometimes alone. It has been suggested that Eva and her mother spent several years in Newark, New Jersey, perhaps while Eva was attached to a stock company based there. In 1903, Eva was listed as residing at a large house on Pleasant Street, even though she was actively working on Broadway at the time. Perhaps she had purchased or leased the place for her mother several years earlier and still held title. For Pleasant Street was Holyoke's wealthy district, far above the canals, removed from the bustling, immigrant-crowded Main Street and Race Street of her youth.[58]

Eva's sister Blanche had moved on too. By 1901, Blanche's marriage to the traveling theater man Alfred Skelding was finished. In the second week of December, she married a local grocer, Elwin T. Howes, twenty-eight years of age. In marrying Elwin Howes, Blanche was hardly settling for an unlettered shopkeeper. Elwin Tyler Howes was the scion of a large and well-regarded Massachusetts family, descended from Myles Standish of *Mayflower* fame, via the Howes clan of Yarmouth on Cape Cod. Elwin Tyler Howes, third child of Robert Howes and Clara Arabel (Clark) was born November 29, 1874. Nancy Garvin of the Ashfield Historical Society theorized that Elwin T. Howes met Blanche Tanguay as a customer in his shop, an eminently reasonable suspicion. "Everyone liked him," it was said of Elwin. He had a reputation as "an honest and honorable merchant" possessed of a "sunny nature." Among shopkeepers in the region he loomed large.[59]

In time, not everyone in the proud, old Howes family would be thrilled about being linked, even if only by marriage, to a scandalous upstart of the vaudeville stage. Marsha Harris, Elwin's niece, was embarrassed by the "impropriety of Eva," according to Roger Howes, grandson of Elwin's brother Raymond Howes.[60]

With her remaining parent gone and a likely illegitimate daughter whom she could not publicly acknowledge, Eva's time in western Massachusetts had drawn to a close. Though she would continue to visit and, in some measure, provide for Florence, her world was now that of Broadway, New York, and the theatrical circuits that sprang from there.

2

The Sambo Girl in New York

IN 1901, Eva got the chance to move up the professional ladder from notable itinerant performer to praiseworthy supporting player when she was cast in a Broadway show called *My Lady*. Although billed as a musical comedy, *My Lady* in fact fell somewhere in between loosely cobbled vaudeville fare, relying heavily on recognizable personalities doing their signature specialties, and a scripted musical revue. The "musical comedy" of our era, based on a clear, cause-and-effect narrative, had not yet risen to popularity. Back then, the form was a tasty yet inelegant stew of blackface minstrel show (which was itself made up of music, jokes, and dance routines), variety program, and operetta. Though musical comedy has been hailed as a distinctly U.S. genre, the truth is that it received its biggest shot in the arm in its early years from the Englishmen William Gilbert and Arthur Sullivan, whose clever *H.M.S. Pinafore* hit the New York stage in 1878 and did much to clean up and legitimize the form.[1]

In the jargon of the era, it would probably be most accurate to call *My Lady* a *burlesque*. At the time, "burlesque" did not yet mean the kind of prurient skin show we think of it as today. Burlesque had first risen to popularity on the British stage of the 1850s and 1860s. It was a patchwork parody of topical subjects, popular songs, pretty scenery, prettier chorus girls, literary send-up, myriad puns (few of them successful), and high-energy comedy. It was extravagant, over the top, and eclectic, with high production values and little plot. Because of its satirical conceit, the form was said to "burlesque," or joke on, whatever it took into its purview. Lydia Thompson of the "British Blondes" extravaganza was the most famous burlesquer of the nineteenth century. She usually played male characters in travesties of the literary canon with tongue-twisting titles like *Sinbad the Sailor; or, The Ungenial Geni and the Little Cabin Boy; Robin Hood; or, The Maid That Was Arch, and the Youth That Was Archer;* and *The Very Latest Edition of Robinson Crusoe.*[2]

My Lady was a parody of *The Three Musketeers* in three acts. Although its structure generally followed the storyline of Alexandre Dumas' vastly popular serialized novel of 1844, it was, like other burlesques of the era, not the storyline that kept the audience's attention. The *Brooklyn Eagle* reckoned *My Lady* a "spectacle, pure and complex, with Broadway jokes, Forty-second street jingles, variety stunts, some of which have been in Hyde & Behman's [vaudeville and burlesque theater] in the past and others which will reach the Orpheum [vaudeville circuit out west] next year." One critic felt the show's main appeal was to be found in the "clever specialties and choruses with which the entertainment is interspersed." Like a modular vaudeville show, *My Lady* was all about the parts rather than the whole.[3]

The book—what there was of it—was written by R. A. Barnet. H. L. Heartz wrote the music, with song contributions from E. W. Corliss, Robert G. Morse, D. K. Stevens, and Clinton Crawford. As with a present-day movie soundtrack, it was not uncommon for one composer to be credited with the score even though many of the numbers were either adaptations of popular hits or songs written specially for the show's star personalities by featured tunesmiths. The music was termed "light, tuneful, spirited, and so catchy that one can't help remembering it." The dialogue was another matter. Though bowdlerized, it was deemed "a too-long and doleful affair" that was not helped by attempts at highbrow punning. At one point, a musketeer cried into his handkerchief, which he then shook, causing bits of lead to fall to the ground. "Look, he weeps bullets!" announced another character. "No," replied the weeper, "they are musket-tears." Such banter led the *New York Times* to fret, "And this is 1901." Because the modern director as we know it had not yet come fully into existence, it was to the show's producer, A. H. Chamberlyn, a respected theatrical figure of his day, that the credit—or blame—largely went.[4]

In addition to marvelous scenery, *My Lady* had a few other elements that were important in burlesque. First, it featured an abundance of good-looking chorines for the (heterosexual) men in the crowd to gaze at. The *New York Dramatic Mirror* felt that if *My Lady* were to be "a go in New York," it would be chiefly thanks to its "dazzling display of feminine beauty," its "plenitude of pulchritude." Still young and comely, Eva Tanguay could meet this requirement while also meriting praise for her character work.[5]

The cast of *My Lady* also provided Eva with a model of how to fashion a role around one's own self rather than simply stepping into a character's shoes, a tactic she would find increasingly crucial in her career, for this was the way to become a hit solo player in vaudeville. For tutelage, she looked to the show's star, Charles J. Ross. Though he enacted the character of Richelieu, Ross really played himself, using the part to showcase his personality and his prior, beloved stage personae. He also peppered his performance with jokes and references to his private life, upping his PR value. Ross, known for his "admirable stage presence," had arrived in New York, much like Eva, after years spent touring the country. In the hinterlands, he did everything from boxing demonstrations—popular in the vaudeville and variety theater of the time—to blackface acts. He also understood that beneath the liveliness and gaiety of it all, variety and burlesque constituted "a very serious proposition." You had a short span of time in which to win over the crowd. If you did not score a victory during that brief window, you were dead. Ultimately it was not the scenery, leggy chorus girls, or fellow clowns that were going to make you a hit. "One must protect himself; everyone stands or falls alone," he once said. In Ross, young Eva Tanguay had a model for performance that she would soon take further than anyone else of her day. Already, Sarah Bernhardt had been both pilloried and idolized for being "always the same" onstage in whatever role she filled. Now the popular entertainment market, a part of it anyway, was elevating the individual above the role. The rising tide of vaudeville that Eva would soon crest provided a perfect platform for the realization of such tendencies.[6]

My Lady premiered in New York in January 1901 at the Columbia Theatre. Lillian Green played D'Artagnan, in keeping with the common burlesque practice of cross-gender casting. As with other burlesques, the names of supporting characters were satirical versions of names in the original source. Will Sloan was "Ah-Those," Gilbert Gregory was "Pork-House," and W. A. McCart was "Arrah-Miss." There were guardsmen and "Cantaniers" (singers), maids-in-waiting, and messengers. There was even an "Intelligent Donkey" played by, it would seem, an intelligent donkey.[7] There was also Eva Tanguay as Gabrielle du Chalus, confidante to the queen. It was a small role but one that Eva was determined to make shine. Alongside Eva, Violet Hollis and Mlle. Proto added to the onslaught of female beauty onstage at the Columbia. Two weeks after its opening, *My Lady* traded up to Hammerstein's Victoria—it was not uncommon for shows of the era to begin with a short, trial run at a smaller venue—with an expanded cast. The audience at Hammerstein's was "not stingy with laughter and applause," according to a reporter. And at least one critic found Eva Tanguay deserving of special mention.[8]

On the whole, *My Lady* received mixed reviews. "The book is quite good and the music is commendable," wrote a New York critic who saw the premiere at the Victoria in February of 1901. The same writer, however, felt the jokes were "worn-out." A jollier peer at another paper was less equivocal, reporting that *My Lady* "abounds in fun, sparkle and absurdity." Alan Dale, the cantankerous and influential critic for the *New York Journal,* made his feelings quite plain: "Some events occur better late than never. Others would be preferable better never than late. 'My Lady,' at the Victoria, belongs to the latter class." Nonetheless, the production enjoyed a modestly successful run.[9]

It was also during the course of *My Lady* that Eva first threw aside any expectation of submissiveness. She began to see that suffering stoically at the bottom of her profession's food chain suited neither her personality nor her talents and professional aims, for she was no longer content to submerge herself among the lot of chorus girls—which was her assignment in addition to the small role of Gabrielle du Chalus. As theater scholars have noted, the position of chorine increasingly meant becoming little more than a faceless body, a sexualized but anonymous part of an unthreatening mass. Though hugely popular as a cultural phenomenon, the chorus girl of the era was expected to do little more than exude two-dimensional beauty from the anonymity of her station as a way to get wined and dined by millionaires, then retire at a young age to a life of plush seclusion, supported by whatever mining magnate or banking bigwig had rescued her from the stage. Perhaps the most famous chorus girls of the era, the six women who glided about the stage in a 1900 musical called *Floradora,* all ended up marrying millionaires. It made sense considering that the average chorine earned perhaps $15 a week at the time, or some $350 in current terms. This was hardly Eva Tanguay's vision of a good career or the good life. She had no interest in become Mrs. So-and-So or making due with a measly $15 a week. Eva nursed a burning desire to become her own agent in life, to climb in status and gather riches and recognition on her own. As for anonymity, no matter how glamorous, it was anathema to the young actress from Holyoke. She had paid her dues toiling on the road for over a decade. It was now time to break loose.[10]

Eva looked with increasing suspicion on her fellow chorus line members in *My Lady.* She saw them as the enemy rather than her peers.

In a sense, this was accurate: any performer who wanted to graduate from the chorus had to view the others as her rivals. But in Eva's case, it also marked the first major, recorded instance of her odd paranoia playing out in full report. Throughout her career, Eva Tanguay looked at many of the women in her profession as willfully encroaching on her spotlight, even if it was not actually the case. Something beyond professional assertiveness was bursting forth, something that suggested deep emotional wounds and a vulnerability she could never quite reconcile.

In particular, Eva focused her animosity on Lotta Faust, a girlish beauty who had appeared in *The Liberty Belles* and would go on to win regard as "the girl with the luminous eyes and a valuable laugh" after her appearance in *The Wizard of Oz,* in 1903. In *My Lady,* Faust played the small, curvaceously cross-dressed role of George Villiers, the Duke of Buckingham, in addition to taking up her chorus duties.[11]

In rehearsals, Lotta Faust, whose very name indicated trouble, was chosen to step forth from the kick line and sing a tune called "Miss Virginia." During a break one afternoon, Eva crackled into her own rendition of the song. The future queen of vaudeville even added a few quirky dance steps. "Hey, you, Tanguay," shouted the stage manager, "Do that again." She did. Faust lost the number and Eva got it. The girl from Holyoke who had started out as an itinerant Fauntleroy now had a featured song and dance on Broadway. And Lotta Faust had a new enemy.[12]

When the show began its preliminary out-of-town trial in Boston, Faust made fast friends with a number of love-struck "rah-rah boys" from Harvard. At the time, Ivy League students, Harvard and Yale men in particular, seemed to have made a habit of chasing shapely actresses. Harvard students were famous as stage-door Johnnies, so it didn't take much to mobilize a fraternity-sized platoon of them to do the bidding of an appealing starlet. Having recruited her crimson army of champions, Lotta Faust now summoned them to New York to exact revenge. One night as Eva sang, one of the college pranksters who had traveled down from Cambridge hurled a biscuit onstage. (Curiously, it wasn't aimed at Eva but at Frances Belmont.) Jesse Jordan, another chorus beauty and ally of Faust's, stepped forward and threw the cookie back at the crowd, causing the house to erupt into peels of laughter. The curtain was brought down and the performance temporarily halted. When Eva later uncovered the scheme—it is said the Ivy League confederates got fifty dollars for their part—she went ballistic. Any notion of prudish, Victorian victimization went out the window. Eva Tanguay was not a chorus drone, nor would she tame herself for the sake of decorum. When Eva finally found Jesse Jordan in her dressing room, she grabbed Jordan's throat and choked her "until her tongue hung out as far as that," in the words of the *Evening World's* Charles Darnton. Jesse Jordan allegedly lost consciousness for several hours, and Eva Tanguay gained a reputation as an "awful fiend"—perfect and enticing stageland gossip. Stagehands and fellow performers granted her wide berth. The newspapers ate it up, calling her crazy, highly emotional, unpredictable. Eva was learning how to play up a public persona that allowed her greater professional freedom and enlarged her profile in the burgeoning celebrity marketplace. Soon the crowds were paying not just for Charles J. Ross and his inside jokes, but for a remarkable if allegedly unstable young entertainer named Eva Tanguay as well. In the economy of personality, the developing currency of the theater business, Eva Tanguay had ratcheted up her value by choking a chorus girl for all to see.[13]

MY LADY HAD GIVEN EVA TANGUAY a brief, if memorable, opportunity to shine. It also gave her the chance to show some public moxie and grab a role beyond that of mere line dancer, staking out new turf for women on the stage. Still, after the burlesque closed, she might just as easily have slipped back into the quasi anonymity of stock company wanderings. But fate provided the young actress with another opportunity, a show that hungered for Eva's peculiar talents. It was called *The Chaperons,* and whatever shortcomings it had as a work of drama—and it had many—it transformed her into a rising star. Perhaps it is more accurate to say that *The Chaperons* gave Eva the perfect platform on which to establish a vital emotional and libidinal connection with her audience, free from the trappings of conventional stage portrayals. Although Eva was not the lead in *The Chaperons,* to judge from press reports of the day you would never know it. It was *her* picture rather than photos of the show's lead players, May Boley, Trixie Friganza, Walter Jones, and Harry Conor, that often illustrated newspaper reviews and features. Well into the run of *The Chaperons,* the Dayton, Ohio, *Herald* wrote, "The now famous Tanguay romped through those two acts and worked her way down deep into the hearts of her audience." The *Kansas City World,* which reported that Eva was now on "the high road to stardom," wrote, "The attention this little French girl has attracted in 'The Chaperons' is all the more surprising because of the many well known people in the company" whom she, by inference, had outshined. She had turned a corner and in so doing redefined what it meant to "entertain."[14]

Like *My Lady, The Chaperons* was a lively bit of stage frivolity that was in total less than the assemblage of its parts—much less. It was not a burlesque per se. But like the *Musketeers* satire *My Lady,* it lay somewhere between a narrative entity and a piecemeal variety extravaganza. One headline declared, "'The Chaperons' a Nondescript Affair but Chock Full of Good Vaudeville." Audiences were not really seeking a story but, like a present-day moviegoer who goes to see a favorite stand-up comic in a mediocre movie, looking for individual performers to do what they were famous for.[15]

Frederic Ranken wrote the libretto for *The Chaperons* and Isidore Witmark the music. George W. Lederer directed, and the production was staged by one of the era's prominent small-time impresarios, Frank Perley. Witmark went on to earn regard as the founder of The House of Witmark music publishers. Frederic Ranken, described as "one of our most promising librettists," enjoyed brief glory as the writer of the hit musicals *The Gingerbread Man* and *Happyland* (cowritten with Reginald De Koven) before succumbing to typhoid fever at the age of thirty-six, in 1905. Perley, however, was the chief creative force behind *The Chaperons.*[16]

Born in 1858 in Erie, Pennsylvania, Frank Perley first learned his trade in the circus like many showmen of his day. He worked for the Doris Great Inter-Ocean Circus and put in several seasons as a "sawdust evangel"—that is, a press agent—with Barnum and Bailey's Greatest Show on Earth. He later formed Frank L. Perley's Singing Comedians, the troupe that would later produce *The Chaperons.* Perley saw in Eva Tanguay some kind of raw potential, though even he could not have realized just how much. He believed, it was written, that he had "a priceless jewel in the Tanguay laugh, and so all the merry soubrette has to do is to look happy and draw her salary, which is said to be a handsome sum." The oversimplification of Tanguay's talents in this press report suggested the writer's (and perhaps Perley's) inability to pin down what exactly the young actress brought to the stage. It was something potent yet ineffable, influenced by the past yet pointing toward things to come.[17]

The play's title, *The Chaperons,* referred to an organization called the "English and Continental Order of Trained Chaperons," a fictitious conservatory school located in Paris's Latin Quarter and lorded over by mistress Aramanthe Dedincourt. Violet Smilax, one of Dedincourt's students, has a crush on Tom Schuyler, whom she has run away to see. Adam Hogg, Violet's uncle, is a U.S. pork magnate and moral crusader. Fearing, correctly, that his niece, who is also his heiress, may not be dedicating herself fully to the study of chaperonage, he decides to pay her a surprise transatlantic visit. Having "made a Sunday School town of Cincinnati," Hogg also figures he can wipe Paris clean of its bawdiness and license.

No sooner has Hogg come to the City of Light, though, than he finds the seal missing on his will. For a constellation of nonsensical reasons, the discovery triggers Hogg to confiscate his niece's inheritance and hand it promptly over Signor Ricardo Bassini, owner of the Ancient and Honorable Parisians opera company. Bassini believes the missing seal to be in, of all places, Egypt. Thus the action shifts from fashionable Paris to exotic Alexandria (or Cairo, depending on which version of the script one has), where a painted backdrop depicted a hotel courtyard flanked by arabesque arches and parapets reminiscent of a North African fortress. There, another seal is missing, but not of the wax variety. Rather, this missing seal is the kind that swims, yelps, and eats fish. A sleuth named Phrosia played by Eva Tanguay is hot on the case. In her role, Eva wore a thick, dark skirt, a cream-colored, college-girl sweater, crude vagabond boots, and a felt hat like a gnome's with a brim and a high peak, resembling an absurd Halloween adornment. Around her neck was slung a copy of *Old Sleuth,* a collection of detective stories popular with readers in the United States in the 1870s. Her chubby, girlish face and mad laugh completed the effect. If the proceedings seemed ridiculous, confused, or both, to audiences of the day it mattered not. As one reviewer aptly put it, "The plot has really nothing to do with what Mr. Perley's comedians say and sing." In other words, it was the comedians themselves, pouring out their respective talents, that merited the price of admission. The show also parodied the growing popularity of chaperonage, a practice that reflected the increasing number of young urban women, sometimes called "bachelor girls," who had the income and cultural freedom to actively seek fun out on the town. Some middle-class social reformers felt these women needed supervision as they haunted big-city amusement spots like restaurants and dance halls, sparking a chaperoning movement. Though actual chaperones might have been looking over the shoulders of the young women who saw *The Chaperons* and other leisure fare, the free-spirited, rule-bending Eva Tanguay stared back from the stage with a metaphoric wink of encouragement for her youthful, female theatergoers' freewheeling desires.[18]

Often, what "Mr. Perley's comedians say and sing" was what they already said and sang in vaudeville. At any moment, cast members would break into routines for which they were already well-known such as the minstrel-like song "Bloomin' Lize." "No one knows what 'The Chaperons' is," observed journalist Miriam Michelson. "It is vaudeville strung on a pretense of a plot. Its songs have, of course, to pry open an opportunity to be heard with a crowbar. And its dances have, like the flowers that bloom in the spring, nothing whatever to do with the case." Such a description suggested, of course, that Miriam Michelson knew very much what *The Chaperons* was.[19]

In *The Chaperons,* Eva witnessed and further developed the art of the performer as an autonomous agent even within the artifice of narrative. As was common in the day, she designed many of her own costumes, notably those she wore when in secondary or chorus parts (as she would famously come to do in vaudeville proper), which she slipped on and off at lightning speed. Made of "spangles hanging on beads," Eva claimed her getup resembled "a blaze of dancing lights" when caught under the spotlight. Eva also learned how to put together costumes that were sexy and alluring in creative ways. She wore "tattered trousers and a shirt so negligee that it is almost negligent." She was discovering the powerful appeal of freakish, kinesthetic energy mixed with a useful show of leg and curve. She was mastering what others, notably Adah Isaacs Menken, had in prior decades: the delicate balance between risqué and respectable. It would lead a young Brooklyn woman named Mae West to consciously pattern herself after Eva. But in Eva's case sexuality never overshadowed personality, her prime object of fascination.[20]

Of the eighteen songs in *The Chaperons,* Eva was accorded two solos, "Billie Is Very Good to Me" and "My Sambo." Crowds and critics went nuts over the latter. "My Sambo," as its name suggested, was a "coon song," meaning a white appropriation and interpretation of supposedly authentic African American musical stylings. The corpulent songstress May Irwin pioneered the practice of white women singing such syncopated numbers in vaudeville. Scott Joplin was perhaps the most famous composer of coon songs and their close cousin, ragtime melodies. Sophie Tucker, later to become deeply involved in Eva's life, was perhaps the most famous singer in the genre in the 1910s. According to Tucker's biographer Armond Fields, coon songs differed from ragtime largely in their lyrics, which focused on "love, loss, and heartbreak," and were sung in "up-tempo, but unhurried" melody.[21]

The relationship between white performers and black-inflected popular entertainment genres is complicated to say the least and has been widely considered by scholars and historians. Donning the figurative blackface of a "coon" number afforded Eva and other middle-class white women a degree of frenetic, sexual abandon they might not have enjoyed in different roles. As some have noted, coon and ragtime numbers were most potent in the hands of stage women like Eva Tanguay who used such black-penned or black-inspired songs to create the image of a self-confident modern woman. They were also clearly racist, suggesting that African Americans were intrinsically different than middle-class whites by virtue of the former's lusty, almost adolescent attitudes. Musicologist Gillian M. Rodger points out that blackface minstrel characters in variety showed white performers and spectators that "black Americans could appear only as foolish and lesser beings," contributing to a consolidation of whites' feelings of cultural superiority. Playing the ethnic could also embolden a performer to break out of the confines and restrictions expected of her while still retaining respectability. She could be more energetic, sexual, outrageous, and titillating by playing a character from a different class and race.[22]

Eva's "Sambo" song boasted lines like, "I got a beau, I love him so, He's my sweet 'lasses Sam, I love him like rasper' jam, I never cared for a man but Sambo!" She complemented her singing by whirling about the stage with frightening speed and agility. "Eva Tanguay made the individual hit of the proceedings by her amazing display of vivacity in an infectious coon song, 'My Sambo,'" wrote the *New York Dramatic Mirror,* "which earned so many encores that even the composer must have lost count." Witmark estimated that Eva earned an average of twelve encores a night for "Sambo," and a Cincinnati theater where she played reported its long-standing encore record broken. The song, according to the *Mirror,* "completely captivated the house and [Eva Tanguay's] exploitation of unlimited 'ginger' was a revelation." In those days, "ginger" meant a combination of energy and effervescence tinged with naughtiness. Because of "Sambo" Eva was called "that booming rubber doll" and the "jiggly soubrette." When she got offstage, she noticed how stressed and overworked her legs felt. But she was young and able to recuperate quickly.[23]

The Chaperons premiered at the Middlesex Theatre in Middletown, Connecticut, on September 28, 1901. Digby Bell played the role of Hogg, Marie Cahill was Aramanthe Dedincourt, Joseph Miron was Bassini, and Louise Gunning filled the shoes of Violet Smilax. Eva, of course, was Phrosia, "An Admirer of Old Sleuth." During the rehearsal period, the show's musicians, with some free time on their hands, bought up "what looked like the entire beer supply of Middletown," according to one reporter. Boozed up good, they began hurling empties from the window of their rooming house onto the street below with unhappy consequences. Instead of playing at that evening's dress rehearsal, the whole orchestra found itself languishing in the local jail. Without a full and proper orchestra backing them up, Eva and her peers had but a lone piano.[24]

The show bounced around the pre–New York tryout circuit in early 1902, landing in eastern Canada, Eva's ancestral homeland, and several midwestern cities, including Kansas City and Saint Louis, where Eva's performance caused at least one newspaper to report, "Laughing is the newest way of earning a livlihood [sic] for women," alongside several photos in which Eva appeared to be guffawing uncontrollably. After a spell in Boston in early spring 1902, *The Chaperons* arrived in Newark, a crucial last stop on the way to Broadway. There, it tanked. At one performance there were so few people in the seats that Walter Jones, one of the production's character comics, walked to the lip of the wooden stage and said, "Gosh, folks, you must be lonesome down there. Why don't you all come up here with us?" The few patrons may have been amused, but Mark Klaw and Abraham Erlanger, the powerful producing team backing the show's New York run, were not. To direct, they brought in George Lederer, who at once insisted it be cut down to two acts. Songs were added and tweaks made. Thus repaired, *The Chaperons* moved to Providence, where it happily grew into a hit. By the time it made its Gotham debut, at the New York Theatre in June 1902, Trixie Friganza, called by the historian Susan A. Glenn "one of the earliest predecessors of modern stand-up comedians," had replaced Marie Cahill in the role of Dedincourt. Harry Conor was Hogg, and the character of Alphonse de Graft had been transmuted into Algernon O'Shaunessy, "one of those deplorable stage Irishmen of the chimpanzee type," according to a journalist of the day. Indelicate as the characterization might have been, the Irish stage caricature was drawn straight out of vaudeville and nineteenth-century popular theater. In Walter Jones's hands it was an audience favorite. After New York, *The Chaperons* went on to enjoy a successful run at other theaters, adding numbers and bits, cutting others, morphing and reinventing itself from venue to venue, like a vaudeville act learning from its mistakes. In July, *The Theatre* magazine ran a short feature on *The Chaperons,* calling it "a lively show" with "an irresistible combination" of performers, including "Miss Tanguay," who "sings and dances with amazing *entrain.*" Whether in French or English, Eva showed lots of "spirit" and "drive."[25]

From near anonymity, Eva Tanguay and her fellow trouper Trixie Friganza, emerged as the show's powerhouse talents. "'The Chaperons' Has Made Young Actress Famous," shouted a newspaper headline shortly after the show's New York debut. The article went on to report: "Probably the two most discussed young women on Broadway yesterday were Eva Tanguay and Trixie Friganza, the unknowns, who jumped into fame at a bound by reason of their clever work in 'The Chaperons' at the New York Theatre Thursday night." Another journalist chose to single out only Eva, remarking, "We have not had anybody for a long time who is her equal in eccentric comedy, and she has a walk that is simply immense."[26]

Although the show itself underwent significant changes, enjoying ups and downs, Eva's part in it gathered speed and magnetism. By 1903, her Phrosia was becoming the stuff of legend. As she gained fame, she staked out a new kind of performance aesthetic: a powerhouse singing-and-dancing oddity and leg show. The *Brooklyn Eagle* credited her with evincing a "new style," finding her every "word and action...novel," especially her "freak work." She was regarded as "a brilliant character actress" worthy of "extravagant praise...the hit of the show." Other spectators were less enthralled, including one who termed Eva a "jerky, grotesque, nervous young woman" sporting a "coiffure that baffles description." Still others condemned Eva for violating perceived codes of decency and decorum, adding unwittingly to Eva's mystique and appeal. A journalist who saw her in New York accused Eva of mistaking "violent forwardness for vivaciousness," and of being "offensive with her monkeyshines." It might be okay to pull off that lowbrow "sort of thing" in a Bowery music hall or a Coney Island sideshow, but it was improper on Broadway. The times, however, were on Eva's side. In the wake of her Phrosia, a publication of the day argued that "while heretofore the women in the casts of farcical productions have had to look prim and pretty and be satisfied with that, nowadays they must furnish food for risibility." The "day of the comic actress has dawned," proclaimed one newspaper. Eva bounded over new territory. She was crazy and wild with little need for the self-restraint expected of respectable middle-class white women in early twentieth century.[27]

Eva was also introducing an athletic sexuality that suggested startling energy and virtuosic endurance. Austin Latchaw, columnist for the *Kansas City Star* in the late 1930s, long after Eva's heyday, wrote that he had recently seen a magazine cover with a picture of two drum majorettes. "The girls, with heads thrown back, with arm and leg muscles taut, with bodies apparently moving in perfect unison, with faces smiling in jubilant happiness...surging with vitality" instantly brought back to him memories of Eva Tanguay in *The Chaperons*. His words conjured an orgasmic vibrancy, an acrobatics of abandon choreographed to perfection. "For all the dancers I have seen, no one matched Eva Tanguay in tireless energy, and no topical singer with quite such gusto." Predictably, Latchaw recalled (at some length) Eva's marvelous bare legs. But Eva's display should not be seen as mere pandering or self-objectification. If the grotesque body, one that made "jerky" movements, broke down barriers, so too did a woman daring to perform with such vitality and speed that she was something of an actress and athlete combined in one body.[28]

With *The Chaperons,* Eva broke out further from behind the role. When the show hit Muncie, Indiana, Eva arranged to serve dishes to the locals at Le Clede Café, a tastefully decorated popular restaurant on Muncie's Main Street. Her salary with Perley's company was so low, she claimed, she had no choice but to pick up a few shifts as a waitress. The gambit worked, getting her (more) press coverage as a cheeky jokester who loved her public, not to mention a few nice tips. The masquerade not only played out like a vaudeville sketch but also offered a sardonic commentary on women's place in the economic pecking order. It was at once entertaining, subversive, and timely, paving the way for women of our present era to combine comedy with a political statement of sorts. Though such "pseudoevents" would be decried by social critics of later ages, there is no doubt that Eva's press-attracting shenanigans played nicely into the hands of a national media increasingly more interested in performers' personalities than their artistic achievements. In Eva's hands, to be sure, personality itself had become an artistic achievement.[29]

The tour of *The Chaperons* progressed through the heartland: Chicago; La Crosse, Wisconsin; the plains of Iowa. As it did, Eva's fame as the coon-singing, seal-hunting, madcap detective Phrosia swelled. So notable had she become that by the time the show hit Des Moines, retail merchants there hired a squad of undercover female security agents to sniff out shoplifters, prompting the *Des Moines Register* to announce, "The Eva Tanguays are coming." Would-be filchers were warned they "must look out for Eva Tanguays," plainclothes lady detectives quietly on the lookout for wrongdoing at local stores. "Have a care lest just as your business is at its best," the *Register* warned, "there comes a soft touch on your elbow and a sweet voice whispers in your ear, 'I am Phrosia, the female detective. Kindly hold out your hands for the cold embrace of my iron bracelets.'" Since vaudeville aimed for the same crowd that frequented big retail establishments—indeed, theaters were often carefully placed near major shopping districts—it was an ideal gambit. Eva Tanguay had entered the cultural lexicon.[30]

BOTH ON TOUR AND IN NEW YORK, *The Chaperons* had been a hit, in no small measure because of Eva. By the time the production wound down, Eva not only found herself with a growing legion of fans but also her first sugar daddy. Literally. Frederick C. Havemeyer owed his fortune to sugar. His father, Theodore Havemeyer, had been one of the country's great monopolists in the sugar trade, helping organize the American Sugar Refineries Company, sometimes called the "Sugar Trust." Frederick was said to have millions in the bank, though one report suggested his net worth to have been around $275,000, some $6 million in today's purchasing power.[31]

Havemeyer doted on Eva in a way that was both heartwarming and slightly disturbing. "I was sort of a pet of his," Eva later wrote. Havemeyer first met Eva when she was rehearsing *The Chaperons* in New York City. The stage manager, Al Morgan, walked onstage one day as the cast was going through its paces and introduced them to an aged gentleman by his side. "I want you to meet Mr. Havemeyer," said Morgan. "He will be with us for a while. I want you to be nice to him." In the dressing room and backstage the players gossiped—"Wonder who Mr. Gotrocks is?"—figuring him one of the show's backers. In time, they discovered his real identity and dubbed him "The Sugar King." Havemeyer was in his early seventies, a widower for seventeen years already, with no children and "nothing but money and time to spend it." Quite soon, he would choose to spend it on Eva Tanguay. He gave her a seven-thousand-dollar diamond tiara and, fittingly, a two-thousand-dollar sealskin coat. Throughout it all she insisted there was no funny business. "He was just a kindly, eccentric old man, a grandpa type," she claimed. Havemeyer had a slightly different fantasy in mind, casting Eva in a diamond-studded Electra complex of his own making. Eva would sometimes approach the footlights, look at the old man and say, "Hello Nunkey. That's my Nunkey down there." When she did, Havemeyer would turn to the people around him and declare, "She's my daughter. Isn't she wonderful?" Sometimes he offered her a thousand dollars just to smile at him from onstage.

Havemeyer's dotage also conferred a kind of cultural capital on Eva, not so much because he was rich and male (though that did not hurt) but because via such public interactions, whether onstage or as reported in the press, Eva's "personal life" became an object of interest. In the absence of a husband or any other visible partner, the press would have to focus on Eva's ambiguous relations with men like Havemeyer. And in this case, it was just weird enough to suffice. The narrative of Eva's life, fueled by her "unique" personality, was increasingly on display. If the conventional chorus-girl story involved a younger man plucking a beauty from the stage for good, Eva's version was different, and much more professionally ambitious. She happily took what she could get and kept right on performing. Public interactions such as those with the

Sugar King, however curious, made the rising stage star less a "distant social figure," and more someone "with whom spectators perceive[d] themselves as sharing a personal relationship," to borrow Renée Sentilles's observations on the phenomenon of celebrity.[32]

Eva's relations with the Sugar King were, like many of her relationships with men, unconventional, hazily defined, and ultimately attenuated. Throughout her adult life, she demonstrated a decided ambivalence about traditional coupling with men. She clearly enjoyed men as sexual partners and short-term boyfriends. Sometimes she liked the attention of older men and the gifts and favors that accompanied it. But her deepest, most intimate, and most durable emotional and personal bonds were with women: family, friends, and perhaps most important, her female peers in show business. Together, the women in vaudeville formed a sorority of companions who would long remain in touch. Their elder members now tutored Eva on the challenges of show business, as Francesca Redding had once done. Indeed, the mere act of being on the road earning money and fame was itself a social transgression, as it placed Eva far from the cloistered, economically dependent space of the middle-class home.[33]

One who helped her learn the ropes was Trixie Friganza, Eva's costar in *The Chaperons*. "Who carried off the show in a dancing specialty with a chorus in 'The Chaperons' last night?" asked the *New York World* in June 1902. "Eva Tanguay, no less." It went on: "And who, after a service in the choruses of Broadway successes, extending over several seasons, went out West to take the star part of 'The Chaperons,' made good in a resoundingly emphatic manner and came into New York last night to establish herself as a favorite of the first rank? Trixie Friganza, also no less." Eva and Trixie had emerged together in the national spotlight.[34]

Friganza was born Brigid O'Callaghan, on November 20, 1870, in Grenola, Kansas. Like Eva's, her parents also were immigrants. Her father was Irish and her mother was Spanish; the latter's maiden name was Friganza. After some Catholic schooling, Trixie set off in her late teens to become an actress. Tall and slender, she made her first appearance in the chorus of *The Pearl of Pekin* in 1889. But young Friganza soon began putting on pounds, which she tried in vain to shed. "The added weight served merely to increase the lightness of her comedy and the gaiety of her spirit," observed the *New York Times* many years later. It did not help that her dancing was offbeat as well. "I couldn't keep time, or jig the right jiggle or kick the right kick," she said. Such tactful self-deprecation was very much in sync with Eva's rhetoric. Friganza tried diet tricks, everything from nearly starving herself to downing pitchers full of warm water and lemon juice. But she only grew fatter. Rather than give up, though, Friganza decided to make her heft work in her favor. Laying aside dreams of Lady Macbeth and Juliet, she focused on making "people giggle" as she executed one fabulous song after another in a voice graced with stunning clarity. Her figure ironically commented on the voluptuous beauties popular in the second half of the nineteenth century, and would provide a mocking take on the skinny flapper beauties in the decades to come. Friganza's dances were intentionally grotesque and indelicate but never vulgar. She wore sumptuous gowns, backed herself with a slew of talented musical accompanists, and erected gorgeous scenery when the act called for it. As a comic actress, she scored a major success in Charles Hoyt's comic melodrama *A Trip to Chinatown*.[35]

Trixie Friganza thus increasingly saw her girth not as an impediment to be overcome but as a kind of actual and cultural costume that she used to subvert prevailing social norms. In so doing, she both advanced the notion of personal appeal over accepted skill and made a crucial link to the women in her audience. She padded herself up to appear even portlier, told countless fat jokes, and tried to forge a universal link among women in her audiences via their shared concerns. Friganza realized that skinny women were objects of desire and recipients of pathos. By contrast, a fat woman falling down evoked only laughter. Her admirable and unabashed girth was said to embody "the sensuality of unrestrained appetites." Though such a pose could lead many (male, middle-class) observers to see her as an exemplar of failed self-will, it could also motivate unconscious fears of women's power and desires associated, as it continues to be, with what some literary critics might call "carnivalesque excess." Eva would learn well from her friend Trixie Friganza's use of self-presentation and her ability to turn a potentially negative personal characteristic into a unique and valuable asset.[36]

Trixie and Eva roomed together on the road. One evening, Friganza showed her younger disciple how a traveling woman might need to take care of herself. As Eva tended to personal matters in her bathroom at the New Sherman Hotel in Jamestown, New York, she heard a noise. Looking through a window that opened into an adjoining room, she saw a man "calmly observing her." (It is unclear whether he was calmly doing anything else at the same time.) Eva yelped. The voyeur took off down the hallway, but not before the portly and powerful Friganza tore after him with a battle cry, striking him with her fists when proximity allowed. At first unsure what to do, Eva, clad only in her bathrobe, gave chase. The two women soon overpowered the hapless intruder, their blows subduing him, their screams calling others to their aid. Cast member Walter Jones gave the villain "a sound thrashing." Face bleeding and clothing torn, the man who dared look at Eva Tanguay in her private boudoir was then turned over to the police.[37]

BACK FROM the perils and excitement of touring with *The Chaperons,* Eva was ready for bigger things. For the moment, though, she would have to mark time as a notable ensemble character in yet another lightweight musical. But even there, her star potential continued to brighten and those in the theatrical hierarchy took note.

Her role was that of Claire De Lune in *The Office Boy.* The show premiered at the Colonial Theatre in New York in the last week of October 1903, moving to Hammerstein's Victoria in November. Based on a peculiarly titled French farce *Le jockey malgre lui* (*The Jockey in Spite of Himself*) by Maurice Ordonneau and Paul Gavault, *The Office Boy* featured music by Ludwig Englander and a book Harry B. Smith. Smith would soon play an important part in Eva's career. Charles B. Dillingham produced.[38]

The first act of *The Office Boy* is set in the law offices of Ketcham & Cheatham, where "an extraordinary number of pretty typewriters and clerks are employed." Unhappy about their low pay, they are about to go on strike when two burglars arrive intending to blow open the firm's safe. From the cracked vault emerges a sleepy, recently napping outsider named Noah Little, portrayed by the hugely popular Frank Daniels. Little promptly falls in love with an office girl named Euphemia, but to get her he must pass himself off as a bona fide member of the firm rather than an itinerant napper. The second act finds Little at the country estate of Euphemia's father, delivering a message like a good office boy of his era. In a plot twist that must be wondered at, he "is mistaken for a famous jockey." He ends up riding a "fiery steed" and emerges in "very much battered condition." Still, everything resolves happily in the end. "The story is rather flimsy," admitted the *New York Dramatic Mirror.* But "it does not seem necessary to have much of a plot in pieces of this sort, as long as there is plenty of fun and several songs." Like *The Chaperons* and so many other similar stage confections of its day, *The Office Boy* had both.[39]

The Office Boy gave Eva another opportunity to watch a performer use a scripted role as a pedestal from which to display personal charm and magnetism, like Charles J. Ross in *My Lady.* The main character was played by Frank Daniels. "The amount of fun contained in the average Frank Daniels show is generally in direct ratio to the amount of time which that comedian spends on the stage," reasoned the *New York Times*. "If the number of minutes in which he is off the scene exceeds the number in which he is 'among those present' his audiences are pretty apt to feel that something is lacking." The crowd loved Daniels's signature gags and mugs. He "interpolated" his songs, such that they became as much his as the composer's, or arguably more so. He demonstrated that in musical comedy and vaudeville, the book wasn't the thing, nor were the songs. *You* were the thing. "It is a habit in the case of comedians of the Daniels order to refer to them as being themselves, which is generally considered sufficient for all purposes," observed the *Times*.[40]

Although Frank Daniels got the most attention for *The Office Boy,* among the secondary leads, none shined brighter than Eva Tanguay, who "made a great hit in her specialties." If her fellow females were possessed of "sweet voice" and played "dainty soubrettes," Eva won favor by contrast. "Eva Tanguay…is quite as lively as ever," wrote the *New York Times,* "and [her] dancing, while it does not at any time suggest the poetry of motion, has a quality of abandon that many people like just as much." As Claire De Lune in *The Office Boy,* Eva was "a fresh bottle of fizz" whose "songs went with a snap and whose feet went like a recordmaking motor." Eva was so magnetic in her triumphant number "Summer Proposals" that impresario Charles Frohman expressed interest in taking *The Office Boy* to London. "Miss Tanguay's personality is so peculiarly her own that it is believed she would make a genuine sensation over there and would strike the English as something decidedly novel in the actress line," wrote one newspaper. It is unclear whether Frohman's intentions were genuine or some version of a ploy commonly used to increase a performer's worth. If the latter, Eva got another lesson in raising one's stock in the entertainment marketplace.[41]

The Office Boy toured with modest success. In Buffalo, a local reporter was surprised to find the book "actually funny" and free of "cheap horseplay…stale joke[s], and…empty jests." In addition to the training and paycheck working as a featured player afforded her, Eva became further acclimated to the culture of the traveling show. She saw the way players could form a fraternity knit together with merry pranks. On at least one occasion, a glass of lemonade that Frank Daniels drank during his signature number, "I'm on the Water Wagon Now," was replaced with a whiskey highball. Other unexpected shenanigans occurred in Portland, Oregon. Ten minutes before he was to go on in the role of a policeman, the trouper Leavitt James discovered to his shock that his costume had been sent to the tailor for cleaning and repair. Thinking fast, he convinced an actual policeman stationed just outside the theater to lend him his uniform. The constable happily complied and the show went off with "not a hitch," despite the fact that the real officer was a few sizes larger than the actor. Stories like these, unabashedly publicized and probably embroidered, suggested an effort at what might be called the vaudevillization of public life. In such tales, the world outside the theater was depicted as a gag-filled extension of the stage's skits and bits, played out under streetlights rather than klieg lights.[42]

After her turn as Phrosia in *The Chaperons, The Office Boy* was a lateral move for Eva, no matter that it won her further recognition. She would have to wait for her next opportunity to rise above the rabble. As for *The Office Boy,* it almost sank into obscurity after Daniels, Tanguay, and their peers were done with it. Remarkably, for a musical comedy of its sort, *The Office Boy* was revived in 1915 with Eddie Carr in the Daniels role. Carr "carries the audience" wrote the *Springfield Mirror.* But whoever played Claire De Lune went unmentioned.[43]

3

❧

I Don't Care

EVA RODE out the remainder of *The Office Boy,* touring and taking her salary while learning what she could from the masterful Frank Daniels. But she yearned for more. *The Chaperons* had shown her a first twinkling of stardom and she liked it. Though catchy songs and hit musicals had a breathtakingly short shelf life in the days before recording technology, somehow her edgy "Sambo" number was still popular. Noting this fact, some canny backers decided to build a spin-off production around the song and its quirky chanteuse. But they had to act fast, lest "Sambo" die and its corpse fade beyond recognition.

Chief among the Broadway powers backing the "Sambo" project was George W. Lederer. Like Frank Perley, the producer of *The Chaperons,* George Lederer was an artistic and entrepreneurial impresario, such as the theater of the era, not quite so heavily specialized as it would become in subsequent years, allowed. Rather than start from scratch, Lederer, the man who had been brought in to save *The Chaperons,* did what he knew best: he took an ailing but promising script and reworked it into something better. The play in which Lederer saw promise was *The Blonde in Black;* it had debuted in June 1903 with Blanche Ring, a notable talent, in the lead role of Flossie Featherly, a woman "who goes to Paris to teach the cake-walk, but whose ambition is to play Camille." This time around, George Lederer was not a hired gun on someone else's turf. He was now a full-on producer-manager and as such enjoyed the highest degree of creative control offered in his day. He was free to disassemble *The Blonde in Black* and rebuild it as he saw fit until it shined like a pearl. Fortunately, he knew where to look for help.[1]

To reinvent *The Blonde in Black* as a proper Eva Tanguay vehicle, Lederer brought in librettist Harry B. Smith, who had written the book for *The Office Boy,* and composer Gustave Kerker to write the music. In so doing, he was recruiting two of the most eminent talents Broadway had to offer. Harry Bache Smith, later remembered as "the most prolific librettist of his day," was born in Buffalo on December 28, 1860. After working as a humor columnist for the *Chicago Daily News,* he moved on to writing dialogue and lyrics, the first being his 1883 work *Rosita; or, Cupid and Cupidity.* Others, including *Amaryllis; or, Mammon and Gammon,* soon followed. Teaming up with the songwriter Reginald De Koven, a former dry-goods shipping clerk, Smith scored a hit with *The Begum,* termed "a kind of panjandrum of comic operetta in the United States." Smith and De Koven formed a temporary partnership. Their follow-up to *The Begum*—an adaptation of *Robin Hood* (not to be confused with an 1872 burlesque of similar name written expressly for Lydia Thompson)—would prove to be a smash hit. Smith went on to become one of the most prolific and top-earning lyricists of his day, later working with Jerome Kern and Irving Berlin, and contributing heavily to the legendary showman Florenz Ziegfeld's first *Follies* in 1907.

Nor was Gustave Kerker, Smith's partner in *The Sambo Girl,* short on talent or reputation. Kerker, born in Westphalia, Germany, in 1857, came to the United States at the age of ten. As an adult, he went on to write such successful (though largely forgotten) shows as *Castles in the Air, The Belle of New York,* and *The Telephone Girl.* Kerker saw possibilities for musical comedy that went beyond the conceit of slapdash burlesques like *My Lady* and fluff pieces like *The Chaperons.* "Musical comedy as it has existed for some time," he said, "is simply a thing of shreds and patches. The public is certainly tired of it." Perhaps some sector of "the public" yearned for something more. At the moment, however, it was hungry for the vaudeville-like informality of *The Sambo Girl,* featuring, as it did, star personalities like Eva. "Threads and patches" in her hands could be potentially spun with gold.[2]

The Blonde in Black was thoroughly reworked to make way for Eva Tanguay. First, the main character was rewritten and renamed to suggest Eva's zest and vitality. In *The Sambo Girl,* the character of Flossie Featherly had now become Carlotta Dashington, an outspoken, enterprising American who finds herself in Paris. The first act is set in Henri Du Pont's clothing boutique. Du Pont does more than sell upmarket hats and dresses to fancy Parisian women. He is also a "matrimonial agent." As such, he calculates the odds of a particular woman cheating on her husband within the first three years of their marriage. He sniffs around, looks into her past, tempts her in the present, and if she passes, Du Pont gets a tidy sum from the man who is to be her mate. Of course if he is wrong, it means a hefty payout to his client.[3]

The last thing on Carlotta Dashington's mind, however, is marriage. She has cabled ahead to Du Pont's shop requesting forty gowns. It has been a busy day for Carlotta, having just bested a male competitor in a car race. "It was all on account of trying to get away from a man," offers Carlotta by way of an excuse. The character's competitiveness, her drive, and the way she rejects couplehood were all a salute to Eva Tanguay. Carlotta Dashington allowed Eva to further pierce the already flimsy fourth wall and state her opinions and desires directly to the audience, relegating the story to secondary importance. Just as Sarah Bernhardt had learned how to "engineer her own celebrity" a generation earlier, so too was Eva Tanguay forging a relationship with her public that transcended the playscript.[4]

Costarring with Eva was the pianist, composer, and sometime actor Melville Collins. Little is known about Collins, though he was to play an important part in Eva's life. Before *The Sambo Girl*, Collins had appeared in a Broadway show called *The Princess Chic* in the role of Louis XI. Wes Eichenwald, a longtime investigator into Eva's life, wrote an article about her for the magazine *American History*, in December 2001. In the article, he described Collins as "a gentlemanly composer" who was the "greatest love of Eva's life." Eichenwald did not provide further evidence or a source for this amazing claim—certainly Eva never said much about him in the press or privately—but he had interviewed one of Eva's surviving nieces in the 1970s. Collins would continue to be associated with Eva and her family, both professionally and personally, for over a decade. But as far as the Eichenwald article goes, Melville Collins merely "liked" Eva and never returned her passion. If so, it would seem that Eva's greatest longing was for a man who did not want her.[5]

Collins played Raphael Rubens, an artist who is about to debut a painting titled *The Sambo Girl*. It is an idealized rendering based on an American dancer he has seen strutting in the theater. So taken was he when he saw her that he threw roses onstage, causing the actress to blush and forget her lines. But Carlotta Dashington will have nothing to do with sentiment. "My dear sir," she says, "the milk of human kindness grows sour as soon as it is taken from the refrigerator." It turns out, of course, that Dashington is the very "Sambo Girl" Rubens had seen onstage during a trip to New York one year earlier. He begs her to come to his studio and sit for him so he can finally finish his masterpiece. She agrees, but only if "no word of love will pass your lips."

There is, meanwhile, another plot involving a man Du Pont has insured but whose wife appears dangerously close to straying before the three-year mark. If she does, Du Pont will have to pay out on the matrimonial insurance claim he sold her husband—and that will ruin him. By dint of several harebrained plot complications, the plan Du Pont concocts to save himself dovetails perfectly with the push-pull machinations between Dashington and Rubens. In the end, Carlotta and Raphael end up headed for the altar and Du Pont's business is saved. The coupling of Eva's Carlotta Dashington and Collins's Rubens, however, seems anything but inevitable. Rather, like a series of odd jokes about dentistry tossed in throughout the script, their matrimonial union feels stuck on, artificial, there for the appearance of closure before respectable, middle-class audiences. Fittingly, Eva was recognized as an individual player with star power rather than one half of a man-woman combination act. "Miss Tanguay as Carlotta, the Sambo Girl, so dominated the whole thing that it is hard to say what her work was like," wrote one reviewer. Despite her character's participation in wedded union, her portrayal and the awkwardness of the plot device has Eva Tanguay essentially laughing at marriage. In her offstage life, Eva long resisted marriage or any identity based on coupling with a man. In her first major starring role, she articulated her ambivalence toward cultural norms framed in the fiercely effective conceit of comedy.[6]

The Sambo Girl was yet another example of fractured vaudeville fare clumped together as a narrative musical comedy. Its piecemeal nature was made perhaps most obvious by the fact that it was based on a song from another musical comedy. In addition, Melville Collins contributed a tune called "I'm for You." Among the other compositions put in for the woman "whose riotous curls were always in her eyes and who sang in a queer little voice and danced like a drunken fairy" were "Sparks," "A Ragtime Hit," "The Girl with the Wink," and "If I Had a Theater on Broadway." Some of these would become part of Eva's vaudeville repertoire for years to come.[7]

But there was one song more than any other in *The Sambo Girl* that caught the public's attention. It was her first number in the show, and it would become her trademark, as well as the devil on her shoulder and the albatross around her neck. The song was "I Don't Care." It went like this:

Figure 10. A riot of golden curls.
Though she often downplayed her beauty, Eva knew how to make the most
of her often alluring—sometimes even soft—feminine side as the performance
demanded. From the 1870s onward, blond hair increasingly symbolized the
sexiness and independent bombast of the showgirl.
(Private collection, courtesy of Beth Touchton.)

· · · · · · · · ·

They say I'm crazy, got no sense,
But I don't care.
They may or may not mean offense,
But I don't care;
You see I'm sort of independent,
Of a clever race descendent,
My star is on the ascendant,
That's why I don't care.

I don't care,
I don't care,
What they may think of me.
I'm happy go lucky,
Men say I am plucky,
So jolly and care free.
I don't care,
I don't care,
If I do get the mean and stony stare.
If I'm never successful,
It won't be distressful,
'Cos I don't care.

There are other verses, other lines full of wicked pluck and wanton mirth. There are rhymes that would have been inadmissible before ragtime, such as "'Cos my good nature effervescing,/Is one, there is no distressing," and "So no one can 'Phase' me,/By calling me 'Crazy.'"

It is difficult to grasp the song's raggish, carnivalesque appeal merely by looking at the words. When she performed it in Florenz Ziegfeld's *Follies of 1909,* the first words out of her mouth were "Hello everybody," but uttered in a tone at once devilish and girlish. She drew out and warbled the word "care" so it became "CAY-uhhhh." Eva giggled the words, but not in an infantile manner. Rather, they were sung with the mesmerizing allure of the snake charmer's flute. In Eva's routine, "I Don't Care" shuddered from her vocal chords in the same frenzied, cakewalking, barely controlled way that she herself skipped and trotted about the stage. It was a perfect marriage of performer and song.[8]

"From the minute she sang her first song, a new one called 'I Don't Care,' the charm of her unique talent asserted itself over the audience," wrote a Pennsylvania newspaperman, while another journalist who saw Eva do "I Don't Care" interpreted it as "a sort of index to her hair, eyes, face, figure and character, in which she confided to the audience that she did not care what they thought about her looks." The song was the perfect platform for Eva's innovative style. It set her apart and established her presence as an object of fascination. She would sometimes customize the number for different crowds. In Pittsburgh, she included a verse about how glad she was to be in Pittsburgh again. She tacked on lines and stanzas about her favorite subject—herself. "I Don't Care" led one awestruck journalist to conclude: "Miss Tanguay is perhaps the most remarkable person on the stage."[9]

"I Don't Care," sprang from the pen of Jean Lenox, "a versatile little woman song writer, newspaper woman and magazine contributor," and the piano of Harry O. Sutton. Lenox later tried to capitalize on Eva's blossoming fame by taking her own rendition of "I Don't Care" onstage. She did two versions, one "as she intended it to be rendered when she wrote it, and then as Miss Tanguay perpetrates it." Lenox's act failed.[10]

"I Don't Care" seemed to be Eva's unending source of fame and wealth. But it was also a burden. When she entered vaudeville, her contracts specified that she had to sing "I Don't Care." In 1908, a Philadelphia vaudeville audience "refused to let her go" until she performed her signature tune. "That wretched song has been the cause of all my trouble," Eva once complained. She even came up with a musical response, "I Really Do Care After All":

> *When you see an "Arrow,"*
> *You think of "Coca-Cola."*
> *When you see "His Master's Voice,"*
> *You think of a "Victrola."*
> *When you see a "B.V.D.,"*
> *You think of underwear.*
> *And when you think of "Eva"*
> *You think of "I Don't Care."*
> *Sometimes I just wonder if*
> *You really believe it. . . .*
> *But I hope you understand*
>
> *That I really do care if you like me*
> *And I really do care if you applaud*
> *And I really do care if you're smiling out there.*
> *In my heart I say,*
> *"Thank Goodness they are with me."*

And I really do care if my salary
Isn't waiting at the box office when I call.
I may sing "I don't care, I don't care,"
But I really do care after all.

It didn't work. She was still and would forever be Eva Tanguay, the siren of "I Don't Care."[11]

Out of Eva Tanguay's hands, "I Don't Care" could mean anything to anybody. It could be taken as a playful romp of the Jazz Age. Or it could be interpreted as something sterner. Many years after she debuted it, in 1918, a conservative booster of U.S. war morale felt "that song as interpreted by Miss Tanguay is, after all, the spirit of America." Eva's assertion of "I Don't Care" meant, according to this gentleman, that she was not afraid of sacrifice in order to make the world "safe for democracy," which had become essential in the face of "the threat of the Huns, and the menace of militarism, the terror of the aeroplane and the horror of the submarine." But those who opposed U.S. entry into the raging European war, those who apathetically said, "I don't care," were taking away the *wrong* message, in his eyes. Such an attitude could be "seen in the slacker, the pacifist and the mollycoddle—who does not care what happens so long as he is protected and comfortable and who cares not who does the fighting so long as the slumberous routine of his selfish respectability is not disturbed," according to this flag-waving Eva acolyte.[12]

In the wake of *The Sambo Girl,* Eva told a journalist that she received so many letters from fans inquiring what a "Sambo" was that she was thinking of printing a standardized reply postcard: "Dear Miss Blank or Mr. Addle-Pate—In response to your inquiry of even date [*sic*] I need only tell you that Mr. Webster defines 'The Sambo Girl' as the 'offspring of a dark person and a mulatto.' And I may add, in conclusion, that the term is of East-Indian derivation: If you will come to the _____ theater this week *The Sambo Girl* will be glad to entertain you. Very truly, Eva Tanguay." The journalists following Eva's rising star loved it. She was iconoclastic, self-promoting, and always possessed of a few choice words for a newspaper quote.[13]

MONUMENTAL AS *The Sambo Girl* was—indeed, because of its massive success and Eva's "I Don't Care" hit number—it heralded Eva's departure from musical comedy. Though she would appear in several scripted musicals and revues over the next decade, Eva now understood that she herself was the only show she needed. That meant taking on vaudeville as a full-time concern.

In fact, Eva had already dipped her toes, and then some, into vaudeville. In 1902, she played at the Cherry Blossom Grove Atop the New York Theatre. Though billed as "The Most Vivacious of All," she was not the headliner, nor was she even a solo act, but appeared with the chorus girls she so disliked. Top credits for the show went to hugely popular blackface minstrels McIntyre & Heath. Two years later, Eva again cropped up in vaudeville. Now her profile was larger but she was still not a star. Billed as "The pet of the Vaudevilles" at Cleveland's New Theatre, "devoted to high class vaudeville," she appeared in the number-five position out of nine total acts. Though audiences liked her, Eva had to bide her time while the crowd cheered soon-to-be-forgotten headliner Edna Aug, at the time dubbed "The Funniest Woman in Vaudeville."[14]

By early 1905, Eva had hit on a plan that would let her headline vaudeville shows. It would carry enough of the capital she had earned as Carlotta Dashington while permitting her to ultimately shed that skin, revealing the full, unmediated Eva underneath. At the time, it was not uncommon for vaudeville shows to feature shortened, freestanding versions of popular plays and musicals, stuck in amid the other variety acts on the bill. Eva pared *The Sambo Girl* down to twenty-five minutes and turned it into a vaudeville act that she took on the road. Melville Collins took over from Frank Norcross as Eva's manager following reports that Eva was "dissatisfied" with Norcross. Where there had been twenty-eight songs, there were now sixteen. Though Collins may not have offered Eva the romantic relationship she wanted, he appears to have helped her build an advertising scheme that would not only draw in audiences but would build her star "brand" as well. "There is them what said she couldn't but she has made good and then some in that ringing swinging dancing singing lyric gem The Sambo Girl," boasted one advertisement. The vaudeville-ized version of *The Sambo Girl* also took a page from the burlesque-inspired stage revues of the day, with "scenic accessories, gorgeous costumes, and Oh, My! Gars and Starters, oodles & oodles of the swaggerest girls." The chorus girls could stay for the time being, especially since they were now mere pawns beside the queen.[15]

The vaudeville theater Eva dove into was eclectic in its offerings. E. F. Albee, one of the most powerful businessmen behind the scenes, constantly played up the mongrel nature of his enterprise. "What an epitome of the graces and humors of humanity is represented by an adroit vaudeville program! Acrobats, song and dance men, serio-comics, musicians, buffoons, beauties, the specialists in all the varied forms of vaudeville—they are wonderful," declared Albee.[16] But vaudeville bills also needed an anchor, a "headliner," someone who could please as many tastes as possible and fill theaters night after night. In time, Eva Tanguay would be the most famous headliner on the North American vaudeville circuits. Managers and producers would discover that she was valuable not only because different parts of her act appealed to nearly everyone in the audience, but also because she could improve the tone and pacing of the overall bill, even repair it, if need be.

Consider a program starring Eva at the Temple Theater in Detroit the night of March 28, 1904, before she had devoted her full energies to vaudeville. The LaMonts, an "excellent acrobatic act," according to the manager of the theater in his report to the head office, consisting of "two men and a girl," opened the show. Nine minutes after the LaMonts demonstrated their first feat, they were off, making way for Max Waldon, "one of the best, if not the best act of the female impersonation type we ever played." Waldon did four or five different characters in drag over fourteen minutes. The manager, who found Waldon's voice "exceptionally good," admired that he "dressed stunningly" as well. He was followed by McIntyre and Primrose, blackface minstrels who joked and gagged in burned cork and greasepaint for fourteen minutes. Alas, they were "far from being strong." Actress Mary Norman then came on and for seventeen minutes tried to win over the crowd by "caricaturing society women" in all their gorgeous pretense. She was "artistic" but the audience didn't go for it. Their disappointment was becoming palpable. Now came a turn for more refined patrons as the Metropolitan Opera Quartet demonstrated their vocal styling for another fourteen minutes. They were "a good singing act" but of strictly limited appeal.

Any dispiritedness, however, was quickly washed away by the sixth performer on the bill: Eva Tanguay. From the moment she took the stage, at both the afternoon and evening shows, Eva was "an instantaneous hit." Her costumes were elegant, though not yet the racy, outrageous, or even legally objectionable getups she would don in the decade to come. Her songs delighted. She was recalled to the stage several times by a mesmerized crowd. One spectator called her "the queen of all soubrettes." What a difference nine minutes made! The unfortunate "Harry Glazier & Co." followed, whereupon the crowd discovered that the "Co." was but a lone sideman (actually, a woman). If you had to follow Eva Tanguay, you had better have at least an extra dollop of talent. But neither Harry Glazier nor his decidedly meager backup troupe did.

At this point, the spectators would have begun filing out of the theater, sharing awestruck retellings of Eva's triumph, and perhaps snorting disapproval of Mary Norman and Harry Glazier. As they did so, the Sid Hassan Ben Ali Troupe of Arabs hit the boards and put on a "marvelous and inspiring" demonstration of gymnastics and contortionism. Acts that were largely visual in their appeal like Sid Hassan were sometimes called "chasers," designed either to actively encourage, or at least not conflict with, the theatergoers' rumblings of departure. But for those in the Temple vaudeville house who stuck around for that last spectacle, or who simply turned their heads as they made for the exit, what they got was the very best performance of its kind. "As tumblers this troupe begins where all others leave off," the manager happily wrote to executives in the head office.[17]

Because of vaudeville's modular nature, a performer like Eva Tanguay was of special value. Not only could she turn a show around, she could also make the audience practically forget what had come earlier. Her presence erased or at least made up for the previous acts. Such abrupt transitions, usually avoided at all costs in "classical" Hollywood film and the naturalistic theater of psychological realism, were for vaudeville a major asset.[18]

By the time Eva Tanguay came on the scene, vaudeville was also seen as a safer, less-rough affair than the various variety-format entertainments it had come from. Though vaudeville was actually to become more morally ambiguous than its big-name producers so often proclaimed—in part because of Eva's antics—for the time being, it passed the judgment of most moral censors.

Legendary showman Tony Pastor was the figure most closely associated with the initial separation of vaudeville from its less respectable ancestor, lowly "v'riety." While variety theater was said to be coarse and vulgar, vaudeville was supposedly fit for respectable audiences. Pastor was hailed in his later years as the "dean of vaudeville," its "godfather." Though this obscures the significance of numerous other individuals and organizations that played a role in developing the genre, Tony Pastor's contributions were nonetheless remarkable.[19]

Antonio Pastor was born on Greenwich Street in lower Manhattan, May 28, 1832. Like Eva Tanguay, Pastor hit the boards early, singing duets with partner Christian B. Woodruff at public temperance meetings at the Dey Street Church when he was a lad of six. Woodruff went on to a career in state politics but Pastor stuck to showbiz. By fourteen, Pastor was a regular at P. T. Barnum's famous oddity-filled "museum." He appeared in "corked face" and shook a tambourine in a minstrel troupe. Like other important showmen of his era, Tony Pastor continued his apprenticeship in the entertainment trade by working for a circus. In addition to the classic circus fare of animal stunts and tightrope walking, the circus of the 1800s featured sketches and short plays. Tony Pastor enacted roles in many. Eventually tiring of the circus man's wandering life, he settled in New York as a singer, troupe leader, and theater owner, opening Tony Pastor's Opera House at 201 Bowery on July 31, 1865, along with partner Sam Sharpley. The nation, barely four months out of the horrors of the Civil War, was aching for diversion and wishful fantasies about the future. The popular theater would play a vital role in providing both.[20]

In New York, Pastor had been mulling over the problem of how to attract middle-class women to his venue. In an age when a woman in the theater was understood to be an actress, a prostitute, or both, this was no simple maneuver. But if he could do it, Pastor might effectively double the size of his audiences, as well as earn respectability, thus linking his enterprise to the solid financial base of the theatergoing middle classes. He offered hams, flowers, chocolates, baking ingredients, even sewing machines to get the ladies. In the end, it was the awarding of cheap silk dresses that broke the gender barrier as no variety producer had quite done before.[21]

Continuing to successfully attract (at least some) middle-class women to his theater, Pastor went a step further. He leased the Germania Theatre on Fourteenth Street at Third Avenue and took the chance of insisting it be "free from smoking, drinking, and carousing," according to historian Robert Snyder. The opening program was given on October 24, 1881, and its success signaled that playing variety to a mixed-gender (if not racially mixed) middle-class audience had become a reality. For their part, women patrons also embarked on a new cultural experiment. Female theatergoers could increasingly see themselves reflected back from the stage as they watched actresses take chances and gain a following, though they themselves could still enjoy the comparative safety and anonymity of the crowd.[22]

Increasingly, the female performer became the focal point of vaudeville, a spectacle for men, an object of admiration for women, and a way for managers to keep crowds at least somewhat balanced. With other fields of public endeavor largely closed off to women, the popular theater became a place where at least some could prosper mightily. The press noticed that, increasingly, the biggest paychecks in vaudeville were going to women. As nostalgic, onetime vaudevillian Joe Laurie Jr. wrote in the 1950s: "A vaudeville show without the 'single woman' was like a jet plane that doesn't jet!" In time, Eva Tanguay would become perhaps the most famous single woman on the vaudeville boards. But in order to do so, she would have to leave behind the smaller circuits and limited tours she played in 1904–1905 and gain entry into vaudeville's major leagues. That meant forging a relationship with a huge, powerful entertainment organization controlled by two men who had enlarged on Tony Pastor's strategy and combined it with a national business framework. In so doing, they ushered in a new and truly modern era, that of the entertainment "industry." Their names were B. F. Keith and E. F. Albee.[23]

The early life of B. F. Keith could have come from the pen of Dickens or perhaps Horatio Alger. Benjamin Franklin Keith was born on January 26, 1846, in Hillsboro Bridge, New Hampshire, a tiny hamlet some thirty-five miles north of the Massachusetts border. After ascending to wealth, power, and notoriety, Keith spoke little about his childhood, the myth of the self-made titan encouraging his silence. What is known is that he was the last of eight children of Samuel C. and Rhoda S. Keith. Keith's mother may actually have been of French-Canadian lineage, her maiden name having been Gerould.[24]

Keith left home at the painfully early age of seven, and somehow moved to a farm in western Massachusetts not far from Holyoke. He spent a decade there and subsequently, like so many other budding showmen of his era, took to the road with the circus, in this case Van Amburgh's. After the circus, Keith made his way to the major cities of the East Coast and familiarized himself with the rising world of urban popular entertainment, taking a management position at Bunnell's Museum, a circuslike attraction of curios and freaks, minstrels and variety performers. Bunnell's was home to wax effigies, bearded women, and many-headed chickens. From there, he moved on to that most famous of nineteenth-century dime museums, Barnum's.

After another circus tour, Keith rented the space upstairs from a confectioner's shop on Boston's Washington Street with a partner, a man of some theatrical experience named Col. William Austin. The two opened their Hub Museum on January 8, 1883. For ten cents, visitors could gaze upon Baby Alice, a three-month-old baby who allegedly weighed only one and a half pounds. Keith's modest enterprise soon expanded and an impromptu stage was erected to feature some variety entertainers along with more freak offerings including a chicken with a man's face and a beast said to be the biggest dog in the United States. The show hall now became the Gaiety. In 1885, the Gaiety introduced a new innovation in variety entertainment, so-called continuous performance. "As Keith knew from his days with the circus, nothing attracted a crowd like a crowd," in the words of historian David Nasaw. The name changed yet again and Keith bumped up the price. For fifteen cents, patrons could take in a show in addition to the oddities at the once-again-renamed Gaiety & Bijou.[25]

To endow his modest resort with an air of respectability, and to follow the shrewd marketing plan pioneered by Tony Pastor, Keith tried to separate his fare from the raunchy or suggestive vibe of the concert saloon and low-class variety house. He insisted, or at least he *insisted* he insisted, that everything be tasteful and free of anything that might be construed as a breach of decorum. To further reinforce the appearance of moral cleanliness, Keith manically endeavored to keep his venue free of grime, dirt, dust, and other evidence of ubiquitous urban filth. By September 1886, the Bijou was drawing a more respectable clientele, including customers of some nearby fancy hotels, department stores, and legitimate theaters. Increasingly, his shows featured well-known dramatic and operatic stars.[26]

Enter E. F. Albee.

Edward Franklin Albee shared not only a middle name with his future business partner but a proud Yankee heritage as well. Albee hailed from Machias, Maine, hard by Machias Bay near the state's eastern thumb. He was born on October 8, 1857, to Nathaniel S. and Amanda Albee. His father was a successful shipbuilder and grandson of one of the original minutemen of the American Revolution, William Albee. The Albees moved to Boston, where Edward went to grade school and sold newspapers. He also worked in a dry-goods store for a spell. But so prosaic a path was not for E. F. Albee. Unlike B. F. Keith, who was said to be bland and unimpressive in person, Albee was able to parlay his charisma into a brief stage career. He played a foundling in the melodrama *No Thoroughfare* starring Charles Fechter, earning seventy-five cents for each performance. But the actor's life apparently did not entice young Albee, and there is no further evidence of his having appeared in any other productions.[27]

Like B. F. Keith, E. F. Albee had left home young. Also like his future partner, it was the circus, specifically Barnum's Greatest Show on Earth, that hooked him. Landing a job as a tent boy, he found himself feeding and watering the lions, elephants, and hippos. He hawked peanuts and popcorn and brewed vats of pink, white, and red lemonade for the thirsty crowd. He packed tents when the show was over. Occasionally, Albee was called on to ride a camel or a donkey in the circus's street parade, devised to let everyone know that the circus had indeed come to town.[28]

Albee regarded the circus as the greatest education an aspiring impresario could get. "In my opinion," he said, "the advantages gained which fit a man for later years in business cannot be found in any other calling: the diverse experiences which one encounters in traveling with a circus—the novelty, the contact with all classes, the knowledge of the condition of the country, its finances, its industries, its farming." In a sense he was right. If the modern era of mass-market entertainment would come to involve using an identifiable but differentiated "brand" to best competitors, much as retailers, soft-drink purveyors, and other businessmen were then learning to do on a national scale, the circus provided an opportunity to apply such a template to popular amusement. The Great London, Sells Brothers, Burr Robins, Bachelor and Doris, all outfits Albee worked for, had both to situate their fare within the known constellation of offerings and yet define themselves as just different enough to spark competition. Vaudeville houses and movie studios would later learn to do the same.[29]

According to one story, when Albee was in his midtwenties he wandered into Keith's storefront museum and theater in Boston, and without inquiring, simply began moving things around, sweeping, and performing other menial tasks. Someone asked the boss who the new guy was, to which Keith responded, "I dunno." However the association began, Albee would soon become Keith's chief adviser, devising schemes of all sorts to sell more tickets. One of his more successful moves involved replacing a menagerie of decaying stuffed animals with lifelike models that he called Living Statues.[30]

But it was Albee's next gambit that sowed the seeds of his and B. F. Keith's future success. A nearby theater was producing Gilbert and Sullivan's *Mikado* and turning away hundreds of people who could not get tickets. Keith and Albee put up a slapdash version of their own that played five times daily starting at eleven o'clock in the morning, all at a lower ticket price than the $1.50 the competition was charging. Gaps between shows and acts were filled with comparatively wholesome variety fare.[31]

With Albee in its employ, the Keith machine kicked into high gear. Keith's Gaiety Museum opened in Providence in 1887, and the Bijou Theatre in Philadelphia in 1889. In 1893, B. F. Keith and E. F. Albee inaugurated big-time vaudeville in New York with the opening of the Union Square Theatre. Built—or refurbished, really—at a reported cost of $1 million, the Union Square boasted an electrically lit, stained-glass facade and ushers decked out like Turkish royal courtiers. In a sense, Keith's Union Square was following the public craze for ostentatious, high-value entertainment environments that had been ignited by the massively popular World's Columbian Exposition, or World's Fair, which had opened in Chicago in October 1892. In 1893, Keith's Colonial in Boston got a $670,000 makeover, allegedly gaining the interest of upper-class clients as much as the masses, or as Albee himself later put it, everyone "from aristocrat to newsboy." The bulk of the crowd was probably somewhere in between, though likely tilted toward the newsboy.[32]

Thus had Keith and Albee articulated what might in modern business parlance be termed their brand's *strategy*. For all the talk of stained glass and costumed ushers, Keith-Albee vaudeville was really more a fantastical simulation, a resort environment which suggested European classiness and luxury, even if was all just a façade. Splashy appointments intoxicated bourgeois patrons into forgetting that the form had risen from the slums of variety but a generation earlier. As historian Robert Allen put it, the environment in Keith vaudeville theaters erased "any hint of its proletarian origins."[33]

Opulent Keith "Palace" theaters, featuring stained glass, frescoes, and china collections, followed in other major cities. Sight lines were scientifically calculated and hygienic conditions were tended to by an army of custodians and charwomen, as the company constantly reminded its customers. Though Keith's name was on the outside of the theater, Albee was credited with having built the guts inside into the "most efficient and powerful organization known in the amusement world," according to a newspaper profile of the early 1910s. Seat heights, the angle of stairs, heating and ventilation, and countless other details were "precisely charted and planned when a new Keith vaudeville theatre is under way." So professed E. F. Albee with the glee of an executive managing a large and growing business concern in the age of Frederick Taylor's 1911 classic text, *The Principles of Scientific Management*.[34]

Along with the purification of sight lines and the cleansing of floor tiles, Keith and Albee made the appearance of moral sobriety a major element of their brand. In an era when progressive activists and troubled clergy increasingly feared the ill effects of urban entertainment on city dwellers, especially youth and women, the two vaudeville impresarios crafted a well-publicized friendship with the Catholic Church.

According to one source, it was the deeply Catholic Mrs. Keith who was behind a sign famously posted backstage at Keith theaters—which by 1899 had become known as "The Sunday School Circuit":

Don't say "slob" or "son-of-a-gun" or "hully gee" on this stage unless you want to be canceled peremptorily. Do not address anyone in the audience in any manner.... If you have not the ability to entertain Mr. Keith's audience without risk of offending them, do the best you can. Lack of talent will be less censured than would be an insult to a patron.... If you are guilty of uttering anything sacrilegious or even suggestive you will be immediately closed and will never again be allowed to appear in a theatre where Mr. Keith is in authority.[35]

Perhaps there would be no shouts of "hully gee" from vaudevillians. But the climate of sexual permissiveness and vulgarity came to be anything but fixed and sanitized on the Keith stage. It was ever in negotiation between performer, audience, manager, and those like Keith and Albee in the boardroom and head office. Keith and Albee were primarily concerned with maintaining and growing their market share; they were less moralists than businessmen. The vaudevillian turned lay historian Joe Laurie Jr. likewise suggested that E. F. Albee's religious inclination went only as far as its market utility. "Had Boston boasted a larger Jewish population," joked Laurie, "it is certain that Albee would have worked a rabbi into the scheme of things." In the words of the historian Marybeth Hamilton, the Keith vaudeville circuit's censoring practices sought to walk the line between hawking "an openly salacious act" and avoiding "a wholly clean bill of fare" that would elicit yawns. Though Eva initially fit well into this strategy, she was interested in appealing to the adventurous, not the traditional. Indeed, she sought to turn the traditional *into* the adventurous. In the end, it was more vaudeville that adjusted to Eva than the reverse.[36]

For its part, the Keith-Albee head office in New York maintained and updated a list of jokes and words that were supposedly verboten. Vaudevillians were advised to steer clear of characters with names like "Lord Epsom of the Interior" (a laxative joke) and double entendres about "taking a tramp through the woods." Lines like this got huge laughs so players would fight tooth and nail to retain them. On some occasions, management was happy to acquiesce, though usually with a covert wink, even as it bunched its fist in moral outrage.[37]

WITH HER REPACKAGED VERSION of *The Sambo Girl* and its centerpiece "I Don't Care" gaining steam, Eva, by late 1905 was able to negotiate her entrance into the vast Keith-Albee machine. She was initially given a four-week contract to tour part of the big-time circuit for a total paycheck of sixteen hundred dollars. Eva more than earned her salary. The manager of Keith's Detroit theater wired Albee in New York, reporting her a "sensational hit" and advising she be booked for a longer term. Albee ignored the advice and let her compensation remain where it was. Eva next moved on to New York as specified, debuting at Keith & Proctor's Twenty-Third Street Theatre. Now there was "a riot" as the house sold out to capacity for all shows. Still Albee remained unmoved. It took two more weeks of stellar business to finally get his attention. Just before the start of her fourth week, Albee called a meeting with Eva. He offered her a longer tour for the following season. Eva politely thanked Albee and turned him down. According to Albee's right-hand executive, Edward Darling, "She couldn't think of remaining in vaudeville—it was too hard and that people standing in the wings made her nervous." It was true that Eva would, throughout her career, suffer an odd paranoia about people watching her from offstage. But she was also learning to play hardball, no mean feat for a lone woman in a male-controlled business. Albee called her bluff, and Eva backed off for the time being. Tired of dealing with the excitable young lady vaudevillian but not wanting to alienate her, for he could see her potential, he assigned Darling to manage her and to "look after her every wish." Edward Darling carefully developed a personal rapport with Eva and talked her into signing with the Keith organization for the longer haul, even if it meant no raise just yet.[38]

After her success at Keith & Proctor's, Eva appeared at that most important of venues, Hammerstein's Victoria, not a Keith-owned house but nonetheless booked by the powerful Keith-controlled United Booking Offices.[39] At the Victoria, Eva was a sensation. An interim hit at the Union Square theater didn't hurt either. With Edward Darling's help, Eva started to realize her worth as an entertainer. She also began more carefully, even zealously, demanding star billing and commensurate pay. Headlining an early tour, she was upset to discover her name in second position at Hammerstein's. "I was hurt and decided I wasn't big enough for Broadway," she confided to Darling. As much as Eva made blustery combativeness a big part of her public allure, she also admitted she was vulnerable to the caprices of show business.[40]

Witnessing her popularity, Albee finally relented. He upped Eva's weekly check from $400 to $600. On her first, full starring vaudeville tour, she was "a terrific attraction especially at that money," in Darling's estimation. Eva caught on quickly. She knew that another popular solo female in vaudeville, the British-born Vesta Victoria, was pulling in $2,500 a week. She called a meeting with Albee and asked him for a salary bump. He offered $750. Eva's eyes welled up. Through the mist she looked at Albee and said, "I have played all season and packed your theaters at six hundred a week, and you have been playing Vesta Victoria at twenty-five hundred, and you offer me only a hundred and fifty more?" Eva gave Albee twenty-four hours to raise her to $1,500. Albee came back with $1,250. He underestimated who he was dealing with, but was also keenly aware of her rising popularity. "I'm sick of doing business," she replied. "Now I demand $2,000." E. F. Albee gave it to her.[41]

As her popularity grew, so too did Eva's reputation as an iconoclast, a wily rebel who played her own game even if it meant being or seeming combative. "Eva's particular pose this season is that of being just as big a 'devil' off the stage as she is on," wrote a gossip reporter in 1905. Tanguay, the playfully destructive gremlin, "wearing a bunch of bun-like curls and that toothy smile of hers that couldn't be removed with a derrick," had taken to purloining potatoes from the corner grocery and commandeering hansom cabs through Central Park after nightfall. "I'd tell you a real spicy story U know in connection with this little lady, but I live in mortal fear of her sky rocket temper," added the journalist.[42]

In December of that year, Eva was on a train steaming for Des Moines, Iowa. Finding it stuffy, the curly-haired comedienne got up, walked over to the door and flung it open—without consulting the forty other passengers on the Chicago Burlington & Quincy railroad car. Had she done so, she might have found them unhappy about letting a "heavy draught" of the midwestern winter rush in. The railroad car, a hefty, olive-drab box on wheels with a crested roof fitted out with ventilation grates for the summer months (some of which may have inadvertently been left open), was a relic from the golden age of rail travel. Despite having over thirty windows of various sizes, Eva somehow felt confined. She had to have the door open. No sooner had Eva let in the icy blast, however, than the car's brakeman stomped over and shut the door. (In trains of the day, each car usually had its own brake operator.)

So Eva got up, went to the door, and flung it back open.

And the brakeman duly shut it again. Now Eva reportedly "jumped up and down and delivered herself a piece of her mind." She screamed and bellowed, her voice damped by the carpeted floor and challenged by the chug of the engine. The row turned physical. A nearby passenger was hit and wounded. The actress later claimed she hadn't drawn first blood. Rather, she alleged, the agitated brake operator pushed her "against the side of the car," leaving her "injured…badly."[43]

According to another version, however, things went down differently. Somewhere during the dispute, a man known only as "Mr. Leach" and incorrectly thought to be her husband, sprang up to defend his lady friend by brandishing a revolver, which he pointed at the brake operator, shouting the usual threats. No shots were fired and the brakeman managed to request the police meet them when the train pulled into Des Moines station.

Eva stepped off the car in an expensive white fur coat, "a picture delightful to behold," in the words of a local newspaper that perhaps had sent a drama critic rather than a crime reporter to cover the event. The brake operator was not so blinded by her glamour. "I want you to put that man and woman under arrest," he told Harry Morris, the Des Moines police officer who had met them at the depot, adding, "He threatened to shoot me and pointed a revolver at me." The railroad man then pointed a finger at Eva, alleging, "She created a terrible disturbance." Eva said nothing, for she knew when to pause for effect. Her man Leach admitted, "I've got a gun in my pocket, but I never pulled it on the brakeman." This statement did not have the exculpatory effect Eva and her beau had hoped for. Officer Morris told Eva and her "husband" that the two "had better come down to the station" and have a talk with Police Chief Jones, which they agreed to do with all speed.[44]

Morris escorted the two to police headquarters, where the chief was said to be "startled almost out of his Altoona boots by what he first thought was an apparition." Yes, it was the country's hottest rising theatrical star right there in his office. The more one reads coverage of the event from the press reports of the day, the more it seems like a farcical vaudeville sketch. This was hardly a coincidence.[45]

After Morris related to his boss the facts of the imbroglio as best he understood them, Eva offered her version of what had gone down. "It's all a mistake, chief," she blurted. "Oh, Mr. Jones," Eva further implored, "you would never think of locking me up on such a silly charge. I never would get over the disgrace, and I've just got to get to the hotel and get some rest before the performance tonight."[46]

Asked to give her version of the scuffle as truthfully as she was able—and surely Police Chief Jones had suspicions about its extent—Eva held that she and her fellow passengers were feeling "almost suffocated" in the stuffy train car. It was not she but one of her chorus girls who got up and opened the door "to let in a little fresh air." (Scapegoating chorus girls, even her own, was practically one of Eva's pastimes.) This, the brakeman promptly closed. Eva said she took it on herself to reopen the door, but the obstreperous train employee just "shut it in my face" immediately, she said. "Well, I just wasn't going to stand for any such foolishness," she explained. Her third and final assault on the door resulted in the brake operator forcibly removing her and blocking it so no one could open it again. It was only then that her champion Leach sprang into action and swore to the hapless railroad man that he "would put him in the bad for keeps." This threat, cloaked in the wonderfully ambiguous moxie of a bygone era, finally made the railroad employee desist. In Eva's recounting, there was no mention of a gun. Rather, she said, this "uniformed nonentity" simply left the train car and returned a short while later with a club or a bat, whereupon the chorus girls in the car "jollied him awfully." His ego taunted, the brakeman called the cops. That was Eva's story. It was almost certainly more entertaining, both in the detail and the telling, than whatever *did* in fact happen aboard that Burlington & Quincy train coursing over the plains of Iowa.[47]

At this point, Leach then took out his gun and showed it to the police there at the station house. He said he carried it to protect Eva, whom he called his "wife," and her thousands of dollars' worth of diamonds. With Eva in a lush, white fur, this argument must have carried a certain heft. But no, Leach insisted, he had never pointed it at the brakeman. And so Eva was done explaining herself. If the police wanted to press the matter further, Eva told them, all they had to do was head over to the Hotel Chamberlain and ask for Mr. and Mrs. Leach. "We are so pleased with your treatment of us," she claimed, then added, "By the way, can't you take luncheon with us after the performance to-night?" No further charges were made. Eva Tanguay had apparently found the plaintiff and the police not guilty. Two months later, she filed suit against the Chicago Burlington & Quincy train line for one hundred thousand dollars, claiming their employee had "injured her badly." There is nothing, however, to suggest she missed so much as a day of work due to her hundred thousand dollar's worth of injuries.[48]

There is also no further mention from Eva, either in the press or in her few surviving private letters, of the mysterious "Mr. Leach." Perhaps he was a fling to salve the wound of Melville Collins's rejection. Perhaps he was a hanger-on, partly in her employ as a handler. What seems clear, though, is that Eva had begun what would be a more or less continual pattern for her throughout her adult life: taking one semianonymous lover after another for various spells. Sometimes the affairs lasted a few months, sometimes longer, sometimes shorter. Indeed, the very absence of information on her romantic relationships, even right down to the actual names of her paramours, may suggest Eva's fundamental anxiety toward coupling.

The gun-toting Leach was soon out of Eva's life. She now forged a more serious romance with her representative at the Keith organization,

Edward Darling. He went on to manage her affairs, give her counsel, and look out for her business interests. As Darling recounted in his private memoirs, "Fortunately or otherwise, we fell in love." Thus began an on-again, off-again romance that Eva, typical for her, spoke little about, publicly or privately. Darling may have been in love, but Eva seemed equivocal as ever.[49]

With Darling's help, Eva learned to counterbalance her growing reputation for conflict with something softer and more culturally acceptable when the situation called for it. "Eva Tanguay, whose 'moods' are gradually assuming the importance once given to [her contemporary, the actor and light-opera star] Richard Mansfield's, isn't squabbling all the time. Occasionally, she is what the rural reporter describes as 'gracious.'" So wrote *Vanity Fair* in 1906. It turned out that Eva had conveniently received several hundred carnations from an association of lumber workers in Davenport, Iowa, not long after the brakeman affair outside Des Moines. Having seen her perform in Rock Island, the workingmen were permitted to meet vaudeville's rising princess in person after the show for a meet and greet that smacked of well-orchestrated informality. They reportedly left "enhanced by their insight into her character off the stage."[50]

4

⟨~⟩

The Cyclonic Comedienne;
or, Genius Properly Advertised

EVA FINISHED out her 1905–1906 Keith obligations and now found herself in a new sphere of budding stardom. She had become an established name in vaudeville, an intrinsic part of the genre, each shaping the other's style and popularity. Everything about Eva's career, from her paychecks to her increasingly lavish tastes to her first scandalous romance, indicated that she was a bona fide celebrity. With the transition to vaudeville, Eva also learned to marshal the apparatus of publicity and image making to heighten her appeal in the marketplace. More and more, she became an individual worthy of fascination. She also began to pay a price for her mushrooming performance schedule. As she cast about for her next, more lucrative vaudeville deal, Eva unpredictably decided to dabble briefly in musical comedy. The show she took on did not require a long commitment; had it, she would have turned it down. More important, it was less a musical with its own merits than a vehicle for her star talents. She would now wrap a script around her popular vaudeville personality as her predecessors had done in *My Lady, The Chaperons,* and *The Office Boy.* Eva now had the credibility as a solo vaudeville act to make the show follow her. After this gig, it would be a long time before Eva Tanguay would once again agree to take on a scripted role, no matter how well it lent itself to her persona.

The musical dalliance Eva chose was called *A Good Fellow,* and whatever misgivings she might have had about doing it were laid to rest by the fact that its cocreator was Melville Collins, her unrequited love interest and sometime manager.

A Good Fellow had started out as a nonmusical farce starring Cecil Spooner in 1904. Collins added songs and extracted a book or something like it from librettist Mark Swan. It bowed in 1906 and was deemed by at least one critic "a clever enough concoction," as it toured upstate New York in preparation for a Broadway run. But the show's success had everything to do with Eva. "Miss Tanguay is a bundle of all the saucier theatrical characteristics," gushed the *Rochester Post,* which found her "small and good looking," nothing short of "merriment personified," an actress who could "carry through a ridiculous situation with perfect ease." She was seen as a playful girl on the one hand, an enticing woman on the other.

Eva played Dolly Sevier, a city gal who weds secretly without telling her aunt Prudence. As her name suggests, Prudence is not the freewheeling sort. Fleeing her disapproving aunt, Dolly secrets herself away in a downtown hotel. Somewhere along the way, her plan goes awry, as plans like this pretty much have to in romantic farces, when something unexpected happens: the cops raid the hotel for running a gambling ring. One of the unlucky gamers takes refuge in Dolly's apartment, and she covers for him by telling the police they are married. The cops meanwhile end up hauling Dolly's actual husband off to jail in a separate incident. To make matters worse, Aunt Prudence gets wind of the arrest and now Dolly must explain her tangled web of deceit involving not one but seemingly *two* husbands to a woman who did not favor her marrying in the first place. Much of the subsequent plot, in the words of one theater critic, was made up of "the bewilderment and perplexity which follow" from this marvelously scatterbrained scenario.[1]

To be sure, such shortcomings in no way interfered with the favorable impression Eva made on audiences. "She is sprightly and full of life," wrote one critic, while another described how she "cavorts about the stage like a house afire, and seems to enjoy the rapid transit locomotion as much as the audience." Though she played a silly part in a silly, forgettable musical, there was something mesmerizing about Eva. Something about her near-manic state mimicked a bustling, urban scene replete with subways, retail stores, automobiles, and looming office buildings. The *Post-Standard* of Syracuse found Eva "as effervescent as a newly opened bottle of champagne but the bubbles do not vanish, and she is as fresh at the finish as when she makes her stage entrance in the first act." She was "about as near perpetual motion as can be imagined in a small package." Professionally, personally, and artistically, Eva Tanguay was indeed in a state of constant movement.[2]

With the closing of *A Good Fellow,* Eva had finally shed her need for all trappings of narrative, no matter how lightweight. When it came to spending, she also began playing the part of a newly birthed celebrity. In addition to plush furs and glittering diamonds, she developed a taste for lavish real estate. In 1906, she offered seven hundred thousand dollars for a turreted, medieval-looking mansion with twelve rooms and an "unparalleled" view of the Connecticut River Valley, according to one newspaper, in her hometown of Holyoke, Massachusetts. The property was called Kenilworth Castle. She also reportedly bought "one of the most productive water melon farms in Massachusetts," and was famously generous to friends and family who were wanting. "Her heart always reaches out in sympathy to any trouble or need," a professional contemporary wrote of her. As she got older, Eva would become as impulsive in her spending as in her giving. For the time being, though, and for at least several decades to come, her bulging purse would allow it.[3]

IN 1907, Eva returned to the Keith circuit, playing the country's top vaudeville houses and doing what she did best: giving crowds the unalloyed energy and charm that was Eva Tanguay. She was now a one-woman show, figuratively if not always literally. At Keith & Proctor's Twenty-Third Street Theatre in New York, she delivered songs, dances, and jokes that were described as a "whirlwind of whimsicalities," in July. The crowd demanded encore after encore from the frenetic entertainer. Finally exhausted, Eva was at last "compelled," in the words of one reviewer, to step before the curtain and give a "neat little speech" about how grateful she was to her fans. It was the kind of personal connection that vaudeville-goers, increasingly used to the bustling anonymity of urban life, came to love. It was also part of a well-orchestrated publicity gambit. After her speech, the question "Who is your favorite?" was projected onto a screen. The throng was asked to cheer after each of three names appeared on the screen—Vesta Victoria, Alice Lloyd, another English music-hall transplant, and Eva Tanguay—to indicate their enthusiasm. "The applause that greeted the last left no doubt of the opinion of the audience," according to Robert Speare of the *New York Telegraph*.[4]

Eva continued to prove her worth in vaudeville by running onstage and picking up a waning program or infusing further life into a bristling bill of talent. She seemed to complement either kind of show, with her "piercing" voice and "dashing and cyclonic" moves. She had the ability to cast a kind of temporary amnesia on the crowd, making them forget what had come earlier and focus their attention on her.[5]

On the night of August 5, 1907, a pleasantly cool one in New York that year, Eva pulled off a major rescue feat. Onstage were Milton and Dolly Nobles, trying desperately to put over an "alleged one-act farce" called "Fads and Fancies." (The title itself should have been the first sign of trouble.) The audience shifted about unhappily in their seats at Keith & Proctor's 125th Street Theatre. For what must have seemed an eternity, "Fads and Fancies" droned on, devoid of "life, action, or business." Some patrons permitted themselves a recess. Finally, the agony, the "disastrous failure," was over.

And then, like manna raining down from heaven, Eva came out and made it better. In fact, she hadn't even walked onstage before things began to look up; the mere indication that she was on her way brought applause. When she finally came on, Eva had to wait "some few minutes" until the house grew quiet enough for her do her thing. For seventeen minutes, she held sway and the patrons expressed their noisy delight after each song. In addition to her trademark "I Don't Care," Eva introduced new songs. They were fresh, topical, and focused on subjects to which her city-dwelling fans could easily relate. In "I'm Not a Cross Word Fan," by Edwin J. Weber she sang:

> Everywhere you go these days, on the trolleys or subways,
> You will see the latest craze, it's cross word puzzling.
> Every face has a vacant stare hunting for some word that's rare
> To fill in an empty square, they're cookoo I declare:
> They may say I'm completely off my nut but I'm not a cross word fan.
> I don't go round with my forehead in a frown and thoughts in Hindustan.
> Such words as "ort" and "oaf" and "gnu" and "syzsygy" are pie for some,
> But I'd rather be dumb, ignorance is bliss to me.

One can imagine Eva today singing a playful snarl about iPods or Sudoku.[6]

AS HER STAR POWER and utility within vaudeville's mode of production increased, so too did Eva's penchant for moodiness and conflict. In particular, she was becoming prone to bouts of frustration when she did not receive the adulation she wanted, which admittedly was rare. Though played up in the press, her tantrums were very real, even if they were offset often by beaming warmth and charisma. Playing Chase's Washington Theater in the nation's capital in September 1907, Eva unpleasantly surprised her managers by failing to appear for a show in the middle of her run. "We knew her peculiarities and everyone waited on her like a queen," wrote a shocked manager who had been walking on eggshells all week. Eva had been accustomed to New York audiences boosting her ego with hurricane peals of applause and cheers. The Washingtonians, however, proved a more sedate lot. "At every performance she was given a most respectful hearing, nothing done to offend but gloves were not torn in applause." But Eva was looking for more than respectful applause.[7]

A temper tantrum, while unpleasant to behold or suffer, could be managed with stoical detachment and hand-holding. But the threat of Eva Tanguay actually canceling an engagement was another matter entirely. When he discovered that Eva would not be appearing at an engagement as promised, a fan named L. V. Fletcher went to the box office in a huff and "requested that either my money be refunded or another ticket be given me for a performance at which Miss Tanguay was sure to appear." Accordingly, managers had indeed to *manage* the erratic star as best they could, a difficult task considering Eva's unpredictability and irritability. Carl Lothrop, who ran Keith's Boston theater, confessed that while "Miss Tanguay gave us an extremely unpleasant morning," he had no choice but to coddle the star who had provided his venue with "the biggest hit that I have ever seen . . . a positive triumph." He noted, "I guess it pays to be crazy. I sincerely hope we shall be able to keep her in good humor throughout the week. It will certainly not be through lack of effort on our part, as we thoroughly appreciate her drawing power." Those who dealt with Eva professionally had to learn to grin and bear it the best they could. The box office had to be protected. "She is simply a wilful and spoiled woman and will ever be found doing as she pleases regardless." So noted the manager of Chase's Washington vaudeville theater. As Eva's professional life blossomed, so too did the myth of her temper—sometimes real, sometimes just feared, but as tangible an accoutrement of her persona as her costumes, gestures, and songs.[8]

The combination of vivacity, energy, and emotion Eva brought to her shows and offstage interactions had, by 1907, earned her a new moniker: "cyclonic." She was billed, promoted, and referred to in articles as "The Cyclonic Comedienne," or perhaps simply "the Cyclonic One." In the third week of September, Chase's Washington vaudeville theater described Eva Tanguay as "The Cyclonic Comedienne" in its advertising. That same month, Keith's Philadelphia announced the return of "the Cyclonic Brain-Storming Comedienne Eva Tanguay." Keith's Cleveland added other forces of nature, boasting of "The Cyclonic Comedienne EVA TANGUAY World's Greatest Magnetic Singer."[9]

Other performers of Eva's day had occasionally been dubbed "cyclonic." When the acclaimed actor Otis Skinner played Laertes in an 1890 production of *Hamlet,* a critic for the *Brooklyn Daily Eagle* found that when Laertes' "young blood flames against the slayer of his father he was cyclonic."[10]

High, Shakespearean tragedy wasn't the only thing capable of garnering such praise. The 1896 play *Rush City* was called a "great cyclonic spectacular farce-comedy," while a vaudeville act known as The Lilliputians—probably a children's troupe—were promoted for their "Latest Cyclonic Success," a sprightly dance revue called *Merry Tramps.* There was even a vaudeville act called The Cyclonic Six who put on short farces with titles such as *The Husband's Return.* Meanwhile, a play called *The Tornado* "whiffled" across the stage of Brooklyn's Star Theater and was so named for the wave of "cyclonic happenings that follow each other in rapid and noisy succession." Urban audiences were increasingly attracted to entertainers whose rapid-fire energy seemed to mimic the milieu in which they lived, a world replete with new motorcars coursing down city avenues and subways rumbling beneath them. Indeed, Boston's subway system had opened in 1897, running the length of a mile beneath Tremont Street, not far from at least one Keith vaudeville house, while New York City's own subway had been born in 1904.[11]

The temper of stage folk might also garner the epithet "cyclonic." George Bernard Shaw declared that his 1908 play *Getting Married* would be "revenge on the critics for their gross ingratitude, ardent philistinism, shameless and intellectual laziness, low tastes, puerile romanticism, stupendous ignorance, susceptibility to cheap sentiment, insensibility to honor, virtue, intellectual honesty, and everything that constitutes strength and dignity in human character." The *New York Times* reporter interviewing Shaw admitted to feeling "overwhelmed" by the Irish playwright's "cyclonic outburst," which was of course mild compared to some of Eva's.[12]

Helping Eva craft her cyclonic image in vaudeville was her latest ally on the PR front, C. F. Zittel. Carl Florian Zittel, also known variously as "C. F. Zittell" and "Zit," depending on where you look, was born in 1877. As a youth, he sold newspapers on the corner of Fourth Avenue (today Lexington) and Twenty-third Street in New York City. He soon moved into office positions at various New York papers, including the *Morning Telegraph* and *Evening Mail,* before joining the ranks of the *New York Journal* where he both wrote about theater and solicited ads. At the *Journal,* Zit hit on the idea of publishing a weekly list "modeled on the performance charts in horse racing" in which he gave vaudeville performers grades. It was this innovation, a kind of early *Billboard* chart for vaudevillians, that won him notoriety.[13]

Zit not only helped make Eva further aware of the importance of fighting for one's slice of the publicity pie, but he also helped apprise her competitors (and the reading public) of the fact that in the era of modern communications and mass advertising it was not enough to simply appeal to one's fans while onstage. The performer had, instead, to constantly reach out to them. "I do not claim that Miss Tanguay proves the case for everyone, but she does prove that only genius properly advertised is sure of the success that genius deserves," declared Zittel.[14]

Zit claimed to be Eva's spokesman, possessing "an intimate knowledge of her remarkable career." Much to the chagrin of Mrs. Zittel, he also had an intimate knowledge of Eva's womanhood. Suspecting her husband might have been providing more than business advice to the shapely vaudevillian, Martha B. Zittel hired a couple of detectives including her brother to dress up as bellhops and infiltrate a room at Riccadonna's Hotel in Brighton Beach, Brooklyn, where her husband had rented a room. It may be hard for a man adept at grabbing exposure, headlines, and publicity to manage stealth as well. The hotel register made no secret of the fact that Zittel had taken room 152 on August 8, 1907, six days after Eva had taken up residence in the adjoining room, 154. As if in a vaudeville sketch, by August 16, the hotel register listed "Tanguay and wife—Room 154." This made for decidedly easier sleuthing. Armed with a target destination, the investigators delivered ice water to the Tanguay-Zittel love nest clad in their bellboy costumes. On entering room 154 in the wee hours of August 31 they found Zit in his pajamas and Tanguay "even more scantily clad than she has ever appeared in any of her stage productions." The jig was most definitely up. But there is no evidence that the affair negatively impacted the careers of either Eva Tanguay or C. F. Zittel, though Martha Zittel filed an alienation-of-affection suit against her husband, one more man who failed to resist the cyclonic allure of Eva Tanguay. It would be the first of many times that Eva Tanguay openly, even mockingly, transgressed cultural norms of gender and sexual behavior without paying a noticeable price. Something about Eva marked her as a new kind of celebrity, one who could write her own rules and thereby encourage her public to do the same.[15]

Eva had also, thus, thrown over Edward Darling for the time being. He was last year's manager, last year's lover. Eva often blurred the line between paramour and business handler. When it came to men, loyalty took a distinct second place to utility and the impulses of the moment.

EVA CONTINUED to work her cyclonic magic, week after week, mostly in New York, though occasionally out of town. By the following year, her frenetic style and its attendant agitations began to have adverse effects.

It was June 1908, not quite summer yet, when she had to cancel several big New York dates, notably at Keith & Proctor's Fifth Avenue and 125th Street venues. Eva was loath to take downtime, especially now that her career was hitting full stride. It was an approach that led her to wear down her body. But Eva's doctor served up an "ultimatum" and told the cyclonic star that if she continued to work at such a pace, he would not be responsible for the results. It was an omen of things to come. After some back and forth, Eva finally relented. She also cabled London and offered regrets over a lucrative contract arranged there for July.[16]

The press termed Eva's breakdown "a severe blow" to the circuits she was playing, reporting that she had become "the biggest money maker" in the history of vaudeville. The day before she announced that she had to take time off, Eva played Keith's Fifth Avenue to an "immense audience." She carried on through song and dance with her usual abandon. She even whipped up a timely new verse referring to a recent horse-racing law and wove it into "I Don't Care." She sang: "To bet on a horse is now a crime. But they never got a cent of mine. So nothing, nothing, ever bothers me." The audience went nuts and gave her a rousing ovation.[17]

But those who really knew her could see something was amiss. When the clapping had subsided enough for her to be heard, Eva addressed her fans directly. "I thank you for your applause," she told the masses. "I have been unfortunate enough to contract a severe cold. Nevertheless, I have tried to do my best and I am pleased to see that all of you appreciate it." When it seemed as if she might dive into another encore, her physician, who had been nervously waiting in the wings, stepped out and declared, "You're a wonderful little woman, but I won't allow this to go any further. You must have rest, unless you want to break down entirely, and I know the management won't permit that." It was a sort of lightweight drama between a lettered, male authority figure and a self-made woman of the stage. This time she relented. The management of Keith & Proctor's was happy to oblige. Better a recuperating Eva than a permanently blown-out cyclone. The next day it was announced that she was not seriously ill and at worst would require "a slight operation" on her vocal cords; a vague "nervous tension" was blamed. After treatment, Eva departed for the foothills of the Berkshires in western Massachusetts, near where she had grown up and close to family, including an unclaimed daughter. She then repaired to the home of her sister Blanche, who now lived in Westfield, Massachusetts, about ten miles southwest of Holyoke, where she was said to enjoy "a complete rest." The time off, away from the pressure and publicity of New York and big-time vaudeville, did her good. At least that was the impression she tried to make when the press inquired. For now anyway, she would listen to those who had her longer-term interests in mind rather than succumbing to a self-defeating urge to work herself into the ground.[18]

While Eva had been making a name for herself in New York and around the country as a hyperactive vaudevillian and enchantress, her sister Blanche's domestic life was playing out with nearly as much drama. She and the loveable grocer of grand heritage, Elwin T. Howes, had had a daughter, Ruth Madeleine, born April 22, 1903. Blanche now had two girls, Lillian Mary Skelding and Ruth Madeline Howes, half sisters. Sadly, Blanche and Elwin were married less than four years when he succumbed both to the grippe and a brain tumor. He passed away on March 29, 1905. Though she doted on Florence, her other niece, who was likely her daughter, Eva developed a relationship with her sister's girls that would prove in many ways the most durable bond of her life. "Her little nieces are her special pets," observed Ullie Akerstrom, a stage contemporary who knew Eva well.[19]

Two years after she lost Elwin, Blanche married Frederick Howard Glanville. Not much is known about Glanville except that he too, like Blanche's first husband, Alfred Skelding, hailed from Philadelphia. The union lasted just a couple of years, after which Blanche wed Walter E. Gifford of New Haven. She was thirty-four, while he was only twenty-one. "This is Mrs. Gifford's fourth matrimonial venture," wrote the *Holyoke Daily Transcript,* its sneering disapproval betrayed by the factually incorrect headline, "Groom 21, Bride 45."[20]

BY JULY, Eva had endured all the recuperating she could stand. In addition to C. F. Zittel, she now teamed with well-known newspaper columnist and PR man—a common professional combination in Eva's day—Sam M'Kee. Working with Eva, M'Kee crafted an article for the *New York Telegraph* full of booming declarations. "'To say I never was better in my life doesn't half tell the story,' chirped the whirlwind comedienne," according to the piece, which was bylined by M'Kee himself. Not only was she supposedly back, full force, but her first performance since the breakdown would be a benefit at the Herald Square Theatre for Mother's Seaside Rest, an institution so charitably named that not even the cleverest press agent could have dreamed it up. Eva's doctor urged her to take another week up in Westfield. But she would have none of it.[21]

It was clear that Eva was determined to be back in full strength as a moneymaking crowd-pleaser on the big-time vaudeville boards. She also seemed further to demonstrate her willingness to fight for her share of the public eye. No doubt this was partly at the urging of M'Kee and her advisers. But she brought to it a zeal from deep in her character, one that often overrode perhaps wiser counsels of moderation. Later in July 1908, Eva secured a high-profile engagement at the Brighton Beach Music Hall, always a popular venue but especially so during the summer months when crowds visited nearby Coney Island and its beaches. David L. Robinson, manager of the Brighton Beach, was excited to have signed her and began publicizing the show.

Unfortunately, one ad—*one*—failed to place Eva's name above that of the boxing legend James J. Corbett, who was also on the bill. The two celebrities instead shared the same line. (Boxers and other athletes were common fixtures on the vaudeville stage.) To make matters worse, their names were displayed in typeface of the same size. Somehow, an advertising agent, in "his zeal to say as much as possible in the space," according to a newspaper report, was unaware that Eva Tanguay shared font size with no one. When she saw it, Eva had one of her handlers (probably M'Kee himself) call Robinson on the telephone. "Miss Tanguay will not play with you this week," a voice barked from the other end of the receiver. The hapless Robinson barely knew what hit him. Eva had read that she was to "divide the honors with some one else" and thus immediately demanded "that it must be clearly set forth in billing and in all the notices in newspapers that *she* is the leading attraction" (italics added). Robinson was stunned. Stumbling for words, he muttered, "So I, but—" But Eva's representative gave no quarter. "Never mind, I'm not through," announced Tanguay's champion. "You wrote back you understood and it would be all right. Look at the papers this morning." Robinson tried to pick himself up. He could perhaps more easily have sustained a roundhouse punch from James J. Corbett. "I have, at all, and—," babbled Robinson for naught. "The point is this," decreed Eva's rep. "The point is that Miss Tanguay must have recognition as the leading attraction. If some one else is entitled to the same recognition it must not be on the same programme with her. Miss Tanguay has tried to honestly earn the position she has attained and cannot afford to sacrifice it by appearing on a bill where she shares the lead with any one else." Robinson was thunderstruck. "Do you mean…that Miss Tanguay won't play the engagements?" he asked. "That's exactly what I mean. Good-bye." It took him a moment to recover, but when he did, David L. Robinson dived headlong into reparation mode. The ad agent who had placed the ad was sacked, a squadron of messengers was dispatched to every paper in town to see that Eva's name appeared in unmistakably huge lettering in banner ads the next morning, and by dint of some twenty go-betweens, manager Robinson begged, pleaded, cajoled, and otherwise interceded with the vaudeville starlet to convince her that the error was definitely not his, but that he begged her forgiveness anyway. David L. Robinson got his box office, the fans got "I Don't Care," and Eva got paid. Handsomely.[22]

It was clear that Eva Tanguay was back. Whatever breakdown or collapse she had suffered in the late spring now seemed a thing of ancient history, almost a misfortune that had befallen someone else entirely. The Brighton Beach affair, rather than rendering her somehow unladylike and therefore undesirable in the eyes of the public, seemed to have had the opposite effect. At the beginning of August, she was elected queen of the Coney Carnival, getting almost as many votes from fans as the second-, third-, and fourth-place contenders, all popular vaudevillians, combined. She also took the laurel as the most popular act in vaudeville according to a survey of ticket holders at the Colonial, Alhambra, and Orpheum theaters. At 2,513 votes, Eva way outstripped her nearest competitor, the highly popular Irene Franklin, who got 1,808. At a mere 945 votes, the famed Vesta Victoria could not hold a candle. At the Fifth Avenue Theater in August, when the orchestra broke into "I Don't Care," *Variety* reported that "one might have imagined the result of the Presidential election had been announced." (One can imagine Teddy Roosevelt, president at the time, finding himself impressed at Eva's swagger and bravado.) Eva added songs that were increasingly about herself. Numbers like "Tanguay Spells Success," "The Tanguay Rag," and "That Tanguay Girl" put her own unique persona in the front and center of her stagecraft.[23]

Her songs, created specifically for her by some of the era's top tunesmiths, could also be gently self-mocking, revealing her likes, dislikes, tastes, and personal observations along the way. They were a further bridge between her zany but tangible personality and a crowd hungering for individual connection. She played up her love of animals in "I'd Like to Be an Animal in the Zoo," by John G. Collins (not to be confused with Melville Collins), which suggested a playful, untamable nature:

> *A human being has it awful tough,*
> *He has to worry and work and lie,*
> *His life, you see, is just a daily bluff,*
> *And you know he must even pay to die,*
> *It's not worth while as you can plainly see,*
> *And just between me and you,*

I really think that I'd rather be
An animal in the zoo.

For many urban workers who navigated crowded trolleys and bustling sidewalks only to be confined to a lowly desk or factory floor, hearing Eva sing about being an animal in a zoo must have held special resonance. It may also have been her connection to animals, not to mention her reputation as a surefire moneymaker, that led a horse breeder in Kentucky with his sights set on Churchill Downs to name a filly after the cyclonic vaudevillian. In three starts, 750-pound Eva Tanguay galloped to two wins—rendering her nearly as bankable as her namesake.[24]

The Tanguay name increasingly came to be associated with vitality and personal success. It appealed not only to horse breeders but to corporations that began using her name to market their wares. One of the first was the Scott L. Snyder Company of Minneapolis, makers of tobacco products, who marketed the "Eva Tanguay" five-cent cigar. The company sponsored a contest to see who could supply the five best reasons to smoke Tanguays. One Edgar Nash, of 1422 Vine Place, Minneapolis, claimed victory with his entry:

> **First**—Because, after smoking 40 years, I think the Eva Tanguay the best nickel cigar I ever smoked.
> **Second**—Because it is not made by a trust.
> **Third**—I have so high an opinion of the good qualities of the Eva Tanguay cigars that I would give $5,000 for the exclusive sale of them in the Twin Cities.
> **Fourth**—Because I believe there is better stock in them than in seven-tenths of the cigars that sell for 10 cents.
> **Fifth**—Because it is a pleasure to smoke an Eva Tanguay at any time. But the real, deep, satisfying enjoyment is, after a hungry man has eaten a good hearty meal, to sit down with a clear conscience and an Eva Tanguay cigar. Then truly "it makes you happy."

Eva herself never touched tobacco. But as the nation's czarina of mirth, she could hardly disapprove of others seeking pleasure and diversion, especially if it involved her receiving royalties and licensing fees.[25]

Eva not only revealed her inner life, however humorously, through her songs. She also used musical numbers to make clear how strong a connection she felt to her fans. She played herself up as their ally, their knowing older sister, their girlfriend. Her songs told those seated before her, in a sense, "I want you, I like you, I need you." She was in their corner. "I'd Like to Give You Something" expressed it perfectly:

> *Most everybody here has seen a circus in their day,*
> *They've been amused and entertained in every different way.*
> *There's vaudeville, melodrama grand, opera so fine and*
> *Comedy and tragedy together combined.*
> *To satisfy the public you must give them something*
> *New in style and dress, original likewise, creations too and*
> *Individualities that differ from the rest.*
> *To please you I always do my best.*
>
> *I'd like to give you something that you've never had before.*
> *I'd like to be the everlasting thing that you adore.*
> *I'd like to hug and kiss you all a thousand times.*
> *What's more, I'd like to give you something that*
> *You've never had before.*

Eva was expressing her commitment to an anonymous yet adoring crowd in a way she rarely could to individuals she knew personally. It was a perfect symbiosis of artist and followers.

PERHAPS EVA'S most brilliant publicity stunt in the late summer of 1908 came in the form of a marriage proposal—or maybe it is more accurate to say, in the satirical performance of one.

In August of 1908, Eva Tanguay took to the stage of Keith's popular Alhambra Theater. The Alhambra was a gaudy affair, a tall edifice with vaguely Moorish features looming over 116th Street in New York City and designed to give the impression of the famous palace in Granada, Spain, for which it was named. (The building still stands; today it is the First Corinthian Baptist Church.) It was therefore appropriate, in this theatrical space with a showy facade, that Eva should have dressed up as a man and accepted a proposal of marriage from the era's most famous female impersonator, Julian Eltinge. It was a bizarre, hilarious, and uniquely vaudevillian sight that hit home on many levels. Though most in the audience knew it to be fake, the engagement ring that passed from Eltinge's hand to Eva's finger nonetheless played with, satirized, and ultimately called into question what the historian and cultural critic Marjorie Garber has called "that cornerstone of normatively heterosexual institutions." In covering her curvy, female form with male garb and accepting the ring of a man known for credibly assuming a woman's cultural stance, Eva was ironically distancing herself from prevailing notions of bourgeois womanhood. As a successful professional and an individual, she had neither economic nor emotional need for marriage.[26]

Julian Eltinge—it is generally agreed his name rhymes with "bing" rather than "hinge"—was a hugely popular figure in his day. Despite his fame and renown, it has been written that "Julian Eltinge's life remains a mystery wrapped in an enigma." The details of his background seem to bear that out. Eltinge's birthday is commonly given as May 14, 1883. But research published on a website devoted to Eltinge puts his real birth date exactly two years earlier. He was born in Newton or "Newtonville," Massachusetts, outside Boston, depending on the date of the account. His mother was Julia Edna Baker and his father a man named Dalton, either Joseph or Michael. Joseph/Michael Dalton worked as either a mining engineer or a barber or possibly both. To such hazy origins was Julian Eltinge born. His given name was William J. Dalton. He may have adopted "Eltinge" as homage to the popular but "strange" 1860s-era actress Rose Eytinge, who had once famously played for Abraham Lincoln.[27]

Interestingly, one of Eltinge's first breaks came when he was recruited for an amateur theatrical event produced by the Boston Cadets, an all-male troupe sponsored by the Boston Bank Officer's Association. The show, which debuted February 5, 1900, was called *Miladi and the Musketeers* and was the inspiration for *My Lady,* the very production that would give Eva her first taste of the spotlight the following year. R. A. Barnet, the show's composer, was also the Cadets' artistic director. It was not easy to find young men both willing and able to play a woman onstage. He was therefore lucky to find Eltinge, who was duly cast as Mignonette, Richelieu's spy.[28]

Eltinge eventually trouped with Harvard's famous cross-dressing Hasty Pudding players, then appeared in female parts in a number of plays including 1904's *Mr. Wix of Wickham* featuring music by Jerome Kern. He confounded audiences by enacting the cultural and behavioral expectations of women with remarkable dexterity, somehow conveying the notion that "being natural was itself a pose," in the words of the historian Kathy Peiss. He "had them guessing for a while" at a vaudeville show in Cleveland. A journalist who once knocked on Eltinge's dressing-room door was greeted with a bassy, "indisputably masculine" voice, then "gasped" when he entered and saw the famous gender illusionist "whitening his neck and shoulders" with powder, rendering his skin soft and "velvety."

Julian Eltinge made a big deal about beating up anyone who doubted his true manhood, which he had to trumpet in an era when female impersonation, once seen as a lively and appropriate form of entertainment for the respectable classes, had become increasingly associated with suspect homosexuality. It did not help matters when the cross-dressing marvel launched the successful *Julian Eltinge Magazine and Beauty Hints,* an odd mix of vaudeville jokes, prefeminist wisdom, and straight-up, irony-free advice on how women could make themselves more attractive. What both perplexed and delighted audiences was Eltinge's ability to, in the words of Marybeth Hamilton, "conjure himself across what spectators believed to be an immutable gender divide"—that is, the then-common belief that men and women were practically two different species. Though Eva Tanguay mocked conventional couplehood, a subject that inspired deep anxiety in her, she never sought to truly evade femininity, only to pry open its social confines. As for Julian Eltinge, he was said to have earned twelve thousand dollars a week at the height of his career. In 1911 ground was broken to build the Julian Eltinge Theater on West Forty-second Street in Manhattan.[29]

Eva's betrothal to a storied cross-dresser kept her public focused on the actress's playful disregard for the conventions of marriage. In May of the year she and Eltinge became "engaged," Eva had debuted a new song at Hammerstein's in New York. Called "That Wouldn't Make a Hit with Me," it pilloried the institution of marriage in grand comedic style. She sang:

> *When you marry some old guy*
> *Who hasn't the decency to die,*
> *Or you marry some old pill*
> *Who you can neither cure nor kill,*
> *That wouldn't make a hit with me.*

Of course, it *did* make a hit at Hammerstein's, in part because Eva infused her delivery with "charming naiveté." Songs like Eva's helped pave the way in vaudeville for an onslaught of jokes about marriage. "Marriage is an institution. So is a lunatic asylum," went one popular jest. Though many such gag lines played on the trope of the henpecked husband who now resented his cash-grabbing, misery-causing wife, there were other clever lines that positioned women as independent and unwilling to sub-mit to the self-indulgent sexual desires of men.[30]

The big hoax staged by Eva Tanguay and Julian Eltinge worked, keeping them both squarely in the public eye. "Eva Tanguay's Coming Wedding

Talk of the Stage," read a headline in the *Evening World*. The ceremony was to take place in the early fall of 1908. It was all cannily announced at about the same time that Eva had played her thirty-third consecutive week in New York. The box office take for her opening at the Colonial at the end of August 1908 broke records. This capped four weeks at the Alhambra where just under a hundred thousand tickets were sold for her shows.[31]

Eva then fulfilled her fans' expectations by calling off the wedding in the name of professional, economic, and psychological autonomy. "I have decided that it would be folly for me to sacrifice my independence by marrying any one. Not even a millionaire could supply me with any comforts that I can't secure alone with my salary," she told the *New York Telegraph*. Though she hardly needed such an excuse to call off a staged betrothal to a famed cross-dresser, it was a stance she was to maintain when more serious suitors came her way.[32]

The Eltinge betrothal also suggested Eva's keen ability as a pioneer, albeit a highly entertaining one, in the area of gender relations. On one hand, she clearly preferred the company of women in a way that harked back to homosocial—that is, men-with-men and women-with-women—friendship patterns of the nineteenth century. But on the other hand, she was very much a creature of modernity with no need for a staid, couple-based home life. In the Julian Eltinge episode, Eva had suggested that her personal life could be acted out just as well in reality as it could onstage and in the newspapers. She was not afraid to be linked, even romantically, with a cross-dresser so effective he evoked deep cultural anxieties and many clawing suspicions of homosexuality (which proved correct). In all this, Eva not only lampooned marriage but placed freely defined companionate relationships in the fore of her social life. Relationships, whether sexual, promotional, or business, were shopped for and reassessed regularly; as such, they belonged firmly to the consumerist present rather than the traditionalist past. Just as important, the Eltinge bluff celebrated her lifelong ambivalence toward conventional, heterosexual intimacy. Whatever emotional wounds she may have suffered growing up as the daughter of the absent, apparently alcoholic Dr. Tanguay, the person she had become—temperamental, driven, emotionally capable of brief public relationships of questionable sincerity—was an individual who was simultaneously able to pursue a career ambitiously and inch society toward a future of bold, if sometimes lonely, relational choices.

As with the Zittel affair, the Eltinge betrothal, potentially damaging to another star, resulted only in Eva's continued fascination with her public and its desire to see her onstage. Whatever personal feelings Keith or Albee might have had about Eva's odd romantic doings, they knew she was the top prize on any vaudeville circuit and so did their best to make sure she played "Keith time." In November 1908, *Keith's Theatre News,* a PR vehicle, featured Eva on its cover and hailed her as "The Madcap Genius of Comedy and Song." Like storms, cyclones, and magnetism, she was cast as a veritable force of nature. "To place her name at the top of the list of headliners before any theatre of the country is enough to jam the house.... Miss Tanguay is now in the very zenith of her career." Hyperbolic and self-serving though it was, the claim was essentially true. Appearing at Keith & Proctor's 125th Street theater, the manager conceded in a memo to the head office, "This woman is the greatest artist in the profession today." When she took the stage, the crowd gave a thunderous ovation, compelling the cyclonic comedienne to "bow for quite a while before they would allow her to sing." Every seat at Keith & Proctor's 125th Street, including "the box chairs," was sold out at every performance. The management added four rows of standing in both orchestra and balcony in order to sell even more tickets. Eva sang seven songs, gave a short "recitation," and was then compelled to take six encore bows and make "three speeches" of thanks to frenzied fans who were "yelling from all parts of the house."[33]

She continued adding new songs, even though audiences demanded "I Don't Care" at every show. Referencing a topical news story about a quack European doctor who transplanted monkey glands into his patients, she sang "When the Doc Makes a Monkey Out of Me":

> *Have you heard the rumor, some sort of gland or tumor*
> *Will make us live a thousand years or more;*
> *It seems in France some wizard, found in a Monkey's gizzard,*
> *A gland that made him shout "excelsior."*
> *So now before the price goes up I'll buy a little monk,*
> *I'll soon find out beyond a doubt if this thing is the bunk.*
>
> *I'm going to get a gland from a monkey,*
> *A monkey's life is the only one for me.*
> *Up in the branches I'll go running around,*
> *Laughing at the tax collectors down on the ground,*
> *I'll never worry 'bout the butcher or the baker,*
> *My restaurant will be a cocoanut tree...*

I've got a gland that comes from a monkey,
The change should be an easy one for me.
Lots of the people who see me on the stage,
Say I'd looked much better locked up safe in a cage.

She was the urban jungle's prize pet: playful, loyal, unpredictable, and somehow wild. Her references suggested other amusements for city dwellers such as zoos, circuses, and animal "freak" acts at dime museums. In short order, Eva would find a way to make herself more exotic yet.

5

Riding Salome to the Top

WITH HER star rising in 1908, Eva could have simply maintained the act she had perfected, a combination of lively topical songs based around "I Don't Care," combined with some jokes and pitches to the audience. She had achieved in less than two years what thousands of other vaudevillians longed for in vain: a mass following and a schedule of appearances as full as her body could stand. But for Eva, standing still was not an option. She had recuperated from her breakdown, which now seemed a thing of the past, never to return. Now she focused on her next triumph. To come back even bigger than before, she needed to cultivate novelty—a feature every vaudevillian knew to be essential—while never letting go of her core stage persona. Much as the pop star Madonna would do eighty years later, Eva began trying on different versions of herself, all fanciful and new, yet all essentially Eva. She had played the soubrette, the chorus girl, the mirthful sleuth, the tuxedoed man in a mock engagement to a cross-dresser, and the siren of "I Don't Care." Her experimentation showed her fun-seeking fans that they might be able to wear their own identities a bit more loosely than previous generations could. Now Eva looked for the next big gag. Surprisingly, it came in the form of a popular sensation whose roots could be traced back to biblical history. For by late 1908, the United States had become obsessed with something called Salome dancing. But it was not just a U.S. phenomenon. In London, Paris, and Moscow, performers of all types were hawking interpretations of the biblical tale of the infamous Salome. The thirty-year-old comedienne who had started out at an amateur night in

Holyoke now decided it was time to enter the ranks of a hugely popular international fad.

The Salome craze of Eva's era had actually begun to take shape several decades earlier and was far from her invention. But Eva's ability to capitalize on the movement and bend it to her vision, combined with an audacious publicity campaign, would help boost her to new heights in vaudeville's firmament, redefining what it meant to be a star in terms of salary, influence, morals, and sheer power.

Although the story of Salome had been turned into popular fare since at least the Middle Ages, contemporary interest in the story of King Herod's daughter, who danced in return for the head of John the Baptist, was rekindled by Oscar Wilde's play of the same name, which went into rehearsal in London in 1892. Wilde, who had penned it for Sarah Bernhardt, was not alone in taking on Salome: Heinrich Heine, Nathaniel Hawthorne, Stéphane Mallarmé, Walter Pater, Gustave Flaubert, Joris-Karl Huysmans, and others had all taken an interest in the subject. So had the composer Jules Massenet with his 1881 opera *Hérodiade*. Even painters, such as Gustave Moreau and Edvard Munch, were exploring the Salome trope. But it was undoubtedly Oscar Wilde who most fanned the flames of Salome's popularity, owing in part to public fascination with its central character's Dance of the Seven Veils. Wilde and his literary and artistic peers shared an interest in Salome's sexual power. Some have said that Salome became popular because she personified broader changes taking place in society at the time, including the beginnings of the modern women's movement, which many still viewed as immoral rebellion. From an entertainment perspective, Salome dancers fit well into the rising popularity of sensual, vaguely freakish, exotic dancers who were said to have been recruited from the Middle East or thereabouts, and presented in vaudeville palaces such as Hammerstein's Victoria.[1]

Influenced by the popularity of Wilde's project, the German composer Richard Strauss strengthened the wave with his opera *Salome*. Debuting in Dresden in 1905, it proved a hit but stirred controversy for its iconoclasm. The music was considered by many to be "discordant and disturbing," according to the historian Richard Bizot, the erotic content unmistakable, in particular Salome's desire for John the Baptist, which led her to fondle and kiss his severed head. The Dance of the Seven Veils was its enormously popular centerpiece, and the basis of countless modern-dance and vaudeville versions.[2]

The interpretive dancer Maud Allan was reputedly the first to seize on Salome as a stand-alone act. She debuted it in Vienna on December 26,

1906. Allan was soon onstage in London in a concoction titled *The Vision of Salome*. In it, she was fitted out in a costume of "astonishing brevity." Sounding remarkably Tanguay-like, she presented a decidedly unbiblical, "pretty and very sexy Salome." Allan's routine started with a number of stark postures and movements, before the disembodied head alighted on a nearby pedestal. "She sees it and folds up like a recoiling serpent," according to one account. A moment later, she was uncoiling, hesitantly lurching toward the object of her fascination. Then, in a whirl, Allan grabbed the head and carried it downstage to the footlights. Once there, she went into what was described by an onlooker as "a spasm of physical raptures over it." The routine climaxed when she held the head at arm's length, swung it around a few times, then touched its lips to hers, seeming to "drink obscene kisses from them as from the brim of a cup." She would then shudder and drop to her knees. In *The Vision of Salome*'s final moment, Maud Allan would rise while her "whole nude figure quiver[ed]," as she "wreathe[d] fantastic figures with her arms, her legs, her gleaming body." She staggered, reeled, and, finally, "in the pallid moonlight," fell.[3]

This became the template for nearly all future interpretations of Salome. Ultimately, what made Allan's *Vision of Salome* so influential and popular was its winning combination of sex and spirituality, all "wrapped up in the rhetoric of High Aesthetic purpose," according to Bizot.[4] For Maud Allan, that was what sold it. As Eva Tanguay would soon discover, the "High Aesthetic purpose" proved dispensable.

In many ways, Allan's *Vision* was but an extension of the burgeoning modern dance. The new art form celebrated liberation and artistic and social freedom. Paradoxically, it looked back to an imagined version of ancient history and repackaged it for the present. Dancers in this young tradition, chief among them Ruth St. Denis and Isadora Duncan, combined bodily display with loose or brief drapery, often turning to archaic and non-Western sources for inspiration. It led to creations such as St. Denis's *Radha*, which was allegedly Indian in origin.[5]

Popular vaudevillian Gertrude Hoffman brought a close imitation of Maud Allan's number to the United States, and was credited by many as the first to land Salome in the New World. By July 1908, Hoffman was appearing at Hammerstein's in what *Variety* called "dignified cooch" punctuated with "a most perceptible wriggle," linking the act with seamy burlesque rather than allegedly respectable vaudeville. Filmy garments betrayed Hoffman's bare form, save for short, white minipants. Soon, mobs intoxicated with "mid-Summer Madness" were flocking to the theater to see Hoffman's scant attire. With Hoffman headlining the bill, Hammerstein's enjoyed its biggest week to date, no matter that the performer was arrested for "violating a section of the Penal Code, which relates to an offense against 'public decency,'" according to news reports. Undaunted and otherwise unpunished, Hoffman whipped up a version of St. Denis's *Radha* that featured a "Hindoo Temple dance" and an even greater emphasis on her striking figure.[6]

By the late summer of 1908, Salome had hit its frenzied peak. From a curiosity with aesthetic roots in shady burlesque and the world of sideshow oddities, Salome dancing, by virtue of its simultaneous association with high art, had come into its own. "Even the 'rubberneck' ballyhoos have changed their cry," wrote *Variety*. "Now it's 'Take the automobile and go Saloming.'" The Salome craze in vaudeville typified the emergent urban amusement. It was, like audiences enjoying new automotive technology, unshackled from its roots and mobile in every way. It could round the circuits thanks to the industrial organization of big-time vaudeville. It was an aesthetic bastard reaching back both to the Bible and the concert saloon. It was a moral tempest in a teapot whose raciness drew big crowds. "And still the Salomes rush upon us!" wrote the *New York Clipper* in August of 1908. Despite presenting a dancer deemed "neither supple nor graceful," Keith & Proctor's 125th Street vaudeville theater drew full, enthusiastic crowds for the Salome flavor of the week. "Truly," marveled the *Clipper*, "there seems to be no stemming the tide of nearly naked dancers of this description, and the public is not yet satiated with the terpsichorean novelty" that was the Salome dance.[7]

The movie producer and motion-picture machine manufacturer (there being little distinction between the two in film's early days) S. Lubin even shot a cinematic rendering called *Salome: The Dance of the Seven Veils*. For forty-four dollars, exhibitors got, on four hundred feet of film, "the play the whole country is talking about," depicting "in vivid scenes the drunken feast given to the Senators by Herod." It of course had Salome doing her famous unveiling, and, in the end, "the hurried entry of Salome's mother, throwing a leopard skin around her daughter." Interested buyers were counseled: "Be Quick."[8]

Yet no Salome dancer made a bigger hit than Eva Tanguay. In many ways, Salome's caricature as understood in the popular imagination fit Eva's ends perfectly. Despite the fascination with some Salome dancers' alluring striptease moves, the character was more than just a spectacle for voyeurs to enjoy. She was also somehow powerful, self-directed, and able to control men. She was expressive and assertive. Eva's Salome emphasized all of these aspects of the character while also reminding spectators that it was she, their beloved, cyclonic vaudevillian, there beneath the veils. A New York–based critic called it "the most rapid method of crossing the stage ever witnessed."[9]

According to Eva, the idea of playing Salome came to her while she was sitting in a dentist's chair. "Everybody was talking about it. I jumped up with a tooth half-filled and told the dentist he would have to finish the job some other day." A half hour later, she claimed, she signed a contract with the vaudeville producer Percy Williams, who had recently returned from London having seen Maud Allan's *Vision of Salome.*[10]

It seems more likely that Eva waited for the trend to show signs of reaching a height, then pounced on it with the help of her handlers and publicists, notably C. F. Zittel, with whom she had enjoyed a scandalous and well-publicized tryst barely a year earlier. Edward Darling, still technically Eva's fiancé, suggested that Eva turn to Percy Williams rather than Keith and Albee, because the latter would raise her pay no higher. Williams, an impresario who owned a string of theaters in and around New York City, including the Colonial and several others, was purportedly more sympathetic to performers than were his rival vaudeville producers. Although long depicted as David to the Keith/Albee Goliath, Percy Williams had stunned the theater world a year earlier by agreeing to book talent at his independent chain via the United Booking Offices, a monopolistic, Keith-controlled syndicate. Thus, Keith and Albee would see good money from Eva's Salome turn without having to finance it directly. (Williams sold his theaters outright to the Keith organization in 1912 for $5 million.) For bringing her Dance of the Seven Veils to the Williams circuit, Eva got $3,500 a week—close to $70,000 a week in current terms. It was reported to be the biggest money ever paid a vaudevillian.[11]

In Darling's reminiscences, "[Eva's] 'Salome' was one to end all 'Salomes.'" Eva wanted producer Williams to furnish her with a large fountain, the type one might find in an Italian piazza, and position it center stage. Her idea was to cap a lengthy dance routine with the hurling of John the Baptist's head into the fountain. Then, presumably to show remorse, she'd throw herself in as well. But Williams rejected the idea of a "damp" Salome. What finally emerged was an act that had Eva prancing about the stage cradling John the Baptist's head in her arms, which she presently kicked about like a soccer ball. "She yelled, screamed, danced and what not," before pulling off one of her signature quick costume changes and steamrolling into her hit musical numbers, which the audience expected anyway. In other words, a millennia-old Bible story had its appeal, but in the end it worked best as a vehicle for Eva's vaudeville routine.[12]

Eva's Salome boasted something else special. Rather than a papier-mâché head, she used a real, live one—for part of the act, anyway. The cyclonic performer had a "Negro boy" crouch in a large box disguised to look like a piece of Roman architectural decor, his head poking out the top "as if on a platter" and draped in a black, silk coverlet. Eva sang to the shrouded head and, at the climactic moment, pulled off the cover. Though supposedly severed, the head nonetheless pivoted and rolled its eyes, suggesting that not even the dead were immune to Eva Tanguay's incantations.[13]

Eva debuted her act, *A Vision of Salome,* in August 1908. She spared nothing in creating a lavish set, complete with torches, a marble-floored temple, and a massive stairway that she used to show off her dancing skills—or lack thereof. In one of her more preposterous PR claims, she said that she had studied a "fourteenth-century manuscript" in researching the role. The ancient document told her that the real Salome came to an end when a sheet of ice on which she stood gave way, ironically resulting in her own decapitation. Thus, a river was added to her already elaborate set. So impressive was Eva's scenery that rather than scrap it when she was ready to move on to her next big thing, she kept it to rent out to other would-be Salomes, including dancer Mimi Aguglia in 1913, long after the Salome craze had faded.[14]

The stage designer P. Dodd Ackerman was the man behind all the set dressing, and another outside artist, the composer Melville Gideon, had been brought in to score the piece. Gideon would go on to enjoy mild recognition as the composer of *The Optimists,* a "musical novelty" in twenty-four scenes that saw a lengthy run in London before relocating to the Century Roof Theatre in New York in 1928.[15]

While the stage was lavishly draped for Eva's Salome, not so the actress. She variously donned a flesh-colored sheath dotted with a few gems, or something a little less revealing when civic authorities came to check her out—and then check her out again. Her costume, which she remembered as consisting of "strings of rhinestones and pearls...but not much else," was not so much a pandering to unbridled lust as yet another way Eva participated in and yet differentiated herself from a popular phenomenon with literally hundreds of players. It also showed Eva honing a unique approach to sexuality, one that let her push the envelope without being sidelined as immoral or perverted. While her body was on display, it was not simply presented as an erotic object. Her fleshy, sometimes overweight form moved with such abandon through so many ludicrous narrative twists that she indeed conveyed her usual impression, not of "lewdness but of lunacy," to borrow from Marybeth Hamilton. Eva did not so much walk a fine line as shimmy, run, and leap all over it.[16]

Still, Eva's Dance of the Seven Veils was undeniably steamy. Her Salome act was sometimes promoted with the tagline: "Eva Tanguay. The Naked Truth." It was not Salome whom audiences saw, according to a Brooklyn newspaper, so much as Eva "clad in Biblical garb—or what there is of it." Eva's sister, Blanche, seeing her kid sister "with more than a Highlander's display of shin and little less than a pugilist's display of 'buff,'" supposedly fainted in shock.[17]

The whole combination—spectacular scenery, near nudity, and flailing dance moves, held loosely together by Melville Gideon's score plus a few of Eva's greatest hits—showed Eva attempting to reach a new level of cultural appreciation. The costs and risks were immense but they paid off. Police had to keep the entryway clear at the 125th Street theater so that patrons could deposit their nickels in a specially built, pay-as-you-enter admission box. "Was it a 'hit'? Most emphatically it was." So declared Ashton Stevens in the *New York Journal*. The audience was "spellbound" wrote Sam M'Kee, the reporter who also worked as a booster for Eva when she returned from her bout of exhaustion earlier that year.[18]

Not surprisingly, some Salome dancers attempted to claim ownership of the act, not because they expected to win but rather to claim some of the public spotlight, however briefly. Millie De Leon, who called herself "The Original Girl in Blue," issued a public challenge in the pages of the sporting and theatrical newspaper the *New York Clipper* in September 1908, a month after Eva's Salome debut. To all Salomes, De Leon declared herself the "originator of this peculiar style of dancing." She warned potential rivals that she could "outdance [all] imitators, in style and execution, for any amount of money," billing herself "The Real Salome Dancer."[19]

The following month, Eva struck back. Taking out a large display ad in *Variety,* she insisted that she alone among vaudevillians had legitimate rights to Salome. The advertisement offered abundant evidence of her popularity though no clear reason why rivals were legally or ethically obliged to steer clear. Pull-quotes from her reviews mentioned "ponderous music and strong scenic effects." One critic was said to find "absolutely no vulgarity to it," while another focused on Eva's scanty costume, pointing out that "if the real daughter of Herodias was as cute and pretty and lithesome as her latter-day imitator, why, then the little lady can't be blamed for a good many things that are charged against her." In her PR efforts, Eva tried to cover all the bases. The musicians reportedly "banged away as though they were playing the overture to the day of judgment." Spectators gazed through opera glasses at the performer in a body stocking, training their lenses "where they will do the most good." Eva may be seen as engaging in a kind of self-parody. But she was also learning, with the help of advisors like M'Kee, that publicity and controversy were to be cultivated just like new material for her shows. Like P. T. Barnum, who stirred controversies, then actively took part in the debates that his outrageous claims had sparked, Eva was learning how to provoke a strong response to her performances, and then step into the center of those responses, in effect making the show go on even longer.[20]

In Eva's wake, the Salomes continued to come, unfazed by her pugnacious claims of ownership and adding their own marvelous and absurd touches. Julian Eltinge, the fabulously popular female impersonator and Eva's pretend suitor, donned and then doffed the veils of Salome, while comedienne Jessica Preston drew peals of laughter at the Colonial with an intentional mockery of the whole thing.[21]

In addition to gender-bending Salomes, there were ethnic interpretations of the character as well. Famed funny lady Fanny Brice, a comic songstress who had cut her teeth in burlesque, unleashed the first identifiably Jewish interpretation of Herod's daughter. Brice sang a tune called "Sadie Salome, Go Home!" penned by none other than Irving Berlin (with lyrics by Edgar Leslie). Rendered with a Yiddish lilt, "Sadie Salome" told the story of Sadie Cohen, "a nice Jewish girl," who has left her home and sweetheart to make it big as a Salome dancer. It both capitalized and commented on the Salome frenzy, and proved Brice's first notable success.[22]

A more culturally complicated and sophisticated rendering of Salome came from the actress, singer, and dancer Aida Overton Walker. Walker, born in Manhattan in 1880, had by her late teens become a member of a popular African American vaudeville show captained by the legendary comedians George Walker and Bert Williams. (Walker eventually became her husband.) The three starred in the groundbreaking musical *In Dahomey* in 1903, enjoying crossover success with white, middle-class audiences on Broadway, and even garnering a command performance for the British royal family at Buckingham Palace. Aida Overton Walker first played her Salome in a musical called *Bandanna Land* (to whose plot it was unrelated) in Brooklyn in 1908. Observers lauded her for comparative modesty of dress and a hint of realist acting style.[23]

Part parody, part high art, and part exotic treat, Overton Walker's Salome was further praised for "eliminating the gruesomeness," in the words of one newspaperman, associated with so many of the stripping, snake-dancing, head-flinging Salomes. She merely touched her lips to those of the Baptist at the very last moment before falling prostrate. *Variety's* Sime Silverman called it the best "parody" of Salome he had ever seen. But he may have been missing a subtle interplay of divergent aesthetic codes that blended modernism and primitivism. Aida Overton Walker was one of the few African Americans to gain widespread popularity in the largely white, Keith-style vaudeville circuits not by denying her ethnicity but by appealing to unconscious, often competing desires in many of her spectators. She deliberately melded African and Western forms to manifest a "studied ambiguity," in the words of the theater scholar David Krasner, which delighted audiences accustomed to exotic dancers and increasingly playful, unabashed displays of the energetic female figure.[24]

Aida Overton Walker may have shared something more than Salome with Eva Tanguay—namely, her husband, George. Vaudevillian-turned-Hollywood-personality George Jessel suggested an affair between Eva and George in *Elegy in Manhattan*, a compendium of semihumorous verse patterned after Edgar Lee Masters's *Spoon River Anthology*. In *Elegy*, Jessel has George Walker declare:

> *Bert was always*
> *Reading books.*
> *I was dancin'* . . .
> *And livin'.* . . .
> *There was whisperin' about me*
> *And the "I don't care" gal, Eva Tanguay;*
> *I guess it's a good thing*
> *That the whisperin'*
> *didn't get louder,*
> *For it could've been*
> *Awfully bad for me.* . . .
> *A dark man,*
> *And a white gal!*

Perhaps to protect her in a racist culture, Jessel's "elegy" of Eva denied an emotional connection, while playing up what Jessel imagined to be her sexual fascination with the comedian:

> *In actors' green rooms*
> *And 5th Avenue mansions,*
> *Where it was whispered*

> *I'd fallen in love*
> *With the dark-skinned George Walker*
> *Of the famous "Williams and Walker"...*
> *But it was not so!*
> *I just admired him.*
> *He was so tall...*
> *And strong...*
> *And handsome...*
> *He looked like the song he sang:*
> *"Bonbon Buddy—The Chocolate Drop."*[25]

Apart from Jessel's poetic history, there is no direct evidence of an affair between George Walker and Eva Tanguay. But those intimately familiar with Tanguay, Walker, and vaudeville today find Jessel's assertion credible. The vaudeville historian and editor of the *Vaudeville Times* Frank Cullen believes George Walker and Eva Tanguay carried on a full-fledged affair. David Krasner seems to agree, though he sounds a note of caution. Those who suspect a sexual liaison between Tanguay and Walker are "definitely onto something," he feels. "But locating who said what and where it happened is as hard then as it is now (that's why we have the *National Inquirer*)."[26]

John Graziano, a professor at the City College of New York who has written on early African American musical forms, is less convinced. He calls the evidence of a sexual relationship between Walker and Tanguay "anecdotal at best." But Graziano notes that George Walker was a prodigious "ladies' man" who enjoyed many women on both sides of the racial divide. "He was certainly at ease with both races," says Graziano. George Walker contracted syphilis and died at the tragically young age of thirty-eight, in 1911.[27]

In courting George Walker, whether for professional reasons alone or a combination of professional and personal, Eva Tanguay was again pushing the limits of what a respectable vaudeville performer was allowed to do. While the 1920s would see the rise of "respectable" white folks' fascination with the culture and nightlife of Harlem, at the time of Eva's Salome turn, a white woman's sexual involvement with a black man could be scandalous to the point of professional fatality. While sexual encounters between black men and white women in the antebellum South were, often covertly, tolerated (if not condoned), things changed drastically after the Civil War. Thus, argues the historian Martha Hodes, racist whites, concentrated mostly in the South, increasingly judged any romantic encounter between white women and black men as, perforce, rape. The result was a tragic epidemic of lynchings carried out by paranoid, murderous white populations who had conjured a myth that black men were "bestial," brutal creatures incapable of controlling themselves. Though the Civil War had ended over a quarter-century earlier, the number of lynchings reached its feverish, bloodthirsty peak in 1892, with "rape" often cited as the justifying charge. As late as 1899, a very nervous and very racist white woman named Corra Harris warned, "At no time, in no place, is the white woman safe from the insults and assaults of these creatures." Those with intellectual and political acumen tried to fight back. "The charge of rape against colored Americans was invented by the white South after Reconstruction to excuse mob violence," wrote the intellectual and civil rights pioneer W. E. B. Du Bois as he continued to wrangle with the issue in 1919. As late as 1967, at least sixteen U.S. states had laws prohibiting marriage between blacks and whites.[28]

As a performer and celebrity who existed in the firmament of professional entertainment, Eva Tanguay was somewhat exempt from certain prohibitions that might pertain to a civilian white woman consorting with an African American lover. But she was nonetheless engaging in risky behavior (though riskier yet for George Walker) and exploring the outer edges of what a rising mass-entertainment industry controlled by middle-class white businessmen could tolerate. Whatever the truth of her affair with George Walker, Eva Tanguay suffered no economic or social consequences. She managed to present a self that combined opposites— white and black, respectable and lowbrow, prudish yet promiscuous—into one improbable persona that starred both onstage and off.

With Eva Tanguay leading the Salome fad, it was only a matter of time before a reactionary band of moralizers tried to put an end to it. In Newark, New Jersey, police threatened to arrest a Salome dancer, who promptly "put aside" her costume and instead offered up a routine "that could not offend even a deacon from Ocean Grove," according to a newspaper report. Vaudevillians were nothing if not protean, having an array of substitute jokes, maneuvers, and routines always at the ready. In New York, the police commissioner had his captains check out Salome dancers in response to a complaint he had received about their scanty costumes. Martin Beck, the chief of the powerful Orpheum chain of vaudeville theaters— which was to the West Coast what the Keith/Albee organization was back East—proclaimed Salome dancers "degrading" and swore his circuit was "diverting its energies to the higher and loftier plane of entertainment." There is little evidence that Beck ever backed up his words with deeds.[29]

Figure 11. An editorial cartoon from *Variety*, July 13, 1909.
The cartoonist suggested Eva should appear in a box to protect the
"I Don't Care" comedienne from moral censure.
*(From the General Research Division, The New York Public Library,
Astor, Lenox, and Tilden Foundations.)*

. . . .

As the Salome wave started to subside, about a year after it first took
vaudeville by storm, several things became clear. Big-time vaudeville, now
a quarter-century old, less and less claimed to be a chaste or inoffensive
undertaking. The Salomes, Eva chief among them, had pulled middle-
class-approved mass entertainment into the realm of sexual fascination more
fully than at any time in U.S. history. "Ten years ago, B. F. Keith held a
place of high esteem in the hearts of American vaudeville-goers," wrote an
editorialist in the *New York Dramatic Mirror* in 1909. "The husband was glad
to take his wife. Where is the standard today? Vaudeville is deteriorating.
What is tolerated to-day would have been impossible two or three years
ago." The "man of high ideals" and the "mother of refined daughters" had
now to cast "a critical eye" on the form that once offered safe haven from
the unpredictable and scandalous tumult of urban amusement.[30]

Eva continued intermittently with Salome but began to phase it out
in favor of routines, costumes, and patter that were no less unique and

provocative. Her outlandish interpretation of the Dance of the Seven Veils had honed her sense of what novelty-seeking crowds (and the businessmen who appealed to them) demanded, while her deft if unsubtle approach to publicity helped her stay atop the pack. The vaudevillian, no matter how popular or well paid during a particular season, could not afford to rest on his or her laurels. Freshness was always the core ingredient of success in the "two-a-day," as big-time vaudeville, with its two shows each day, was sometimes called.

In 1909, amid much fanfare, the U.S. treasury department issued a new penny with the face of President Abraham Lincoln. The coins had barely begun to circulate when Eva got the idea of making them into a stage costume. As part of a well-orchestrated promotional scheme, she let fans know that the penny dress weighed forty-five pounds and had somehow cost two thousand dollars to make. But that wasn't all. During her vaudeville act, she'd pull off the coins and toss them one at a time into the audience. Here was a strange take on striptease, a reversal of power and money relations, however low the stakes. Fans loved it. Thomas J. Flynn of Brooklyn wrote Eva an adoring letter after seeing her do the Lincoln-penny striptease: "My Dear Madam: While sitting in the Auditory at Keith's yesterday, I received the sum of TWO CENTS, and while it has been my custom in the past to acknowledge remittances of money, I take the pleasure at this time to thank you for the same." Hilton Thomas, who described himself as "your ardent admirer in vaudeville," had an even better tale. Sitting in a Keith vaudeville house in New York City, Thomas was struck "on top of the nose" by an Eva-flung penny. Determined that no one else should suffer the same blow, he nailed the offending projectile to his office desk. That very afternoon, Thomas made a handsome one thousand dollars, he said, "on some stock which I had invested in." The very next day, the lucky investor received word that a property in Connecticut he'd been trying to unload for eight years had finally gotten snapped up, netting him nine thousand dollars more. He thus implored "that if you ever hit me on the nose again I see right now that John D. [Rockefeller] and [J. P.] Morgan are liable to get sore." Next time, he requested, she should not only send a penny his way, but "please hit me a little harder…as I feel now that instead of hitting me with a cent you hit me with a bank," mixing money and sadomasochism into a fetish not unthinkable with the Wall Street crowd.[31]

Vaudeville censors kept a watchful eye on Eva, not necessarily looking for what she was doing wrong but trying to come up with a calculus for what she and they could reasonably get away with. In early 1909, Ned Hastings, manager of Keith's Hippodrome in New York, admitted in a short memorandum that "we might like to make some changes in her material," though he appeared hesitant to tamper with box-office gold, labeling Eva a "phenomenal drawing card." Hastings offered the following rationalization, probably designed to ease the minds of superiors: "I think the fact that it is Tanguay makes the people forget what in another might offend." Though he did not describe the specific material he might, under other circumstances, like to have altered, in all likelihood it was a combination of suggestive dance moves and revealing costumes, both of which would irk civic authorities in the months to come. Still, following Salome, Eva was in a stratosphere of her own. Perhaps a bit like Janis Joplin, Madonna, or Lady Gaga, she was increasingly able to write her own rules, to define acceptability as much as be defined by it.[32]

It was not only that Eva brought daring costumes to her vaudeville turns, but also that she made costume changes with lightning speed several times during her act—all on the stage. It lent her act an element of burlesque and striptease, as though Eva's private boudoir were now in public view. At the same time, it was something out of the circus sideshow, the quick-change artist, the freakish novelty, combined with an athleticism that was both erotic and yet culturally unwomanly. On at least one occasion, playing New York's Fifth Avenue Theatre, Eva changed her costume for each song. Every show was standing room only, "probably...the 'record-breaker' of the season," in the estimation of the theater manager. The dancer and stage producer Leonard Sillman saw Eva perform in the late 1920s when she was past her physical and theatrical prime. He swore that she pulled off eight full changes during an eighteen-minute show. Under the spotlight, she used the piano as a changing lounge, "achieving effects that are beautiful and bizarre," according to the *Los Angeles Times*. A male dresser had helped shoehorn the increasingly plump vaudeville star into a length of inner tube, thereby "squeezing the waist down to proportions acceptable for public display."[33]

She continued debuting outfits that were hilarious and culturally relevant. In addition to the penny dress, Eva had one made of dollar bills. In *The Encyclopedia of Vaudeville,* Anthony Slide termed Eva's stage wear "deliberately outrageous." One of her outfits was nothing more than an assemblage of memo pads and pencils, no doubt appealing to the class of clerical workers who populated the urban workforce and spent their leisure dime on vaudeville.[34]

Figure 12. Kooky costume, kooky lady.
Eva could play the sex card. But she preferred to play the queen of nuts.
(Author's private collection.)

· · · · · · · · · ·

6

Rivals, Imitators, and Censors

A S HER FAME GREW in the wake of Salome, Eva struggled to maintain her personal and professional equilibrium. She would face this challenge throughout her career: trying to push herself to the limit—physically and emotionally—without flaming out and crashing. But balance was never Eva Tanguay's strong suit. Her will, determination, and talent at pleasing audiences and promoting herself had paid off handsomely with Salome. At the edges, however, she was beginning to fray. She increasingly saw the world around her as a battleground full of rivals and opponents. To be sure, there were dozens if not hundreds of Salomes. But it was not only these direct competitors that Eva viewed with fear and loathing. To Eva, it more and more seemed that every vaudevillian, save a small circle of intimates, was grabbing for her turf, even if in reality they could never hope to capture her essence. Her animus, no matter how amusing or tinged with PR value, betrayed a core of deep insecurity. Presently, that core would erupt, raining hot anger on those who happened to be near.

She also felt alone. Planning, touring, publicizing, and negotiating left her with little time for sojourns to the relative calm of her family in Massachusetts, where she herself no longer kept a house. And she had no reliable partner or family of her own. Eva had turned thirty in 1908 just as her Salome was taking off. Yet she seemed to have no satisfactory private life to balance out the emotional and physical rigors of her job. Something had to give.

In October 1908, a musician named Willa Holt Wakefield gained notoriety for winning a second straight week at Keith & Proctor's Fifth

Avenue Theater thanks to her unexpected popularity. As the papers eagerly noted, such an honor had not been bestowed on a female vaudevillian since the previous July, when Eva Tanguay had managed just such a doubleheader. Wakefield went on to score bigger and bigger successes with her "parlor entertainments," genteel renditions of songs from a bygone era that, popular as they were, still resonated as, at best, inoffensive museum pieces. Perhaps the theater's manager liked the air of class and decorum that Wakefield lent his program. Maybe her novelty was briefly popular with a crowd normally accustomed to fast-paced, fun-poking ditties that vibrated with citified energy. Whatever Wakefield's appeal, Eva, though silent for the moment, began nursing a smoldering resentment against the parlor singer. It did not help that the press played up Willa Holt Wakefield as somehow possessing everything that Eva Tanguay seemed to lack—elegance, refinement, self-control, and dignity.[1]

Wakefield was billed in the press as "a society woman hailing from one of the best families in Georgia," reputed to be a descendant of a former governor of that southern state. Whether true or not, Wakefield played the classiness card to her advantage. "One has only to look at her to recognize the refinement of many generations," wrote *The Green Book Album* magazine, a high-profile publication with elaborate fonts and impressive photo spreads. She first came to New York in 1902 to entertain at private gatherings; soon, she was hitting vaudeville with her one-woman piano act. She sang, recited, and played the ivories, "which appeals to the better classes," according to the notes of the New York vaudeville manager F. J. O'Connor, in 1906. In contrast to Eva, Wakefield spoke out against "risqué" songs. She opted instead for "simple melodies," half sung, half spoken, as she accompanied herself at the keyboard displaying her refined musical skills. Critics praised her as a balm for the "too frequent clap trap and obvious vulgarity on the vaudeville stage." Her numbers were "delightfully clean," standing out "like some lustrous jewel in a dark setting." To make matters worse, she was also a reputed investing sharp who rubbed elbows with some of the city's top financial brass. At 4 Wall Street one could find the offices of Willa Holt Wakefield Stocks and Bonds, staffed with stenographers, clerks, and the like, "devoted exclusively to the business of buying and selling securities for Miss Wakefield." She had two cars, two maids, a home on respectable Riverside Drive in Manhattan, and a profitable working farm in the suburban town of Mamaroneck on the Long Island Sound. In 1909 alone, Wakefield enjoyed forty thousand dollars in profits from the sale of securities.[2]

To Eva, this was unbearable; the gauntlet had most definitely been thrown down. Here was a potential rival who was not only complaining about off-color material, but maintaining a respectable profile and, it would seem, cultivating a fan base on Eva's home turf. It would have been better if the two had simply never crossed paths. As fate would have it, however, they were to have a significant collision when both were slated to play at Hammerstein's deluxe vaudeville theater on the evening of March 9, 1909.

Recuperated from her afternoon show (at which Eva was not present), Wakefield left her nearby hotel in a taxicab at nine o'clock, expecting to go on in the number-seven position after intermission, which occurred around nine forty-five, just prior to Eva Tanguay's time slot. When she arrived at Hammerstein's, however, with her personal physician and business manager both in tow, Willa Holt Wakefield was now told that she had the *number-five* spot. The arrangement was simply not workable, she told Mr. Simon, Hammerstein's stage manager, because she needed more time than that to dress and prep for her act. Wakefield assumed she would be changed back to her original position on the program. What she did not know, though, was that Eva had been spreading rumors that Wakefield had a claque ready to hiss her, Eva, off the stage as soon as she opened her mouth. Wakefield had some friends from back home in the theater. But there is no evidence that they were involved in the plot as Eva charged. Nonetheless, Eva used it as an argument to have her rival bumped to the earlier spot in the night's program.[3]

It was shortly before ten o'clock and Willa Holt Wakefield was finally ready to take the stage. She assumed the earlier misunderstanding regarding her spot had been mended—a misunderstanding, nothing more. But as she headed to the wings the management informed her that she would not be going on *at all*. She was also told that her manager, Louis Newman, and her personal physician had both been ejected outright from the theater. Wakefield was at a loss. She offered to go on in *any* position, if that were the problem, even after the show-closing short movies. But stage manager Simon told her there would be no negotiating. He politely, but in no uncertain terms, asked her to leave. It was now intermission. Not knowing what else to do, Wakefield, in full stage regalia, strutted down to the theater lobby. The crowd recognized her at once, and by one account—a story probably embellished by Wakefield's press representatives—police reservists had to be called in to keep the throng at bay. Willa Holt Wakefield bid the throng adieu and returned to her hotel.[4]

Away from the scene of the battle, the pianist realized she had lost the skirmish with Eva Tanguay, though she would not yet concede the all-out war for hearts and minds. She cancelled further engagements that week at Hammerstein's and declared publicly that she knew Eva Tanguay was behind her ouster. Her popularity had quite simply threatened a very popular but very insecure Eva Tanguay, Wakefield explained to the *New York Times*. A prominent banker friend of Wakefield's offered twenty thousand dollars to take legal action against Eva Tanguay "for what he considered a gross insult to Miss Wakefield." For Eva it was a mixed blessing. She did not have to share the stage with Willa Holt Wakefield and she had further defined herself, for better or worse, as a deeply competitive, adversarial performer. The press loved the coverage but also painted her as a willful and selfish schemer. "Eva Tanguay has once more given evidence of the fact that she can master a situation to her own liking," wrote a reporter who felt it was "a crying shame to vaudeville. To attempt to cite the tantrums that Tanguay has indulged in during the past season would be like attempting to count the stars." Eva's publicity-seeking drive was, on the one hand, keeping her in the spotlight. But it was also beginning to backfire, the first signs of an internal compass starting to spin off course. It could have been nearly anything that set Eva off—and increasingly, it would be. For now, something about Willa Holt Wakefield's association with the supposedly "better" classes had triggered Eva's demons. Eva was increasingly looking at the world as a ladder to be climbed: there were those above her whom she sought to vanquish and those below whom she could tolerate as inferiors. But her rung was a lonely place. Eva, of course, failed to see that her own appeal lay in her decided difference from Willa Holt Wakefield. Though the daughter of a doctor, Eva had nonetheless known alcoholism and near poverty after her father's death, and perhaps before it too. That she was of "indeterminate social origin," in the words of the cultural historian Lois Banner, added to her fascination. But she did not see it that way. For her part, Willa Holt Wakefield was immediately signed on to the competing William Morris circuit with a "considerable" salary bump. She continued to play vaudeville, and continued to boast that she brought an element of "class" to the show. But her star soon grew dim. Her clash with the cyclonic one proved the high point of Willa Holt Wakefield's notoriety.[5]

EVA CONTINUED to strike out against rivals or those she saw as rivals. After the Wakefield incident, that suspect group might have included just about everyone on the two-a-day boards. But something else drew her attention, and for the moment it was one of vaudeville's most interesting species: imitators.

As vaudeville grew in popularity, new theaters were added to nearly every town of size throughout the United States and Canada. Unlike mass-reproducible movies in the years to come, however, a popular act could appear at only one venue on a given night. Nation-sweeping train lines and efficient, industrialized routing could help ensure that a top player would cover wide swaths of the continent during a tour. But there was no way to put a sought-after entertainer in two theaters at once—at least not exactly. Seeing a need to be filled, in a short time, any number of would-be vaudevillians devised clever and sometimes astoundingly accurate (or, on occasion, brilliantly satirical) imitations of big-time star acts. Curiously, their efforts pointed to the fact that vaudeville, despite its systematization, was indeed based on the ephemeral charm of a live performer. Perhaps for that very reason, audiences loved the phenomenon of seeing and hearing their favorite star in facsimile, for the star was both obviously absent and yet seemingly present at the same time. Among vaudevillians, none was more widely imitated than Eva Tanguay, again reflecting a paradoxical urge to capture and re-create her very uniqueness.

As early as 1908, Gertrude Hoffman added Eva to the roster of stars she imitated, a list that came to include Ethel Barrymore, George M. Cohan, Isadora Duncan, and Valeska Suratt. But Eva was her biggest put-on. With a repertoire of high-precision copy routines, Hoffman scored big on Keith time.[6]

Such was the state of the industry that the *New York Clipper* could say, in 1909, that "Tanguay is so often imitated and usually so badly done, that it is a relief to see a good imitation of the 'whirlwind' every once in a while," referring to Tanguay impressionist Bessie Browning. (By now, Eva's fame was such that even her nicknames had nicknames, "whirlwind" being merely another version of "cyclone.") Browning not only copied Eva but claimed to have discovered an unknown Milwaukee girl singing in a café whom she promised to train up as "a second Eva Tanguay." The performer Harry Breen, a Brooklyn native, famous for coming up with impromptu songs of jumbled nonsense, dubbed himself "the male Eva Tanguay," while the couture-sporting Frenchwoman Gaby Deslys sang Eva's "I Don't Care" as part of her own act. A hip-shaking stripper named Babe La Tour billed herself as "The Eva Tanguay of Burlesque." And a curious young woman named Mae West, who was just starting out in vaudeville, studiously copied Eva for her own performances.[7]

Also among the early "second Tanguays" on the scene was a woman named Miss Maurice Wood. By the fall of 1908, Wood was enjoying "conspicuous success" pulling off imitations of both Eva and the popular British import Vesta Victoria with "consummate skill." The daughter of Dr. Willis Wood, one of Chicago's top surgeons, Wood was taken as a girl to see Eva's winning turn as Phrosia in *The Chaperons*. She recounted that, on watching the cyclonic comedienne onstage, she was seized with the idea that when she grew up, "I would be a second Tanguay." Flattering though it may sound, attempting to become a "second Tanguay" called into question the value of the original, both upping its value and simultaneously depreciating it in the eyes of some. Would a "second Tanguay" make crowds hungrier for the original? Or would imitators simply steal unprotected creative material and lead the public to tire of the actual item? "[Wood's] 'Tanguay' is really remarkable, so good that no one excepting the original has approached it," wrote *Variety*. Wood even mimicked Eva's famous publicity poses, with back arched, legs covered in nothing but a thin film of silk, and a naughty grin stretching across her face.[8]

Wood was soon eclipsed by Billie Seaton, another of the throng copying "the most imitated woman on our stage to-day," according to the *New York Star*. To her credit, Seaton successfully, if briefly, clawed her way to the top. She started doing her Tanguay act in the live portion of small-time vaudeville shows, which sprinkled live acts amid a program of short movies. Deemed a leading talent in the "army" of Tanguay mimickers, Seaton sang songs "as it might be supposed Eva Tanguay would." But not all observers saw it that way. "Billie Seaton is wrong in continuing to be an imitation of Eva Tanguay," wrote the *New York Telegraph*. "At the same time it must be confessed that of all the countless young women who have tried to be like Eva Tanguay, the one having copied this wonderful comedienne's style and manner more effectively than all her competitors is Billie Seaton." When she played, Seaton's name was only slightly larger on the marquee than her specialty, "Eva Tanguay," making it seem to some unsuspecting passersby that perhaps she *and* the queen of vaudeville were doubling on the bill. None of this bothered Billie Seaton. "Oh, I know I am 'copping an act' all right," she said. "But that ain't nothing. Don't they all do it? I have seen fifty with acts of others." It was true. Mimicry was a growing fad on the vaudeville stage, with subgenres ranging from reverent to mocking to out-and-out bizarre. Eventually, to spice up an act that ultimately could not capture the essence of another individual, Billie Seaton peeled off most of her clothes onstage, capitalizing on the unalloyed sexual allure that Eva herself would have mixed with farce and fancy.[9]

On rare occasions, Eva encouraged imitators if she did not perceive them as a threat. She helped launch the songwriting career of Blanche Merrill by performing a tune Merrill had written especially for her titled "Give an Imitation of Me."[10]

Most of the vast throng who played the circuits with a Tanguay act avoided direct conflict with the cyclonic star. But of all the imitators, Eva was most threatened by Gertrude Hoffman, perhaps because she was not merely an Eva copier but a hugely popular artist in her own right. The two had in fact sparred over Salome. Eva now inaugurated a very public feud with Hoffman, challenging and counterchallenging her rival to various performance duels and showdowns, none of which ever came to pass. Though some have judged the sparring match between Tanguay and Hoffman to be fake, staged for publicity's sake, it also seems that Hoffman's efforts pushed deep emotional buttons in the cyclonic one.[11]

"Authors of books are protected; why not an originator of his or her line of work?" argued Eva in the pages of *Variety* in 1909. "Fifteen years it has taken to obtain my present position in my profession. Night and day I plan and worry and pay out most of what I earn only to have it stolen by *imitators*. It is the material they want, for not in any other way could they use my songs or costumes." To be sure, Eva made good use of hyperbole. By no means "most" of what she earned had been, or ever would be, raided by imitators. But her public rhetoric betrayed a sense of threat. Mimicry could, by its very nature, call into the question of the idea of individuality, which was precisely what Eva's professional life and identity were based on. This was how Eva saw it, anyway.[12]

Appropriating a battle plan pioneered by her rival, Gertrude Hoffman struck back. In the pages of a theater trade paper, Hoffman challenged Eva to "stop four-flushing and make good." If she thought herself "so extremely clever," Eva ought to appear side by side on a bill with her. Should that come to pass, Hoffman declared boldly, "I will receive as much genuine applause as you do."[13]

Though she publicly gave no quarter to imitators, Eva Tanguay was both canny and insecure enough to at least toy with the idea of capitalizing on the vast sea of Eva imitation that at once detracted from and yet enhanced her own star value. In 1909, she briefly added one such imitator to her very *own* bill, perhaps hoping to keep fans away from Gertrude Hoffman's shows. On an even weirder note, on finding out that Hoffman was reenacting her childhood victory at amateur night in Holyoke, Tanguay whipped up her *own* imitation of *Hoffman's* imitation of her. Despite the unlikelihood of Eva satirizing a rival's fanciful rendition of her very own childhood, the gambit actually worked. It was testament to the cyclonic comedienne's versatility and resilience, demonstrating an ability to turn challenges to her own advantage. At the same time, it revealed Eva's deep need to control the market around her. She spent huge quantities of psychic and physical energy warding off or absorbing threats that could be looked at as merely lifting the tide on which her own flagship sailed.[14]

In their official rhetoric, performers and those who spoke on their behalf decried mimicry. The White Rats, vaudeville's labor union, generally counseled originality rather than imitation, since legal protections for their material were sparse. "All artists should remember that in originality lies strength.... It is far better to do a bad, but original act, and to continue to improve it, than to do a stolen or partly stolen one," decreed the Rats in an editorial. Maybe to some with high ideals it was. But to many hungry vaudevillians, whatever secured work was strength enough. Sime Silverman of *Variety,* the most solidly pro-performer theatrical paper of the era, made known his wish that "actors would be discreet in the matter of purloining what cost some one else the labor of his mind or his money." Few were, however. It was this sort of infighting and competition that ultimately rendered vaudevillians unable to effectively organize, even in their own best interests.[15]

Amid the frenzy of Tanguay imitating, Bill Delaney, the manager of New York's Majestic Theater, hatched a clever plan. With so many performers imitating Eva Tanguay, rumors began to spread that the cyclonic vaudevillian owed her success largely to publicity and flashy promotions rather than talent. If Eva rose above the army of copiers, the argument went, it was only because she advertised herself more effectively. It reflected a bizarre logic, to say the least, but some began to believe it. Delaney would therefore organize a "tryout" night at the Majestic featuring unknown performers attempting to impress a typical crowd. As far as the patrons knew, this was little more than an amateur night permitting management to assess new talent. Without benefit of any announcement or publicity, Eva Tanguay went on, not as herself but in disguise as yet another lowly foot soldier in the huge brigade of Eva Tanguay imitators. The audience loved her. Eva's makeup and garb were such that they "DEFINITELY did not know" the genuine article had sauntered onstage amid the clones. So wrote Delaney in a private letter written decades later to Edward Darling. Eva the "imitator," playing herself, went on at the Majestic and did her best Eva Tanguay. The audience went nuts, regarding her act a "veritable sensation." According to Delaney, "She never received greater applause...at Hammerstein's...when the audience KNEW she was Tanguay." They thought her just another impersonator, and heaped cheers and applause on top of cheers and applause. Eva, in a singularly remarkable act of self-restraint, did not give away her identity. She did, however, walk offstage in tears.[16]

AS HER POPULARITY MUSHROOMED, as indicated by swarms of imitators and rivals, Eva increasingly began to see civic and legal restrictions as unjust encroachments. Again, it made for good press. But it also betrayed her growing unwillingness to fit in, and a penchant to take personally and bitterly what others in her field faced as well. In addition, it added further friction to her increasingly disharmonious life, for while rivals and imitators could be squarely met and bested, it was another matter when facing law-enforcement authorities. Eva never quite mastered the art of squaring off against these foes, though she had many PR handlers and attorneys who were eager to help.

Beginning in February 1909, the New York police spent months "carefully" examining Eva's frenetic gyrations, her panting and running onstage. They were trying to build a case against Eva proving she was in violation of the so-called Sunday Law, a series of statutes that limited what performers could do and wear on that supposedly sacred day of the week. Eva, having played more or less continuously for fourteen months in New York, was in no mood to tame herself in the city she had conquered.[17]

It was just before her Sunday matinee at Keith & Proctor's 125th Street Theatre in July when the officers came knocking. On entering her dressing room, they told the actress she had to cut the dancing out of her routine, noting that they had been watching her for close to six months. Eva donned a cheery aspect and replied to the gentlemen in blue, "Oh, you mean not do the hornpipe in showing the act I presented at my first appearance onstage. All right." No, they clarified. She was not to dance *at all,* not on Sunday anyway. Eva's tone changed in a flash; sticky sweetness gave way to fangs. With Eva, there was rarely a middle ground. "Perhaps you don't want me to appear at all," she threatened. The police explained that she was to desist from the waltz during "Who Discovered Love." That was all.

Another performer might have let it go at that. But Eva had a penchant for taking things as personally as possible, as if the law had been passed specifically to frustrate *her.* She retorted, "What of it? Surely that's not criminal." In fact, explained the policemen, it was. "I certainly shall sing the song properly, if I sing it at all. It's not my temperament to keep still. I don't see why I should and I intend to do my act exactly as I always have."

As one newspaper reported it, Eva simply "refused to accept the police interpretation of the law." The law may have been a silly one, evidence of Victorian prudishness combined with Progressive Era hand-wringing. But the threat was serious. Since the rise of urban amusements in the 1890s, social reformers had become increasingly worried about the effects of inexpensive, readily available, "unchristian" amusements, especially on impressionable youth and the poorer classes, who were seen as unable to manage their response to cultural influences. Furthermore, it could hardly be said that Eva was being charged without due research or preparation. None of this really mattered to the cyclonic star. To Eva Tanguay, it was all yet another personal affront and a challenge to her will, one that merited neither negotiation nor compromise. She seemed to remain unaware that the past several years had seen a rash of show closings and theater shutdowns spurred by anxiously crusading moral reformers and grandstanding politicians. Nickelodeon movie theaters and some vaudeville houses in New York were even shut down for a time in late 1908.[18]

After more squabbling with the officers, Eva appeared to back down—for the moment, anyway. She claimed that getting hauled into court would have interrupted her travel the next day to Boston for an engagement. "I'll go on the stage and do my best to give my act as you wish," she sighed to the police. But, she added, "I am doing this solely because I don't want to make trouble for managers who have always been kind to me. I never had the disposition of a stone image and I never like to be bossed." That last bit was certainly true. But Eva Tanguay was hardly in danger of being perceived as a stone image. Indeed, the press played up the incident as a feisty prank pulled off by an actress who never gave quarter. "Eva Tanguay's 'I-really-can't-keep-still' temperament caused the argument about her act," wrote the *New York Telegraph,* glibly but accurately.

The cause célèbre grew. "To-day I'll come as near doing what you ask as I can, but this will be the last time," she announced both to the authorities and her public. "On my return from Boston, with my own money and under my own direction, I'll find out whether it is a crime to be gay and natural on any day in the year." She then swore to "give a performance of my own and I'll do my act exactly as I do it on week days and as the people have shown they wish it done. Then if I'm arrested I'll fight the case. This nonsense has gone on long enough and I'm going to put a stop to it for the benefit of others if an independent effort on my part can accomplish it." Eva went onstage and, perhaps drained of bile for the moment, gave no offense to the Sunday Law. She never did challenge the statute as she had promised, perhaps because the vow had already yielded its publicity payout. But later in July, Eva was arrested for dancing about the stage in a bathing suit during a song called "The Country Club." She was charged in the borough of Queens, where she was working, with violating section 2152 of the penal code, which forbade "any one appearing on the stage on Sundays in costume that would not be used on the street." Eva screamed at the hapless policeman who was trying to arrest her and ordered him out of her dressing room. Five hundred dollars in fines and several interventions by her lawyers and managers later, the matter was resolved.[19]

Eva's antics onstage and off altered not only public perceptions of her, from energetic soubrette to iconoclastic and sometimes exasperating rebel, but the way vaudeville itself was now seen. Once a family-safe form of entertainment, approved for audiences of all ages and for women as well as men, vaudeville had now become suspect, daring, and morally unpredictable. "It is somewhat disconcerting to find vaudeville, that versatile and once careful form of amusement, dropping into the evil habits of some of the older and more hardened sins of so-called variety," lamented the writer of an editorial in the *New York Dramatic Mirror* in 1909. Aghast, the paper reported that in New York there had recently appeared "an act that is a reeking offense to the morals of even that hardened community." Vaudeville had clearly hit bottom, for it was now capable of offending even New Yorkers, in the *Dramatic Mirror's* panicky opinion.[20]

With Eva Tanguay pushing the limits of censure, even those who had once banked on the idea of clean entertainment began to change with the times. When the swimming star and aquatic beauty Annette Kellerman, famous for appearing in the briefest of bathing suits tolerable at the time, appeared on the Keith circuit, E. F. Albee ordered a phalanx of mirrors set up behind her onstage. After at least one theater manager looked askance, Albee told him, "Don't you know that what we are selling here is backsides, and that a hundred backsides are better than one?" On another occasion, Albee enthusiastically approved a Lady Godiva act, one of many vaudeville presentations that used the gilt frame of highbrow culture to deliver the illusion of nudity. Albee said he felt his patrons "ought to have a little fun." Without "fun," why would customers, increasingly offered no shortage of places to spend their leisure dollar, keep coming? The rhetorical backlash continued. "Ten years ago, B. F. Keith held a place of high esteem in the hearts of American vaudeville-goers," wrote another editorialist in the *New York Dramatic Mirror* in November 1909. "The husband was glad to take his wife. Where is the standard today? Vaudeville is deteriorating. What is tolerated to-day would have been impossible two or three years ago." The "man of high ideals" and the "mother of refined daughters" had now to cast "a critical eye" on the amusement that once offered safe haven from the unpredictable and scandalous tumult of urban leisure.[21]

AMID THE BATTLES with rivals and the police, not to mention the non-stop need to develop new material following her Salome triumph, Eva tried to make at least some time for her so-called niece, Eva Adela, now more commonly called Florence or Flossie. Because Eva could hardly leave her battleground headquarters of New York City, the girl, now on the cusp of her teenage years, had taken to spending summers with her famous "aunt" in the big city. Despite its challenges, for Florence it beat the cold comfort of life with Mark Tanguay, Eva's brother and the man temporarily cast in the role of her father. While life with Aunt Eva was anything but calm, it had its perks. Many, in fact. Eva had her assistants shop for Florence, giving the girl lavish beauty and fashion accessories almost unknown in rural Ashfield. To the girl, it was like being in a marvelous, distant world, and made returning to Massachusetts all the more disconcerting.

In September 1909, having just returned from summering with Aunt Eva, Florence attended the annual Ashfield Children's Fair. She was so gussied up in the latest cosmopolitan fashions that her playmate Ruth Sears did not recognize her until she spoke. "She had a new coat and her hair was done different and her old dress was either lengthened or she had a new one," wrote Sears in her diary. A week and a half later, Florence showed Ruth an assortment of forty-five face powders and perfumes Eva had bought her in New York. During a visit to Ashfield the following summer, Eva replaced Florence's entire wardrobe. "Florence was [in school, and] her aunt Eva Tanguay the actress has been here and brought her many new clothes," recalled Sears. Eva had even promised Florence a trip with her to Europe. "They were all packed and ready to go," according to Barbara Johnson, Florence's daughter. But some type of contractual snag—par for the course in the peripatetic world of vaudeville—nixed it. "As mom said, that was the closest she ever got to Europe," recalled Johnson. If Eva came to be regarded by her family as the absentee parent figure who never did quite enough for Florence, sometimes it was not for want of trying.[22]

As much as she loved the attention and the glamorous gifts Eva bestowed on her, Florence Tanguay also loved the simpler pursuits of rural life in small-town New England. She got together with her friends Ruth and Viola to sing from time to time, until the latter, for no apparent reason, decided she had "given up her music!" in the reminiscences of a shocked Ruth Sears.[23]

Despite the makeup, gowns, and other New York finery, courtesy of her celebrity aunt, Florence had, like Eva, a tomboyish side. She favored sledding, playing hide-and-seek, climbing trees, and picking checkerberries (the fruit of the wintergreen plant) when the urge arose. Sometimes she was the target of practical jokes. On one occasion, Ruth and Viola, having shared some candy, happened upon "a funny post card" in the latter's attic. The girls decided to mail the card to Florence but make it seem as if their school chum, a boy named Raymond, had in fact posted it. The ruse had apparently worked once before, and it was just as effective this time. On receipt of the card, Florence thanked Raymond, who, though confused, didn't let on that he had not the foggiest idea what she was talking about.[24]

Also like her purported aunt, young Florence didn't back down from a quarrel. In arithmetic class one day, a girl named Hazel thought she saw Florence copying from someone else's test. After class, in the creaking, wooden halls of the simple country school they attended, Hazel asked Florence why she'd done it. The girl fired back that if Hazel minded her own business as well as she did other people's, then "she would get along very well." Hazel retreated from the argument, but nonetheless spread a rumor of the Tanguay girl's alleged cheating. When the leak made its way back to Florence, she confronted her accuser on the snowy playground during recess. It is unclear whether the conflict grew physical, but there were definitely tears, and Florence left disconsolate, too upset to go "sliding" on the snow with her friends later that afternoon.[25]

Though Eva was not around, she continued to provide for the girl. She plunked down three thousand dollars to buy a prominent home in Ashfield known as "the Gardner house," which a local resident, Susie B. Kelly, had bought for twenty-five hundred dollars in 1903 from the estate of the late Jacob L. Gardner prior to her marriage to Joseph Green. Florence was installed in the house with Anne Howes, a widow and aunt of the now-deceased Elwin T. Howes, who had been married to Eva's sister, Blanche. Also living with them was Lizzie Howes, forty-five years of age in 1910 when Eva bought the Gardner house for Florence. Flossie wasn't crazy about Lizzie—"Miss Lizzie was a typical spinster, as mom would say," according to Barbara Johnson—but it was better than living with Mark Tanguay. In time, yet another Howes, Ethel Mary, former sister-in-law of Blanche Tanguay, came to live in the Gardner house as well.[26]

Though Eva rarely visited, the rumor that she was Florence's mother never quit. Perhaps trying to assuage charges of neglect or her own sense of guilt, she not only bought the girl a house in which to live but also paid her tuition at the prestigious Sanderson Academy, located in the nearby foothills of the Berkshires. Florence earned mostly As and Bs in subjects like English, French, economics, and chemistry. As a sophomore, she and her pals participated in the ritual of making the freshman boys stand atop their rough-hewn, wooden desks and sing "Mary Had a Little Lamb," before getting dunked in the coal bin. Florence's friend Ruth reckoned it "a circus and a half." Had she seen it, Flossie's famous "aunt" might well have come to the same conclusion.[27]

WHILE EVA MAINTAINED ties to her niece in Ashfield, by 1909 things had fully soured between her and her on-again, off-again paramour Edward Darling. Though there had been rumors of their engagement for at least a year, Eva called a halt to their romance by May. Certainly the affairs with C. F. Zittel and possibly George Walker provided a reality check for Darling. But even in the absence of such scandal, he must have come to see her deep ambivalence about marriage. Indeed, the fact that there is so little information about Eva's romantic involvements, even the significant ones, may suggest just how clandestine and anxiety-producing the issue was for the vaudeville star. When the papers began to run stories of their engagement, Darling "refused either to affirm or to deny" whether they were true. When Eva caught wind of the headlines, however, she called the whole thing merely "a press agent's dream." Still, it must have hurt Edward Darling, who, despite being cast aside by Eva, would continue to advise her intermittently for years to come. It was not an easy role, being Eva's friend and fiancé. But clearly he had come to care about her.[28]

It was not enough for Eva to have merely severed her romantic ties to Edward Darling. She felt she had to make a public declaration of her opposition to marriage. She sent a telegram to the papers in her hometown of Holyoke pleading, "Please tell my friends that I am not to be married, never have been, and don't intend to be." Rather than brazenly decry the institution of marriage—a risky move at the time, even for a rebellious celebrity—she chalked it up to economics. "I have never yet been able to find the man who could give me to spend what I earn myself." That much was probably true. "Anyway, wedding bells don't sound like music to me," she quipped. Eva was said to have one hundred thousand dollars in cash at the time, but aspired to see that number grow to $1 million. As for her diamonds, they alone were worth seventy-five thousand dollars.[29]

Her romance with Edward Darling was officially over. As for her future choices in men, they would never be as good as the Keith executive who helped manage her career and, in the course of that weighty task, fell in love with Eva Tanguay.

7

Follies and Fortunes

B Y THE FALL OF 1909, Eva may have imagined the world around her swirling with threats and rivals. But the truth was quite different. She inhabited a lofty sphere of success and celebrity enjoyed by few others. As far as vaudeville was concerned, she commanded a following, a salary, and a degree of artistic freedom hitherto unknown. As the first decade of the twentieth century wound down, Eva Tanguay was not so much a player *in* vaudeville as she was the definition *of* it. If she could hold herself together—physically, emotionally, professionally—there was no limit to what she could achieve.

Eva was understandably determined, as ever, to move forward and up. But the question was, where? One possibility was England. Playing the music-hall circuit and maybe even some larger, time-honored British theatrical venues could increase her star appeal and allow her to raise her asking price. She had her people look into it. As Eva cast her gaze across the Atlantic, however, another entertainment supermogul trained his sights on Eva, though she did not yet know it. He would offer Eva the chance to move up the cultural and economic ladder, rising higher than even big-time Keith vaudeville without ever leaving New York. His name was Florenz Ziegfeld Jr.

Ziegfeld was something of a newcomer to the New York entertainment scene, but in a short time he made a big splash. The first production of his vaunted *Follies* musical revue premiered on July 8, 1907. Ziegfeld staged it on the roof garden above the New York and Criterion theaters between Forty-fourth and Forty-fifth streets on Broadway. He cannily renamed the elevated venue the "Jardin de Paris," giving it an air of continental sophistication, and promising cool breezes to patrons daunted by the pre–air conditioning stuffiness of indoor forums. From this aerie above the world's most important theater district, Ziegfeld aimed to compete directly with big-time vaudeville by capturing a market that Keith and Albee wanted more of: upper-echelon theatergoers with elevated tastes and bulging wallets. But Florenz Ziegfeld was also aiming for something higher, something more rarified than his rivals in top-tier vaudeville were seeking, even if so much of what he eventually put onstage resembled dressed-up Keith fare—or, as we will see, undressed. Ziegfeld's first *Follies* was, like other concoctions of its era, such as *The Passing Show* and *Scandals,* a song-and-dance extravaganza of elaborately staged, loosely connected scenes featuring shapely chorus girls and the top talent of the day. Ziegfeld's 1907 *Follies* fittingly spoofed Strauss's opera *Salome,* with both a chubby Emma Carus and a slender Mlle. Dazie each playing the biblical dancer. Celebrated New York millionaire Diamond Jim Brady was said to have procured ten opening-night tickets at the stratospheric scalper's rate of seventy-five dollars each.[1]

The 1907 *Follies* has since been called the first Broadway revue, which probably says more about Ziegfeld's genius at promotion than it does about the historical truth. What is certain is that the *Follies,* like Keith's most elaborately decorated vaudeville theaters, appropriated an air of upper-crust, European-style classiness that it used to legitimize so many beautiful, barely clad chorus girls. Ziegfeld's idea was to produce a show that would make audiences feel both artistically grandiose, as if they were at the opera, and at the same time titillated by the brief costumes and double entendres suggestive of the concert saloon and burlesque house. It worked. The success of the *Follies* and ensuing lack of moral censure urged vaudeville's bigwigs to take notice. As a result, big-time vaudeville and Ziegfeld's *Follies* began sharing many of the same performers for the next two decades.[2]

The first two *Follies* were huge hits, attracting top talent to the stage and society's biggest names to the seats. In short order, Ziegfeld's extravaganza became the place to see and be seen. His third edition, properly known as *F. Ziegfeld, Jr.'s Revue on the Follies of 1909,* had everything—well-known stars, fabulously costumed and scandalously uncostumed chorus beauties, sensational settings, and a classy venue—everything, that is, except the most popular entertainer in the country. The producer of the *Follies* may have sent mixed messages by looking down on vaudeville while happily borrowing its biggest talent. But one thing Florenz Ziegfeld never wavered on was a desire to reach for the brightest, the biggest, the very best. Such ambitions earned him a new status in popular culture: Ziegfeld had become the first full-fledged celebrity *producer* of the modern era, a larger-than-life impresario who picked up his gold-plated phone and made things happen. He was a mover and shaker who took bold steps even when simpler gestures might have sufficed. He liked wearing the crown of entertainment power broker and buffed it to a shiny gloss. B. F. Keith's name may have been on the outside of his theaters, but Florenz Ziegfeld's name was all over the program and woven into the titles of his productions; it was a brand name with a Midas touch. Over the twenty-five seasons of the *Follies,* there was no doubt about who the star of the show really was.[3]

Florenz Ziegfeld Jr. was born March 21, 1868, to a middle-class German family in Chicago. His father was known as Dr. Ziegfeld, reflecting an honorific title many bandleaders and highbrow musical types enjoyed back then. The good "doctor" had earned a measure of credibility producing the composer Johann Strauss's 1872 tour of the United States (not to be confused with the *Salome* composer, Richard Strauss). Ziegfeld *pere* had high hopes for Ziegfeld *fils,* believing his son might in fact be the next Johann Strauss. As is so often the case with fathers who misread their sons, the boy did not flourish as dad wished and never seriously took up the study of music. In fact, Ziegfeld the younger seemed destined for glory nowhere. Often sick, he was "anemic, frail [and] apathetic," possessing "about as much vitality and imagination as overcooked spinach," according to Marjorie Farnsworth, a writer who chronicled the impresario's work in the 1950s.[4]

Troubled that his son might end up a lost soul, dad packed seventeen-year-old Florenz off to a Wyoming cattle ranch for some toughening up. In the father's imagination, limp spinach would return as seasoned rawhide, even though the elder Ziegfeld privately had scant hope of his plan's success. But it actually worked. Florenz Jr. returned a changed young man. When the circus came to Chicago not long after the young man's return, it featured Buffalo Bill's Wild West Show. Having roped a few, saddled a few, and swept up after a few back in Wyoming, Ziegfeld landed a job with the famed lariat-wielding stuntman. He now shared with B. F. Keith and E. F. Albee that exposure to a circus-style amusement so crucial to entertainment pioneers of the late nineteenth and early twentieth centuries.[5]

With his first taste of show business, Florenz Ziegfeld Jr. was as eager to get out of the gate as a hyperactive bronco. His father was the musical director of the famed, massive 1892–93 Columbian Exposition in Chicago. Florenz Junior was dispatched across the pond to find military bands, opera singers, and whatever Euro-talent would help make this greatest of cultural events, this so-called world's fair, that much greater. After the fair, he promoted the strongman and bodybuilder Eugene Sandow, famous in vaudeville as much for his brief, fig-leaf-like costume as for his breathtaking feats of strength. Young Ziegfeld managed to get some of society's most respected ladies to come backstage and inspect, palpate, and otherwise observe firsthand Sandow's bulging muscles. Like an erotic freak act, one that had to be seen (and touched) to be believed, the gambit paid off. Soon, fondling Sandow was the thing to do among the highbrow set. "You were no one, really no one, my dear, unless you had felt Sandow's muscles," according to Farnsworth.[6]

After a producing stint at Weber's Music Hall—Weber being half of the famed Weber & Fields musical-comedy duo—Ziegfeld went back to Europe, poking around for the next big talent. He found it in a Paris music hall. Anna Held was a singer of hazy origins and middling ability, but Ziegfeld promoted her as "the epitome of Gallic spice and naughtiness." This set the tone for classic Ziegfeld glorification—especially considering that Anna Held was not Gallic at all but, it would seem, of humble Polish Jewish extraction. Some even said she had been born in Indiana. Anna Held's true background did not matter. In Ziegfeld's hands, and in a consumer culture where supposedly high-class French cosmetics and fragrances were now extremely desirable, she was whatever he could make of her.[7]

Ziegfeld brought Anna Held back to the States and produced a series of shows built specially around her. He lent her an aura of noble, European elegance and refinement by publicizing her beauty regimen, which supposedly involved extravagant baths in gallons of fresh milk. He also played up her derring-do and independence by making sure she drove her own car, a gutsy move for a woman in those days. With Ziegfeld's help, Anna Held began promoting her personality rather than her specific talents, following Eva Tanguay's lead. In subsequent productions, Ziegfeld continued to make Held, by this time his wife, the centerpiece in a bouquet of sensual, female beauty. He surrounded her with gorgeous chorus girls, who collectively became a star element in shows like *The Little Duchess, Mlle. Napoleon,* and *A Parisian Model.* The loosely knit musical extravaganzas, close cousins of productions like *My Lady,* which had brought Eva to the fore were the embryo of Ziegfeld's *Follies.*[8]

The inaugural *Follies,* put up in 1907, like the one two years later, indeed had little in the way of a unified book or story. The "plot" of a

Ziegfeld *Follies* typically followed a visitor to New York checking out the city's most fabled sights; each interlude was its own scene, usually accompanied by a musical number. In a formal sense, the *Follies* were barely distinguishable from Keith and other big-time vaudeville shows. To play up the distinction and thereby justify higher ticket prices, Ziegfeld relied on continental elegance and suggestions of elite refinement. Nothing in the *Follies* was small or dear. If choosing between silk at five dollars a yard for costumes and silk at thirty dollars a yard, Ziegfeld would unflinchingly pick the latter. Hardly surprising for a man whose desk boasted three golden telephones and who delighted in handing out bags of gold coins to friends and acquaintances, like a nobleman bestowing largesse on the masses.[9]

For the 1909 *Follies,* Ziegfeld gathered an impressive array of talent. He made Herbert Gresham the chief artistic director—then remained steadfastly by Gresham's side nixing anything he disliked. To write lyrics, libretto, and music, Ziegfeld recruited Maurice Levi and Harry Bache Smith. The latter, it may be recalled, was among the era's leading librettists and had contributed the book to *The Sambo Girl* and *The Office Boy.*[10]

The star of the 1909 *Follies* was Nora Bayes, one of the best-known vaudeville headliners of her day, a peer and rival to Eva Tanguay. Though slightly younger than Eva, Bayes had in fact reached the spotlight earlier, though she never commanded it the way Eva did. In truth, the two had much in common.

Nora Bayes was born Dora Goldberg, about 1880, in Joliet, Illinois, though she sometimes claimed to have been from Los Angeles. Like Eva, she had a sharp and clever tongue, an unconventional attitude toward men and marriage, and a penchant for self-neglect. Also like Eva Tanguay, Nora Bayes cut her teeth with a traveling stock company, the nineteenth-century theater's equivalent of minor league baseball or a niche cable TV show or Web series. And, like Eva, who never returned to her small Quebec hometown, Nora Bayes left Joliet with a disdainful turn and never glanced back: "Many people remain in Joliet for twenty and even thirty years and life, unable to tear themselves away," she once joked, adding, "Joliet and the Tombs are somewhat alike in that respect," referring to New York City's infamous jail (and the legendary Joliet Prison).[11]

Though she would be married five times over the course of her life, at the time of Ziegfeld's 1909 extravaganza, she was paired with Jack Norworth (aka Jack Knaupf), who wrote such classics as "Take Me Out to the Ball Game" and "Shine on Harvest Moon" and performed alongside Bayes.[12]

Ziegfeld's 1909 *Follies,* "musical farce, burlesque, travesty and what not" according to the *New York Dramatic Mirror,* consisted of sixteen elaborate and zany scenes in two acts. Nora Bayes enjoyed five production numbers, including "Mad Opera House," "I Wish I Was a Boy and I Wish I Was a Girl" (with Norworth), "Falling Stars," and "Blarney." The settings were as eclectic as Ziegfeld's whimsical imagination. From the Court of Venus to the Metropolitan Opera House to the offices of fellow impresario Oscar Hammerstein to the wilds of Africa, there was nowhere the *Follies* did not gaily tread. It was the theatrical equivalent of the world's fair and its myriad exotic pavilions. "One can't realize how delightfully foolish we all were during the past Winter until one glances into the mirror Mr. Ziegfeld, Mr. Smith and Mr. Levi have set up on the roof of the New York Theatre, and then, like the foolish one of the popular saying, we laugh joyfully at the mirrored reflection of our own folly." So wrote the *Dramatic Mirror.* Critics marveled at richly detailed scenery that changed so often—at least once every fifteen minutes—"that it almost makes one's head swim." There was a female chorus "of rare pulchritudinous distinction" to boot. The *Follies,* said the critics, wasn't "intended for old ladies, but if you've got good red blood in you and a sense of humor you'll enjoy it from the first scene to the sixteenth." By his third outing, in 1909, Ziegfeld had mastered the blend of sauciness and luxury served up in a golden chalice. It was an intoxicating and successful formula that would be copied by others, though none quite as successfully as the originator, for years to come.[13]

Yet from the beginning of the 1909 *Follies,* there was trouble afoot. All was not glittering behind the gold-encrusted facade. Barely a month into its heady run, star Nora Bayes suddenly fell "ill," according to newspaper headlines, and suddenly bowed out of the show. It was reported that Bayes had succumbed to "a rather severe attack of nervous prostration," but a subsequent, very public squabble between Bayes and Ziegfeld suggested instead a severe case of salary woes. Bayes was making twelve hundred dollars a week but believed she was worth more. To make matters worse, her husband, Jack Norworth, was pulling in only two hundred a week.[14]

It is unclear just how much more money and what additional perks Bayes and Norworth were asking for, but what is abundantly clear is that Ziegfeld would not budge, likely more out of ego than tight purse strings. Faced with the possibility of a *Follies* without headliners, he picked up the phone and called vaudeville's leading lady. At the time, Eva was playing an engagement in Brooklyn at the popular Brighton Beach Music Hall, not far from the site of her headline-grabbing romantic entanglement with

C. F. Zittel in 1907. After her gig at the Brighton, Eva was due to sail for London to reap what was purported to be the largest salary ever paid a U.S. entertainer in Britain, on a tour arranged by E. F. Albee and the Theatrical Syndicate bigwig Abraham Erlanger.

Ziegfeld immediately offered Eva terms "so liberal that he thought she could not refuse it," according to a press report. But Ziegfeld had miscalculated. For Eva's asking price had been rising so rapidly that no sum of money would keep her in New York. For Eva, it was no longer just about pay. It was about venturing across the ocean to convert a new legion of the faithful. As for the *Follies,* they would be there next year.[15]

It says something quite remarkable about Florenz Ziegfeld Jr. that he would not take Eva's refusal as final. Few in the entertainment business had either the temerity or status to argue with the feisty superstar. But Ziegfeld was both desperate and, much like the entertainer he wanted so badly, unwilling to back down. He put down the receiver and, deciding that a face-to-face encounter would do the trick, jumped in his car and headed to Brooklyn.

Ziegfeld had summoned his associate Frank McKee to ride along with him, and the two motored from Manhattan across the East River. The Manhattan Bridge would not be completed until later that year, but the Brooklyn Bridge had spanned the waterway since 1883. Arriving late that evening, they approached Eva after her show at the Brighton. She was surprised to see the fabled impresario all the way out there, but she remained skeptical. The man behind the *Follies* offered even more "liberal" terms, according to a news item. Whatever Ziegfeld offered to pony up, garnished with copious personal charm, it did the trick. Eva changed her mind. England would simply have to wait. With a phone call made on the spot, Eva secured legal permission from Albee and Erlanger to put off her transatlantic tour. Both men probably realized the hot property she would be after a star turn in the *Follies* and, therefore, the even richer purse they might then harvest from Eva's British adventure.

To christen the start of their professional journey together, Ziegfeld offered his new queen a ride back to Manhattan. It would have been a smooth denouement had not the clutch broken on Ziegfeld's car barely halfway back to the city. It may seem like a minor mishap, but lesser things had soured deals with the unpredictable Eva Tanguay. The thought of vaudeville's moodiest superstar stranded with Broadway's biggest impresario in the summer heat was a troubling one, particularly after a painstaking negotiation. But the wind was at Florenz Ziegfeld's back. As it turned out, the automobile had rolled to a dead halt just fifteen feet from the Prospect Park subway stop in Brooklyn. The fare to ride the train back into Manhattan was five cents. It seemed a worthwhile investment.[16]

Ziegfeld had found the only thing to make his *Follies* shine brighter than they already did: Eva Tanguay. Predictably, she made sure that in addition to a sumptuous salary, the 1909 *Follies* would be reshaped into a vehicle for her own personality, from song numbers to publicity. Indeed, onlookers wondered how she and the storied producer, two souls never famous for humility, would find enough room for both their egos. Wrote one editorialist: "Several people expected to see the play's description evolve on the billboards into 'Eva Tanguay and the handsomest chorus in the world.'" The new Jardin de Paris program headline now read:

F. Ziegfeld, Jr's

REVUE

On The

FOLLIES OF 1909

Special Engagement

EVA TANGUAY

Ziegfeld's name was over Eva's. But Nora Bayes had enjoyed no such placement.

The first act still began with the elaborately staged Court of Venus numbers, with scenography by the prestigious Lee Lash design studio. It then moved to the Metropolitan Opera and, in the third scene, to the Hammersteins' office. In it, Eva, playing herself, made her first appearance in the show and sang several rousing numbers. Subsequent scenes were set in a wheat field, a fanciful Millionaires' Ward at the Tombs prison, the stage door of the New York Theatre where the *Follies* itself was playing, and the famous New York Polo Grounds, then home to the New York Giants baseball team (and, a few years later, the Yankees). The audience got to enjoy "Play Ball with Me" by Gus Edwards at the close of act 1, at which point theatergoers were furnished with actual baseballs and urged to engage in a game of catch.

After intermission, the second half of the *Follies* featured an equally dizzying array of settings both realistic and fantastical, from the streets of New York to the throne room in a palace of a faraway land. There were airplanes, bathing beauties, and Eva riding an elephant. The new star, "dressed in the most vivid red imaginable," according to one press report, not only got Nora

Bayes's musical numbers but belted out an assortment of her own vaudeville favorites, including the suggestive "Go as Far as You Like" and, of course, "I Don't Care." She was hailed a "triumph." Ziegfeld realized that dumping Nora Bayes, his founding star just two years earlier, might have been the best thing that had ever happened to his beloved *Follies*.[17]

One of the tastiest delicacies of the 1909 *Follies* was a song-and-dance sketch called "Moving Day in Jungle Town." It featured plenty of scantily clad so-called jungle girls and was inspired by Teddy Roosevelt's recent return from hunting in Africa. At the center of the number was a rising talent named Sophie Tucker. Born Sonya Kalish to a Russian Jewish family that somehow became known as Abuza by the time they had immigrated to the United States shortly after her birth in 1886, Sophie Tucker, as she would later be known, initially started singing to entertain patrons at her parents' kosher restaurant in Hartford, Connecticut, a city not terribly far or different from the Holyoke of Eva Tanguay's youth. Tucker eventually donned blackface and made a name for herself as a coon shouter who brought ragtime melodies to life and played cafes, burlesque halls, and the vaudeville circuit.

By 1908, she was appearing at Tony Pastor's famous vaudeville house. Shortly after that, she became one of the first singers to gain a following in the emerging medium of recorded sound, laying down "Rosie, My Dusky Georgia Rosie," a blackface favorite, for Atlas Advertising, a recording company. In the early part of 1909, she toured with Gus Hill's famous burlesque troupe, The Gay Masqueraders. Taking a cue from minstrelsy and drawing inspiration from both the Yiddish theater and the bawdy, over-the-top stylings of Eva Tanguay, Tucker was noticed by Ziegfeld during her "Masqueraders" stint and recruited for his *Follies*. She would earn sixty dollars a week.[18]

For nine weeks, Sophie Tucker wowed the *Follies* audience with "Moving Day in Jungle Town." It was popular and timely, an unabashed mix of parody, exoticism, spectacle, and sexuality brewed up according to the classic Ziegfeld recipe. There was just one problem. When Eva arrived, she wanted it for herself. Having wooed vaudeville's hottest star, the hotshot impresario had little choice. Sophie Tucker was peremptorily let go.[19]

Tucker was thus bounced out of a top job in late summer, a difficult time of year to nab a new vaudeville contract. To make matters worse, a bout of nerves had caused her throat to tighten up, robbing her of her main talent and income source. Thanks largely to the ministrations of her assistant and nurse, Mollie, Tucker's voice eventually returned. "You can't afford to let yourself get bitter," Mollie told Tucker. "Getting bitter never did nobody no good." Sophie listened to her nursemaid's earthy advice, despite how justified her resentment may have been. She was down for the count after sustaining a body blow from the queen of vaudeville. In time, though, Sophie Tucker would pick herself back up.[20]

Florenz Ziegfeld Jr. would go on to produce twenty-two more seasons of *Follies,* dropping out when the Roaring Twenties succumbed to the Depressing Thirties. He was to make and use stars such as Bert Williams, Fanny Brice, W. C. Fields, Louise Brooks, and others. He died less than a year after the curtain descended on his last production, passing away July 22, 1932, almost twenty-five years to the day since he had driven out to Brighton Beach and entreated Eva into joining the most glamorous gig on Broadway. Like his onetime leading lady, he too, just before his death, was down at the heels. A man who had once surrounded himself with gold now passed into eternity virtually insolvent. Anna Held died in 1918, six years after her divorce from Ziegfeld. It was reported that she had died in part from the obsessive dieting and brutal waist cinching that Ziegfeld had forced her to endure.[21]

As for Eva, her stint in the 1909 Ziegfeld *Follies* elevated her to new professional heights. The ten years to come would see her ascend to a level known by few in the field of modern entertainment. She was a megastar, the beneficiary of many before her yet a pioneer for many to come. The era would also see changes and upheavals in the landscape of culture and popular amusement, which would in many ways mirror the life course of vaudeville's cyclonic wonder. In the 1890s, the presence of respectable middle-class women onstage and in the crowd, notably at big-time Keith theaters, had symbolized advancement, marking vaudeville as a place where people could seek amusement without fear of being sullied or seated close to society's baser elements.

Things were now different, and perhaps no artist's contribution to that transformation was more important than Eva's. She and other women had come in as a kind of Trojan horse. Having breached the walls, Eva and others who followed played the part of a woman "ruled by her libido," in the words of the historian M. Alison Kibler. Eva certainly played at being ruled by hers. As we have seen, she did this and more. The climate around Eva was changing, to some degree because of her efforts. It might be said that following the Ziegfeld *Follies* of 1909, the dawn of the modern female celebrity had given way to its bright, sometimes blinding, midday sun.[22]

The New York production of the *Follies* closed by late December 1909. Eva disliked the feeling of being confined, whether to a particular show, a relationship, or even a specific venue. Yet her Ziegfeld time had given her highly marketable material that crowds around the nation would eagerly pay to see. She arranged a show featuring some of her more popular *Follies* numbers and her standard favorites into a slimmed-down, vaudeville-sized routine. This she could take on the road, thus avoiding the rut of inertia. But the constant traveling and rehearsing came with its stresses too.

BY FEBRUARY OF 1910, Eva's *Follies* package was ready to go. The tour took her across the country, to the major venues of cities large and small. On one occasion, she was appearing at McCauley's Theater in Louisville, Kentucky. As usual, her routine required a series of quick costume changes, which had by now become one of her trademark talents. She was given the theater's only dressing room located directly backstage to facilitate her changes. Worried that her way on and off the stage might be obstructed, she recruited a prop handler named Harry Ruff (or Rough, depending on the source), described in the press as "a little fellow," to help keep the way clear.

The show itself went off without a hitch. As Eva herself later recounted it, she was in her dressing room following the last curtain call, changing into her street attire, when she heard a scuffle. "Look! There's a big fight on the stage," someone yelled. On one side was Ruff. Facing him were some forty local hoodlums who had been hanging around the back alley behind the theater. Heading the mob was a bruiser named Clarence Hess. Hess was a backstage scenery handler who had been knocked down a flight of stairs by Ruff in the course of keeping the way clear for Eva. There was nothing to suggest Ruff was acting maliciously or that there had been prior bad blood between him and Hess. The stress, strain, and demands Eva had placed on Ruff simply led him to play his part with a heavy hand. Between angering a local thug and angering Eva, Ruff unhesitatingly chose the former.

Hearing the ruckus, Eva charged onto the stage, slapping blindly "right and left to protect her champion," according to a local newspaper. She later said that going instantly into attack mode was "the natural thing, at least it was the natural thing for me." Whatever blows Eva managed to land, her man Ruff remained in peril. The ruffian Hess had him by the collar and was preparing to deliver him to the fate of a gang that had become even more agitated thanks to Eva's impulsive pummeling. Just as Hess's men were about to deliver the coup de grace, however, Eva Tanguay reached the inner circle of the fight, clawing her way to Ruff's side.[23]

It was then that someone made the observation, "Hey! Look out! She's got a hatpin!"

Eva later claimed she "hadn't realized it." But indeed, she had launched into the melee clutching more than a few hatpins, which she herself reckoned "a pretty wicked weapon." According to Eva, her brandishing of hatpins caused the crowd to disperse and Hess to let go of his prey.

At seven o'clock the next morning Eva was awakened by her tour manager. She was then led into a police car and taken to court. There, the following charge was read to her: assault with intent to kill.

Clarence Hess, his abdomen amply bandaged, not only leveled criminal accusations but also filed a personal-injury claim against Eva for the curiously precise sum of $1,909.09 (about $37,000 today).[24] The scene at the hearing was no shorter on drama than the epic battle the night before. Add a few songs, and it could have been Ziegfeld's *Follies* for 1910. Told that she was being held on bail, Eva took out a golden purse that had her initials, "E. T.," marked on it in diamonds and produced a roll of hundreds, "enough to choke a horse," one of her intimates later remembered. "Take it all and let me go," she shouted, for it was mealtime. The trial took place the following day, and it played out better than many scripted courtroom sketches. Anxious with worry, having been informed by the prosecutor that "the victim was in critical condition," Eva began to wonder, "What was prison life like?" Fortunately, she would never find out.[25]

As Eva's peculiar luck would have it, just down the hallway was a man named Dr. Robert Kingsley. He had been a childhood sweetheart of Eva's, the two having met years earlier riding the rails as theatrical urchins with the Redding Stanton repertory troupe. (He eventually left acting to pursue medicine.) Kingsley had once even asked Eva to marry him. "Now this grand friend had come to my aid in my hour of need," she recalled. Somehow, the doctor inveigled his way onto the stand as an expert witness. He testified to the judge that Clarence Hess's wounds were superficial at best, "but bandaged in a manner to give the appearance of serious injury." The assessment swayed, the gavel pounded, and Eva got off. Hess had likely been quietly offered a generous settlement on the sidelines. The encore: Dr. Kingsley once more asked Eva to marry him. Thanks, Doc, but no thanks, she replied. Did the good doctor know nothing of Eva Tanguay?[26]

After the *Follies,* and especially on tour, Eva's paranoia grew. The McCauley's affair would not be the last hatpin incident. Perhaps it was being out on her own, fending for herself from the top of the mountain, that catalyzed her bouts of mania. Or maybe they were spawned by wounds and ill feelings long submerged, the terrifying powerlessness over her father's alcoholism. Whatever the root cause, Eva developed an intense aversion to being watched or, in her view, distracted from backstage. "She couldn't have anybody, ever, watch her from [behind] the proscenium— never!" her accompanist Al Parado later recalled. Even though Parado often tried to downplay Eva's combativeness, he conceded, "She'd pick up a chair and bat you over the head. She was so concentrated, so taut, so tight—so concentrated on what she was doing that she couldn't have anything to disrupt her." Increasingly, if she felt threatened or subverted by some random occurrence offstage, she would threaten to walk out in the middle of a show.[27]

On one occasion, Eva was sharing a bill with the legendary bandleader John Philip Sousa. They were playing the Palace, vaudeville's crème de la crème, in Times Square, the so-called Valhalla of Vaudeville. Sousa was to follow Eva on the program. The queen of vaudeville was on in front of the drop curtain, while the bandleader and his brass militia assembled behind it.[28]

As Eva sang, Sousa and his men occasionally, accidentally, bumped their backsides into the curtain. Chances are it was unnoticeable to the crowd, considering the heft of old theater curtains designed to ward off fire. But Eva noticed the protrusion and removed a hatpin from her elaborate and weighty headdress. Lance in hand, she jabbed Sousa right through the curtain. The hapless bandleader howled in pain. Eva interpreted the mishap as being somehow intentionally directed at her rather than simply a chance occurrence. She believed people were leagued against her and felt backed into a corner. It was, in the estimation of her onetime fiancé Edward Darling, "a thing she could not overcome."[29]

The myth of Eva's explosive, combative personality was hard to separate from the reality. The press delighted in the drama that swirled around her, even though Eva was often cast as an unpredictable, highly emotional diva in newspaper reports of the day. Yet she also lived in a way that increasingly defied cultural norms and played out like a theatrical melodrama. One adventure after another awaited Eva Tanguay, as suitors, producers, wannabes, and rivals chased her around the country.

IN 1910, not long after she had officially called things off romantically with Edward Darling, Eva found herself the object of yet another man's affections, under circumstances that were anything but usual.

She was in the middle of a midwestern tour and had just finished a show at a vaudeville theater in Saint Louis when a knock came on her dressing-room door. Opening it, Eva found herself faced with, in her words, a "handsome chap" by the name of Sylvester L. "Tony" von Phul.

Before she could speak, the gentleman posed a question: "Miss Tanguay," he asked, "how would you like to make a balloon ascension with me?" This was not sexual lingo from the golden age of aviation. In fact, von Phul, in addition to being a wine dealer, was better known as a balloonist, having set several speed records including a journey from Saint Louis to Charleston, South Carolina, some seven hundred miles, in fifteen hours. Eva, perfectly comfortable in automobiles, was less at ease with the notion of sailing through the sky. After all, the Wright brothers had inaugurated heavier-than-air aviation less than seven years earlier. And balloons seemed like something out of a storybook. Still, she found the prospect "exciting," as she later recalled it, and might have even remembered that the legendary Sarah Bernhardt won front-page headlines for ascending in a balloon over the City of Light during the 1878 Paris Exposition.[30]

Eva awoke to a bout of nerves the next morning in her hotel room, regretting her decision to fly with Tony von Phul but with no intention of backing out. She had her maid drive her to the sprawling grounds of the Saint Louis Aero Club, arriving there in the late morning. Eva trembled as she saw the balloon tethered to several thick, knotted ropes. The sphere itself was impressive, some eighty thousand cubic feet, and the aircraft boasted sixteen heavy sacks for ballast. Still, she was unnerved at a high wind "whipping" the craft as it awaited ascent. Collecting herself, Eva handed her valuables to her assistant and mounted the passenger basket accompanied by Captain von Phul and a paying customer from Alton, Illinois, named Horatio Bowman. At 11:55 a.m., Tony von Phul gave the word and the ground crew loosened the tethers. The craft shot heavenward. They climbed to three thousand feet and crossed the broad, silty band of the Mississippi. "I was petrified," Eva later recalled. Von Phul took the rig two thousand feet higher and leveled off, nearly a mile above the earth. Below her, Eva could see the expanse of the city, noticing in particular the huge Anheuser-Busch brewery. She claimed that despite the height, she could hear cars honking and crowds shouting. Imagining herself on the loftiest of stages, Eva felt as if she ought to "take a bow." Close to three o'clock in the afternoon, Tony von Phul began releasing hot air from the balloon and the craft began gently returning to earth. It was then that things took a turn for the strange.[31]

Not far from the ground, perhaps a few hundred feet up, the balloonist suddenly turned to Eva and declared, "Miss Tanguay, you are the bravest girl I ever met. Will you marry me?" Eva laughed. But she immediately realized he was serious, even if his proposal was based on a fantasy image of her stage persona. She thanked him but politely turned down the offer.

They landed near Turkey Hill in Illinois. "My three-hour courtship was over," Eva later recounted.[32]

Comical though the whole episode may seem, Eva Tanguay, though reticent about men and romance, nonetheless had a knack for attracting members of the opposite sex who were often slippery, unreliable, or morally complicated. Barely a year later, Tony von Phul was fatally shot in the bar of Denver's Brown Palace Hotel. He had apparently been carrying on an affair with a married woman named Isabel Springer, who, in addition to having recently married John W. Springer, was also romantically linked to a family friend named Francis Harold Henwood. It was Henwood, not John Springer, who fired at von Phul three times as they quarreled over the much sought-after Isabel.[33]

In time, Eva would attract more suitors. By 1911, she was thirty-two and her sex appeal seemed undiminished, a combination of womanly curves and girlish energy. "She was very good looking, with a mop of light brown curls, a piquant face, and a stunning figure," remembered a newspaper in Holyoke, Massachusetts, while another publication in the nearby city of Springfield wrote of her "famous red blonde hair" and praised legs that Eva often showed off in see-through tights onstage.[34]

The writer and vaudeville watcher Caroline Caffin, both irked and dazzled on seeing Eva at the height of her popularity in the early 1910s, found her to have a "saucy, broad, good-humored face, with large, smiling mouth and pertly upturned nose." She found the cyclonic performer's eyes "small and impudent," seeming to "snap and sparkle," appearing black, though really dark blue. "Every inch of her from the topmost spike of yellow hair to the tip of her never-resting toe is alive, nervous, vital," observed Caffin.[35]

The Encyclopedia of Vaudeville, published in 1994, described Eva as "overweight and ugly," but others who knew her saw different. As a little girl, Barbara Johnson, daughter of Eva's niece, caught her famous great-aunt's show in Springfield, Massachusetts. She remembers Eva as having a well-proportioned figure at the time and nice legs. Johnson estimates Eva's height at roughly five foot two. Edward Marks, a music publisher and peer of Eva Tanguay's, said she weighed 126 pounds, "all muscle," held up by "incomparable white silk legs" that were nothing but "trim and taper." Dan Johansson, Barbara Johnson's son and something of the family historian, admits Eva "had a yo-yo weight problem." But for the time being, every inch of Eva's body, from her golden-red curls to her finely toned legs, was fetching.[36]

Marshaling all the elements of her appeal, Eva turned her attention back to upping her star value. She had spent enough time on the road, complete with odd incidents such as the amorous balloonist, and was ready to bask in her post-*Follies* stardom back in New York. Her new self-promotion wave began with Eva openly boasting that her box-office receipts proved she was the most popular act in vaudeville. In early 1911, she took on the perennial vaudeville favorite Valeska Suratt, who was known for displaying fashionable, elegant gowns during her stage turns. Eva obtained a sworn statement from the business manager and treasurer of the Keith vaudeville house she was playing in New York to prove her status in cold dollars and cents. The affidavit, which Eva of course passed along to the press, read: "THAT the gross receipts during Miss EVA TANGUAY's engagement beginning on February 6th and ending on February 12th, 1911 did exceed the gross receipts of either of the three preceding weeks during which Miss Adeline Genee and Company, Miss Valeska Suratt & Company and Mr. Nat C. Goodwin & Company were the headline attractions." Not only was Eva beloved; she was even more beloved than those who sparred with her for the spotlight.[37]

However boastful her box-office claims may have been, it was clear that Eva commanded fees matched by few in the business. Many mythic sums have been thrown around over the years by those impressed with Eva's earning power. Sophie Tucker claimed Eva made $5,000 a week in her prime, while Eva's would-be biographer in the 1940s, the journalist Elza Schallert, claimed she made $7,000. These estimates seem high, but they are not out of the question. A more reliable source, *Variety*'s founding editor, Sime Silverman, says Eva once got $4,700 for a week at the 44th Street Music Hall in New York. What is certain is that by August 1911, the United Booking Offices, a Keith-controlled booking syndicate that was the most powerful in vaudeville, was throwing $3,500 a week at Eva Tanguay. The contract, signed by the theater manager, Charles S. Breed, required the cyclonic comedienne to perform two shows a day every day of the week. In equivalent purchasing-power terms today, that would be roughly $72,000 a week. Each show saw Eva changing costumes for nearly every number. In April, playing the Fifth Avenue Theater in Manhattan, the manager reckoned Eva "the 'record-breaker' of the season," as she performed to standing-room-only audiences.[38]

With heaps of cash at the ready, Eva allowed herself to indulge in the kind of showy lifestyle for which celebrities were increasingly becoming known. Her gem-spangled purse was said to carry between five and fifteen thousand dollars in cash on any given day. For a home, she bought two flats in an elegant, six-story, brick-and-stone building on the corner of Morningside Drive and West 116th Street in Manhattan, combining them into a palatial dwelling atop "a swagger apartment house," according to a reporter who saw them. Perched above sloping, tree-lined Morningside Park, the Tanguay residence, thirteen rooms in all, was judged "one of the handsomest homes owned by any of our American players" by *Stage Pictorial* magazine. Each room conveyed not only "elegance" and "good taste" but its own unique design motif. "Costly, graceful divans, fine heavy book-cases, rich curtains and tapestries, beautiful chandeliers, a magnificent grand piano—all these and other things give distinction and a note of individuality to the entire establishment." The confluence of individuality and affluence served the performer's professional aims well, as it has done for many of her famous successors.[39]

Though almost neurotically tight-lipped about men, when it came to luxury, Eva Tanguay had no problem telling her story. Her descriptions reaffirmed her sense that she had succeeded, receding ever further from

Figure 13. A room in Eva's lavish New York City apartment.
From about 1908 to 1913, Eva lived in this apartment
on Morningside Drive near what is today the main Columbia University
campus. This photo came from an album she had published showing her
personal palace decorated with silver, mahogany, velvet,
and other lush finery—only fitting for vaudeville's reigning queen.
(Author's private collection.)

• • • • • • • •

the financial neglect Dr. Tanguay inflicted on his brood. She published a *Souvenir Album* whose cover bore the inscription "My effort to please you is my only happiness" in what appeared to be the actress's own hand. In addition to the usual publicity shots, there were sumptuous photos of her home's lavish reception hall, lined with silks and artwork; her sleeping quarters with regal brass bed, gilt-edged furniture, rich lavender drapes, and a small illuminated fountain that sprayed a gentle mist of perfume in the air; and her dining room, which had enough silver and china to satisfy a family of at least middling nobility. "Miss Tanguay's apartment would be voted 'a dream' without hesitation," wrote a journalist who visited. Though Eva thought it "the last word in elegance," it was not without its garish touches. There was the fourteen-foot tiger rug, for example, not to mention a room clad almost entirely in red velvet. One part stage set, one part celebrity redoubt, the Tanguay residence was anything but a modestly decorated, middle-class household of the sort many of her female fans were expected to keep for their husbands.[40]

If Eva's possessions now reflected her celebrity, wealth, and fame, her star status was also increasingly inflated by her habit of throwing away big-ticket luxury items as if they were worn-out socks. She sold the Gardner house in Ashfield, for which she had paid three thousand dollars in order to provide Florence with a place to live several years earlier, for a mere one dollar. It went to an elderly New York silk merchant named Milo Belding. Belding in turn deeded the property directly back to the small, rural town for the "building of a suitable library," according to a legal document from the transaction, intending it as a memorial to his parents. Eva was just as casual about cars. "When I got tired of one, and that was often, I gave it away and bought another. I never thought of selling one," she recalled.[41]

Her top-notch celebrity status was also cemented by her associations, both personal and professional, with the leading luminaries of the day. In 1912, she partnered with vaudeville legend Lew Fields in a production called *The Sun Dodgers*. A musical comedy in name only, *Dodgers* was billed as simply a "Fanfare of Frivolity." What passed for a book was penned by Edgar Smith with music by E. Ray Goetz. Eva played a woman named Praline Nutleigh. In fact, as her character's name suggested, Eva was really just playing herself. Indeed, Nutleigh was described in reviews as "a footlight goddess of the vaudeville persuasion, to whom sunshine is a novelty." Eva decided to push the limit by selecting an exotic costume with jewel-trimmed shorts that left her knees and much of her thighs temptingly bare. Fields approached Eva in high dudgeon, beseeching her to throw on stockings or something to cover her legs. Predictably, Eva would not budge. "I guess I was just ahead of my time," Eva speculated many years later. The disagreement over covering up, no doubt combined with other conflicts between her and Fields, led to the show's early closing.[42]

It was not merely comedians and producers who sought out Eva Tanguay and her bare thighs. She had by now caught the attention of men of stature. In May 1912, Alexander P. Moore, a newspaper publisher and the future U.S. ambassador to both Spain and Peru, asked for Eva's hand in marriage. She declined. Eighteen days later, Moore wed his presumed second choice, the renowned beauty, actress Lillian Russell.[43]

Eva Tanguay had arrived. A theatrical journey begun one night on an amateur stage in Holyoke, followed by a decade on the road and in Broadway musicals and vaudeville, had landed her on top. Producers of eminence sought her talents and men of power sought her affections. Both groups often did so vainly, as she remained somehow just out of reach. It was thus especially odd that an unknown wayfarer should have made his way so deeply into Eva's life at the very pinnacle of her success.

8

❧

Men and Other Travails

NOT LONG AFTER ALEXANDER P. MOORE'S marriage proposal, Eva was in New York playing a Keith house. She fired off her usual salvo of songs, including "I Don't Care," and dressed herself in outrageous costumes, one fashioned to look like tree branches, another resembling a chandelier. Romance, she would later claim, was the furthest thing from her mind. The truth was a bit more complex. As her success grew, so too did Eva's appetite for sexual companionship—along with her deep-seated aversion to being part of anything like a traditional male-female couple. With notoriety came the opportunity to be seen by millions: onstage, in the press, in advertisements. More and more men made her an object of fantasy; more and more women made her an idol of admiration. Eva seemed a symbol of the times, in which sexual economics had taken a new turn. She also now traveled in circles inhabited by more than a few charming, stylish, and complicated men of the sort showbiz is famous for. Among them, Eva could pick and choose as she wished.

As she took her copious bows at the big-time Keith vaudeville venue, an usher rushed down the aisle with a beautiful basket of red roses. She acknowledged the bouquet and blew a kiss out to the audience. Later, changing in her dressing room, she looked at the lovely floral arrangement and saw a note nestled amid its petals. Something about its formal tone struck her as tantalizingly unique.

"Dear Miss Tanguay," read the message. "This is my first visit to New York City. I was fortunate enough to see your performance. I am only a wanderer but at present fascinated to the extreme and desire your presence at dinner." The writer claimed he had "no motive only to sit with you." Would she join him, he wondered, the following evening at the Waldorf-Astoria Hotel at six thirty, for he had to be out of town by eight. The generosity was odd. Something about the note left the queen of vaudeville "intrigued"; this "wanderer" had penned, in her estimation, no "ordinary mash note." Wondering "what possible harm" could come from dining with her new admirer, she jotted a response in white ink on lavender paper, bound it with a matching lavender ribbon, and handed it to a messenger boy.[1]

Eva put on a nice but understated dress the following evening to meet her mystery man. As she made her way to the Waldorf, she wondered what he would look like. Would be heavyset? Ugly? "If he were disreputable-looking I could make up an excuse to get away," she reasoned. Eva entered the venerable hotel via its famous Peacock Alley, a corridor so named because it led to a lobby where fashionable men and women strutted stylishly like plumed birds. Her suitor had chosen an auspicious meeting spot. The Alley led to the equally famous Palm Room, perhaps New York's most prestigious restaurant, which was nightly jammed with stars and stargazers, the latter straining to get a look at the nation's royalty of finance, industry, politics, and the stage. It was said to be nearly impossible to get a table at The Palm. How had this wanderer managed such a feat? She found herself impressed.

Striding to the end of Peacock Alley, beneath a high, arched ceiling hung with elegant chandeliers and past abundant potted palms, she anxiously looked around for the "wanderer."

He spotted her first.

At that moment, any second thoughts she might have had vanished. The man was six feet tall, handsome, and equipped with "fine hair" and "beautiful teeth," in Eva's words. He wore an impeccable top hat, was impressively groomed, and displayed courtly manners. She immediately dubbed him Prince Charming.

The charming gentleman accompanied Eva into the hotel's Peacock Room, fitted out with burnished wood paneling and an Eastern-inspired mural of two exotic birds in flight. As they entered, heads turned to glimpse the queen of vaudeville and her prince.

Yet something was not right. A voice in Eva whispered that it was too good to be true. The wanderer's putative worldliness did not match the facts he soon gave about himself. How could a first timer to the big city be this polished, this sophisticated, she wondered? Nonetheless, because she was "stunned by his charm," Eva pressed on with the evening. He told her he had never met an actress before and that he worked for a cigarette company that wanted to transfer him to London, despite his desire to head out west. After a meal in which he ordered everything and demanded "perfection" in all details, he took her to the theater for that night's engagement. He doffed his hat and smiled as the cab took him away. During her performance, Eva could not get him out of her mind.

That night she slept with the wanderer's note under her pillow. Although he had not explicitly wooed her and had not shown overt sexual interest, she was thoroughly smitten. Weeks and months passed. Eva tried to forget him but could not. She heard nothing from the mysterious, gallant, handsome gentleman who had given her the roses.

Eva returned to the rigors of her professional life. She signed another Keith contract and took to the road. Later that year, she found herself in Boston. After opening night, one of the stage managers brought her another note. "I am here," it read. "Will you see me? The Wanderer." Excited "as a schoolgirl," Eva had him shown to her dressing room and flung her arms around him. He seemed embarrassed and explained that he was living in a nearby bachelor apartment. Would she like to "come up and see the colorings of my lights" tonight? he inquired, employing one of the early twentieth century's saucier pickup lines. She declined but suggested breakfast the next day instead. This time she dolled up good. His bachelor pad was every bit as striking as its tenant. Plush tiger rugs adorned the floor. There were rare antiques and fine paintings. Expensive silver lined the breakfast table. And yes, she conceded, the colored lights were impressive. Again the wanderer did not try anything physical. In the days that followed, he sent her telegrams, books, and more flowers. For the first time in her life, Eva began to wonder whether she might give up her career for a relationship.

On Saturday evening, Eva planned to take a late train back to New York. The wanderer picked her up at the hotel. As they approached the station, Eva felt weepy, "disconsolate" at the thought of leaving her perfect man. But Prince Charming had other plans. Then and there he surprised Eva by telling her he was going back to New York with her. Not to chase her, he said, but because he had business matters there. As the train trundled out of Boston, she reclined in his powerful arms, feeling as if she never wanted to be apart from her new beau. He arranged for chicken and champagne to be brought to their compartment. (In the late 1920s, Eva claimed to be a teetotaler. With the wanderer, she alludes to having champagne served to her on several occasions, though she never indicated whether she indulged or merely watched him drink.) They talked, laughed, and watched the lights of Massachusetts twinkle in the distance. "Yes, I thought: I'd gladly give up my success for this man." She didn't care if she ever set foot onstage again. "It was glorious," she later remembered.[2]

The day after arriving in New York, the gentleman paid a call and she invited him over to her palatial apartment on Morningside Drive. She expected him to be impressed if not speechless at her luxurious home. But as the wanderer strode into the queen's palace, he regarded it coolly, casually, "as if he had always lived there," in Eva's reminiscence. She thought he would rave about her furnishings and finery, the rugs, velvet, and silver. Alas, he did not. It hurt. She had feathered her nest impressively thanks to her hard work and talent. Her home was the chief trophy of all that was important to her; she had even put it on display in a souvenir album for all to see. Now it was being ignored by an ordinary civilian.

But when it came to Eva herself—her body, her face, her heartstrings—the wanderer paid plenty of attention.

Their hitherto chaste relationship turned decidedly carnal. Over the next few weeks, Eva and her wanderer became nearly inseparable. It was a dizzying detour from her usual love-'em-and-leave-'em routine. Not only was he her sexual partner, but her new beau catered to her every other need as well: whispering the right things in her ear, promising to protect her with masculine bravado, fetching her what she wanted, and surprising her with unexpected delights. She soon found him indispensable. Then, when things seemed perfect, just as Eva began to live the kind of coupled life that she had never really imagined or even wanted, the wanderer broke the news that he had to leave on business. What was more, he could not be sure when he would be back.

Eva was devastated. Determined to show her he would be absent in person only, the charming wanderer comforted her with candy, poems, books, and yet more flowers. "His technique was perfect," she later recalled.[3]

Though she mused fancifully that she was ready to abandon the stage for her new love interest, Eva nonetheless accepted a nearly yearlong vaudeville contract that would take her across the country. She was distraught at the idea that she might not see her man during this grueling, busy stretch. But the money could have been nothing less than fantastic. She telegrammed the wanderer to tell him and got as immediate a response as could be had in the era of wired messages. "Am resigning my position at once to go with you," read the return. Eva was beside herself with joy. The wanderer wandered back to New York and helped her prepare for her tour. Then something odd happened.

Eva was rushing about her apartment getting ready for a special hometown engagement before embarking on her theatrical pilgrimage, while the wanderer lounged around playing cards with a friend. She said she'd see him when she got back and headed out. At the theater, Eva scrambled into costume, then opened her bag to get out diamond jewelry, worth some forty thousand dollars, that she had planned to wear onstage.

It was gone.

The queen of vaudeville was apoplectic. As her cue sounded, she tried to reassure herself that she must have left the precious stones at home. For Eva Tanguay, left penniless and fatherless as a child, the diamonds signified even more than their hefty dollar value. When her stage turn ended, she changed and frantically prepared to return home, hopefully to be reunited with her jewels. Her man was waiting for her at the stage door. He acted even kinder and more attentive than usual.

Together they ransacked the apartment, searching everywhere for Eva's missing diamonds. They turned up nowhere. Eva's suitor soothed the frantic actress telling her they would surely be found the next day or the day after that. Eva called the police. When they arrived, she explained what had happened to several curious New York City detectives. "Aha! What about this boy friend? Looks to me like he's in the middle on this [*sic*]," sniffed one of the investigating cops. Eva bellowed at the policeman, calling his suggestion "preposterous." She was infuriated. Still the precious stones remained lost.

Several days passed. The diamonds failed to appear. Eva had to pick herself up from the blow and carry on as best she could. She had a tour to begin and needed all the help she could get. In short order, the wanderer became her de facto manager. He doted on her, calling cabs, bundling her so she wouldn't catch cold, painting her into the center of his world. He was sweet, she recalled, but also somehow distant. As vague and noncommittal as she was in day-to-day life about her affairs, Eva never detailed his specific duties or gave him a job title. He was simply there for her, emotionally, sexually, and logistically.

Whatever distance he may have conveyed, Eva's new lover and secretary nonetheless spent lavishly on her. He bought her expensive dresses and frilly, high-class lingerie. She noticed how quickly her cash was departing but said nothing of it. After all, he was seeing to her every need and then some. One day, her man told Eva how much he wanted to bring his dear old mother and father to live in New York but that he could not afford to do so because he was no longer employed with the cigarette company. Would Eva mind helping out, he wondered? "Certainly, my love," she told him, at once agreeing to hand over a year's rent on an apartment in the city.

Not long thereafter, her suitor-cum-manager had a proposition for her. He adored being her manager but without an income of his own he would soon be obliged to return to his old job. "Of course," he added, "if you feel that my services are worth it, and could pay me a salary, I would feel more independent." She granted him his independence and put him on the payroll. She never revealed how much she paid him, but Eva was undoubtedly generous. "I was his golden baby," she later wrote. "And I mean golden!"[4]

Toward the finish of her tour, Eva noticed that she was ending up with very little cash in hand each week despite an average paycheck of twenty-five hundred dollars. She never seemed to have questioned the wanderer about it, though, in part because the tour left her feeling overwhelmed and exhausted. Her lover suggested an overseas trip; Eva found the idea delicious. She dug into her savings and converted a few thousand in cash into traveler's checks. Soon they were steaming out of New York harbor bound for Europe.[5]

Several days after setting sail, the queen of vaudeville and her companion were in the ship's luxurious dining salon when an actor she knew recognized her and approached to say hello. But not a moment after he had opened his mouth, a dinner plate that had been launched into the air at high speed flew by within an inch of the actor's face. The china exploded into shards against a wall. Everyone in the dining room looked around to see what had happened. Eva glanced up. There was Prince Charming, his face purple with rage. Stewards hastily ushered him out of the dining area and Eva followed, shocked, confused, and seeking some kind of explanation. "Understand this," he shouted. "You are not to talk to anyone else. You belong to me." The gallant, attentive man for whom Eva had fallen seemed now to betray a jealous monster within. The incident shook her so much that she stayed in her stateroom for most of the rest of the trip, only occasionally seeing her paramour at night on the upper decks. She tried to tell herself—or so she later claimed—that his militant possessiveness must have equaled true devotion. In the depths of her being, however, Eva knew better. Since girlhood, she had known how imbalanced and unreliable men could be. But somehow, perhaps out of sheer geographical necessity, she managed to tell herself things would be okay. They sailed on to France. Shortly after docking, Mr. Hyde went into remission. The wanderer charmed and doted on Eva once again. She convinced herself that it had been the upset of the ocean voyage that accounted for his rapid, violent change of mood.

Their first night in Paris, Eva and her lover went to the famous Maxim's restaurant. Eva was decked out in her best frock. "It was heavenly," she remembered. As they feasted on gourmet fare and sipped French champagne amid the restaurant's quasi-modernist decor of striped wood and globe-shaped lighting fixtures, Eva's fears receded—even if her partner's champagne sips were more like wolfish gulps. Then it all came to a head.

The wanderer, by now quite lubricated with drink, had struck up a flirtatious conversation with a pretty young Frenchwoman at the next table. Eva didn't like it but stifled what she considered unwarranted jealousy. As the vaudeville star and her man prepared to leave the swank eatery, her lover turned to her and, slurring his words, declared, "That girl—s-s-he's gorgeous. Let's take her with ush." Eva was dumbstruck. "What are you talking about?" she demanded. "How can you suggest such a thing when you don't even know her?" "Bet she'd like to get acquainted," he replied. Eva leaped to her feet, but the wanderer grabbed her with such fury and ferocity that it tore her evening gown. That was it. Eva caught a train back to the boat, fled to England, and from there returned home to New York, fearing the whole way that he was chasing her. The romance was over, though not its fallout.[6]

By the time she got back, Eva was a wreck. "The bottom had dropped out of my world," she recalled. Weeks passed. She put the fragile pieces of her life back together. Then one day she got a phone call. It was him. In silken tones, he entreated her to meet. He pleaded. She felt nothing for him, no love, but agreed to see him anyway. When they saw each other, the wanderer fell to his knees. He wept. He begged. "The man should have been an actor," recalled Eva. "He played a scene that day that would have melted the heart of an image." But it did not melt hers. It was over. "Now get out!" she ordered. She soon made a discovery. During her tour, the money she had been allotting her companion was being used to ferry his secret lover around the country with them. Years later, the wanderer's mother called Eva to tell her that her son had died. There was no money for a proper burial; he lay in a public morgue. Could she help? Eva Tanguay agreed to finance his final journey.[7]

Who was this wanderer, other than a dangerous man who seduced Eva then turned against her? Eva never hinted in her own writings or in magazine interviews. Indeed, much about her woman-scorned narrative left out the fact that she remained an active participant in her own misery. Eva's recap smoothed out the messy contours of her deep dive into the arms of a man who emerges from the evidence as at least something of a sociopath. That was Eva's choice, as it would often continue to be. Men like the unavailable C. F. Zittel and the abusive wanderer were ever more enticing to Eva Tanguay than the attentive Edward Darlings.

It is possible that the wanderer was one Albert Donald Walk, a scammer arrested for con artistry in Buffalo, New York, and subsequently visited in jail by Eva who, according to the papers, was touring in the city and swore she would "stand by him to the end."[8] It is unclear why Eva promised to champion Walk's cause, spending an hour with him in the jailhouse though never offering to post bail. Curiously, it seems the police gave Eva a six-hundred-dollar diamond ring that belonged to her and had been found on Albert Donald Walk at the time of his arrest. It is not impossible to imagine Eva being charmed by a small-time drifter who displayed just the right amount of boyish regret and beaming admiration.

Further investigation revealed that Walk had been impersonating a U.S. naval officer, which somehow permitted him to swindle banks and hotels. At the time, playing the part of a naval officer carried with it a notable ability to impress, manipulate—and defraud. In 1911, an ordinary Brooklyn civilian named Stephen Jacob Weinberg made headlines by approaching the Afghan royal family when they visited New York and representing himself as a naval officer assigned to aid the U.S. State Department; he renamed himself Rodney Sterling Wyman. (Some years later, Weinberg also successfully posed as the actress Pola Negri's personal physician, despite never having received medical training of any kind.)

Not long after his troubles in Buffalo, Walk again found himself in hot water, this time awaiting trial in the famous Tombs prison for "abstracting" two diamond rings from the actress Beatrice Brevaine's purse as he and Brevaine lunched at the Hotel Majestic. There was no way Walk could have done it, insisted Eva—despite the fact that he had done it to *her* just a short while earlier—then publicly denounced Brevaine as "a fat little thing." This time Eva put up eight hundred dollars of Walk's bail money and the accused's father fronted the other three thousand. Though she did not offer evidence or even a logical argument for his innocence, Eva nonetheless protested loudly to all who would listen that Walk was not guilty of the Brevaine theft. She further told reporters that there was nothing but "a friendly interest on her part," while caressing a rabbit's foot, no matter that she had brought a sumptuous Christmas dinner to Albert Donald Walk and spent several hours of the holiday with him in the jailhouse. Eva said she had met him in Buffalo and that he had been introduced to her by a U.S. naval lieutenant named Kinney who assured her that Walk was a Princeton man. After being released on bond by the Buffalo authorities, Walk followed Eva to Toronto—where he was promptly arrested yet again for diamond theft. From his jail cell in Canada, he wrote the cyclonic actress letters she deemed "perfectly beautiful and sentimental and just like a Princeton man would write." Somehow he was released and made his way to New York, where again he could not control his desire for other people's diamonds. If the wanderer was in fact Albert Donald Walk, Eva omitted many important details from her narrative of the affair in the serialized autobiography published in the pages of *American Weekly* magazine shortly before her death in 1947. But then again, when it came to her personal life, Eva Tanguay left behind a frustratingly brief and redacted tale.[9]

THOUGH SALOME was now four years behind her, and it had been nearly a decade since she first sang "I Don't Care," Eva felt full of vim, ready to plunge back into work to rid her mind of the entire "wanderer" episode and no doubt to refill her coffers. The wanderer had inflicted significant emotional and financial damage, but Eva, having absorbed the blows, now lifted herself from the floor. In part to show she was back, and in part perhaps to vent some anger intended for the wanderer, Eva picked a new professional fight. Her target was once again, as in the case of her feud with Willa Holt Wakefield, not only a woman who differed drastically from Eva in her stage appeal but one who was perceived as refined, lettered, and dignified.

Eva's new nemesis was the renowned actress Ethel Barrymore. Born in Philadelphia on August 15, 1879, Ethel Barrymore, unlike Eva Tanguay, came from one of the country's great theatrical families. Her father was Herbert Arthur Chamberlayne Blythe, a popular leading man of his day, and her mother was the well-regarded comedienne Georgiana Emma Drew Barrymore. Ethel's siblings included Lionel Barrymore and John Barrymore. The latter was the so-called first gentleman of the American theater and grandfather of the popular film actress Drew Barrymore. Ethel's grandmother, Mrs. John Drew, had been a star of the early American stage, descended from the Lanes, a well-known clan of English actors and balladeers.

Like Eva, Ethel Barrymore hit the stage young. She was fourteen when she took a small role in a production of Sheridan's *The Rivals*. From there she worked her way through an assortment of melodramas and Shakespeare productions, gaining skill, winning praise, and building a working relationship with the theater magnate Charles Frohman. With Frohman's help, she became an actress of the top tier. Barrymore famously ad-libbed the line "That's all there is, there isn't any more" while playing the title role in Frohman's production *Sunday* in 1904. Though unquestionably a thespian of the scripted dramatic stage, her talent for spontaneity and her ability to read an audience would serve her well eight years later when, poring over one bad script after another, she decided to take a stab at vaudeville. Frohman let her play Martin Beck's Orpheum circuit, western rival to the Keith chain. Barrymore had enjoyed a popular run in J. M. Barrie's *The Twelve Pound Look,* and Frohman suggested she condense it down to vaudeville size and take it on the Orpheum trail. She did, to the tune of three thousand dollars a week. For good measure, she threw in a cut-down version of Barrie's *Alice Sit-by-the-Fire* as well.[10]

For Barrymore, vaudeville was a step down, but one she made graciously, like a society woman deigning to shop at a popular market for a glimpse at the local color. You could call it noblesse oblige. In any case, three thousand dollars a week took the sting out of slumming. "I found that you have to be awfully good in vaudeville," she later wrote. "It is a real taskmaster because there are so many acts in it...that require absolute perfection." Not only was talent required, but, to her shock, vaudeville theaters "proved to be beautiful, not only in the front of the house, but in the back as well," she would later reflect.[11]

The pretensions and pay of "La Barrymore," as starstruck critics called her, irked Eva on a deep, personal level. In logical terms, Eva did not have much to worry about. Vaudeville crowds were amused, though not awestruck like the critics, to see a well-known dramatic star who hailed from a well-known theatrical family. And though Barrymore provided The Colonial Theater in New York with "a prosperous week" when she played there, the *New York Dramatic Mirror* felt that Barrymore, despite her appeal, was "not the drawing curiosity that Eva Tanguay was." Besides, *The Twelve Pound Look,* whatever its lofty social intentions, was not the stuff of vaudeville. "I feel as if I were preaching a sermon to every married man and woman in the world," Barrymore once said of her performances in *The Twelve Pound Look,* with its insightful messages about domestic life and calls for "female independence." Vaudeville crowds were looking for many things, but heavy-handed sermonizing was not one of them.[12]

Perhaps it was Ethel Barrymore's quasi-aristocratic background that pushed Eva's buttons; Barrymore had even retained an English accent from her time as a schoolgirl in Britain, not to mention hanging about at family gatherings with what she called the "cream of Philadelphia society." Maybe it was that Barrymore came from a different world, the legitimate (that is, dramatic, nonvaudeville) stage, and was therefore an outsider in

Eva's eyes. By virtue of her artistic position, Barrymore enjoyed social status and cachet that a vaudevillian never could. Whatever the precise motivation—Eva never revealed it—the cyclonic wonder "nursed a grudge against Ethel Barrymore and carried it on in public to the stars' mutual gain," according to theater historian Leigh Woods. Within a year, Ethel Barrymore announced she was done with vaudeville. In a farewell interview, she graciously acknowledged that vaudevillians were people too. "I had been told that vaudeville was not class, and that the artists were more or less bounders. I found the contrary to be the case." In addition to the skill of the acrobats and the "accurate comedy of the comedian," she even paid homage to "the finesse of the single singing woman." Besides, some of her best friends were vaudevillians. "As comrades and fellow workers they are loyal, helpful and generous. I have made scores of fast friends in vaudeville of whom I am proud," recounted La Barrymore.

From Eva's standpoint, it was good-bye and good riddance. Perhaps Eva would later have bonded with Barrymore when the leading lady of legitimate theater hit a rough patch in the early 1920s. It was then, six years after her departure from vaudeville, that Ethel Barrymore finally went public with the news that she had been suffering violent abuse at the hands of her husband, Russell Griswold Colt. The son of Samuel Pomeroy Colt, known as "the rubber king of Rhode Island," Russell Colt, it turned out, had long been beating his actress wife. On one occasion, in 1920, he gave her two black eyes and slashed her face so severely that Barrymore had to retire to the care of a doctor for several days. It also came out that Colt, despite his moneyed background, had never supported her financially throughout their chaotic, abusive marriage.[13]

IF EVA HAD bitterly disliked rivals in several of her contemporaries, she also had troves of worshipful emulators in an upcoming generation of performers. Increasingly, young women who sought fame, glory, and money looked to Eva Tanguay as their prime inspiration. She had demonstrated that it did not necessarily require prodigious musical or dancing skills or years of professional training resulting in technical mastery. But what Eva made look easy—exuding the glowing power of one's personality in a marketable way—was of course anything but. Still, a young Mae West was determined to follow as closely in Eva Tanguay's footsteps as possible.

What Holyoke had been to Eva Tanguay—an urban crucible of inspiration—working-class Brooklyn was to Mae West. Born Mary Jane West to a German-immigrant mother Matilda Delker Doelger and

John West, a bruising, brawling father of lower social status than his wife, on August 17, 1893, in the Greenpoint section of Brooklyn, Mae spent her early years much as Eva had hers. Mae's mother, like Eva's, was not raised in the United States. (Mrs. Tanguay, it may be recalled, was born in the United States, but to a French-Canadian family that quickly pulled up stakes and settled in Quebec.) And while Mae West at one point said her father was a doctor practicing in the then-classy Richmond Hill neighborhood in Queens, much as Eva had once declared her father a Parisian physician, he was an itinerant worker who traded jobs frequently—mechanic, coffee salesman, night watchman, and professional gambler—and was likely a heavy drinker. John West's ancestry may in fact have been part Canadian, and some have speculated that Mae was also part Jewish on her mother's side, though West herself never admitted it. While Matilda West, known as Tillie, focused her energy on helping her daughter Mae succeed in show business, father John, who lacked any formal schooling, devoted much of his time to the company of "roughnecks, sharpies, gamblers, and confidence men," in the words of Emily Wortis Leider, one of Mae West's biographers. If Eva knew a father who was drunk, neglectful, and disappointing, Mae's was a surly, working-class version who engaged in barroom dustups, street boxing, and, of course, interminable boozing. Like Eva Tanguay, Mae West would long decry those who drank too much, including her famous costar in the 1940 film *My Little Chickadee,* W. C. Fields. Mae also had to withstand her sister Beverly's alcoholism.[14]

A the age of seven, Mae made her stage debut as Baby Mae, at Brooklyn's Royal Theater on Willoughby Street during an amateur talent night sponsored by a local chapter of the Elks fraternal order. The amateur-night beginning not only mimicked Eva's start but so too did her odd getup, a pink-and-green satin affair decorated with gold spangles. Like Eva, she also walked away with first prize. Mae continued to play the Brooklyn amateur-night circuit before joining a local stock company where she assumed roles in such popular hits as *Uncle Tom's Cabin, East Lynne,* and, again like Eva, *Little Lord Fauntleroy.* In talent contests, she often won by impersonating major vaudeville talents such as Bert Williams and Eddie Foy. Mae preferred impersonating entertainers who focused on personality rather than standard acting talent. She portrayed her subjects satirically—as one might expect from a little girl playing an adult man in blackface, in the case of her Bert Williams impersonation, for example—though always lovingly. Mae had no interest in losing herself in a classic character such as Ophelia or Hedda Gabler. She sought to perform rather than act, to entertain by drawing on herself rather than depicting someone else's creation. Given these aims, there was no one better to study—and copy— than the queen of vaudeville herself.[15]

It was Mae's mother, Tillie, who first urged her daughter to observe Eva onstage and pay close attention. Tillie West repeatedly took the girl to see Eva, telling her that one day she could be just as big a star if she worked at it. In time, Mae developed a routine that was an unabashed imitation of Eva. Mae West was soon identified by one theater critic as "nearly an Eva Tanguay," and even began opening her show with a song called "I've Got a Style All My Own," which was ironic since it was little more than her take on Eva's "It's All Been Done Before, But Not the Way I Do It," a paean to originality.[16]

By 1911, with her juvenile stock days behind her, Mae West hit vaudeville. She was barely eighteen, but vaudeville was mushrooming thanks in part to the outsized popularity of her idol, Eva Tanguay. In short order, there would be close to five thousand big- and small-time vaudeville houses in the United States. In New York alone, some seven hundred thousand people visited vaudeville each week, according to one study. In addition to her Eva-inspired act, Mae availed herself of the popular "coon" shouting trend that would be made popular by Sophie Tucker, Fanny Brice, and others. Mae made a splash with "Lovin' Honey Man" and other hymns to a jazzy Eros.[17]

Though she managed to win time on the Keith, Orpheum, and Loew circuits, Mae never came anywhere close to Eva's level of success in vaudeville. Sometimes she appeared alone, sometimes as part of a male-female two act, and often in a larger ensemble known as Mae West and the Shooting Stars. Almost everywhere she played, she was compared to Eva, though not always favorably. She continued to boost her artistic and symbolic links to the cyclonic one, promoting herself on one occasion as "America's Youngest Temperamental Comedienne" and enlisting the songwriting services of Blanche Merrill, who also supplied material to Eva. So ardent was her aping of Eva Tanguay that a San Antonio, Texas, review identified her as, inexplicably, "the Eva Tanguay of vaudeville"— as though she were trying to out-Eva Eva.

In 1913, after Mae played the Keith theater he managed in Columbus, Ohio, W. W. Prosser informed the head office in a memo that West "must be credited with possessing unusual individuality and style that is peculiarly her own," echoing comments that had been made some years earlier about Eva Tanguay. Following Eva's lead, Mae latched onto notions of "individuality" and "style." Prosser found Mae West interesting, believing that her "methods and personality are such that will be sure to attract anyone with an eye for the unusual." Still, he confessed to his corporate superiors, she had not scored a hit. Others saw more accurately why Mae West, despite her best efforts to copy vaudeville's most popular artist, was falling short. "This woman is all that is coarse in Eva Tanguay without that player's ability," wrote a disapproving Detroit critic. Increasingly, it seemed that Mae West was, for all her study of Eva, failing to properly understand Eva's true appeal. At the same time, she was minimizing her own special qualities that audiences would come to love—and over which censors would eventually go haywire.[18]

The truth was that while Eva played with sexuality like a kitten batting a ball of string, Mae West fastened onto sex with the claws of a wildcat. She had been a streetwise girl known for sexual adventure and exhibitionism. Try as she might to temper, submerge, or redirect her eroticism, as Eva skillfully had, Mae could not hide who she was. Mae West's "appeal was openly one of sexual impropriety, [while] Tanguay's was not," wrote Marybeth Hamilton in her authoritative book on Mae West, aptly titled *When I'm Bad, I'm Better: Mae West, Sex, and American Entertainment.* West earned her keep in vaudeville for a spell, but she never headlined. After six years of trying unsuccessfully to sell a dirtier vision of Eva in the two-a-day and small-time circuits, Mae finally threw in the towel. It seems likely that for the duration of the decade and well into the 1920s, she submitted to playing the nation's seamy, skin-oriented burlesque wheels, that less-reputable industry's version of vaudeville circuits. In 1926, however, Mae West began the remarkable run that would render her, by the mid-1930s, the most famous woman in show business. Unleashing her unvarnished sexuality and no longer tethered to sheer Eva mimicry, she wrote, produced, and starred as a Montreal brothel's chief madam in the play *Sex,* which despite being called "offensive" and a "monstrosity" by some outraged observers of the day, became one of the three longest-running shows then on Broadway, closing in March 1927.[19]

Though Mae West was actually tried, convicted, and sentenced to ten days in prison for *Sex's* alleged filthiness, she nonetheless followed up with an even riskier play of her own device, *The Drag,* in 1927, which openly depicted New York's campy gay underworld using performers drawn from its recesses. As with *Sex,* Mae did not depict something potentially shocking with judgmental, moral distance for middle-class audiences to enjoy from afar. Rather, she thrust it under the Broadway spotlight, illuminating it for all to see. She had, in effect, placed prostitution and gay male subculture on the boards not as freakish oddities but as fellow citizens of the very city in which the well-heeled classes dwelled. To be sure, some members of those high-flown classes must also have secretly yearned to join their ranks.[20]

West moved toward more acceptable fare with her hit play *Diamond Lil,* which premiered on April 9, 1928, and eventually became the popular movie *She Done Him Wrong* (1933). She followed with a string of successful films including *I'm No Angel* (also 1933), *Belle of the Nineties* (1934), *Klondike Annie* (1936), and *My Little Chickadee* (1940), which she either cowrote or otherwise managed to receive authorship credit for. By the mid-1930s, Mae was lauded for single-handedly keeping Hollywood afloat during the bleak, early years of the Great Depression, while simultaneously whipping up moral backlash to such a point that the entire film industry was forced to inaugurate its infamous Production Code. The code, administered by Joseph Breen, a lay Catholic reformer whose job it was to remove all hint of moral ambiguity from Hollywood's already suspect product, battered the likes of Mae West, whose films were rife with social and religious iconoclasm, spicy double entendres, and busty, hip-swinging sexual moxie. By the 1940s, Mae West's career as a major player in Hollywood was dead. She turned to various creative endeavors involving stage and screen, but sank into relative obscurity until the liberating force of the 1960s scooped her up as a nostalgic, ahead-of-her-time icon. Her ultrafeminine shimmying and pugnacious sex appeal became a kind of symbol for the gender politics of both gay men and culturally oppressed women. "With buttons, pin-ups, and works of pop art lavishing attention on her hourglass figure," wrote Marybeth Hamilton, "West found herself suddenly hip." She tried to parlay her rediscovered visibility into a revivified career with two films, the X-rated *Myra Breckinridge* (1970) and the tamer *Sextette* (1978). Both tanked. Mae West died at her home in the Ravenswood Apartments in Los Angeles, the very same development where Eva Tanguay had once lived, in 1980.[21]

Though she failed to enter Eva's orbit in vaudeville, or even come close to it, Mae West scored her biggest victories, even at the price of institutional censure, when she stopped trying to be someone else and dished up what had long been simmering within. She had clearly learned much from her days gazing at Eva in rapt admiration. West had learned, paradoxically, that bringing oneself to the fore was the only real route to stardom, which she could not do by channeling another. To Mae West, Eva's virtual one-woman show shouted, "Be yourself! Just like me!" Though she had fully come out from beneath Eva's shadow, the two maintained a friendship over the years.

In the decades closer to our own, many know the name Mae West while only a handful remember Eva Tanguay. It is an enigma to which some commentators have paid attention. In 2009 the online magazine *Slate* ran a feature article on Eva written by its music critic, Jody Rosen, who lamented, "Tanguay is forgotten.... How did such a big star, such a heady period, slip from our view, and slide out of the history books?" Similarly, Wes Eichenwald, who wrote a piece on Tanguay for the magazine *American History,* saw her as a "missing link" between soubrette Lotta Crabtree and West.[22]

In terms of overall success, Eva could be called the bigger star. While Mae West crested Hollywood's peak for perhaps five years, roughly 1933 to 1938, Eva Tanguay was the country's biggest live act for nearly a decade, beginning around 1906. Mae West's movie career, meteoric though it was, was abruptly halted by social and economic forces that denied West her most potent tools and kicked her into a marginality from which she would never come back, except as a museum-like effigy.[23]

To be sure, Mae West's image survives in part because she played a more active role than Eva did in creating the sort of artifacts that live on in the annals of popular memory. In addition to her screenwriting credits, West authored perhaps a half-dozen plays, some unproduced, as well as the novel *Babe Gordon,* which focused on interracial sex in New York and later became a play called *The Constant Sinner.* She was also credited with an autobiography titled *Goodness Had Nothing to Do with It.* Though nearly all her written works were composed with generous assistance from skillful editors, interpreters, and ghostwriters, they nonetheless indicate West's desire to command and control her own career, and to do so within our society's accepted rules of evidence.[24]

And yet of course, it is not Mae West the writer or even the rule-breaking actress–producer so many today remember—or think they remember. Rather, it is Mae West the icon of film, the self-possessed femme fatale whose ultrafeminine curves never obscured the wily tough girl underneath. To suggest that Eva failed as an icon, however, would be to miss the point. By her very nature, Eva eschewed the artifacts of recall. She was decidedly not of the screen, nor of the printed word nor even the scripted play. Her brilliance, to its glory and detriment, would not come across on a wax record or silent movie. It is not, then, that Eva was forgettable but that she was evanescent. She was tied to her time, place, and creative form in a way few artists in our era have managed to be. Unlike playwriting, movie-starring Mae West, Eva Tanguay was the mistress of a disappearing kingdom. But to truly know Mae West is to know Eva Tanguay.

Vaudeville women like Eva showed the young Mae Wests of the world that you did not have to follow in your mother's or grandmother's footsteps. With Eva leading the pack, women entertainers in the first decades of the twentieth century articulated a life path that did not entail being a wife and mother in a traditional family unit. In the nineteenth century, many women in North America saw their roles transition from active coagent, along with their husbands, in a family's financial and strategic affairs, to cosseted, sheltered wife whose realm was that of affection, emotion, and rigid humility. In the words of the well-known historian Ann Douglas, by midcentury, "the independent woman with a mind and a life of her own slowly ceased to be considered of high value." Whereas in earlier colonial and frontier days, wives flanked their spouses as thinkers and doers, they now married not "to help their husbands get a living, but to help them spend their income." In time, they would turn to fashion (among other arenas) as an outlet for individual expression. With Eva and, in her wake, Mae West and others, the image of woman as not much more than a passive, complementary element in her husband's household would fall away, at least until the renewed conservatism that followed World War II. But by then, Eva would be gone.[25]

WITH NO ROMANTIC LIFE to speak of, and with Florence taken care of and attending school in Massachusetts, Eva put together her own touring outfit, the Eva Tanguay Vaudeville Company, which she took on the road in the latter half of 1913. The company was an assemblage of comics, dancers, and singers who either backed up Eva or provided entertainment between her numbers. Sometimes the unit was promoted as "Eva Tanguay and Her Own Volcanic Vaudeville Company."

Little is known about her ongoing relations with Melville Collins, the man some supposed she had fallen in love with. What is certain is that the gentlemanly composer and pianist was by now courting Eva's niece Lillian Skelding, eighteen years old and endowed with a gentle smile, chestnut hair, and a broad visage with soft, pretty features. Collins would wed Lillian the following year. Eva left no record of her feelings about the romance, though she must have been torn. On one hand, Melville Collins was no longer a viable prospect. On the other hand, he was still very much in her life, part of the family, and joined to her nieces, Ruth and Lillian (both daughters of Eva's sister Blanche, by different fathers), to whom she too was increasingly emotionally bound. Ruth, still a girl of ten, with her raven locks and black eyes, looked less a part of the Tanguay clan than her fair-featured aunt, her mother, and her half sister all did. As for Eva's business affairs, they were now in the hands of Jack Edwards. When it came to management, Eva was as promiscuous as she was in her love life.

In charge of her own touring company, Eva took more chances with sexual brazenness. It was no longer 1900. The decade in which she had come up professionally saw big changes in both the demographics and cultural tastes of urban life in the United States. Between 1900 and 1910, the total number of white-collar workers—those professionals, managers, clerical workers, salespeople, and the like, who more than any other single group had time and money to spend on novel amusements—rose 55 percent, from 5.1 million to 7.9 million. Less bound to traditional mores, they both sought out and were wooed by a city life that was increasingly libidinal and theatrical. Department-store windows, for example, began to feature clothing, even underwear, on mannequins resembling women, suggesting the woman's body as something to be costumed, shown, and leered at. Though she was hardly a lifeless mannequin onstage, Eva's choice of attire made it clear that she was part of the new urban morality rather than some Sunday-School-approved vaudeville circuit. *Variety* wrote that Eva's new costumes "fit even tighter with more form revelation than ever before, impossible though this may seem," suggesting as well that the cyclonic performer had gained a few pounds.[26]

To reach for the easy reference, Eva began to embody the essence of "I Don't Care." She challenged authorities and aligned herself with an emergent ethos of self-determination and individual morality. When her Vaudeville Company ambled into New York as part of its 1913 tour, theater impresario Lee Shubert requested that Eva make several cuts to her act when playing his 44th Street Music Hall. Rather than reply herself, she had manager Edwards fire back. The letter to Lee Shubert was clear but curt, tinged with Eva's trademark indignation. First, it argued, a Shubert representative had seen the Eva Tanguay Vaudeville Company on the road and had no complaints about it then. Second, the reviews were in the papers and critics found nothing wanting on Eva's entire bill. Therefore, Eva informed Shubert, she would "retain all of her acts for this week, in addition to the two acts which you furnished." In other words, no cuts.[27]

Shubert backed off, wisely choosing not to go head-to-head with Eva and her team. The cyclonic actress agreed to add two more Shubert-managed acts to her Vaudeville Company when it appeared at his 44th Street Music Hall. But even this concession soon piqued her fury. One of the Shubert performers was a man who sang songs and told jokes while doing tricks on roller skates. Accomplished as he may have been, the rolling vaudevillian took only two minutes of stage time before, according to Eva, "thoughtlessly" wheeling back offstage amid the applause. The trouble was that the next act was not yet ready to go. Eva had a conniption. She either had not been aware of the routine's brevity or, in her mind, considered its effect on what followed ruinous. Either way, reacting strongly, but without much consideration, she fired the skater as soon as he glided offstage. As luck would have it, the comedy team of Brady & Mahoney happened to be in the theater picking up some personal items at the time. Eva pleaded with them to go on and fill the remaining time until the next act on her bill was ready to go. In a flash, the comedians did some of their famous "Hebrew act," a popular genre on the vaudeville stage, in which performers played Jewish ethnic stereotypes. So successful were Brady & Mahoney that Eva decided to retain them for the rest of the run. She even paid their salary that week out of her own pocket, apparently not wanting further tension with the management. "I am having enough trouble without worrying over this," she declared, making plain her resentment against Lee Shubert.[28]

With the money to make her own choices and call the shots in her industry's power structure, Eva came to embody the idea of the "new woman" emerging in U.S. society at the time. Rather than passively fulfilling traditional expectations, the new woman was viewed as an empowered agent who chose to lead rather than follow. Not everyone was so enthusiastic about such women; many considered them appetitive and capricious. In 1912, a writer for *American Magazine* wrote of the new woman:

> She has found out that with education and freedom, pursuits of all sorts are open to her, and by following these pursuits she can preserve her personal liberty, avoid the grave responsibility, the almost inevitable sorrows and anxieties which belong to family life. She can choose her friends and change them. She can travel, and gratify her tastes, satisfy her personal ambitions. The snare has been too great, the beauty and joy of free individual life have dulled the sober sense of national obligation. The result is that she is frequently failing to discharge satisfactorily some of the most imperative demands the nation makes upon her.

Of course, *American Magazine* failed to recognize that such a profile might appeal to house- and culture-bound women of the late nineteenth and early twentieth centuries. After the turn of the nineteenth century, women came more and more to see themselves as consumers and chose to define themselves in part by their choices in makeup, clothing, amusements, and even dates. Eva Tanguay and others like her showed and indeed publicly professed the pleasures of such a life.[29]

Enjoying her freedom, success, and wealth at this particular moment in her career, Eva Tanguay made a decision—if one can call such a whim a decision—to do something that was anything but unconventional. In 1913, for the first time in her life, Eva Tanguay got married.

9

❧

Mrs. John Ford

AMID THE COMEDIANS, musicians, and chorus girls of the rambling Eva Tanguay Vaudeville Company—not to mention its eponymous star—was an entertainer named John W. Ford (no relation to the famous film director of westerns such as *Stagecoach* and *Rio Grande*). Neither in Eva's company nor in his vaudeville career up to then had John Ford distinguished himself as headliner material. But he was resourceful enough to know what might please a crowd along the way. Perhaps more important, he understood how to hitch his star to someone else's when the opportunity presented itself, and, just as important, when to cut ties. Honing one's craft and keeping abreast of the latest tactical options, no matter how Machiavellian, were simply part of the drill for midlevel vaudevillians.

John W. "Johnny" Ford was born into a theatrical family in Covington, Kentucky, just across the river from Cincinnati, about 1881. His father, William Ford, was a blackface minstrel comedian of some renown, and his mother, Emily Forrester, a noted actress. Johnny was the middle of five children, with two older brothers, Edwin and Max, and two younger sisters, Dora—also known as Deborah—and Mabel, the youngest. In addition to having been performers, the Fords owned and managed theaters in Ohio and Kentucky. As children, the three Ford boys would dance around the living room of the family home. As soon as they were able, they began performing in Cincinnati theaters. Sometimes dancing by themselves, sometimes with girls from the famous Dockstader minstrel troupe, they perfected a subspecialty known as wooden-shoe dancing, or clog dancing. To do it, they strapped on shoes with solid wood soles and made a marvelous racket stomping, slapping, and clacking about the stage.[1]

As the Ford children burnished their skills, Edwin, Max, Dora, and Mabel formed an act showcasing their talents. The boys gave a nautical-themed dance in which they wore sailors' attire. They wove in some comedy, one playing a wisecracking tippler, the other a typical straight man. Dora and Mabel cooked up a number based on Homer's story of Nausicaa from the *Odyssey*. Johnny Ford would sometimes join his siblings onstage. Usually, though, he chose to hoof it alone. Without Johnny they called themselves The Four Fords and gained a following. When he did drop in and perform with his siblings, they still called themselves The Four Fords. Johnny was a maverick, sometimes in, sometimes out of the family dance fraternity. His talent and ambition, both considerable, were thwarted by his inconsistency and ambivalence. Had it "not been for Johnny's stubbornness it might have been the 'Five Fords,'" noted one journalist. Stubbornness was one word for it. There was a certain egotism governing Johnny's artistic decisions. If clog dancing with his fellow Fords took him where he needed to be, he was up for it. If flying solo landed him closer to glory, he would just as soon do that. In addition to being stubborn, he was simply hard to predict.[2]

By 1902, Johnny Ford was making a name for himself in wooden-shoe dancing. In Boston, the week of November 17, he "scored a solid hit" during his ten-minute turn on the forestage, according to M. J. Keating, manager of the Keith vaudeville house at which Ford appeared. The dancer enjoyed similar success in nearby Providence and six months later "more than made good" again in the Rhode Island capital. "He can play here frequently," a satisfied theater manager allowed. The only complaint managers had about Ford was that his high-energy act, at between seven and ten minutes, was a little too short to let more scenically complicated routines finish setting up behind the drop curtain. Soon Johnny Ford would bill himself as "the champion dancer of the world," using the kind of hyperbole for which Eva Tanguay had become known.[3]

The more his solo career gained steam, the less time he spent dropping in as a guest star with the other Four Fords. Without Johnny, his siblings soldiered on to greater success. Dubbing themselves the "World's Greatest Dancing Carnival," The Four Fords eventually booked a tour on a bill headlined by Eva Tanguay. With Eva as the program's star, the Ford clan enjoyed houses overflowing with standing-room patrons. Sometime in 1907, it seems, brother Johnny showed up with his clogs, willing to dance with his brothers and sisters. Taking advantage of the fifth Ford—it was never clear when or where he might show up again—the Four let him join. That week in all likelihood, Johnny Ford met Eva Tanguay for the first time.[4]

By 1912, the clog-dancing vaudevillian Johnny Ford was making a regular living touring the circuits across North America. It was a regular gig—something to be grateful for in the peripatetic world of vaudeville— but it left him hungry for something bigger. If he wanted to make the leap to headliner, Johnny Ford knew he would have strike soon. He tried remaking himself as a multitalented, singing, dancing, wisecracking one-man show. At B. F. Keith's Union Square Theatre on the night of November 11, 1912, he showed the theatrical capital of New York City what Johnny Ford was also capable of.

Accompanied by the pianist Ray Barton, Ford not only danced but offered jokes and belted out songs. It busted. The manager of the theater watched Ford's new act, unimpressed. He reckoned there to be a good deal of stalling in it. Nor was the manager much taken with the clog dancer's alleged comedy. And however strong a dancer Johnny Ford was, he was judged at best only a fair singer. Bona fide solo stardom seemed just out of his grasp. Maybe he should have remained with his fellow Fords. Or maybe he could join a troupe with more promise, a better vehicle for getting to the top. The following year he got that chance. In 1913 Johnny Ford, failed headliner but popular freak dancer, joined Eva's "Volcanic" company. At once, he saw a new chapter potentially unfolding. But first he would have to do some convincing. He went to work.[5]

Eva's company ambled through the Midwest in the fall of 1913, venturing as far north as Saginaw, Michigan, and also sweeping through southern Ohio not far from Johnny Ford's home town. In addition to singing her patchwork of songs in revealing or tight-fitting costumes, Eva amped up the kinesthetic qualities of her show by running about the stage while shrieking. One theater critic in Ohio found "her particular form of volcanism" beginning to wear thin, too reliant on "freakishness" without recognizable skills. Certainly Eva had made a name for herself by rejecting, even mocking, conventional performance abilities and replacing them with personality, libido, and frenzied energy. But her style was beginning to reach its limits. She leaned on her supporting cast more than she ever had. It must have been hard for the most storied one-woman act in vaudeville to play as part of an ensemble, no matter how prominently. For now, though, the demands of pleasing fickle crowds, combined with the toll her high-velocity antics were beginning to take, led Eva to fall back, if just slightly, on her supporting cast. Johnny Ford rose to the occasion. A critic in Columbus, Ohio, called Ford the "best laugh-producing act on [Eva's] bill," regarding him "a capital dancer and clown." As the company toured, Johnny continued to step up, much to Eva's relief. Each was getting something out of the deal. Ford benefited from the high profile afforded him as a member of Eva's team. Eva got an opportunity to catch her breath, avoid overexposure, and downshift on the production of new material. Helpful as it might have been, it was a relationship that probably should have remained purely professional.[6]

In late fall of 1913, Eva and her company arrived in Ann Arbor, Michigan, to play an engagement at the Whitney Theatre. By now, Johnny Ford had grown away from his vaguely hillbilly, clog-dancing past, at least on the outside, and cultivated the look of a dapper dandy with a cane and spats. He liked being surrounded by the glamour of vaudeville's leading lady. For once, he was connected to something bigger than The Four Fords of Covington, Kentucky. As for Eva, "I liked him," she later recalled, though she insisted that their relationship had been, up to that point, strictly professional.

That was not how Johnny Ford saw things.

As Eva approached the theater to prepare for her show one afternoon, Ford, waiting to pounce, stood there twirling his cane, looking "quite the dude," in Eva's recollection, his eyes twinkling with hidden intention. "I've been waiting for you, Eva," Ford said as the cyclonic vaudevillian approached. He pointed to a justice of the peace sign swinging in the breeze across the street. Eva tried to dismiss it as just another one of his amusing pranks. "Very funny," she replied. But though she chuckled, she also discerned a seriousness in his face. Ford grew more persuasive, waxing on about how lonely he was and how much he loved Eva. This time, she bolted for the stage door. Once inside, she tried her best to forget what had just happened by throwing herself into preparations for her afternoon show. As Eva plied herself with makeup and powder, Johnny Ford showed up in the small dressing room and continued to plead his case. Eventually she had to literally push him out the door. But despite her outward protests, something in Eva began to soften—or perhaps loosen. As Johnny Ford performed that night, Eva watched him closely from the wings. His hard sell had begun to sink in. She had to admit, he was clever and handsome. Snapping out of it, though, she still frankly hoped he would forget the whole thing.[7]

He didn't.

At six o'clock that evening, as Eva exited the theater, Ford accosted her and said he had asked the justice of the peace not to close up shop just yet.

"We'll have to hurry," he urged. Eva looked at the man begging her to get married and, in a moment of what can only be called seriously muddled judgment, reflected how "it might be nice after all to have someone around who really cared." He told her once again how much he loved her. Before she had time to reflect further, though, Eva found herself coaxed into the justice's office. They were told to get a license and zipped off to the county clerk, where one was hastily obtained. Events now took on a momentum of their own. Some part of Eva was simply going along for the ride while another was already trying to back out. On their return to the justice of the peace, Eva brooded in a dark corner, blushing, and refusing to go through with it. Twice she stepped toward the altar at Ford's urging, and twice she stepped back. In her heart, Eva Tanguay had no desire to wed Johnny Ford. Finally, Ford looked at his would-be bride and said, "Come Eva, I love you." An uncharacteristic inability to say no overtook the struggling actress. And so she mumbled, "I'll give in, John." The only witnesses were two fellow troupers, Hylda Florian and Edward Sloman, as well as the justice of the peace himself, John D. Thomas, all of whom signed their marriage document. Though there was ample room on it for inscriptions and well-wishes, the space remained blank, the first artifact of a union whose emptiness it reflected. Eva Tanguay had, in her words, made her "first leap into matrimony." The date was November 24, 1913.[8]

Eva returned to her inner sanctum, the place she defended like a tigress from would-be censors and disapproving managers, her dressing room. She burst into tears. "Why had I done such a thing?" she agonized. She had resisted proposals from dozens of other men, many of them more appetizing than the B-level vaudevillian from Kentucky. That night, after word of their elopement had spread, Johnny Ford was met with cries of "Poor John! Poor John!" from the audience as it ribbed him good-naturedly. But Eva wept real tears and wondered why they didn't say, "Poor Eva! Poor Eva!" It must have felt as if the crowd, her favorite ally in life, had deserted her. The wedding dinner was held at a modest local restaurant. On the menu: ham, eggs, and beer.[9]

Not surprisingly, the newly married couple never enjoyed anything approaching a blissful honeymoon period. Three days after the wedding, Eva was already strategizing "a way out of it." Two days after that, it was Johnny Ford who left; it was to be first of many such abandonments. She was probably relieved, but each desertion was painful for Eva, perhaps triggering memories of her father's desertion during her childhood. It also probably left her feeling out of control in her personal life, less confident about how to take care of herself and make crucial decisions.

Eva's primary complaint about her husband was his penchant for drink. Abstinence was crucial to her, she told Ford. Many times he promised to put down the bottle. Sometimes he actually did. But it never lasted long. Ford's first stab at sobriety lasted twenty-four hours. When he drank, he would typically go AWOL, disappearing for days at a time after tormented screaming matches with his bride. But Johnny Ford could not walk away from Eva's sizable purse. Though he would leave her some "ten or fifteen times" over the course of their marriage, by Eva's count, he would always beg her to take him back, usually through pity-soaked letters. The missives nearly always included requests for money as well, which she provided along with demands that he sober up. She sent him to an alcohol rehab, or what passed for it in those days, in New Haven.

Scientific and medical authorities of the day generally agreed, as they do in our own, that alcoholism was a disease that affected not just the drinker but his or her whole family as well, including children, spouses, and siblings. Drunken parents were understood to raise children "weak in body and feeble in mind," according to a 1901 journal article. Professor Karl Pearson, a London academic, gathered data to prove that alcoholism in a family member "ruins the physique and mentality of the offspring." But learned men differed on how to treat the problem and how successful the outcomes might be, leaving plenty of room for charlatanism to flourish. Dr. V. A. Ellsworth of the Washingtonian Home for inebriety in Boston claimed in 1909 to have completely cured between 15 and 20 percent of his alcoholic patients, while Dr. Leslie E. Keeley insisted that his "Gold Cure," based on a "secret formula" free of the atropia, strychnia, aloes, and other antialcohol drugs popular in the era, had "treated and cured" no fewer than 110,000 inebriates. Not surprisingly, a week after his return from the New Haven facility, Johnny Ford was back at the bottle, this time worse than ever. He would soon turn to other drugs, including cocaine, opium, and various preparations in powder and vial.[10]

On Eva's dollar and reputation, the couple soon returned to New York. Perhaps to keep her husband in a calmer frame of mind, the cyclonic queen of vaudeville sold her swanky Morningside Heights duplex and bought a roomy, low-slung ranch-style cottage costing $40,000 (some $900,000 in today's terms) in the exclusive enclave of Sea Gate, Brooklyn. Sea Gate was a ritzy community on the western tip of the Coney Island peninsula, perched on the lapping waves of the ocean. Entry was limited by security gates. Eva bought two cars and a pleasure boat. When her husband complained the vessel wasn't big enough, she bought him another. "Everything was money, money, money," Eva remembered.[11]

There were occasional moments of calm out in Sea Gate, times when the two acted as if they were happy. Perhaps it was a facade they wanted to believe in or show to onlookers. One afternoon, a snooping reporter spied Johnny Ford watering the grass with a garden hose in front of the Sea Gate house. Eva came outside and gently chided her mate, "John-nie." "Yes, darling," he replied. "You're sprinkling the lawn with your Sunday hat on." "Yes, love." "Take it off or I'll kiss you." "I dare you to," replied Ford, probably aware that the press was watching.[12]

To Johnny Ford's delight, and to his wife's nightmarish regret, they formed a couple's act that was touted with great fanfare. In December, the Eva Tanguay Show debuted at the 44th Street Music Hall. It was a lavish spectacle costing $4,700 to produce. When she walked on, Eva was showered with rice from the boxes and addressed as Mrs. Ford by the bandleader. She sang her usual crowd-pleasers. Later in the proceedings, she and Ford danced a tango and a waltz. The Music Hall notched its ticket prices up to $1.50, the highest big-time vaudeville would allow. She and Ford were soon in discussions to costar in a show together, a musical comedy adapted from a French farce, to be produced by the powerful Shubert brothers. Johnny also wrote a tune for Eva's repertoire called "I Was Built for Speed and Not for Comfort." It went:

> I was built for speed and not for comfort,
> Speeding put me where I am right now.
> Some say I exceed the limit fearless,
> And go faster than the law allows.
> I must speed like this to keep on living,
> When I stop you'll know I am dead.
> It sounds strange to hear me state
> I will speed past Hades' gate,
> I was built for speed and not for comfort.

Though the song captured Eva's rush-rush vigor, it did not rise to the top of her playlist. Again, Johnny Ford's talent did not match his ambition. In fact, his biggest coup so far was getting Eva Tanguay to say yes at the altar.[13]

Despite public interest in Johnny and Eva's onstage partnership, their once-promising performances faltered under the flow of liquor. Eva complained that her husband was not only frequently drunk but reliably so every Saturday night. Such a schedule might have been workable for a civilian, but for an entertainer it was a quick ride to the end of the line.

What was more, his addiction appeared to be getting worse. Eva reckoned that over the course of two years, Johnny Ford's alcoholism caused him to miss six months' worth of engagements. One Christmas Eve they had a big show together that featured Ford and Eva dancing together as its highlight. To her dismay, she found her husband drunk, collapsed in a corner of his dressing room. The engagement had to be canceled.[14]

Increasingly, Johnny Ford's behavior became even more erratic, spilling from backstage and home into the glare of the public eye. In April 1914, he was arrested in Schenectady for creating a public disturbance after getting into a tussle with a cabbie over the fare. Bail was posted at twenty-five dollars, but Ford failed to show up at his subsequent trial. That, too, would be a portent of things to come.[15]

At the Euclid Hotel in Toledo, Ohio, Johnny Ford managed to lose a diamond scarfpin, worth a thousand dollars, that Eva had bought him. He had hotel clerks scurry about madly in search of the mislaid item. A local paper deemed it not "a fatal loss, for Eva could earn him a couple of others and a ring thrown in by just one week of her 'I Don't Care' performance." While that was true, it also pointed to the unavoidable fact that Johnny Ford could never match his wife's stellar earning power or even come close. His drunkenness, however, made him unable to hold on to what he earned or contributed to the couple's coffers. In fact, Eva would later testify that her husband had never provided financial support of any kind while they were married.[16]

Under the strain of her husband's behavior, Eva began to regularly lose sleep. According to someone who knew her, she gazed "with her great earnest eyes, deep down under the froth of life, to the dregs beneath—she feels deeply." Many a night, Eva would rise from her bed in Sea Gate, unable to find solace in slumber, grab a flashlight, and saunter around the yard looking for birds savaged by "an old cat" and left to die. When she found the suffering creatures, she would take them inside, rest them on a pillow, and gently pour warm milk down their throats. One night she rescued no fewer than seven injured birds. When they had recuperated, she set them on a branch in her backyard and watched them flutter away. Eva would later compare herself to the stricken birds, but with no one to look after *her*. She had wanted to be taken care of, to be healed, and fed mother's milk. Instead, she had allowed herself to end up with an insolvent drunk who so often disappeared into the night.[17]

In late 1914, Eva and Johnny took another stab at a show featuring both of them. It was a flimsy musical called *Miss Tabasco* in which they played a married couple. Onstage, Eva projected the illusion of "wholesale happiness," an infectious mirth that spilled "in great gobs" over the footlights and into the delighted crowd, according to one reviewer. Ford wrote some "catchy songs" for *Tabasco*. Ironically, or perhaps fittingly, the plot focused on a couple's plan to extract money from a wealthy father-in-law by obtaining a temporary divorce.[18]

But backstage and back home, things continued to deteriorate. The fighting intensified, usually ending only when Ford stormed off in a drunken rage. What bonds there were between the two frayed beyond repair. Lucille Weber, one of Eva's assistants, overheard a heated argument outside the cyclonic star's dressing room one night. Ford demanded money from Eva. "If you don't give it to me, I am through with you for life," he bellowed, his words booming through the door. The request was not unusual, of course, but now Eva could finally muster a "no." Financially dependent on his wife, Johnny Ford fought back by trying to steal some of Eva's spotlight. Playing a vaudeville house in Decatur, Michigan, one night, Ford took one too many encores, propelling Eva into what a local reporter described as "a fit of jealous rage." In challenging his wife's primacy and attention onstage, Johnny Ford knew he was playing with fire.[19]

Their stage partnership was now over, and their marriage, what remained of it, was not far behind. Eva returned to her solo show with a new vigor. In the summer of 1915, she brought out all-new songs, save for "I Don't Care," and a complement of gowns that a theater manager judged "as novel as ever." Eva and her producers were especially pleased with the crowd's reaction to a new number called "Eva, You're All Right." If her husband used and abused her, Eva always had her fans to provide the adoration she hungered for. She had also enjoyed top billing at the Palace, vaudeville's most famous and prestigious venue, in New York City, earlier that year. Even if her marriage was a failing mess, Eva was determined that her career should be quite the opposite.[20]

On August 15, 1915, Johnny Ford left Eva for the last time. He moved into a room at the Princeton Hotel at 116 West Forty-fifth Street in New York City, which he shared with his friend and fellow performer Harry Tighe, a comedian known for what one newspaperman termed a "breezy personality," and who would later direct Buster Keaton movies. With Johnny Ford as his roommate, Tighe found himself in the thankless role of arbitrator between Eva and Ford, which he managed with mixed success. On one occasion, Ford begged Tighe to get Eva to come visit him at the Princeton. Eva relented. When she arrived, she found her husband in his usual state of inebriation. Eva quickly left, though not before shooting

Tighe a withering look. In a letter of apology, Tighe asked Eva's forgiveness and claimed he had no idea Ford had been so liquored up: "I want you to know that had I dreamed John was in that condition I would have been the last person in the world to suggest your going to the Hotel." Tighe, moreover, took full responsibility for the debacle and swore he'd never again play peacemaker. In a vaudeville sketch about a drunken husband and an unhappy wife, it would all have ended happily after twenty minutes of rollicking misadventure. The worst that might have happened: a case of mistaken identity involving a hotel bellboy, his best friend, and a visiting nobleman from Latvia. But that was why people went to vaudeville; reality was scarcely so accommodating. Ford stayed at the Princeton for three months before wandering, without a home base, from gig to gig; letters sent to him at the hotel were returned as undeliverable.[21]

Johnny Ford continued to pick up vaudeville work where he could find it, but stopped asking Eva for money. Effectively if not yet legally single, Eva continued to reassert her artistic viability. In January 1916, she got top billing at the Palace in New York and played there again twice in April. Her pay was down from its Salome-era height of $3,500 to a more modest but certainly comfortable $1,900 a week, or about $39,000 in current terms.[22]

She was successful enough that some predatory businessmen now threatened to release a slapdash movie featuring Eva, which had been filmed back in 1908. The film, titled *Success,* was probably little more than a silent camera trained on one of Eva's vaudeville turns. When she caught wind of the film's release, Eva rushed to get an injunction, telling a judge that "the crude work of seven years ago [captured on film] would be detrimental" if shown today. The movie was never shown to the public. But Eva was reminded of the growing popularity of movies, how their illusory images of projected light were starting to yield bigger money and quicker stardom than the lower-tech, and very human, vaudeville stage she dominated.[23]

THE TURMOIL in Eva's life, her disastrous relationship with the "wanderer," her tortuous marriage, the physical rigors of her stage antics, and the beginnings of a slow but irreversible downturn in her earnings, all triggered an understandable crisis of faith. Peace of mind had always eluded Eva, but now she was determined to grasp some deeper meaning and, moreover, make it well-known to her public.

In mid-1915, not long before Johnny Ford abandoned her for good, Eva publicly professed allegiance to the relatively new religious practice of

Christian Science. A few days before launching a new show at Brooklyn's Orpheum vaudeville theater, she held a press conference. There she promoted not only her new routines but also, and with the same energetic flair, her adherence to Christian Science. Eva declared that she had "embraced" the sect wholeheartedly and now wanted to spread the good word. Impressed, a writer for the *New York Press* observed, "She is not one of the 'halfway' folks about this." The queen of vaudeville, on a kind of zealot's high, even went so far as to say that if given the chance to preach Christian Science every Sunday for the rest of her life, she would happily do it, though only if "people would take [me] seriously." She paused—rare for Eva during a public appearance of any kind—then added: "I'd give up vaudeville for that." To the ears of her managers and handlers, though disinclined as yet to take her conversion too seriously, this was definitely not the Good News.[24]

Eva had actually flirted with Christian Science as early as 1906, at which time it was reported that not only Eva but many of her supporting players were members of the church. It was all part of a trend toward Christian Science that was sweeping the entertainment industry. Nora Bayes, whom Eva had replaced in the Ziegfeld *Follies* of 1909, was a Christian Scientist until her death in 1928, whereupon her body was "buried with the rites of that church." It would be nearly two decades before Bayes's body was moved to Woodlawn Cemetery in Queens so she could lie in eternity by her husband in Jewish burial facility.[25]

Eva described Christian Science as therapeutically useful rather than delving deeply into its theology, identifying it as good for her "disturbed state of mind." While her flirtation with the religion may have comforted Eva, it did not have the same effect on some of those whose livelihoods depended on her. "Her managers were in a panic and feared that if Miss Tanguay lost her 'disturbed state of mind' she would not be just as they billed her—a cyclonic comedienne," reported the *Hartford Courant*. The worry on the part of her promoters and backers, however, turned out to be unfounded, as her drawing power on the latest tour remained strong. As one reporter noted at the time, Eva was "just as able to break a few attendance records as she was before she took up [Christian Science founder Mary Baker] Eddy's teachings." Whatever effect Christian Science may have had on Eva's "disturbed" appeal, it never got the chance to fully do so. Despite the predictable fanfare of her announcement, Eva was hardly a strict adherent. Rather, she took those parts of Christian Science that worked for her and discarded the rest. Eva Tanguay was often full of zeal, but rarely orthodoxy.[26]

Unlike many other Christian Science practitioners, who relied on the faith to cure bodily ills, Eva looked to the religion for relief of anxieties and what today might be termed a mood disorder, such as depression or irritable anxiety. "Probably you know it, I used to be a grouch," she told a reporter shortly after her conversion. "When anything went wrong, I went up in the air. I'm naturally of a nervous temperament and little things used to disturb me. Now not even the big things do." This of course would prove more wishful thinking than reality. But the years of stress, pressure, personal loss and instability, and, most recently, marriage to an abusive alcoholic, led Eva to look for solace where she could find it.[27]

She also felt burdened by the demand to constantly project an upbeat, I-don't-care persona, in part to counteract the swelling reports of her combativeness and unending string of offstage imbroglios. This no doubt added to her psychic strain. Christian Science offered Eva a way out of the spiritual and emotional pain she had known for so long. The creed, she now claimed, had helped her see that her woes were really the result of her own outlook. As she put it, "Now I know that our troubles are only as real as we make them."[28]

Eva sat down with a New York–based journalist and, in a moment of surprising candor, used the interview to vent deeper sorrows:

> I am supposed to be a heedless, foolish, joyous capricious minx...with no more heart than a stone, no more feeling than an electric sign and no more seriousness than a moth....I am supposed to live in a realm of unbounded happiness and be in my daily life the nearest approach to a perpetual laugh. I am supposed to bathe in eternal sunshine and not to have a single care. I am supposed to be so intensely happy that it hurts....Fiction—all fiction....Apart from health, my life is not only wretched but unsatisfactory, not only unsatisfactory but dreary, not only dreary but lacking in a hundred emotions which make me all the time wish I were some other body....I never go a day without a good, old-fashioned cry, the kind that comes when troubles have piled up so high you just can't get over them, the kind that women understand and that men call silly blubbering.

Her many "creature comforts," Eva claimed, did not bring happiness. Her holy grail was simpler, yet more elusive: "I long for real happiness." It was a remarkable admission, a crack in the public facade of a stage personality known for her toughness and nonchalance. She was hitting an aching spot in the depth of her being that she could no longer be troubled to hide. Eva called her life "wretched," all woe "apart from [my] health." In Eva's frank lament there was nothing to spin.[29]

Christian Science offered hope to many spiritually and emotionally hungry souls in Eva Tanguay's heyday. Of particular appeal to Eva must have been the fact that the movement had been started by another remarkable, complicated, and ultimately very successful woman, Mary Baker Eddy. Though she borrowed some of her teachings from the work of the New England faith healer Phineas Quimby, Mary Baker Eddy leavened Quimby's ideas with her own, which addressed the worries of a nation in upheaval after the Civil War. In particular, the middle and upper classes were anxious over changes in social stature, opportunities for success, and emergent notions of what constituted personal satisfaction. Middle-class white women in particular were caught up in a maelstrom of shifting expectations and opportunities. Thus, what some saw as the decidedly maternal, feminine ethos of Christian Science proved, for them in particular, a huge draw over the patriarchy of traditional Christianity. It was not that Christian Science sought specific political or social goals for women, for to do so would have been to surrender its transcendent qualities. Rather, for the first time, a woman's voice was heard resounding from the pulpit and gathering a legion of the faithful.[30]

It is impossible to separate Mary Baker Eddy from the religion she started, which is pretty much how Eddy wanted it. Her charisma and personality informed it, both to the faith's advantage and detriment. While she was in many ways completely different from Eva, it is tempting not to notice similarities as well. It is also worth wondering what Eva Tanguay, the leading lady of vaudeville, might have seen in the alluring figure of Mary Baker Eddy, matriarch of the Christian Science Church. Today celebrities have Oprah, Dr. Phil (or Dr. Drew), and Deepak Chopra. In Eva's day, the options were no less interesting. In January 1888, Mary Baker Eddy addressed Chicago's Central Music Hall, which was packed to the rafters with four thousand attendees, mostly middle-class white women. After holding forth on her belief that sickness and death were but illusions, she was rushed by a multitude of fans who showered her with affection. It has been said that Mary Baker Eddy played to a broad audience for maximum appeal. If it had been Eva—and but for the subject matter, it could have been that day—the crowd would have insisted on an encore of "I Don't Care."[31]

Christian Science offered Eva Tanguay and other women of the late nineteenth and early twentieth centuries an empowering and unconventional view of womanhood. In a society that had come to see women as sickly, overemotional, and incapable of being their own agents in society, Eddy's creed offered "an alternative" to the dominant cultural view of [middle-class] "women as essentially faulty, uterus-driven bodies," according to the cultural critic and historian Alison Piepmeier. Rather than viewing themselves as passive objects of medicine, sickness, and bodily investigation, women equipped with Christian Science could begin to envision different possibilities for their lives. To many female theatergoers, Eva Tanguay similarly offered an alternate and appealing view of womanhood.[32]

Mary Baker was born July 16, 1821, on a "large, neat, well kept farm" belonging to "a much respected New England family," according to an 1899 article in *The New England Magazine*. The Bakers lived in the small, rural town of Bow, New Hampshire, in a house originally belonging to Mary's grandfather, Joseph, who had come from England with his wife, Marion McNeil, shortly before the American Revolution. Mary's own parents, Elizabeth Duncan and Mark Baker were of stout-hearted, deeply principled, Congregationalist, Yankee stock. Her father was driven, moody, and tyrannical, while Mrs. Baker was passive and meek—"wraithlike" by one account—seeming almost to disappear into the background of daily life. Between the two role models, young Mary felt she had little choice.[33]

Mary was the youngest of six. She was, in her youth, described as "delicate and beautiful," though such adjectives suggest the aesthetics of an age when female timidity equaled attractiveness. Adult pictures of Mary Baker Eddy put one in mind of certain prominent nineteenth-century men—perhaps presidents Franklin Pierce or James Knox Polk—with curls carefully packed atop a stolid, mannish face. She was bright, a good student, one who grasped academic subjects almost by instinct with little need of study. Early on in her life, Mary Baker understood the idea that a successful movement must not limit itself to the educated elite or to those of arcane scholarship. For Eva Tanguay, this was another lure of Christian Science. Growing up, Eva did not receive much in the way of formal schooling, a gap she never filled. Her performing career had cut short her academic life. As an adult, she showed little interest in book learning or conventional intellectual pursuits. "No intellectual proficiency is required," wrote Mary Baker Eddy in *Science and Health,* the central text of Christian Science. Here was a club that accepted people looking for comfort and peace. Those wishing to debate fine points of theology were better off looking elsewhere.[34]

When she was twenty-three, Mary Baker married Colonel George Washington Glover and followed her husband to his South Carolina home. There she gave birth to George, the only biological child she would ever have. Six months later, the colonel succumbed to yellow fever.[35]

A decade after Glover's death, Mary married Daniel Patterson, a dentist. Although they remained married for two decades, the union became emotionally null and void early on. In this regard, it resembled Eva's ill-fated marriage to Johnny Ford. Mary did not have children with Patterson, but left her son, George, increasingly in his care. After 1856, she would have little to do with her offspring. This again supplied a curious and painful parallel between the lives of the founder of Christian Science and the cyclonic wonder of vaudeville, who by now had only occasional contact with Florence "Flossie" Tanguay.[36]

Over the years, Mary had suffered from a number of illnesses and maladies. The specifics of her ailments are not always clear from the various accounts of her life, but it seems she was dogged by chronic "dyspepsia," muscular and skeletal "weakness," and a "delicate constitution." Doctors and cures were sought, but none proved enduring. Then, in 1862 at the age of forty-one, Mary met a man who would become the most influential figure in her life after her father. His name was Phineas Quimby, and he was a so-called mental healer, born in 1802 in Lebanon, New Hampshire. Quimby triggered a profound religious awakening in Mary, his faith-healing beliefs impressing on her his own conviction that curing disease had little to do with medication or surgery. To be sure, this would become the central philosophy of Christian Science, not merely the benefit it offered but the keystone of its theology.[37]

Phineas Quimby died in 1866. That same year Mary herself sustained a life-threatening injury. She had slipped on a patch of ice on her way to a Friday-night missionary meeting in the growing industrial town of Lynn, Massachusetts, a mill town much like Holyoke to the west. The story goes that during her recovery Mary summoned what strength she had and undertook deep and constant prayer, Bible in hand. So immediate and full was her restoration that a member of her household was said to have fainted forthwith. Mary later claimed that she had pulled through only by resorting to the "curative powers of Scripture and Christ." A local doctor, however, attributed her recovery to two weeks of bed rest and a ready supply of morphine.[38]

Mary began teaching faith healing a few years later. Her curriculum, which debuted in 1870, drew heavily from Quimby. With a handful of students, who paid one hundred dollars each, in addition to promising to tithe 10 percent of their future income as practitioners, she was under way. She told one of her novices that she would "one day establish a great religion," and declared, "You will live to hear the church-bells ring out my birthday."[39]

Mary Baker became Mary Baker Eddy in 1877 when she married a quiet, unexciting sewing-machine salesman named Asa Gilbert Eddy. He had come to her with a heart condition, been healed, and hastily took up the study of her spiritual arts. By 1882, he was dead. But bigger matters were afoot. For during this time, Eddy was busy writing and refining what would become the foundational text of Christian Science, *Science and Health*. One of the first outside reviewers of *Science and Health,* which was published by Eddy's students in 1875, felt "none but a fool or a woman would have written this book," and "that it was safe enough as no one would ever read it." The prediction turns out to have been off the mark. The church, which had but twenty-six members in 1879, boasted some 86,000 by 1906 and reached 202,000 two decades later. In the years since its first publication, the book has sold some 10 million copies, according to the Christian Science Church.[40]

Science and Health is a lengthy, passionate work. At some points, it is repetitive and scolding. At others, it is an insightful, inspired argument for the unreliability of our worldly perceptions. In the text, Eddy argues— or rather insists—that "the discords of corporeal sense must yield to the harmony of the spiritual sense." In order to overcome suffering, one must not plead, beg, or negotiate with God for comfort and healing. Rather, one must cast off the illusion of "mortal mind" and instead convene with the eternal, that which is of God, and is therefore unshakeable and unerring and knows only of perfection. For while "human experiences show the falsity of all material things," the "divine Mind cannot suffer." To the degree that individuals could establish contact with the divine "Mind" rather than succumb to the falsities of the flesh, they could enjoy the way of health and virtue instead of illness and sin. "All reality is in God and His creation, harmonious and eternal," exhorted Eddy in *Science and Health*. "Therefore the only reality of sin, sickness, or death is the awful fact that unrealities seem real to human, erring belief, until God strips off their disguise." In other words, it is our erroneous, human *belief* in disease that makes us sick. If we accept this for the fearful illusion it is, we will not suffer illness.[41]

Science and Health also found its author revering the "Antediluvians," whom she understood to have lived longer, healthier lives. "Damp atmosphere and freezing snow empurpled the plump cheeks of our ancestors," wrote Eddy, envisioning a race of hearty prehistoric tribesmen, "but they never indulged in the refinement of inflamed bronchial tubes." Jesus himself "took no drugs to allay inflammation. He did not depend upon food or pure air to resuscitate wasted energies. He did not require the skill of a surgeon to heal the torn palms and bind up the wounded side and lacerated feet." There is in such prose a reprimand of the ailing and increasingly doctor-reliant middle classes of her time.[42]

Along with this rejection of belief in disease came, quite logically, the rejection of contemporary Western medicine. To Mary Baker Eddy, doctors were "inquisitive modern Eves," and their patients "unmanly Adams" who followed them blindly. Surgeon and physician, convinced by their training that "matter forms its own conditions and renders them fatal at certain points," were always, at some level, fearing the worst. Because of this, their ministrations were necessarily "tentative." That was why they so often lost patients to injury and disease. One of the appeals of Christian Science, particularly for white middle-class women, was that it seemed a viable "alternative to ineffectual and sometimes brutal medical treatment," in the words of the historian Beryl Satter. The idea that her body and destiny could be in her hands—or at least not in the hands of brutish, disinterested men—held great appeal for Eva Tanguay.[43]

Of course, as with many things in her life other than her profession, Eva's relationship with Christian Science was anything but unflinching and true. She reached out to it in times of spiritual or physical need as she did with other traditions of belief. Yet she also held it lightly, discarding it when her desires beckoned elsewhere. Enjoying a temporary respite from the first of what would turn out to be serious long-term eye problems, she credited "a bit of Christian Science and a lot of patience." In fact, according to Judy Huenneke, a researcher at the church's Mary Baker Eddy Library for the Betterment of Humanity, Eva was never an official member of the Mother Church, as it is sometimes called. Eva's solutions to the many painful and tragic obstacles life had thrown at her, the disorders of body and mind that were their substance and cause, were rarely straightforward. Her coping strategy was always to seek whatever mix of antidotes and emotional support got her through the day, from one music hall to another, and when there were no more music halls to play, from one fantasy to the next.[44]

ALTHOUGH JOHNNY FORD had abandoned Eva for good in their Sea Gate, Brooklyn, home in August 1915, and checked into the Princeton Hotel on West Forty-fifth Street in the city's theatrical epicenter, they remained legally married for two more years. By the fall of 1917, Eva could take it no more. On October 22, 1917, Eva Tanguay's attorney, Edward J. Ader, submitted on her behalf a bill for divorce with the Circuit Court of Cook County (Illinois). The filing, peculiar for a woman who had been living in Manhattan and Brooklyn, listed Eva's home as the Hotel Sherman in Chicago. She claimed the hotel was the closest thing she had to a permanent residence over the past twelve months, which, given her hectic touring schedule, was conceivable if not exactly true. In choosing Chicago's Hotel Sherman, Eva may have been following the lead of Sophie Tucker, her onetime rival, now peer. Tucker had resided at the Sherman in 1913 with her husband-to-be, Frank Westphal. More important, by 1917 Chicago was emerging as the divorce capital of the United States. Other women in entertainment would use Chicago similarly, notably Fanny Brice, who split from her ne'er-do-well husband, Jules "Nicky" Arnstein, in 1927.[45]

Stating that she had been "a true, faithful and affectionate wife," Eva's petition to the Cook County court argued that her husband had "absented himself from [her] without any reasonable or just cause therefor, for the space of two years and upwards." (Sophie Tucker would make an almost identical plea in her Chicago-based divorce suit, in 1920.) She asked to be granted a permanent divorce and to be legally permitted to resume her maiden name. Hearings were scheduled in the court of Judge David M. Brothers. From Eva's perspective, things were going well, largely for two reasons. First, her attorney Ader lined up a claque of sympathetic witnesses who said, truthfully or not, that Eva had been a good wife, and Johnny Ford a miserable, drunken money hound. Second, and perhaps more important, Ford failed to show up for the proceeding. Classified ads had been placed to notify the defendant but to no avail. This was classic Johnny Ford. The man who had decided not to show up in court after posting bail following a taxicab ruckus in Schenectady now neglected to show up for his own divorce hearings. By sheer coincidence, Ford had bumped into Ader on a Manhattan street in September 1917, just a month earlier. Ader explained that he was in a hurry and made an appointment for Ford to see him at his office the next morning. Not surprisingly, Ford "wholly failed to keep said appointment," according to Ader, who was probably relieved.[46]

On December 19, 1917, Eva got her wish. Judge Brothers, no doubt peeved at Ford's no-shows, found him guilty of "wilfully deserting and absenting himself from the Complainant without any reasonable or just cause thereof, for a period of more than two years continuously." The nightmare of a rash marriage to an abusive, financially draining drunk was over—almost.[47]

Although absent from his marriage, Johnny Ford had not been entirely idle after fleeing Eva. He teamed up with Mayme Gehrue for a short tour; it was rumored he would marry her once things with the cyclonic comedienne were finished, though Ford denied it. He took a one-man singing act focusing on patriotic themes on the vaudeville circuits. He even teamed up with Vera Houghton for a musical comedy routine featuring songs he had written and arranged himself. But in 1918, with the ink barely dry on the divorce papers, Ford and his attorney, Leon A. Berezniak, started making trouble for Eva.[48]

In particular, Ford alleged that Eva had had no grounds to sue for divorce. She had not, he claimed, conducted herself as a "true, faithful, affectionate wife," nor had he, as she had charged, absented himself from August 15, 1915, onward. Moreover, his countersuit argued, she had no standing to execute her divorce in the state of Illinois because she had not lived there for the legally requisite one year prior to initiating proceedings. Eva Tanguay had been living in Sea Gate all along—or so claimed Johnny Ford in a desperate last-ditch ploy.[49]

Eva's attorney immediately saw Ford's countersuit for what it was: pure harassment, based not on fact but on a desire for revenge and probably a financial settlement of some sort. It was, in other words, an ugly mix of slander and blackmail. Ader fired back unflinchingly and immediately. He responded to the court that Ford was now questioning Eva's residence claims and charges of absenteeism purely "for the purpose of defaming the character and besmirching the reputation of [Eva] and bringing her into public disrepute, notoriety and shame." Responding to Ford's legal maneuver, which sought only to "annoy, injure and harass" her, Eva stated for the record that two "agents" acting on her ex-husband's behalf had approached her and said he would drop the whole thing, "publicity avoided," if she would deliver a "payment of money" to him. Eva explained to the court that Johnny Ford was not interested in "securing a divorce which he already has" but in "obtaining money if possible." Ford had sunk to a new if predictable low. Furthermore, she argued, the trade paper *Variety* had covered news of her various divorce filings, and Ford, a regular reader, must have seen it there. Hearing both sides, Judge Brothers found Johnny Ford's counterclaims absurd. Eva's legal counsel had done everything required to notify Johnny Ford, from letters that were returned unopened to classified ads in legal newspapers (designed to get Ford's lawyer's attention). Of course, there had also been news of the divorce in the pages of *Variety* and other theatrical trades. Saying he had never heard about it or been given the opportunity to respond was patently absurd. Johnny Ford had been offered his day in court. He had just failed to show up for it.[50]

Ford did eventually get a financial offer from Eva Tanguay, but it was not quite what he was looking for, and it was way too late. In a will drawn up six years later, in 1924, Eva included a bequest for her ex-husband. The amount: five dollars. Given Eva's financial state at the time of her death many years after that, her ex-husband would have been lucky to get five cents. But at the time it was a final slap in the face. Johnny Ford died at age eighty-one in Hot Springs, Arkansas on March 12, 1963. His obituary remembered him, not entirely correctly, as one of the Four Fords. But the onetime wooden-shoe dancer's greatest fame came not from his two-a-day show but from five turbulent years as the husband of Mrs. Eva Ford, way back in the great old days of vaudeville.[51]

10

❧

The Wild Girl

S HER MARRIAGE skidded to an official end, Eva breathed a sigh of relief. She was finally rid of the abusive drunk who was reliable only when it came to hitting her up for cash. To be sure, she had fallen into the mess of her own accord, even though she had never much fancied the idea of a mate for life, never mind one like Johnny Ford. The whole thing left her drained, financially and spiritually. Somehow, a marriage she had never wanted to be in held her captive for five years, from ambivalent vows to messy divorce. During that time, the landscape of popular culture had changed. Eva was still the top star of vaudeville. But it was unclear how long vaudeville itself could withstand the competition from the film industry, a new entertainment that once was considered trifling at best, worthy only of being used to chase crowds from the house at the end of a variety bill. Yet the movies had grown and changed, like a once-sickly newborn becoming a rambunctious teen.[1]

For her part, Eva soldiered on as if nothing had shifted. There was not much else she could do. She headlined the prestigious Palace in New York on March 4, 1918, and again a week later, on March 11. She kicked off her onstage turn with "If They Give Us a Lovingless Day," donned her suit of pennies, and then, "just to show us that the high cost of loving has not effected [sic] her any," in one observer's words, switched to a costume composed entirely of stitched-together one dollar bills for her second number. Responding to the mood of a nation increasingly concerned with Europe's terrible war—thousands of U.S. soldiers would arrive in Europe that summer—she dressed as a navy ship and sang "If

They'd Only Send Eva Tanguay Over There." She then threw on a sailor's uniform and sang "If I Were a Boy You Bet I'd Belong in the Navy" and "Please Don't Forget Me When I'm Gone." Another quick change, and she belted out the "Marseillaise," though many Frenchmen would have cringed at her rendition. Then, after a lengthy wait and just as the crowd grew fidgety, she delivered a racy number called "There's Be a Hot Time for the Old Boys When the Young Men Are Away," later borrowed by Mae West. Sixteen minutes after she came onstage at the Palace, she went off, breathless. The crowd applauded enthusiastically. But Eva could not offer the encores they begged for. She claimed a "sudden illness," when in fact she simply did not have the raucous energy of former days. The Kane Brothers finished out the night with impressive feats of gymnastic balance. Approaching forty, Eva was increasingly unable to deny the fact that cyclonic performing was better suited to the young. And vaudeville in general, with its two to four shows a day, week after week, was more demanding than motion pictures.[2]

As patriotic fever spread, Eva added war-related themes to her publicity campaign. "Eva Tanguay Is to the Vaudeville Stage What a 42-Centimeter Gun Is to the German Army," read one of her promotional ads.[3] The gambit worked. Harry P. Harrison, the manager of the International Lyceum Association, an organization initially founded in 1903 to develop free lecture series on a variety of subjects, requested Eva's participation in the ILA's Smileage campaign. This was a sort of ancestor to the USO, which provides entertainment and morale-boosting efforts for military troops abroad. In a letter to Edward J. Ader, the attorney who had helped Eva through her tempestuous divorce, Harrison suggested, "She could stage all of her old time songs—wear her striking gowns, and thus be doing her part toward winning the ultimate victory." Eva seems to have proven less a committed patriot than an adept interpreter of timely topics; there is no evidence she ever took part in the Smileage project.[4]

By the time the armistice was signed in November 1918, entertainment in the United States had changed drastically compared to the heady days of a decade or so earlier when Eva had savored her first taste of superstardom. Though vaudeville still loomed large, movies were by now the most popular form of entertainment in cities. Originally movies were not projected but were viewed through the lens of an apparatus known as a Kinetoscope, which showed short film loops of dancers, boxers, and other human subjects in motion. The first Kinetoscope parlor opened in New York City on April 14, 1894, at 1155 Broadway, in a former shoe shop.[5]

Though successful at first, largely because of its novelty, interest in the one-viewer-at-a-time Kinetoscope soon waned. By 1896, however, the technology for projected motion pictures had been developed. A device known as the Vitascope debuted at Koster & Bial's Music Hall, a vaudeville and burlesque venue in New York, on April 23, 1896. Though it was promoted as Thomas Edison's "Latest Marvel," the Vitascope had in fact been invented by C. Francis Jenkins and Thomas Armat of Washington, DC. Jenkins and Armat sold their interest in the Vitascope to two businessmen, Norman C. Raff and Frank R. Gammon, who in turn made a deal with Edison. Edison agreed that his organization would supply Raff and Gammon with movies and manufacture Vitascope machines in return for his name going on the device, plus a financial cut. At the end of June that same year, the rival Lumière brothers, who had already demonstrated an all-in-one movie camera and projector in Lyons, France, debuted their movie shows at Keith's Union Square Theatre to much fanfare.[6]

For the first ten years of its existence, the most popular venue for viewing projected motion pictures was the vaudeville theater. A cluster of short motion pictures, usually depicting interesting visuals or newsworthy images of the day, fit well into vaudeville's modular, nonnarrative structure, where visual acts such as magic-lantern displays and gymnastic feats were popular. In 1902–1903, narratives, especially short comedies, began to play an increasingly important role in the film programs featured in vaudeville. Perhaps the most famous and influential narrative (that is, fictional, cause-and-effect-driven) movies of the period were Georges Méliès's *A Trip to the Moon* (1902) and Edwin S. Porter's *The Great Train Robbery* (1903), both of which used the new medium's ability to create impressive, illusionistic special effects.[7]

By 1908, however, the movies had largely graduated from vaudeville. With the remarkable upsurge in their popularity, films increasingly needed to find a home of their own. What emerged to house them were small, cheap, storefront theaters called nickelodeons. They were a far cry from the elegant movie palaces of Hollywood's golden age and were often cited (not unreasonably) as firetraps. For a nickel or less, you could see a program of short movies, usually a mixture of comedies and nonfiction newsreels or demonstration films, accompanied by slides and a pianist who sometimes led sing-alongs. As early as May 1907, it was estimated that some three thousand nickelodeons were in operation in the United States. Urban diversion-seekers now had an abundance of low- or modestly priced options to meet their entertainment needs, which also included burlesque and cheap, so-called small-time vaudeville circuits. Little wonder that Florenz Ziegfeld decided to one-up big-time Keith vaudeville with his *Follies,* whose glamour and production values gave an exciting option to those well-heeled men and women in U.S. cities who would not dare set foot in a nickelodeon.[8]

With the amazing rise in popularity of the movies, thanks in part to the nickelodeon, the need for a ready supply of new films each week to keep audiences coming back rose to a fever pitch. To meet that heightened demand, film producers shifted away from the nonfiction, newsreel-type subjects they had concentrated on earlier and began making fictional narratives. These could be much more easily mass-produced by reusing the same actors, costumes, and settings, and, in many cases, even the same story lines.[9]

Nickelodeon attendance soared. In 1910, between 25 million and 35 million people visited a nickelodeon *each week* in the United States, bringing in gross receipts of $91 million. But much as Tony Pastor, B. F. Keith, and E. F. Albee had done with vaudeville, moviemaker and exhibitors sought to extend their trade to the more economically reliable middle classes, who would also add an element of cultural respectability to their enterprise. Moving away from cheap, if thrilling or hilarious, shorts, moviemakers began to producer longer films, many based on culturally respected works of literature, by Zola, Poe, Dumas, Hugo, and others. If filmmakers and venue owners wanted a higher class of individual to pay a heftier admission for a longer movie, they could not expect the uncomfortable wooden seats and unventilated stuffiness of the nickelodeon to suffice. In place of the repurposed storefronts that had been used up to then, movie theaters were increasingly built afresh, designed for comfort and safety to attract the middle classes. What began to emerge were capacious, carefully designed cinemas showing programs of films usually based around a multireel feature, which had come to be seen as an artistic rather than a purely commercial product. By 1915, so-called feature movies were the norm. D. W. Griffith's *Birth of a Nation,* in the words of film historian Tino Balio, "proved the clincher." Opening at New York's upscale Liberty Theater on March 3, 1915, *Nation* ran forty-four consecutive weeks. Audience members were charged a two-dollar admission, and the movie had a running time of over three hours. There were reserved seats, orchestral accompaniment, and souvenir programs. As a profitable, large-scale commercial and aesthetic enterprise, the movies had definitely arrived.[10]

In this context, it was not surprising that Eva began to consider dabbling in pictures. Equally unsurprising, she was ambivalent from the start. At some level she understood that her particular talents, based on a direct emotional connection to a live audience in front of her, would not lend themselves to the new medium—not to mention that her shrieking, warbling, and manic back talk would all be lost in a silent film. In a sense, Eva was the last great performer of live entertainment before film's arrival as a giant competitor. Historically, it is kind of an honor to serve as the epitaph for a genre. At the time, it cast a chill that Eva could not shake. The monopoly of the live player was over. Those who played in person now had to vie for the attention of a public increasingly interested in the technology of motion pictures and, in the years to come, sound recordings, radio, and eventually television. (Had she been born a bit later, it is not unthinkable that Eva's talents could have been conveyed on TV.) It was a pill that Eva and her vaudeville peers would have to swallow. For Eva, though, unused to sharing the spotlight with other artists much less other technologies of entertainment, it was a pill that would never really go down.

In 1916, the year after *Birth of a Nation* helped transform the expectations of the moviegoing public, Eva shot a picture called *Energetic Eva,* according to records kept by the American Film Institute. There are no extant prints of *Energetic Eva,* and AFI records cannot confirm that the picture was ever released in theaters. In all likelihood, it was a cinematic version of Eva's vaudeville routines. The movie was directed by Joseph Smiley, who would later gain renown for his star turn in Thornton Wilder's classic play *The Skin of Our Teeth.*[11]

It was not until the following year that Eva Tanguay appeared in her first and only feature movie. *The Wild Girl,* released in October 1917 by Selznick Pictures and produced by Harry Weber, one of Eva's many theatrical agents over the years, was an odd mix of pastoral romance and, as the title suggests, energetic Tanguay high jinks. Yet the picture so completely removed Eva from the milieu that had nurtured her stardom— the vaudeville stage—that it's hard to figure out the logic behind the decision to cast her in the picture. A more logical choice for Eva's first starring role in film might have been, say, as a hardworking vaudevillian making her way to the top. But perhaps realizing what an inherent departure the movies would be for her, Eva chose *The Wild Girl,* whose story and setting would force the cyclonic comedienne to depart from the very things she did so well. It was an experiment.

The Wild Girl—at least the sole remaining print, owned by the Museum of Modern Art in New York City—begins with a bit of footage unrelated to the rest of the movie. In the opening, Eva shows off some of her famous, lively costumes after a curtain bearing her initials parts. They are amusing, overblown outfits made of flags, feathers, and glitter. One is little more than a large, fanlike veil covering her midsection, no doubt a nod to her Salome turn. This section of film is either a vestigial shred of *Energetic Eva* or something that film historians might refer to as a spectacle of the "cinema of attractions," an early movie style that prized pure visual delight and optical engagement over story line and character. Possibly it was both. Although interesting, the silent-film capture of Eva parading about in her lively vaudeville garb already heralds the failure of what is to follow, never mind that it had no relation to the plot. Eva clearly seems inhibited and framed by a medium she was never meant to conquer. It somehow resembles a lion taken from the plains of Africa and forced to saunter back and forth in a cage. Eva's stage act, a vital connection between a vibrant woman and a hungry crowd, had become a mere shadow on the wall.[12]

The plot of *The Wild Girl* goes something like this: a baby girl is abandoned at a Gypsy camp with a note explaining that when she turns

Figure 14. Production still from *The Wild Girl* (1917).
The 1917 Selznick Pictures release *The Wild Girl* was Eva's only serious attempt to perform on the silver screen. It failed. She was too perfectly suited for the immediate and vital vaudeville stage.
(Courtesy of the Academy of Motion Picture Arts and Sciences.)

. . . .

eighteen, she is to inherit a Virginia estate. For some unexplained reason—probably to dissuade pretenders to her inheritance—this causes the tribe's chief to rear her as a boy. Named Firefly, she comes of age apparently unaware of her true sex until the chief's son discovers it and demands her hand in marriage. Firefly flees and, in exile, meets a crusading young journalist named Donald MacDonald, a man whose investigative skills may not be terribly keen after all, since he hires her as an errand boy. A series of misadventures involving the scheming Gypsies who want Firefly's inheritance ultimately fails to get in the way of her final, happy union with MacDonald—who now gets that this shapely, prancing Gypsy is in fact a *she*. Sprinkled throughout are scenes of Eva frolicking in scanty costumes, prancing lightheartedly in the countryside, and otherwise flouting the strictures of a suffocating society.

Perhaps as a live vaudeville act with plenty of singing and dancing *The Wild Girl* would have worked. At five reels (about 107 minutes if shown at moderate speed, though it could have been projected faster since there was no standard projection rate in the silent era), however, it exceeded even the charitable limits of silent-film light melodrama. Critics immediately noticed the miscasting of its title character. "Those persons who have long been familiar with that dynamite personality of the vaudeville circuits, Eva Tanguay, will be surprised to find an entirely new Eva when they see her in 'The Wild Girl.'...For the Eva of 'I don't care' fame is lost among the hundred Evas who play the central character in 'The Wild Girl.'" So wrote *The Moving Picture World*. Eva's firefly indeed cavorted about a sylvan countryside, the very opposite of the urban jungle whose culture she knew so well.[13]

Though Eva was *The Wild Girl*'s raison d'être, the picture also owed a great debt to its director, Howard Estabrook. Eva instinctively knew how to go on before a live crowd. But film was a different matter. She needed coaxing and coaching in this newfangled, indirect medium. Howard Estabrook was deemed the man to provide it. Born Howard Bolles in Detroit on July 11, 1884, his father was a prominent industrialist, president of the respectable Bolles Iron and Wire Works. Howard fled to New York City where the big-name producer Charles Frohman took the lad under his wing. In time, Estabrook enjoyed success as an actor in Clyde Fitch's *The Straight Road,* a popular stage version of *Little Women* (he played Laurie), and in David Belasco's production of *The Vanishing Bride,* among others. With the backing of Eva Tanguay's onetime love interest, the show business executive Edward Darling, Estabrook trimmed his famous legitimate roles down to vaudeville size. From there he made the leap to film, unlike so many of his more successful vaudeville brethren, going on to star in the hit movies *Officer 666, Four Feathers, The Closing Net,* and others throughout the 1910s.[14]

One reason why Howard Estabrook was chosen to direct *The Wild Girl* was his belief in movies as, ultimately, escapist entertainment rather than high art. Vaudeville, for all its pretensions to respectability, never sought to be art. "We live in a world of realism, all too sordid and colorless, and the motion picture provides the realm of romance by means of which we can escape from it," Estabrook told a reporter for *Hollywood Filmograph* magazine. Movies, in his view, had to appeal to the "love of fairy lore, of make believe," which, in his view, "resides in every normal person." Moviegoers went to the theater to indulge these innate leanings, and to see a story in which "good is rewarded and evil is punished." Despite the feelings of some of his peers in the movie industry, he did not feel the need to base film on works of high literary and intellectual value. Philosophically, he was a good match for the queen of vaudeville.[15]

The Wild Girl enjoyed only modest success—enough to make Eva ask various studios for a ten-thousand-dollar-a-week, three-year contract, but not enough to make any of them actually give it to her. Decision makers in the young film industry had begun to realize that movies did not necessarily require the same talents as the live stage. Those who made the jump—whether actor, writer, or producer—had to comprehend the new aesthetic demands of the cinema. It was clear from *The Wild Girl* that Eva Tanguay did not. Some have defended Eva Tanguay and other lady vaudevillians who did not flourish onscreen by pointing out that the Hollywood studio system gave these women less room to take risks and spread their wings creatively. Within its more tightly controlled, vertically integrated industrial system, the film companies had no place for Eva "and other New Women of the stage to explore their talents and expose their audacity," in the words of the cultural historian Susan A. Glenn. Women in the early movies owed a great debt to Eva Tanguay. But they had to deploy different talents in different ways. In some sense, the Tanguay energy would return more fully with the rise of variety and sitcom television, where weekly output and audience demand for character distantly mirrored the creative conditions of vaudeville.[16]

The same year as *The Wild Girl*'s release, Eva tried her luck in a strange stage production that attempted to combine elements of motion pictures with live stage performance. *Young Mrs. Sanford,* a "playlet" by Edward Elsner, was described as a "flash drama" by the press. It appeared at the famed Palace vaudeville theater. Making use of gauze, lighting effects, and projected captions, *Sanford* was devised to "suggest the look of a motion picture." Shadows and silhouettes replaced actors in certain moments. In trying to capture both live performance and the motion picture, *Young Mrs. Sanford* merely indicated the existential gulf between the two. The audience did not take to the play's "movie-like melodrama," according to one review, with its facsimile of film edits and camera angles. Eva, on the other hand, was regarded as "undiminished." But she was still out of her depth. She had not made the successful journey to the other shore, which now teemed with new stars.[17]

Nearly two decades after *The Wild Girl*'s release, the social critic Walter Benjamin famously argued that in the age of "mechanical reproduction," works of art would lose their "aura"—that is, their connection to a particular time, place, and creator. As for the actor, he or she now played for the camera. "This permits the audience to take the position of a critic, without experiencing any personal contact with the actor," argued Benjamin. This was hardly Eva Tanguay's strong suit—an entertainment lacking vital, personal contact—and she knew it. In a sense, the fate of *The Wild Girl* indicates that Eva occupied a fault line in the history of pop culture. As it split, Eva remained on the far side. Her influence and spirit stayed alive, but not so her image. Glenn has written that Eva Tanguay "looked backward to the grotesquerie of turn-of-the-century musical comedy and forward to a new era of jokes about women told from a female point of view." Maybe. But Eva herself could not make the leap necessary to reemerge as a spectral motion-picture star.[18]

Following *The Wild Girl* and Eva's unsuccessful bid to join the Hollywood crowd, Eva's career seemed to be slowing down. She turned forty on August 1, 1918. The years of demanding tours and vigorous stage antics and had begun to take their toll, while Eva's fluctuating weight and sagging facial features were making it harder and harder to put over "I Don't Care," a number that to many fans represented heedless eternal youth.

To demonstrate that she was still as glitteringly successful as ever, Eva made a well-publicized trip to western Massachusetts in 1919, the centerpiece of which involved her driving a brand-new car up to her brother Mark's front door and leaving it there. The press loved it. "It was a reminder of the good old days when they used to swap kicks and punches in a regularly brotherly-sisterly way," wrote the Holyoke paper, sentimentally recalling a past that never was. "She may be crazy, but her heart is located right and working overtime," concluded the article. But Eva was in transition: from headlining star to mistress of a fading form; from able-bodied to ailing; and from New York star to Californian newcomer. She exchanged the occasional letter with her putative niece, Flossie, now Florence Tanguay Dufresne since marrying Joe Dufresne, who, like Eva, could trace his roots to French Canada. But Eva's contact with Florence began to diminish and her ties to the region where she first took to the stage as a girl grew increasingly attenuated. In what must have been a heartbreaking observation for Eva, the daughter of an alcoholic, Florence had found a husband who drank, nursed a somber, melancholy outlook, and "cussed a lot," according to his grandson Dan Johansson, who speculates that Joe Dufresne was emotionally if not physically abusive to his wife. According to Johansson, Eva did not consider Joe Dufresne to be "quality goods." But there was little she could do. In her hometown, Eva could never fully escape suspicions that she had given birth to an illegitimate daughter and then abandoned her. By all accounts, Florence remained "nurturing, fun, [and] bubbly." She and her husband moved to a farm in Plainfield, Massachusetts, where she rented out rooms to aging bachelors and toiled over a half-wood, half-gas cookstove. Eva focused her nurturing impulses on her two nieces, Lillian and Ruth, daughters of her sister, Blanche, who themselves would soon relocate to Southern California, leaving snowy, austere New England behind forever.[19]

Eva continued to play vaudeville dates in and around New York City. Her pay had dwindled to the point where she could command about $1,600 a week—a handsome sum, to be sure, but a far cry from the $3,500 she boasted in 1908–1909.

The queen of vaudeville now found herself in a peculiar position: having to beat the bushes for work. To be sure, she was looking for more than mere employment. She was seeking to reestablish her dominance with a high-profile gig. But she now entreated those she had once admonished.

Eva approached the powerful Shubert producing organization. It may be recalled that back in 1913, Eva had given Lee Shubert orders, telling him she was going to cut his acts from her show and extravagantly paying for replacement performers out of her own pocket. It was now 1919 and things had changed. Her tone with Shubert was decidedly more polite, almost coquettish. For the first time in her career since becoming a star, Eva Tanguay pulled her punches.

In February 1919, Eva Tanguay sent a letter to Lee Shubert. She was seeking to play at his flagship venue. "Am I never going to appear in one of the Winter Garden productions? Wouldn't you like to place me in the next one?" she wrote. She pointed out that her current act, consisting of eleven songs, many with accompanying costume changes, resulted in "packed" theaters wherever she played. "This proves I am more popular than ever," argued Eva. But of course the very need to sell herself in what had become a buyer's market for vaudeville talent suggested just the opposite. More telling than her words was her willingness to negotiate on price. "I do not care so much about salary," she confided to Lee Shubert, "because I have accumulated enough." The claim rang false, betraying a neediness Eva had not known since her formative years in the business. "I could be of some service to you," she mused, asking Lee Shubert if he would "think it over and drop me a line." The star who had walked out on contractual obligations because her name was posted in lettering that was too small now offered to let producers name their price. Economic necessity had forced her to play the humility card.[20]

The Shuberts—Lee and his brother J. J.—at first responded positively to Eva's gesture. They would indeed have her in one of their Winter Garden extravaganzas. But as a featured player, not a solo star. Though willing to compromise on pay, this was a concession Eva was not ready to make. "No matter what salary you paid me, I could not afford to go in a small part and have one number to sing," Eva argued to J. J. Shubert. She sugarcoated her demands with appeals to the theatrical clan's ego. "If you could build a show around me—a regular Tanguay production—such as only the Shuberts could produce, it would finally land me to what I have so long been aiming for." She had "stacks of songs" and a line of chorus girls to back her on production numbers like "Pretty Baby." She envisioned "a glorious California number" set in an orange grove, and others too elaborate for mere vaudeville. Clearly she envisioned a *Follies*-like extravaganza. But it was no longer 1909. Again, she bit the bullet when it came to money. "You SET the figure—that's how anxious I am to be with you." To avoid the appearance of desperation, though, Eva wrote that she wanted out of vaudeville not for lack of opportunity—she claimed she had plenty—but because her heart was set on "making a big hit on Broadway," much as she had done long ago in *The Chaperons*.[21]

In the end, Eva needed Lee and J. J. Shubert more than they needed her. They would indeed have her as part of a larger, Ziegfeld-like revue, but not as the centerpiece of her own production. The Shubert brothers may have had a reputation, deserved or otherwise, for treating performers better than other producers did. But in rejecting Eva Tanguay, they were merely demonstrating the business savvy that had brought their enterprise to the fore a decade earlier after winning a much-ballyhooed "war" against a powerful theatrical monopoly known as the Syndicate. While the Syndicate, whose members included the producers Charles Frohman,

Marc Klaw, Abraham Erlanger, and others, was a formidable foe, the Shuberts ultimately triumphed because they better understood modern business practices involving finance and industrial organization. They had even briefly challenged Keith and Albee's United Booking Office by forming a vaudeville-booking company known as the United States Amusement Company (USAC). If the Shubert brothers felt Eva Tanguay could not pack the house on her own, it was significant. It left the onetime undisputed star of the live stage reeling. The movies were unwelcoming and vaudeville was fading. She would have to do her best with what remained.[22]

In late January 1920, Eva headlined at Keith's Alhambra, the gaudy show palace on 116th Street in Harlem. She pulled in $1,575 for that week's work. The following week, she scored top billing at the Palace, seventy blocks south. Although she would again headline the Palace the week of February 28, 1921, Eva had to ink deals with smaller vaudeville circuits eager to net favorable results. The Pantages circuit, whose founder, Alexander Pantages (pronounced "pan-TAY-jez"), had started out with a single, ten-cent vaudeville house located in a storefront on the corner of Second Avenue and Seneca Street in Seattle, gave Eva $2,200 for a week at its Regent Theater in Detroit, in April 1921. The following year, another small-time circuit, the Loew chain, which would eventually turn into movie houses affiliated with Metro-Goldwyn-Mayer's film studio, offered Eva a lucrative $2,500-a-week contract for playing its Metropolitan venue in Brooklyn. It was the highest-paying contract she would enjoy for the remainder of her career.[23]

11

❧

Knockdowns and Comebacks...
and Knockdowns

THOUGH SHE did not make the transition from vaudeville stage to movies, Eva could not help but feel the westward drift of U.S. entertainment. The nation was enjoying unprecedented prosperity, and the fledgling Hollywood studios were doing their best to meet heightened demand. Between 1922 and 1928, U.S. industrial production swelled by 70 percent, the gross national product went up 40 percent, and per-capita income rose 30 percent, while corporate profits and real earnings for wage laborers shot up 62 percent and 22 percent, respectively, during approximately the same period. The nation's workers also had more leisure time, as the average workweek had actually decreased by 4 percent. At the same time, motion picture producers were merging with theater chains to form vertically integrated companies that could regularly deliver vast amounts of product on a national scale. But little of it translated into continued success for Eva. Vaudeville theaters were closing in favor of motion-picture halls, and Eva, rather than leading the entertainment industry, now followed it like an Okie, hoping to harvest her share of the profits, though she was not sure how, or even if, it were possible.[1]

Though she still spent time in New York, especially when paying gigs presented themselves, she decided, for reasons both personal and professional, to switch coasts. She sold off the comfortable home in Sea Gate, Brooklyn, where she had briefly lived a semblance of conventional domestic life with Johnny Ford, and began acquiring property in the Los Angeles area. Though the movie men would not have her, Eva held out hope that the developing entertainment capital would somehow provide a fountain of youth for her career.

There was also her family. Her devoted nieces, Lillian and Ruth, had moved to Southern California by 1924. Lillian lived on Gower Street, in Hollywood. Lillian's husband, Melville Collins, reputed to have been Eva's one true love, died of a stroke in 1923. But the two had a child, a girl named Lilyan Mae, who came to be known as "Babe." Fortunately for Lillian, her sister Ruth and her mother, Blanche, had also relocated to the area. Blanche was now on her fourth husband, a college administrator named Walter Gifford, who was fourteen years her junior. Blanche's daughter Ruth, who turned twenty-one in 1924, was not yet married and lived with her mother and new stepfather.[2]

Though her tours were not netting Eva what she had earned in the glory days—roughly the ten years that began with her Salome success in 1908—her financial health was still sound. She had never been a big speculator in the securities markets, preferring cash instruments and real estate instead. The only major stock play Eva seems ever to have made involved 250 shares of Loew Theatrical Enterprises, purchased in 1913 at eighty-eight dollars a share. Financial documents indicate that by 1924, she no longer owned those securities or any others. Selling off her New York homes had left Eva flush enough to buy an impressive array of properties in the Los Angeles area, both as residences and investments. Eva bought a house overlooking Toluca Lake near what is today Universal Studios in Burbank. She paid $45,000 for it and furnished it with $50,000 worth of her favorite objets d'art.[3] By 1924, she also had several lots, some empty, some with houses that were also hers, on Hillcrest Road in Hollywood, plus a house at 1255 Gower (where Lillian lived) and its "little house in back," according to a financial document. She bought the Bungalow Court complex, with nine living quarters and six garages, at the corner of DeLongpre and Las Palmas, just south of Sunset Boulevard. She also had large but unspecified personal holdings of jewelry and gems.

Financially confident enough to do so, Eva drew up a will in 1924. Its scrawling, handwritten declarations conveyed both a lack of discipline and the emotional solace she found in her dear nieces. She also used the opportunity to take potshots at some of the men in her family, notably her brothers, and her former husband. Eva apportioned a mocking five dollars each to her eldest brother, Joe, and her other brother, Mark, turning her testament into a kind of tough-luck vaudeville routine. But Lillian was singled out for special treatment. "My niece Lillian Collins has kept up a home for me and has been my comfort through my life and she

Figure 15. Eva, Blanche, Lillian, and Ruth.
Though Eva sometimes quibbled with her older sister, Blanche,
the two remained close. But Eva was closer still to Blanche's daughters, Lillian
and Ruth. Clockwise, from top left, Ruth, Lillian, Eva, and Blanche.
(From the Collections of The Henry Ford.)

· · · · · · · · · ·

Lillian Collins is entitled to [what] little I leave after my death—I have
done my share when living towards all the above persons mentioned[.]
Lillian Collins knows my financials and has been instructed how to act
concerning every thing connected with my name[.] Let there be no
arguments regarding this document. I desire one and only *one* Lillian
Collins to inherit *all* and *anything* and everything that was mine. May
God watch over her is my prayer—Eva Tanguay." Even her sister, Blanche,

was to receive but five measly dollars, suggesting the two were in a fight when she had the will drawn up. It was not unlike Eva to act out passing emotional states in the form of dramatic, even hurtful, gestures. But her life had now migrated to Southern California. The Quebec wilderness of her birth, the bustling Holyoke of her youth, and the glamorous and demanding New York City of her professional heyday were all things of the past.[4]

If Eva alienated family members or former professional peers in the course of her career, she also managed to recuperate at least one important relationship by virtue of her robust generous streak.

It had been fifteen years since Eva Tanguay had hijacked Sophie Tucker's featured number in the 1909 Ziegfeld *Follies,* "Moving Day in Jungle Town." Though walloped by the blow, Sophie got up and built herself into one of the most successful performers in show business over the next decade, both following Eva's lead as a racy, outspoken woman in vaudeville and enlarging on it with her own gifts and charms.

Within a few years, Tucker was appearing regularly in big-time Keith vaudeville and rising above the competition. At the Fifth Avenue Theatre in July 1911, her twelve-minute act led the manager to herald her as not just "another of those ragtime comediennes," but "probably the best of the lot. She has always been a big hit with me when there was any audience to play to." Within a few years, her following would grow as impressive and ample as her waistline. W. W. Prosser, the Keith vaudeville manager in Columbus, Ohio, reported to the head office that Tucker was "the biggest hit we have had for a long time." He marveled at the fact that she never seemed to run out of material, performing one new tune after another, accompanied by Frank Westphal on piano. She was a dynamo who just kept going. Her twenty-one minutes onstage left the crowd delirious.[5]

By 1914, Sophie Tucker was successful enough to make her first appearance at New York's Palace vaudeville theater. At the Palace, now a Keith-owned venue, Sophie belted out spicy songs while running her hands over her Rubenesque figure. Management told her to tone it down, but the fans went nuts. She would also make a big hit on the western Orpheum circuit.[6]

In addition to being vaudeville's favorite ragtime singer, Sophie Tucker branched out into the world of cabaret, a subspecies of restaurant featuring dance floors, bandstands, and a stage for more intimate entertainment. There was plenty of liquor, even during Prohibition, and other services could be arranged for those wishing to carry their partying into the wee hours. Some claim that Bustanoby's, which opened in New York in 1911, started the cabaret craze. Other haunts such as Rector's, Shanley's, and Reisenweber's soon followed. Sophie Tucker started appearing regularly at the latter, a four-story establishment at the busy nexus of Eighth Avenue and Columbus Circle, in 1917. By 1919, Reisenweber's was calling her the queen of jazz and had renamed its fancy 400 Room—so called because it attracted New York's four hundred richest and most influential citizens— the Sophie Tucker Room. There, much as Eva had done in vaudeville, Tucker changed gowns for each heated number. She was said to be making some two thousand dollars a week, approximately what Eva was earning in vaudeville at the time.[7]

And though the Shuberts were to turn down Eva Tanguay, the producing brothers had gladly recruited Sophie Tucker at $850 a week in 1917 to appear in their popular *Passing Show,* their own glitzy, *Follies*-like revue. In part Sophie Tucker's career strengthened as Eva's lost steam because her talents lent themselves better to new technologies for reproducing music. By 1920, Sophie Tucker had recorded no fewer than thirty songs, including "That Lovin' Soul Kiss," "Missouri Joe," and "Some of These Days," which was perhaps her signature number, as "I Don't Care" had been for Eva. While Eva's delivery, with its winking and crowing accompanied by cyclonic stage crossings, could not be captured on a recording cylinder or disc, Sophie Tucker's electrifying voice readily lent itself to the medium.[8]

There were other parallels between Eva Tanguay and Sophie Tucker. On October 13, 1917, nine days before Eva would file for divorce from her drunken, abandoning, money-filching husband, Johnny Ford, Tucker married her accompanist, Frank Westphal, with whom she had been living in scandal since her separation from Louis Tuck, her first husband and the father of her only child. (Sophie took his surname, then added "-er" because she felt it made a better stage name.) Sophie and Frank had also lived in the Hotel Sherman in Chicago, the very address Eva would claim as her primary residence in her own divorce suit. In October 1920, Tucker sued for divorce from Westphal in the Cook County Superior Court, the same venue that had executed Eva's case, claiming her husband had deserted her "without any reasonable cause." An enticing mist of scandal began to settle on the voluptuous entertainer, who sang suggestive, African American– influenced songs while running bejeweled hands over her bountiful curves. She had also gained notoriety for telling a woman in the audience to stop knitting, though the knitter claimed she was making sweaters for her boys overseas—leading others to brand Tucker as self-involved and unpatriotic. More famously, she was brought up on charges in Portland, Oregon, for singing "Angle Worm Wiggle," a supposed offense to decency. In many ways it did not help that she was overweight, Jewish, and foreign born.[9]

By the early 1920s, then, Eva Tanguay and Sophie Tucker had a lot in common. They had been through the ups and downs of struggle and success, marriage and divorce, and both were branded misfits, if talented ones, by society. In early 1924, Sophie Tucker was headlining the Majestic Theater in Milwaukee. Eva had starred the week before and, having no immediate touring obligations, remained a day or two after her contract ended to see Tucker hit the boards. It was winter, and a particularly cold Wisconsin night at that, when Sophie took to the stage. After a successful appearance, the buxom coon shouter went back to her dressing room and changed out of her feathery stage garb into a thin, silk kimono and some scanty underwear. She had caught a cold and was sneezing and wiping her nose as she tried to remove her makeup.

Eva came backstage and burst into Tucker's small dressing room. Before Tucker had time to react, Eva expressed alarm at the singer's ailing condition, howling, "You don't dress properly...in the winter,...a girl with your voice.... You should take better care of yourself." It was no wonder Tucker had a cold, said the queen of vaudeville, reprimanding the queen of jazz like a mother scolding her daughter. Before Tucker had a chance to respond, Eva dashed out to a nearby department store. Presently, she returned with a set of silk-and-wool-blend underwear and a bottle of cough syrup. Eva helped Tucker to her feet and into her warm new clothes. She also plied Tucker with medicine, "scolding me the whole time," as Tucker recalled. According to Sophie Tucker, Eva apparently had no idea that this was the same person whose career she had nearly ended one morning back in 1909 by snatching away her number in the vaunted Ziegfeld *Follies*.[10]

The two became fast friends. Unlike Eva's relationships with men, her friendship with Sophie Tucker and other important women in her life—her nieces, some of her fellow vaudevillians—would only deepen and strengthen over time. So much about Eva reflected the onset of the twentieth century, with its newfangled social relations and ethic of individual pleasure. Yet there was something cloistered, and almost nostalgic about her steadfast maintenance of a women-only circle of close friends and relatives. As much as Eva onstage reflected and shaped the changing image of women and femininity in the modern, urban era, her private life was reminiscent of the "homosocial" Victorian age, to borrow a term used by the historian Sharon Marcus.[11]

Eva played tour dates in both big-time and small-time circuits, which had increasingly come to resemble one another in the era of film's dominance. She appeared on the Interstate Circuit, which took Eva to Texas and Arkansas, for some $2,375. In Manhattan in May 1924, she played Keith's massive Hippodrome, which was ringed with flags atop a roof that featured spectacular, globe-topped towers and a had street-side facade of soaring arches. But the pomposity of the structure did not translate into epic pay for Eva, who received a comfortable but unimpressive $1,575 salary for the week.[12]

After a show at the Hippodrome one night, Tucker invited Eva to go out on the town with her and some fellow entertainers. On the town with Tucker's entourage was another well-known vaudevillian, a man, in Eva's reminiscences, "quite noted for his eccentric dancing." Though she never identified him by name, it is clear that the man in question was Roscoe Ails. Ails, a veteran of the two-a-day boards, had once told a reporter that his "true classification" as a dancer was "eccentric...I do a typical 'eccentric dance.'" He was also single.[13]

Much like Johnny Ford, Roscoe Ails was a species unique to vaudeville, a hybrid of dancer, gymnast, and kinetic human freak show. While Ford clattered about the stage in wooden dance shoes, Ails mixed contortionism with comedy and burlesque. A "Southern boy," born in Vanceburg, Kentucky (some ninety miles southeast of Johnny Ford's Covington, Kentucky, birthplace), who considered Atlanta his home, Roscoe Ails had worked in blackface minstrelsy productions, tent shows, nightclubs, dinner-dance venues, and, of course, the vaudeville circuits, where he partnered with Midgie Miller, his hair finely waxed to a cowlick curl on his forehead. Like Eva, he became known as much for endurance as for choreography. Playing Reisenweber's on the same bill as Sophie Tucker, he cooked up a "slow, draggy sort of dance," according to one reporter, complete with leg slides and what seemed to be the dislocation of his limbs. (One envisions a Michael Jackson–like moonwalk years before its time.) It won him attention, prestige, and success in New York and beyond. By 1919, he was said to typify the "astonishing evolution of a present-day Broadway dancing-comedian sensation," according to the *Morning Telegraph* newspaper. In 1920, Ails headlined vaudeville's impressive Palace. He would later share bills with Eva Tanguay, notably at New York's Riverside Theater. Ails was also reputed to have pulled off the mathematically unlikely accomplishment of seventy-eight shows in two weeks at the Palais Royal, a performance space at the Bal Tabarin nightclub in San Francisco.[14]

The night Roscoe Ails joined Sophie Tucker and her retinue, he made his affections for Eva known immediately, even a touch impulsively. At the fancy soiree, he asked her to dance. Eva liked the attention and felt "flattered," as she remembered it. They got along "ideally"—that night, anyway.

As they danced together, Eva felt special in Roscoe Ails's arms. After the song was over, another guest at Tucker's party, whom Eva had also promised a dance, approached the queen of vaudeville and took her arm. Ails shot to his feet and landed his rival such a blow that the unsuspecting suitor crumpled to the floor, though he soon rose to mount a wary counteroffensive. Eva's two would-be bucks scuffled furiously until separated by the crowd and urged to cool down. The rest of the evening passed without further incident, but at night's end Ails turned to Eva and insisted, "I'm taking you home." Eva later claimed that, because she didn't want to make a scene, she agreed. As she had the day she married Johnny Ford, she rationalized the decision. "He was handsome and could be quite gallant," she thought, no matter that mere hours into their relationship he had already exhibited a fit of pique that might have frightened off a more prudent woman. He was definitely exciting.

Eva and Roscoe Ails began seeing a lot of one another, visiting cabarets and New York hot spots until all hours. Eager onlookers greeted the celebrity couple everywhere they went. House orchestras would strike up "I Don't Care" and "Whose Baby Are You?" when the two sauntered into a dinner club or similar fashionable resort. Uncharacteristically, Eva began doing something she never had before—staying out all night and sleeping all day, with just enough energy to make it to her show the following evening. She couldn't keep it up and soon had to cancel bookings. As they spent more time together, Ails's rage again boiled to the surface. One night, walking her dog with her boyfriend on the Upper West Side, Eva turned and noticed her new beau brandishing a pistol. Before she knew it, Ails was firing it willy-nilly into the night sky while doing a dance routine. A policeman approached. "What's going on here?" he demanded. "Why officer," Ails explained, "we're just rehearsing a new act. This is Miss Tanguay." The cop was incredulous, but faced with one of New York's leading celebrity couples—a dancing lunatic with a loaded firearm and a vaudevillian not known for her docility—the constable backed down. Ails, likely drunk, said that the gunfire was "part of the act too." The officer issued a warning. But if he heard any more gunshots, he warned, he would run them downtown. Ails thought it was hilarious, but Eva was scared.

They had been together a little over two months. The late nights, the carrying-on, the brushes with the law, the effect on her career—it was all beginning to take its toll. In a rare moment of financial self-reflection, Eva calculated that her nine-week thrill ride with Roscoe Ails had cost her nearly twenty thousand dollars. Even for the country's favorite live act, this was a steep tab. The end was nigh. Soon after, Ails phoned Eva, asking her to join him and a few friends at the Hotel York, at the corner of Seventh Avenue and West Thirty-sixth Street. She entered a hotel room thick with tobacco smoke and the smell of whiskey. "The men had been drinking," Eva remembered with chagrin. What happened next is not entirely clear, but it seems that one of Ails's barroom buddies made a suggestive, wishful comment involving the cyclonic one and a certain "young girl" Eva knew as well. Rather than express her anger to Ails or his buddies, Eva converted it into a series of unkind remarks about the girl in question. Whatever Eva had said, and in whatever tone, the drunken, raging Roscoe Ails took it personally. Out of nowhere, as Eva described it, he landed a stunning blow to her face, temporarily blinding her. She stumbled out as quickly as her shaking legs and battered eyesight would permit. Much as Johnny Ford had done after fits of booze-induced abuse during their marriage, Ails proffered "apologies and pleas for forgiveness" the next morning, according to Eva. But this time Eva Tanguay did not bite. The affair with her latest lover was over. Eva later claimed the punch she received was so severe that it led to the slow loss of her eyesight, forever crippling her career. While the pummeling didn't help, in all likelihood Eva's sight problems had already begun, and would worsen over the next two decades. It is also possible that the Tanguays may have suffered from a hereditary eye disease; her brother Joe Tanguay, for example, was to go blind later in life.

Things with Roscoe Ails had ended sadly and badly. Despite the severity of his abuse and the insanity of his behavior, it must not have been an easy severance. The two were so closely associated, in fact, that the press later believed, albeit incorrectly, that they were married. They had even been planning to work together onstage, Eva doing her classic numbers and Ails offering "a little 'impromptu turn'" of his own, in the words of a writer at the *New York Dramatic Mirror*.[15]

The women in Roscoe Ails's life who followed Eva fared little better. After things went south with the queen of vaudeville, Ails hooked up both romantically and professionally with the banjo player and fiddler Kate Pullman. In 1928, Pullman gave birth to a child she said belonged to Ails and sued him for a hundred thousand dollars for "breach of promise." It was the celebrity scandal of its day. Certain "advanced thinkers" at the time hailed the couple's decision to raise a "eugenic baby," with no concern for society's customs and strictures. But Roscoe Ails's alleged nonconformity turned out to be mere posturing, a cover story, for he had already taken up with another woman, Shirley Dahl. Dahl and Ails were married in 1930. In time, Dahl described her mate as "a caveman who mauled and kicked" her in front of party guests. On another occasion, she alleged that he hurled her clear across their bathroom, leading her to fight back by throwing a mirror at his head. Roscoe Ails tried to blame it on "evidences of her temperament" and professional jealousy. Few bought it. They split in 1935.[16]

IT WAS ALL BEGINNING to cost more than Eva could pay—not just in money, but in energy, physical well-being, and career management: the demands of performing and traveling, the financial uncertainties, the abusive men, and the moods and bombast that brought her into conflict with those around her. Just before Christmas of 1924, Eva was touring the northeast and had to call off shows in Providence, Rhode Island, because of an unspecified illness. She returned to New York where she convalesced for a week in a small apartment she sometimes rented at the Hotel Embassy. She tried to go back to work but a reported "severe attack of grip [sic]" (flu) forced her back down for another two weeks. Though it was not so, Eva claimed that it was the first time in her career that an illness had sidelined her. She eventually got back on her feet, but five months later, while playing the El Fey Club on West Forty-fifth Street in Manhattan, she suffered a major seizure. She had played two shows on a Wednesday night and, still hanging around the club at five o'clock in the morning, fell ill, a condition deemed "serious" according to Larry Fay, the club's owner. The next day, though, reporters searching for the real story at Eva's Hotel Embassy quarters were told the onetime cyclonic queen of vaudeville was "not seriously ill" after all but had only an "abscess in the throat." She appeared to be out of danger. But it seemed only a matter of time before the specter of failing health would lurk once more.[17]

Eva Tanguay was forty-six years old. Though vaudeville usually allowed performers a longer career than the movies, Eva's act was based on youthful energy and abandon. For these reasons, or perhaps because it was simply becoming too painful to stare in the mirror and see herself aging— and perhaps because she still held out hopes of a movie career—Eva chose a path of rejuvenation that so many celebrities would also take in the years and decades to come. In fact, it would all but become a requirement in the age of Cher, Joan Rivers, and those other vibrant women of stage and screen who, wittingly or unwittingly, owed an artistic debt to Eva Tanguay. In 1925, Eva Tanguay undertook a course of plastic surgery, though Mary Baker Eddy and her Christian Science devotees would surely have disapproved.

Eva was not the first star performer to go under the scalpel, although plastic surgery was still relatively new and rare. The comedienne and singer Fanny Brice, who had gained notoriety as a Yiddish Salome, made headlines in 1923 when she had her nose—understood to be a sign of her Jewish ethnicity—pared down from "prominent" to "merely decorative," in the words of the Brice biographer Barbara W. Grossman. In Brice's case, the press generally regarded it as a necessary if risky move if the Jewish actress wanted to leave behind high comedy for more respectable drawing-room drama where "the nose might distract attention from the play." The ethnic nose, in other words, was appropriate for farce, but not for dramas conveying more "realistic" emotions.[18]

Eva did not cover up the fact that she had had surgery to improve her looks, but made light of it, trying to sound as cavalier—as "I Don't Care"—about her decision to turn back the clock as possible. "Oh, I'd be getting old like everyone else, . . . but I made up my mind that I would not," she told an interviewer as she prepped backstage for a show at Boston's Bowdoin Square Theater. As Eva applied her makeup, the reporter noticed the unusual smoothness of her face. Eva recounted how she had six inches of excess flesh shorn from her neck, her face "ironed," her cheeks and eyebrows lifted, and her wrinkles flattened, all in the interest of a more "youthful" image. Despite the thousands of dollars the surgery had reputedly cost, and no matter that it was all "very painful," in Eva's words, she considered it worth the price on all levels. Attempting to justify what she feared might be seen as needless vanity, even for her, she suggested, with fanciful revision, that after having been "on the stage since I was 2 years old[,] I couldn't help having wrinkles and sagging muscles." Eva, of course, was still an infant in Canada at age of two. But her biographical refashioning served one of her favorite myths: Eva as the perpetual youngster. The New York Dramatic Mirror, after all, had once judged her "distinctly childlike...a sort of girl-who-wouldn't-grow-up...a Peter Pan in real life." She could thus be forgiven, admired even, for having her face doused in carbolic acid and oil to form blisters, which were then peeled away to reveal a reborn, more youthful visage below.[19]

Indulging in plastic surgery might have marked Eva as self-absorbed or undignified—two characteristics she hardly tried to play down throughout her career—but it was also courageous. The risks of the "new surgery" were still largely unknown when Eva chose to submit to its vagaries. Though the practice of face peeling dated back to the 1880s, plastic surgery as we know it had emerged largely from the treatment of devastating, disfiguring wounds suffered by soldiers in World War I. "It is hardly any exaggeration to say that modern plastic surgery dates from 1915," wrote *Good Housekeeping* a few years after Eva had her face and neck done. Eva was thus a daring adventurer into realms the ordinary, housebound woman could only imagine.[20]

Performers, of course, were not ordinary individuals and as such were accorded cultural leeway in dabbling with medical procedures that were otherwise judged a dangerous and vain undertaking. "Certain occupations, particularly those related to the theater, the concert hall, the prize ring or politics," wrote *Hygeia* magazine in the mid-1920s, "which bring their possessor into the public eye, demand an appearance that will at least not excite ridicule, laughter or disgust." As a woman, Eva was also encouraged to make every effort to be beautiful. A 1930 *Good Housekeeping* article on "the widespread interest in face lifting" did not chide women for seeking out the "beauty surgeon" by viewing them as shallow or self-indulgent. Rather, the magazine saw women's interest in cosmetic procedures as arising from "an instinct of self-preservation." Women were blamed only for being "loath to ask advice of regular doctors" about where to find legitimately trained and licensed plastic-surgery specialists rather than falling into the hands of unscrupulous quacks.[21]

In reworking her visage, Eva was also enjoying a newfound freedom that, over the past several decades, had become culturally available to women. Rather than being seen as the result of inner virtue and purity, beauty was now something a woman was expected to go out and buy. The 1910s and 1920s saw sales of cosmetics rise tenfold, to $141 million, as a woman's face was increasingly considered a "style, subject to trends and fads," in the words of the historian Kathy Peiss. Much had changed since Eva first trod the boards as a girl. The sprightly youth she had evoked in song could now be procured if money was available and the doctor knew what he was doing.[22]

THE RISE OF MOVIES also meant a greater need for facial reconditioning, either through makeup or surgery. A face that would have been impossible to see up close in vaudeville could now be splashed onto a huge screen in painful detail for the inspection of everyone in the crowd. Eva knew the movies would never be her true art form. But the possibility of extending her career by acquiescing to an emerging Hollywood notion of beauty had nonetheless to be considered. Her plastic surgery turned out to be a feint in the direction of an unsurprisingly brief film career.

While plastic surgery may have taken the sag out of Eva's cheeks and spruced up her forehead and neck, it did not have the same effect on her career. She found herself booked on smaller vaudeville chains, drawing lower and lower salaries. At the beginning of 1925, she played the James Theatre, part of the Gus Sun circuit, in Columbus, Ohio, for $1,750 a week. When she appeared at the Lyric in Richmond, Virginia, however, she was able to secure only four days of work in May 1926, netting $787.50, which was less than the $250 a day she had been earning the year before. Performing at Brooklyn's Dyker Theatre that October, she managed to get back up to $750 for a three-day engagement, in part because pay rates were higher in the New York area and her following was stronger. But at the Ben Ali vaudeville house in Lexington, Kentucky, in 1927, she made only $625—about $208 a day—for three days of work. It was her lowest draw since she had started out in vaudeville over twenty years earlier.

In addition to her own inevitable aging, Eva could also witness huge changes in demographics and consumption patterns. Vaudeville proper was in its death throes, as movies and radio absorbed more and more of the public's interest (though admittedly in very different ways). By 1930, there would be only a hundred or so vaudeville theaters in the United States, down from several thousand a decade before. As for the city crowds who made up vaudeville's vibrant audiences, they were also increasingly seeking the racial uniformity and perceived security of the suburbs after World War I, taking their leisure dollars with them and leaving a situation in which, according to the historian David Nasaw, "no one could deny that cities were poor and that the suburbs were, relatively speaking, rich." But it was the movies more than anything that had basically brought live vaudeville to its knees.[23]

FACING A WORLD that no longer needed her, Eva made a desperate attempt to get back in the public eye. The vehicle she used to get attention was so radical, for her anyway, that it smacked of desperation. In 1927, her fiftieth birthday not far off, Eva Tanguay, rather than knock down a stagehand or blatantly violate censorship codes, took a more radical step to win headlines.

She got married.

Eva set her sights on a young man less than half her age. He was her accompanist, and his name was Al Parado.

Figure 16. Al Parado and Eva.
Eva was almost twice his age when she married her pianist,
Al Parado, in 1927. A publicity stunt, the marriage did not excite
the interest she had hoped for. It was her last attempt at matrimony.
(Private collection, courtesy of Beth Touchton.)

· · · · · · · · ·

Al Parado was born in 1904 in Budapest, Hungary, to a family that
was part Polish. As a boy, he showed remarkable talent for piano. When
he was still quite young, preparations were made for him to go to Warsaw
to study with the Polish music legend Jan Paderewski. Paderewski (1860–
1941) was more than a virtuoso piano player. Although by the 1890s he
was revered for his musical skills—and mobbed by awestruck female fans,
as a kind of Victorian precursor to Elvis—he would later go on to become

not only prime minister of Poland but also a signatory to the Treaty of Versailles that ended World War I, and, as if that weren't enough, one of the first Europeans to bring Old-World grape plants to the United States in order to successfully cultivate vintage wines in California.

Parado described himself as a "boy prodigy" who "knew nothing but music, serious music, morning, noon and night." He "ate it, drank it, slept it" and "didn't give a hang" about school, in his words. He was skinny, pale, and considered Chopin and Liszt his main sustenance. He practiced finger exercises for hours at a stretch while locked in his room. As for the sports that boys of his age busied themselves with, "I didn't know a darned thing about them; in fact, I wasn't interested." Much like Eva Tanguay, his was the unconventional childhood of a budding performer.[24]

The young Parado never actually made it to Poland to study with the legendary Paderewski, for his family immigrated to Buffalo, New York. He had come from eastern Europe to a bustling U.S. industrial town with a large population of immigrants—in this case, Poles. Again, his story had something in common with Eva's. Parado's father was a local impresario who had himself been a child piano virtuoso and was now friends with Dr. Francis E. Vranschek, Buffalo's health commissioner and an intimate of Paderewski. When Paderewski came to perform, Parado the elder booked him at the city's convention hall and introduced him to his young son. The boy played for his idol and preparations were again made to pack the lad off to study piano, for real this time, in New York City. And yet again, in a curiously Tanguay-esque turn of events, the dream was deferred, for Parado senior suddenly "lost his money in his handling of the local [concert producing] business," Al Parado later said. In a quandary, he turned to his close friend and business peer, Mike Shea. Shea owned a number of theaters, some vaudeville or formerly vaudeville, in upstate New York and the Toronto area. Shea heard the teenage Al Parado at the keyboard playing alongside his sister, Olga, a year his junior. The girl was said to be gifted with a "voice that sounded like a church organ." Olga Parado could sing in five languages and span three octaves. Under Shea's tutelage, brother and sister developed an act that compressed symphonic virtuosity into a five-minute vaudeville routine with orchestral accompaniment. They played selections from Liszt's Hungarian Rhapsody no. 2 and *La Traviata*. A pinspot would follow fifteen-year-old Olga across the stage. At the piano sat her bushy-haired brother, decked out in a "Little Lord Fauntleroy collar and Eton velvet jacket," as he put it, complete with bloomers, leather slippers, and a billowy Windsor tie. The Parado kids were soon playing all the major vaudeville circuits, including Keith, Pantages, Orpheum, and Sullivan-Considine.[25]

As they toured, however, public interest increasingly focused on the female half of the duo. The Shubert organization contacted Olga and inquired whether she would be interested in teaming up with the legendary vaudeville performer Al Jolson for the Broadway production of *Robinson Crusoe, Jr.* It was a golden opportunity for the girl. But for young Al Parado, the separation from his sister, his musical soul mate and best friend, was heart wrenching. "I practically breathed for her, you know what I mean," he recalled in pain. The Shuberts signed Olga to a three-year contract, while brother Al went on his way in vaudeville playing on the same bill as Sophie Tucker, the Four Mortons, Jim and Mary Harkens—and, of course, Eva Tanguay.[26]

After accompanying Eva on a few random gigs, he became her musical director, not to mention yet another handler who picked up the pieces after her emotional earthquakes. In addition to preparing her music, Parado made sure her dressing rooms (in some of her contracts, if she could manage it, Eva insisted on having two) were decorated with fresh flowers. He saw how those around her deferred to her with a seemingly endless stream of "Good evening, Miss Tanguay" and "It's a pleasure to have you, Miss Tanguay." Parado grew adept at anticipating and managing her moods, and the two never quarreled. He even read to her: Eastern philosophy and other ponderous subjects. "Where did you ever learn that stuff?" she would ask the young pianist who once nearly studied with Paderewski.[27]

Keeping the peace between local musicians, who Eva had to hire as she toured, and the cyclonic vaudeville star was a daunting task. Eva would "cuss like a trooper" at the boys in the pit and call them "You dirty lot of shoemakers!" Once she broke a fiddle over a band member's head. Word got around that playing for Eva Tanguay was hardly worth the paycheck. Al Parado knew all this and developed a brilliant tactic to calm the waters. The pianist told Eva that she didn't have to show up early at rehearsals—or even show up at all. He somehow convinced the perfectionist Eva that the $450 a week she was paying him entitled her to do nothing other than get up there at curtain time and wow the crowd. He would prep the band ahead of time. Eva was growing weary and was happy to have the additional downtime. Thus placating his employer, Al Parado would go by himself in the morning to whatever local venue Eva would be playing that day and introduce himself to the orchestra. "My name is Al Parado," he'd say, then supply his musician's union affiliation, "802 New York." Next came the crucial bit: "I know exactly how you feel," he'd say, "but don't feel that way. I'm going to tell you right now, I'm here with you. I'm responsible. This is my job. Now, just listen to me, just work with me. You've got not a damned thing to worry about. Going to have a wonderful week, in fact." His calm empathy soothed anxieties. Plying the musicians with cigars and bottles of whiskey didn't hurt either. He learned their names and told them just to keep up with him and not worry about what Eva was doing onstage. "Drummer," he commanded, "don't watch her; watch me from the side." Eva realized she was deeply in Al Parado's debt.[28]

It is unclear what the nature of their personal relationship was before Eva proposed. But in 1927 she asked him to become, in effect, Mr. Tanguay. The two were wed on July 22 of that year in Santa Clara, California, during a West Coast tour. Following the wedding, Parado headed east ahead of Eva. The plan was to reunite back in Buffalo, meet the groom's folks, then head quickly down to New York City for a gig at the Coliseum Theater on 181st Street and Broadway. Parado's mother prepared a traditional Polish meal at their Buffalo home and waited for Eva Tanguay to arrive.

She never showed.

Al Parado visited the Buffalo train depot hoping to rendezvous with his new bride. All he found waiting there was a bulky telegram from California. The lengthy message confirmed what Parado must have suspected all along: the wedding had been a publicity stunt. When it became clear that it had failed as that, Eva disclosed other ideas to garner the attention of a public that was losing interest in both her and vaudeville. "It wasn't that she loved me," he painfully came to realize. The marriage proposal, he now saw, had been based on nothing more than "a selfish motive." Parado felt used, angry. "I was so baffled, so stunned," he recalled. He read and reread the telegram. The truth sank in. Eva was hitting her financial wall and had recruited her faithful, unwitting young accompanist in a last-ditch effort to avoid the collision. "People who make so much money for so many consecutive years don't stop to realize that someday that steady stream of income is going to stop," he later told an interviewer. "They think it becomes endless. Actually, the people were commencing to change their tastes. New ideas and a new generation were coming in. They commenced to forget about Eva Tanguay. So the only thing that she thought would pop her back in the good graces of her beloved public was to remarry." This was Parado's assessment of the situation. It was selfish and absurd. No publicity stunt could have pushed back the hands of time. On the brink of fifty, Eva Tanguay was staring at a world that no longer cared much about her. It was a vision with which she would never make peace.[29]

After the few, minor, back-page news items announcing Eva "going to altar with boy of 25" had come and gone, Eva sought an annulment. In October 1927, barely three months after her vows, she claimed that she wanted out of the marriage because her husband had never given her his real name, instead going by a number of aliases including Alexander Booke and Chandas Ksiaziewicz. She alleged, too, that he had "deceived her in other ways." Again, Eva's involvement with marriage, an institution for which she had little use, turned out like a bad vaudeville sketch with an inflection of pain and pathos. Eva Tanguay and Al Parado were divorced twelve days later.[30]

Without Al Parado, her accompanist and the man who made for smooth sailing, Eva had to make do as best she could. She managed a few more gigs on the small-time Gus Sun circuit, playing bitterly cold Rochester, New York, at the end of January 1928 for $214 a day. She also had to branch out into smaller venues such as dinner clubs and cabarets. In western Pennsylvania, she appeared at the Nixon Restaurant, located in the Pittsburgh suburb of Oakmont. Heading north that spring to Bradford, Pennsylvania, she played the New Willows café. Though she was perhaps a six-hour train ride from New York City, Eva felt as if she were playing to strangers in a cold, distant, and increasingly uninterested universe.[31]

Though the stock-market crash of 1929 and the ensuing Depression were to devastate the entertainment industry in general and Eva's fortunes in particular, it did not help that throughout 1928, Eva seems to have been bent on sabotaging what remained of her career. Without Al Parado for ballast, and having alienated a slew of managers and handlers, her recklessness grew unchecked. No longer was she merely a high-maintenance eccentric comedienne whose moods were given wide berth by an industry getting rich off her talents. She was on her own. Her closest aide at the moment was neither a musician nor a show-business professional, but a personal secretary and servant named Ted Savage. She was now even willing to throw away what remained of her career over a dog.

Eva adored animals, often bonding with them more comfortably than with people. She always had a pet and was apparently rather fond of a monkey that Florence kept on a farm in Massachusetts. But canines were her true love. "She was so nutty over dogs," Parado observed. Of all her dogs over the years, the one she was nuttiest about was a black Boston bull terrier named Stokie. Stokie had been the gift of one of New York City's famous eccentric millionaires, W. E. D. Stokes. William Earle Dodge

Stokes was born in 1853, the scion of a famous and wealthy mercantile clan. His grandfather Thomas Stokes had partnered with Anson Phelps and William Dodge, eventually forming the Phelps Dodge mining concern in the 1880s. W. E. D. was implicated in a number of juicy scandals during his lifetime. On one occasion he was shot several times (though not fatally) by a singer named Lillian Graham in what seems to have been a lover's quarrel sparked by incriminating mash notes. Another time he was charged by the city with running an illegal "sky farm" rich with geese and a charismatic pig named "Nanki-Poo" atop the Ansonia Hotel, which he owned, on Manhattan's Upper West Side. It was thus somehow natural that Eva Tanguay should have received a beloved pet from New York's amateur, high-rise zookeeper—a man who was no stranger to intrigue involving showgirls and the colorful flouting of laws and conventions.[32]

Stokie the dog became Eva's constant companion and, to outside observers, her protector. When visitors would show up at Eva's dressing room or hotel suite, the dog would bark and refuse them entrance. The creature had apparently absorbed some of its owner's moxie. Stokie got so old he went blind and lost his teeth. But Eva clung to him, her canine security blanket. The dog's health, already poor, took a turn for the worse when Eva played a Nashville, Tennessee, theater in 1928. Just before the curtain was to rise, Eva told the manager she would not go on. He reminded her of her contractual obligation. She told him to go to hell. Eva informed the manager that her dog was in dire need of medical attention and she simply would not perform until it arrived. Realizing Eva, however irrational at this point, would not budge, the manager gave up. She told Ted Savage, her secretary, to summon a veterinarian. It took some scrambling, but Savage managed to find a local vet who made house calls. The doctor came to the theater, went to Eva's dressing room, took one look at the frail, ailing canine and advised in sober tones, "I think you ought to give him gas, Miss Tanguay." Eva exploded. She would hear none of it. "Get out of here!" she shouted at the hapless doctor. She asked for a phone and dialed a veterinarian she had known in Brooklyn, one who had treated many of her pets over the years. It was nearly midnight by now.

The phone rang in the Brooklyn vet's home. Groggily, he answered, "What do you want?" Eva said she needed help. "It's past office hours," he reminded her, wiping sleep from his eyes.

"Well, my Stokie is dying. I want you to come over immediately," she explained.

"Where are you?" asked the vet.

Figure 17. Eva with one of her beloved dogs.
Eva owned a succession of dogs and loved them arguably more than people.
Her attachment to her dog Stokie, a gift from the eccentric millionaire
W. E. D. Stokes, helped end her career.
(From the Collections of The Henry Ford.)

. . . .

"I'm in Nashville, Tennessee," Eva replied.

The veterinarian, no doubt used to Eva's demands and hysterics, explained that Brooklyn was quite a ways from Nashville, and that, in any case, he couldn't just pick up and leave his wife and family. Again, Eva would not hear it.

"I don't give a hang what it costs; I didn't ask you. Come on! Pick up your bag and your wife and come on. You got to see my Stokie." And so, somehow, another otherwise reasonable human being fell sway to the raging temper of the onetime queen of vaudeville. The vet made it out to Tennessee late the next day. But of course there was nothing he could do—no matter how much pain the loss of Stokie caused Eva. The animal passed on. She buried Stokie but first deposited the dog's heart in a small bottle filled with alcohol. She would keep it for years.[33]

Her tour was now all but over. Eva's receding popularity and the damage over the Stokie incident, as well as clashes with musicians in the absence of Al Parado, left few interested in working with the onetime superstar who had defined vaudeville. She was pushing herself to the brink of professional extinction both consciously and unconsciously. She made one last effort to secure some gigs, reaching out to the Keith organization's United Booking Offices. The Keith outfit itself was in transition, having acquired the huge Orpheum chain. In 1928, it was in the process of selling its vaudeville houses to the Radio Corporation of America, RCA, which wanted to wire an existing theater chain for sound in order to produce and project "talkies" using its proprietary Photophone technology. (*The Jazz Singer,* with Al Jolson, typically credited as the first full-length motion picture featuring sound, had been released the year before.) The result would be the end of Keith vaudeville and the rise of the Radio-Keith-Orpheum movie studio and cinema chain, better known as RKO. Thus in name only did Keith vaudeville live on. B. F. Keith himself had died in 1914, and E. F. Albee was to expire in 1930. But in 1928, the UBO still existed and wielded control over the booking of many live performers across North America.[34]

The seeds of the UBO had been planted some three decades earlier. In 1900, Keith, Albee, and other theater owners forged an agreement to jointly book and route talent. This gave them greater bargaining power over the fifty or so venues they controlled at the time. It was positioned as advantageous to the performer, promising that "railroad jumps will be so laid out as to minimize the artists' traveling expenses, and in all other details the best interests of the performers will be conserved," in the words of a Keith PR communiqué. With the UBO, Keith interests were also trying to undermine ambitious, independent agents, especially one named William Morris.[35]

Six years later, Keith and Albee turned their Association of Vaudeville Managers into the United Booking Offices of America, or UBO for short. Incorporated in Maine, the UBO, more than any entity before it, brought entertainment, for better or for worse, squarely into the age of big business. "It is probably the greatest combination of money and power in the entertainment world, and ranks with the most important of America's industrial combinations," wrote the *New York Clipper* in 1907. By that time, the UBO's weekly payroll exceeded five hundred thousand dollars, some $9.7 million in today's terms. Soon it began booking and routing for a number of so-called independent chains, including Shea's and Poli's.[36]

To be sure, the appearance of job security afforded by the UBO was a real lure, holding out the promise of nearly a full year of solid engagements. But as the vaudeville historians Charles and Louise Samuels have pointed out, performers knew full well that they could be "dropped cold" the moment they lost their following or made trouble for management.[37]

It was, then, a difficult transition for the average vaudevillian. "The impulsive and peripatetic player became a specialized agent within an industry," wrote another vaudeville historian, Albert McLean. Eva Tanguay was nothing if not impulsive and peripatetic. Her celebrity and star value permitted her at least the illusion of self-determination. But for the rank-and-file vaudevillian, the change was cataclysmic. Coming largely from either variety-acting families, the circus, and/or touring stock companies, the vaudeville performer was now a tiny piece of a complicated and ever-changing puzzle that someone in an office building in New York, who might as well have been marketing and selling washbasins, pieced together.[38]

Until 1913, when it moved its offices to the very Taj Mahal of vaudeville, the Palace Theatre, at Forty-seventh Street and Broadway, the UBO was headquartered at 1403 Broadway, in the Putnam Building. If the Palace reflected all that was high-class and professional about the vaudeville business, the Putnam offices were not far off. Here, the United Booking Offices took up twelve floors. The top story of the building, a "huge room filled with Circassian walnut desks ranged in close formation," in the words of one impressed journalist, served as the nerve center of the Keith-Albee empire. The UBO offices in the Palace would boast furnishings made only of solid mahogany, a veneer "finer than any bank." This was the domain of E. F. Albee, "the presiding genius and general manager, who made 'big business' out of an amusement." Soon there would be no need to place a halo of quotes around the term "big business" when referring to entertainment. That was perhaps E. F. Albee's chief accomplishment in life.[39]

By the late 1920s, the UBO's luster had faded, though not as much as Eva's. She had always resisted subordinating herself and her demands to the rigors of a highly mechanized industrial system. But she no longer had the box office heft to call the shots. The UBO gave her some performance dates, and Edward Darling, once her fiancé and still her perennial adviser, helped her string together something like a tour. But a detail in her arrangements with the UBO irked Eva. It was unclear what sparked her annoyance, but her feelings of disgust only grew.[40]

Darling managed to book a few non–UBO houses as well, foraging for work for his onetime paramour wherever he could. One night, Eva arrived for a show at the Park Theater, a small venue in Union City, New Jersey. Eva was in a foul mood, her resentment against the UBO brewing over harms both real and imagined. The crowd was thin, sending Eva's mood plummeting even further. As it happened, the Park was run by a man who had been fired some years earlier by E. F. Albee and who, like Eva, now harbored an ugly grudge against the aging vaudeville mogul. Eva and he exchanged some choice trash talk about Albee and the UBO. Thus fueled, she went onstage and delivered what Darling termed a "bad performance." But it was the finale that did her in, for which she sang a song called "Oh That U.B.O." that "bashed" and mocked the booking agency whose time she had recently been playing. Ill-advised though it was, Eva took paranoid delight in smacking the hand that fed. The audience, to be sure, did not get the reference. "[They] thought she was singing about a railroad," remembered Darling. Sated with revenge, Eva wandered off. The audience, bewildered, asked neither for an ovation nor an encore of "I Don't Care." Eva was on her own. The United Booking Offices canceled what remained of her contract.[41]

With little work to scavenge, Eva joined a has-been tour, a collection of human relics nostalgically trying to resurrect the corpse of vaudevillian yesteryear. It was more an oddity show, a novelty, than fresh entertainment. When he learned that Eva had signed on to tour with an "old time unit," Edward Darling picked up the phone and dialed his former fiancée, about whom he still clearly cared, both personally and professionally. "I called her and begged her not to do it for I knew it would be her finish," he recalled. Though he offered wise and generous counsel, Eva responded with suspicion and rage. "She felt I was trying to hurt her," according to Darling. He pleaded with her to no avail. She took the "old time" tour and continued to make a noisy mess, though few cared to listen or respond. "There was so much trouble with her after that nobody wanted to bother with her again," recalled Edward Darling in an unpublished memoir. Eva would scrounge some more work here and there in next few years, but in essence, Darling had it right. Big-time vaudeville and Eva Tanguay. Each had helped make the other what it was. Now both would be unmade.[42]

12

◦⃕₰

Death and Other Endings

HE 1920S had not been good to Eva Tanguay. She had dabbled in plastic surgery and Christian Science, chosen yet another toxic, money-draining mate, and fumbled powerlessly over both a body and an entertainment format whose best years had come and gone. By contrast, the United States, her adoptive country, rode high until it famously hit the skids, and hard. After nearly a decade of unfettered economic growth, the U.S. stock market, as measured by the Dow Jones Industrial Average, peaked at 381.17 on Tuesday, September 3, 1929. Then it started to slide. On what would become known as Black Thursday, October 24, 1929, investors fearing gross overvaluation of securities and overproduction by U.S. companies feverishly sold off their shares. Stock prices tumbled precipitously. Between 1920 and 1929, stocks had more than quadrupled in value. But at the end of trading on October 24, the market was at 299.5, having fallen thirty-three points in a single day. It continued to fall, down to 199 on November 13, plummeting to a 1932 trough in the mid-70s, by which time some U.S. shares had lost up to 90 percent of their peak value. Unemployment, poverty, economic depression, and—perhaps most pernicious of all—a culture of fear and scarcity spread as millions lost work and the hopes of a generation vanished. To put things in historical perspective, the Dow would not recover its pre-1929 levels until 1956.[1]

As we have seen, Eva was not heavily invested in stocks. But as the market sank, it took everything in the economy with it. Her real estate was worth less than it had been, and could be less easily sold, and work of all types was simply harder to come by. Even if Eva had been at the top her game, she would have felt a sharp sting.

In 1929, she signed on for twenty-six weeks with the Pantages circuit. Pantages vaudeville was decidedly small-time compared to the Keith and Orpheum enterprises back in their heyday. Though she somehow managed to pull a decent salary from the engagement, the tour was taxing. Eva was beginning to suffer painful bouts of arthritis and a debilitating loss of vision, which she attributed to Roscoe Ails's pummeling. "The road grew harder. My eyes grew dimmer," she recalled. Everywhere she played, technicians had to install a red light downstage center so Eva could get her bearings. In Baltimore one fateful night, she stepped over the lip of the stage and landed on a bass drum in the pit. She was apparently unhurt, and the manager rushed to her dressing room after the show and urged her, "Keep it in the act!" He said it was the "funniest bit of business" he'd ever seen. Eva broke into tears.[2]

In trying to outrun the brutal truth, Eva hoped for a swansong, a Second Coming in which she could return to the hearts and minds of the nation. Something had to give—she hoped. Her personal finances were in tatters: the $2 million in net worth she was said to have had at her peak was largely gone. This had as much to with her own inability to save as it did with the economic downturn.

She began liquidating the real estate assets she had so proudly acquired in better times. She sold off her North Hollywood home at 245 North Vermont and all its furnishings for a hundred thousand dollars and moved into a modest bungalow at 6887 De Longpre Avenue in eastern Hollywood. Her sister, Blanche, lived in nearby Beverly Hills with her most recent husband, Walter Gifford, by now a college dean. But there was little Blanche either could do or wanted to do for her once high-flying sister. The sheriff's office delivered a notice threatening Eva with eviction; for a time, it looked entirely possible that the onetime queen of vaudeville might end up homeless.[3]

The old-time show of washed-up vaudevillians against which Edward Darling had counseled provided Eva with some work and allowed her to line up gigs at various small taverns and cafés. Called "The Stars of Yesteryear," it allowed Eva to sing "I Don't Care," though without the frenetic running and gyrating that had brought her fame in her salad days. Nowadays, fading vision and arthritic joints rendered her little more than a mannequin belting out her signature tune as best she could. The engagement earned her what she described as a "pittance." But at least it was work. Eva followed the "Yesteryear" shows by traveling back east for a stint at a small cabaret in Brooklyn called the Rockwell Terrace—ironically, across the street from the big-time Orpheum vaudeville house she had once headlined—opening the floor show in April 1931. A *Time* magazine reporter found himself shocked to learn of Eva's small-potatoes gig in an article aptly titled "Not in the Big Time." The *Time* critic sentimentally recalled an era when Eva Tanguay was the biggest name in show business. For her part, Eva claimed to be "glad to be back in the harness." But rather than a large, cheering crowd, she played to a puny house and, to make matters worse, had to mount a flight of stairs merely to get to her dressing room. Several months later, undoubtedly wanting to feel appreciated, she returned to her childhood home of Holyoke, Massachusetts. Appearing at both the outdoor Mountain Park Casino and local RKO vaudeville house and cinema, the no-longer-cyclonic entertainer found herself "vigorously applauded" for turning the stage at both venues into "an arena of mirth," in the words of a reporter at the *Holyoke Transcript*. It is unknown whether Florence, her presumptive daughter, was in the audience. But her brother, Mark Tanguay, the man who played the role of Flossie's father, surely was not, for Mark had died in 1930. Eva's life was no longer connected to New England or New York. She was now a Californian making a mere stopover.[4]

Eva took the train back to Los Angeles, which must have been an agonizing journey, her aching joints jostling about on rocking railroad cars. When she looked out the window, partial blindness rendered her barely able to see the landscape rushing by. In its place, Eva inserted dreams of coming back to conquer the vast terrain of popular entertainment yet again, perhaps also looking back fondly on the days when her battles with an argumentative railroad employee had made headlines.

By 1932, Eva had returned to her modest lodging in Southern California. The papers reported her "nearly blind," the victim of "a combination of diseases." To retain anything like her former sight, Eva would need a miracle. And it seemed she got one—or several, actually. After consulting over a dozen specialists, each of whom told her there was no hope, she brought in a physician from Chicago, Henry Gradle, who offered to operate on her failing eyes. Dr. Gradle removed cataracts and performed other vision-restoring feats. Her recovery was agonizingly slow, but in the end, Eva found herself able to see better than she had in years. In addition to Dr. Gradle, Eva credited "a bit of" Christian Science for her healing. She now was fifty-five years old. Perhaps the worst was over; maybe she could start plotting her comeback in earnest.[5]

Increasingly, she turned to God. "When I was too sick to move, when my bed was a shabby army cot, something bigger and greater than mere personal comfort took possession of my heart and soul. I had always thought I pretty well understood God and His ways. But I had never felt the light of His countenance upon me till then," she told a reporter.[6]

But later that year, even as her eyesight improved, other organs began failing. Lying weak and ill in her small house, she suffered afflictions of rheumatism, heart ailments, and a wrenchingly painful kidney disorder known as Bright's disease (which doctors today would call chronic nephritis). In the late summer of 1932, she was reported to be "near death," surrounded by flowers and notes from former friends and stage associates. The curtain appeared to be descending.

But Eva pulled through. Barely.

Dr. Gradle may have been an expert at repairing eyesight, but for Eva's host of internal maladies, she turned to a new physician, Lucius B. Faires. Dr. Faires administered a series of blood transfusions and other aggressive treatments. That and a heavy dollop of luck let Eva escape the grip of mortality. To aid her recovery, she took the waters at the Como Hotel in Hot Springs, Arkansas. She had also suffered a reported nervous breakdown, and her heart continued to give her trouble. But the fantasy of better days to come buoyed her, even when her spirituality could not.[7]

If she looked forward with some tendril of hope, however unlikely, it was to balance a past that increasingly left Eva feeling little but anguish and regret. "My life has been a tragedy," she wrote to her niece Florence. Eva told the girl who some said was really her daughter how so many friends and acquaintances had come to visit her while she was wracked with arthritis and other ills. But as she slowly got better, it seemed to Eva that "one by one they left greatly disappointed that I didn't die. I soon found myself utterly alone." Her nieces, Lillian and Ruth, were her main companions, not counting the doctors and healers who dropped in when she needed them and could afford to pay.[8]

While Eva's family, aided by Dr. Faires and others, saw to her emotional and physical needs, Eva also needed white knights with deep pockets. She had little in the way of assets, liquid or otherwise. To her rescue came a passel of showbiz folk stirred by hearing of Eva's lamentable condition (and, no doubt, fearing ever finding themselves in such a state one day). First was Sid Grauman. Grauman had famously created the sumptuous Chinese and Egyptian movie palaces in Hollywood (in partnership with United Artists), after having been credited with opening the first "vaude-film" hybrid theater in New York City on 125th Street (more likely myth than reality). Grauman's gaudy, grandiose movie mansions were perhaps the perfect exemplars of an era devoted to overblown exhibition, roughly 1915–1932, when the movie "palace" craze was at its height. Predictably, the crash of 1929 and subsequent Depression heralded the end of that time. Away went lavish stage shows and scores of doting ushers. In their place came toned-down, often Art Deco–style cinemas offering simpler movie fare. Grauman, reportedly worth $6 million before the 1929 crash, was himself in financial free fall shortly after he came to Eva Tanguay's aid.[9]

Another of Eva's benefactors during these desperate days was Lucy Cotton, yet one more of the odd lot of show folk and misfits who seemed to circulate in the cyclonic one's orbit. Born in Houston in 1892, Cotton came to New York to make it big onstage in her late teens. Like Eva, she gained notoriety in musical comedies including *The Quaker Girl*. Also like Eva, she engaged in a succession of failed, high-profile romances and marriages, including one to a Russian noble that rendered her, however unlikely, Princess Eristavi Tchitcherine. Cotton died of a sleeping pill overdose in a Miami Beach hotel in 1948.[10]

Not surprisingly, Mae West furnished Eva with material support in the form of a coat (though not the lavish ermine one reported in the press at the time), a hat, gloves, and shoes. Mae also paid for a hairdressing appointment for Eva and wrote her onetime role model a check for thirty-five dollars. But when the famed radio gossip man Walter Winchell broadcast that Mae West was paying *all* of Tanguay's bills, Eva fired off a letter to Winchell to let him know he had the facts wrong and had falsely reported damaging information. According to Eva—as usual, her logic was questionable—Winchell's report that Mae West was looking after her had halted other charitable sources on which she had been relying, causing her to become even more financially "handicapped."[11]

In fact, Eva wrote to Winchell, in an indignant letter that was neither published nor publicized, her "real benefactress" was none other than Sophie Tucker, the very performer whose career the cyclonic comedienne had nearly crushed back in 1909. "She is paying all my bills," Eva wrote, underscoring her words in thick black ink. She described Sophie Tucker as a "noble creature who knows motherly love and is not all selfishness." Tucker had in fact formed an "Eva Tanguay fund" (probably in alliance with the National Vaudeville Artists, a mutual aid organization that reportedly contributed to Eva's medical and living costs) and was not doing so for publicity or personal gain. "What a wonderful friend," wrote Eva. Though Sophie Tucker struggled with her own financial issues, notably a gambling addiction, she understood what Eva somehow failed to grasp: namely, that a performer's peak may be brief. "Save your money," Tucker exhorted her fellow vaudevillians, "send home your money order every payday; take out insurance and annuities. Remember, there's many a rainy day in show business." The "Last of the Red Hot Mamas," as she came to be known, Sophie Tucker went on to demonstrate a sizable munificent streak. In the years before her death in 1966, she gave generously to charities of all stripes. Vaudevillians and itinerant performers knew they had to look after one another, for they were somehow a breed apart.[12]

With the help of her family, Lucy Cotton, Mae West, Sophie Tucker, sundry show folk, and the various doctors who took care of her, Eva once again nursed dreams of a phoenixlike reemergence. "Three months ago the great comedienne was stricken desperately ill. A month ago her friends despaired of her life. But they reckoned not with her iron will." From her new flat in the modest Ravenswood Apartments, located in the comfortable Hancock Park neighborhood of Los Angeles—the very same condominiums where Mae West would live out her last years—Eva envisioned a one-woman touring show. It would debut in New York. She promised to bring back the "best songs" in her repertoire. "And believe me," she told a journalist, "I'll try to 'panic 'em,' just to show how grateful I am that I am alive and well."[13]

"Alive and well" may have been something of an overstatement. She was, after all, barely solvent and could never hope to dominate a stage as she had in the great days of vaudeville. She also needed a few more eye operations to make it possible for her to even think of treading the boards again. But none of this seemed to matter. Eva reckoned it would take a year or two to "repay all those dear friends of mine who enabled me to have my sight saved and to regain my health." Though she no longer owned property in New York or had much family in New England, in Eva's mind, only a star turn back east would truly signal to the world that the onetime cyclonic wonder of vaudeville had returned from the brink, just as feisty and capable as in her glory years. Eva told reporters that a noted "capitalist" in the city, perhaps a former lover, had promised to bankroll her act. She also let it be known that she took daily constitutionals with her beloved new dog, Kiddie, no doubt to trumpet her improved mobility. Furthermore, she noted that she had put on eighteen pounds since languishing in her sickbed and had been looked after by no fewer than thirteen doctors. "Besides," she said with almost admirable naïveté, "I'm only fifty-six."[14]

Not only would she make a professional comeback and wow them in New York, but Eva, never one for thinking small, also promised to become a benefactor for the blind. Though barely able to pay her own expenses, it helped her battered ego to think that she might someday assist others who suffered as she had. "I'd like to make enough money to endow a hospital to treat the sightless eyes of children," she announced to the press.[15]

Her one-woman show never came to pass. Unable to get financing or match her failing body to the task, she set it aside. Instead, she rested in her Los Angeles home, recuperating and regaining strength. She had a few visitors and took her dog for a walk when she could manage it. In 1933, Eva was stable enough that she could withstand yet another cross-country journey. In New York, she managed a few modest stage appearances, though by now the newspapers largely ignored her. She stayed at the Hotel Woodward, which rose twelve stories above Broadway and West Fifty-fifth Street in Manhattan and boasted at least one quasi-turreted corner not unlike a grand vaudeville palace of yore. Eva penned a letter on hotel stationery to Florence in Massachusetts. "Your Poor old Mark died," Eva wrote, referring to her brother. Mark had been given Florence to raise, and the family had tried to pass him off as the girl's father. But Eva's words—referring to her brother as "your poor old Mark" rather than "your poor old father"—now seemed to let the fiction go.[16]

It was important to Eva to keep Flossie, as she sometimes called her, in the loop, to let her likely illegitimate daughter know that she still cared even if she could not muster a visit. Nor did Eva hesitate to pull heartstrings. "Don't faint dear Baby when I tell you I am in New York and working." "[My] eyes seem better," she assured Flossie, "but my heart is broken." She tried to explain in her own frantic manner that she had been in New York but did not have the funds to make it up to Ashfield, Massachusetts, Florence's home. "There was so much I wanted to do for you, Florence, but it was spend the money and stay in Ashfield or pay my fare to California." She was burdened with "debt after debt over three thousand," she explained, and added—as if it needed saying—"I do not get the big money anymore." Eva, it seems, had consulted some type of psychic or tea-leaf reader because she added the curious comment, "I understand that I have only one more year of bad luck." It was desperation speaking. Eva felt lonely, torn, and disconnected. "I have cried this whole day and wish now I had run in and surprised you for a day or so." Eva assured Florence, "I will always love you—you are so like my self thrown on the world and you have done your best." Perhaps the reference to Florence's having been "thrown on the world" was a nod to her illegitimate birth and patchwork rearing by relatives, spinsters, and overseers. "No one ever knew how I was when a child and it was the same with you," Eva speculated, a possible scent of guilt rising from her words.

Eva queried the songwriter George Spink to see whether he could provide some new material for her. "No one could ever write songs for me as George Spink did," Eva told the *Providence Journal,* which reported, "No ordinary 'Tin pan Alley' ditties will do for the cyclonic Eva. She must have songs to suit to her dynamic personality and method of delivery." Spink, of course, had had nothing to do with Eva's most famous song, "I Don't Care," and it may have been this very fact that made him appealing now.[17]

It is unclear whether George Spink ever came to Eva's aid. Likely he did not. But Eva managed to pick up some special-appearance work with an entity known as Fanchon & Marco. Marco Wolf and his sister, Fanchon (who was also known as Mrs. William Simon), were born Mike and Fanny Wolf in the 1890s in Los Angeles to musician parents. Though Jewish by birth, they later became devout Christian Scientists. The two put together a vaudeville act and eventually moved into cabarets and cafés, and then larger stage revues when shows patterned after Ziegfeld's popular *Follies* took off. By the time Eva Tanguay was in their employ, the Wolfs were providing elaborate, self-contained stage shows as filler for some 350 movie theaters in the western United States. The entertainments produced by the Fanchon & Marco unit were known as the *Ideas.* It was not exactly the *Follies,* but it paid.[18]

The last attempt at a career onstage, a vaunted but unrealized comeback, a last stab at rejoining New York's theatrical royalty—all had failed. Eva was unable to work, and even if her health had been better, the world no longer needed vaudevillians. Her onetime peers had either transitioned to movies and radio, died, or retired in anonymity. Professionally speaking, the curtain had fallen on Eva Tanguay for the last time.

RETURNING TO LOS ANGELES, Eva moved out of her Ravenswood accommodations by April 1936 and into a tiny cottage in Hollywood. She had letterhead printed that bore the address "6702 Lexington Avenue, Hollywood, California." But even that was wrong. Somehow—perhaps because her handwriting was illegible on the order form at the print shop, or maybe because her ever-wandering mind led her to transpose the digits, or possibly just owing to a mistake by the printer—what should have been 6207 Lexington Avenue became twisted and transposed into 6702. She had no money for more stationery; the tainted batch would have to do. When she used the letterhead, she would cross out "6702," and scribble the correct street address, "6207," next to it. Part of the confusion may have come from the fact that a year earlier, Eva had opened a shop to display and sell some of her outrageous costumes, now veritable museum pieces. She rented a small storefront on Hollywood Boulevard, east of Gower, where she tried to hawk the dresses made of feathers, spangles, and pennies that had once won her a reputation for being outrageous. Though the venture soon failed, the store's street address, 6027 Hollywood Boulevard, was a numerical anagram of her home street number.[19]

In the pink stucco bungalow at 6207 Lexington, Eva received few visitors. To cover the peeling plaster on the walls, she pinned up yellowing newspaper clippings from her famous past. One day Florence sent Eva a card that bore the picture of a single bird perched in a tree. Eva wrote back to her niece, "The card made me very sad[,] for the little bird on the *high* stump of a tree is so like my self."[20]

Some days, when the pain in her arthritic legs and aching body lessened, she took walks. She wore a blue cape, the color of a robin's egg. Kiddie followed her on a leash or sometimes enjoyed a ride in Eva's arms if she could summon the strength. Eva's hair, thinning, was dyed the color of corn silk. One afternoon in October 1936, as she lay resting, a snooping journalist, shouting to be heard through her window (for she would not come to the door), asked her how she was doing. "Please tell them," she informed the newsman, "that Eva Tanguay is all right. Just say that. Or say nothing—that's better." After a pause, she added that she would be back onstage by Christmas.[21]

THROUGH 1937, her health was stable enough to permit more walks and regular visits from her nieces, including Ruth, who had married Charles William Weekes in June and had by this point edged out her half sister, Lillian, as Eva's favorite. As 1938 wore on, though, Eva took a turn for the worse. In December, the *New York Times* readied its obituary. "Eva Tanguay Failing," reported the paper in a tiny notice buried in the fourth section. Despite more blood transfusions, even her latest personal physician, Wendell W. Starr, called her case "hopeless." When asked to comment on reports of her dire health, Eva sounded a philosophical note for the press. "My life has been a full one," she announced from her sickbed, surrounded by the clippings of her glory days, "It's all right. The end has to come to every one some time." She was being fed intravenously. An oxygen tube breathed life into a body that was closing up shop.[22]

One morning she awoke in her bungalow to find herself covered in blood, the result of a massive throat hemorrhage. Dr. Starr gave her thirty-three bedside blood transfusions in the weeks that followed, no mean feat considering how many of Eva's veins had collapsed. For ten months, Eva lay in her bed, barely moving and rarely attending to personal hygiene. She wrote to Florence of how her knees had grown "stuck *together* from lying on my back," while her once-glorious mane of gold ringlets had become a matted, filthy tangle that needed to be all but completely shorn. During one three-week stretch, she claimed, she went without food or drink. For companionship she had three cats in addition to her beloved dog.

When her hair started growing back, a friend—Eva did not say who, but very likely Sophie Tucker—paid for her to have it styled every two weeks. The feeling of human contact and whatever restoration of dignity came from such grooming efforts helped raise her spirits a notch. Other times it was not enough. Despite her joint pain, weakness, vision trouble, and general ill health, Eva nonetheless made an effort to articulate her suffering and loneliness in a way she had not done when times were good, as if needing to leave a record of her pain. "Sometimes I feel I'll just have to give up[.] Then I cry for about two days and get a hold on myself and start over again," she wrote in a letter to Flossie. The same people who were paying for her blood transfusions also arranged for a home health aid, a "jewish woman" [*sic*], Eva said, who came in each morning and helped the ailing vaudevillian from her bed onto a chair that had been made into a kind of toilet. The device saved her from the indignity of the bedpan and was, according to Eva, in part her idea. "All the friends I had seem to be dead," Eva lamented in a letter to Florence, to whom she confessed that although she was "still hanging on," she felt unfulfilled, admitting that "someone to take care of me is what I want."

There was one more thing Eva needed from Flossie: mittens. "I want great large ones such as a *man* would wear. The covering of my hands stops the pain a little so large *red* mittens is just the thing." She offered to pay for them, but it is unlikely Florence Tanguay Dufresne ever received any money.[23]

Much as her bodily ailments distressed her, Eva's pitiful financial state tore at her self-image as she languished in bed. In 1938, with vaudeville's corpse cooling, Ed Wynn, at one time a fellow vaudevillian, gave an interview to *Stage* magazine. Born Edwin Leopold Wynn in 1886 in Philadelphia, he started out with the Thurber-Nash repertory company, hit vaudeville with an act called The Rah Rah Boys, and was eventually recruited for the Ziegfeld *Follies of 1914*. He gained a following on radio doing such clownish characters as The Perfect Fool and The Fire Chief. Along with a contingent of other vaudevillians, Ed Wynn took the humor of the variety stage and reconfigured it for the airwaves. His Tuesday-night comedy show was said to be the most popular on the radio in 1933, drawing some 74 percent of all listeners.

Wynn told *Stage* magazine an old story about Eva having a fit when he, appearing with her on the bill, erred by speaking to her as she left the stage and headed into the wings. Enraged, Eva made a scene and threw her diamond tiara on the floor, according to Wynn. After reading the interview, Eva grabbed some of her misaddressed stationery and fired off an angry letter to the editor of *Stage,* claiming that Ed Wynn had indeed accosted her at an inappropriate moment, but that otherwise, "THERE IS NOT ONE WORD OF TRUTH IN [Ed Wynn's] STATEMENT." She admitted that at the time she had indeed owned a tiara consisting of some six hundred stones and bought at a cost of seven thousand dollars at Spaulding's Jewelry Store in Chicago. But she would never have displayed "such thoughtlessness as to throw such an expensive piece of jewelry on the floor under any circumstance." In fact, Eva claimed she never brought that particular tiara to the theater and certainly never used it onstage, as she was sure she had "intelligence enough at all times to cherish valuable things." The reminder of an era when she not only could afford jewel-encrusted tiaras but also throw them to the floor was more than she could bear, and Ed Wynn had had the temerity to remind her of it, even if she denied some of his story.[24]

When curious members of the press occasionally asked Eva for her own story in the early 1940s, they came away desperately wanting to see something different, perhaps too dismayed or overcome with pity to report on what they had actually observed. Eva Tanguay "Refuses to Be Sad," declared one headline. Her spirit was said to be "still blithe" despite a "pain-wracked body," on the occasion of her sixty-fourth birthday in 1942. No big celebration had been planned for the event, just some drop-ins by retired stage folk. The conversation, insisted the article, would focus on "the old days—cheerful talk, because Miss Tanguay won't tolerate any other kind." It was only in her private missives, drenched in pain and regret, that she tolerated talk that was less than cheerful.[25]

The *New York Times* continued the masquerade that other papers had begun. "She has been quick during her long illness to correct any impression of gloom," wrote the *Times,* whose editors must have known it would be a hard sell to those few readers that still cared. "She was cheerful then, and she is cheerful now," insisted the newspaper. The *Times* also took the occasion of Eva's birthday to speculate on the death of vaudeville. The reporter, a veteran of the theater beat, tried to put an upbeat spin on an otherwise decrepit reality. Eva's allegedly buoyant mood was "just one more piece of evidence that the spirit of vaudeville is not dead." No, it was not completely dead, but, like Eva Tanguay, it was pretty close. Alas, conceded the *Times,* the "birthdays of Eva Tanguay and others of those public favorites remind us in melancholy fashion of how time has slipped along." A revival of two-a-day vaudeville that spring had failed to arouse much interest. Many stage veterans were "at liberty"—a euphemism for unemployed—and yet they were said never to lose hope. The performer's suit may be "threadbare," noted the *Times,* but it was always neatly pressed and lint free. Indeed, Eva's very life and well-being were threadbare at best. A Jewish woman kept her thinning hair washed and brushed, and the makeup heir Max Factor Jr. sent bottles of perfume to Eva as well, a small if symbolically important gesture of dignity.[26]

In March 1945, as the Allies crossed the Rhine on their way to the Nazi capital of Berlin, Eva suffered an episode of congestive heart failure that again almost took her out for good. Her latest health-care attendant, Dr. Maurice Kowan, rushed to her aid and somehow pulled her back from the brink. Through that summer, Eva showed a slight improvement. By August of the following year, however, Eva could see the end in sight. "I'm just waiting for it to come any time now," she told a *Time* magazine reporter. Her knees were swollen and her legs bandaged. Several weeks earlier, she had been feeling good enough to be taken out for a drive. The car she was in, however, came to an abrupt stop and jangled the fading actress. She was thrown from her seat and cracked her head on the floor of the automobile. She begged a journalist, "Please, if you're going to write about me, don't say that my hair is grey. It's really pale gold. I don't have grey hair."[27]

It was reported that Eva Tanguay awoke smiling on the morning of January 11, 1947, a foggy day with a light wind and temperatures in the midfifties. Her niece, Ruth Weekes, her nurse, Anna Rubey, and a neighbor were at her bedside when she suffered a sudden, massive stroke. Eva Tanguay died at 9:25 a.m.[28]

A FEW DAYS LATER, on January 14, 1947, a crowd of some five hundred fans, friends, devotees, former colleagues, intimates, and onlookers crowded the Pierce Brothers mortuary in Hollywood, then accompanied the funeral procession to the Hollywood Mausoleum (today the Hollywood Forever Cemetery) on Santa Monica Boulevard for interment. "Some odd people showed up there," remembered Joseph Santley Jr., who covered the event for the *Los Angeles Examiner.* The throng included the assortment of eclectic, side-of-the-road characters Eva had been drawn to during a life that was anything but ordinary. Actress Trixie Friganza was there, and so was Fannie Mae Lockwood. Tex Cooper, a former expert cowpuncher who was said to have been an Oklahoma deputy before turning western star, showed up dressed like a Confederate officer. Little Mate Monday, sideman to the dime-show fabulist Whale Oil Gus, was among the pallbearers. Her onetime manager, one of the many, Harry Leonhardt was also in attendance, as was the stage actress Anna Chandler and the song-and-dance man Joe Whitehead, with whom Eva had once entertained President Harry Truman. The plain-talking president said he had seen "every vaudeville show" there was in Kansas City and had been wowed by "the great ones," notably Eva. Officiating at the proceedings was Elisabeth Carrick-Cook, a minister not of Christian Science but of a related, more humanistic tradition known as Religious Science, also called Science of Mind (and currently part of the United Centers for Spiritual Living), founded by Ernest Holmes in the late 1920s in California.[29]

In Eva's casket was placed an urn containing the ashes of Melville Collins, her niece Lillian's husband, said by some to be the only man she had ever really loved.[30]

Predictably, by this point Eva Tanguay's material contribution to posterity was effectively zero. She died intestate—her 1924 will was no longer even vaguely applicable—with less than six hundred dollars in salvageable assets. Blanche gave the job of administering her sister's final debts and possessions to her daughter Ruth Weekes. According to court papers filed after Eva's death, the onetime star's total estate was worth $584, nearly all of which would go toward fulfilling creditors' demands and paying attorney fees, funeral costs, and other bills. Her assets were scant: a 1937 Ford Standard Club Coupe (worth $400); a player piano; a straight-backed wooden chair; seven trunks; a bed, including a box spring; a chest of drawers; another bed; a vanity and bench; and a few mattresses. The biggest bill to be paid was from Pierce Brothers mortuary: $453.31. There were some other predictable charges. Southern California Gas Company issued a letter to Ruth Weekes asking that the sum of $5.52 be paid so that Eva's account could be closed out for good. Similarly, the telephone company demanded $9.02.[31]

Somehow a trunk full of programs, sheet music, news clippings, sundry documents, and even some costumes remained intact. Ruth Weekes, Eva's niece, seems to have ended up with it, and it eventually made its way to the basement of a home on Ventura Boulevard in Studio City, just north of the Hollywood Hills. This was the home of Lilyan (aka "Babe"), the daughter of Eva's other niece, Lillian. And there it apparently sat. Water damaged the costumes and they had to be thrown out. But the rest was eventually sold at a yard sale after Lilyan—by then Lilyan Mae Collins Musser, for she had married Charles Musser—died in 2003. And whoever bought it put it up for auction on eBay, where it was purchased by the archival division of The Henry Ford Museum, in Dearborn, Michigan, where it resides today, open to researchers since 2006. It is especially interesting that Eva's last physical gifts should have ended up at The Henry Ford, for during Eva's tough times in the 1930s, she had written a hopeful letter to Ford himself, asking for a free automobile.

Her request was denied.

Epilogue

George Jessel and Darryl Zanuck
Don't Care

EVA'S DEATH IN 1947 caused many nostalgic journalists and entertainment-industry watchers to declare, predictably, that along with the cyclonic one's passing, an era had died. Vaudeville could now finally be laid to rest. The golden yesteryear of B. F. Keith, Trixie Friganza, Salome dancing, and the myriad marvels of two-a-day lore were now surely ready to retire for good into the pages of scrapbooks and the recesses of popular memory.

The need to relegate a commercial art form to the quaintness of the past, however, usually says more about those doing the relegating than it does the object of their sentiments. From a practical and economic standpoint, it was certainly true that vaudeville as it had existed from, say, 1890 to 1920 was gone. As we have seen, parts of it lived on or changed shape. But when people describe something as "history" or "back *then,*" they usually have a reason, even if it is an unconscious one, for exiling it to the past in this way. In the case of Eva Tanguay, she had the misfortune, or perhaps good fortune, to die at the beginning of the post–World War II era, a time when many people in the United States wanted to forget the depredations of the past and all that had led up to financial hardship, social instability, and war. It was thus fitting that when Hollywood decided to remember the life of Eva Tanguay in the form of a splashy, big-budget biopic, it consequently erected a dense barrier between the modern, forward-looking, motion-picture present and the complicated, transitional, live-performer past. If today Eva seems to belong to a bygone time, it has as much to do with the ways in which the culture—Hollywood in particular—has chosen to recall her era as it does with Eva's stubborn bond to an evanescent art. Paradoxically, one of the chief players in the official misremembering of Eva Tanguay's life was a vaudeville peer who knew her well.

In 1948, less than eighteen months after Eva's funeral, a memo landed on the desk of a Twentieth Century-Fox producer named George Jessel. Jessel, born 1898, was a Bronx native of Jewish ancestry who made his way up through the ranks of vaudeville with a series of popular comedy sketches. By 1925, Jessel had moved to Broadway and won fame in the lead role of a musical called *The Jazz Singer*. When Warner Bros. wanted to adapt it into the first full-length motion picture featuring not only music but also spoken dialogue—the first of what came to be known as "talkies"—Jessel wanted more than the Warners were willing to pay. The part went to Al Jolson and history was made.

By 1948, though, things had changed. George Jessel knew the world of vaudeville perhaps better than anyone on the sprawling soundstage and Quonset-hut-filled Fox lot just west of Beverly Hills. (Today it is the business and shopping district known as Century City.) He commanded a first-person authority of the world he once traveled and was famous for sentimentally recalling his love affair with all things vaudeville. (Jessel was equally famous for referencing his love affairs with such starlets as Pola Negri, Norma Talmadge—whom he later married—and enough showgirls to make even Florenz Ziegfeld Jr. blush. His book, *Elegy in Manhattan,* it may be recalled, also spread rumors of Eva's love affair with George Walker.) But in the new dawn of the late-1940s United States, George Jessel was determined to remake himself as a movie man. He would go on to produce over a dozen high-profile pictures, such as the 1952 musical *Wait Till the Sun Shines, Nellie,* and to play dramatic roles in nearly twice as many films. In 1948 he was still a fledgling producer, a movie-colony recruit eager to make his mark and impress the imperious, powerful Twentieth Century-Fox production chief—his boss and everyone else's—Darryl Zanuck. He was determined to make vaudeville an artifact, surround it forever in a burnished chunk of amber. The life story of Eva Tanguay would give George Jessel the perfect opportunity to accomplish that task. It would also leave Eva forever on the far side of popular culture, looming huge in her day but hard to see from where we now stand.

It is unclear who initiated contact between Eva's heirs and the Fox studio. But what is certain is that, within a short time of the cyclonic one's passing, Ruth Weekes and Blanche Gifford (nee Tanguay), Eva's niece and sister, were sniffing around for a deal. At Twentieth Century-Fox, Blanche and Ruth, whose surname was misspelled as "Weeks" in studio memos, informed the legal department executive George Wasson that they wanted to sell the studio one hundred of Eva's songs plus some "100 pages of 'unusual incidents' either observed by Mrs. Weeks in her travels with Miss Tanguay or related to her by Miss Tanguay," according to an internal studio document. Ruth not only offered to sell the songs to which Eva may or may not have actually owned the rights since she had not composed them, she also promised to throw in a number of her aunt's famous stage costumes and, to further sweeten the deal, an alleged draft of Eva's memoirs, curiously "written by several different people but uncompleted." According to Ruth Weekes, her mother wanted $50,000 for it all, but not to worry, she could probably talk her down to $35,000.[1]

George Jessel was intrigued. Here was a moldable lump of clay delivered right to his hands. As he had made his way in vaudeville in the 1910s, there was no bigger star than Eva Tanguay. Now he had the chance to tell history, to inscribe Hollywood's epitaph on vaudeville's headstone. From the beginning, he was not especially interested in preserving the truth contained in whatever artifacts Ruth Weekes and Blanche Gifford were hawking. The key, as far as Jessel was concerned, was to quietly pay off Eva's heirs, then show them the exit. While Fox could not libel or otherwise defame Eva, since she was dead, unhappy heirs and offspring had been known to make life unpleasant—and costly—for studios producing biopics about their deceased relatives. Ruth Weekes had retained the powerful, high-profile attorney Mendel Silberberg to represent her interests. Silberberg informed Wasson, Jessel, and Jessel's production associate, Lew Schreiber, that there was "no question in his mind but that [Ruth Weekes] would sue" if not properly compensated for her source materials.[2]

That simply could not happen. George Jessel knew he had to wrest financial, artistic, and historical control of the Eva Tanguay biopic early and fully. "It would be awful to have us all come down to court and go through a great deal of litigation for a very small amount of money," lamented Jessel to his colleagues. To make matters worse, it turned out that an enterprising scribe at Twentieth Century-Fox named Joseph Santley—himself a onetime vaudeville song-and-dance man who liked Eva for being "crazy" and "wild"—had spoken "many, many times" with Ruth Weekes to prepare a treatment of Eva's story. Jessel reflected on the agony of another vaudeville-themed quasi-biopic, *The Dolly Sisters* (1945), starring Betty Grable, because it had to stop shooting for thirty money-bleeding days due to a similar legal impasse. "It wasn't so bad then as I had no pictures in production but if it happens this year it will be awful," groaned Jessel in a memo to Wasson. In short order, Ruth Weekes was paid an undisclosed sum, and from that point forward neither she nor her trove of information about Aunt Eva had much further impact on the movie that would eventually purport to tell the story of vaudeville's onetime queen.[3]

Santley got to work and quickly pounded out the draft of a screenplay called, not surprisingly, *I Don't Care,* which he declared to be "totally fictional." The claim helped protect the studio's legal interests but also gave him and his bosses full control over the narrative, regardless of the materials Eva had left behind. Fox paid Santley $17,500 for a script it understood to be "fictionalized" and tossed in the possibility of some royalties for the writer should the movie actually come out. Furthermore, the studio commissioned a lawyer, Fulton Brylawski, to find out whether they could use the title "I Don't Care." After some digging, it turned out that Eva's signature song, originally copyrighted in 1905, had since lost its protection because of failure to renew. Neither Jean Lenox nor Harry O. Sutton, the song's composers and copyright holders, nor Eva herself, had bothered to reinstate a legal claim to it. "I Don't Care" now belonged, in effect, to George Jessel, Darryl Zanuck, and the film moguls at Twentieth Century-Fox.[4]

Jessel took a close look at Joseph Santley's draft screenplay. He did not like what he saw. The Santley story opened in the early summer of 1901 in Holyoke, Massachusetts, a "thriving New England factory town" with fairgrounds, variety theaters, and dime museums for its "hard-working and fun-loving" inhabitants. A young Eva is employed at a dime museum in a scam freak-show act called "The Bodyless Woman." Losing her temper at a heckler, she lands "a solid right to the yokel's jaw" and decides to head for the real world of acting and theater in New York.[5]

Once there, a hard-drinking theater critic named Oliver Crane takes a professional and personal interest in Eva. Writing provocative reviews and editorials, he plans to "make Eva Tanguay the biggest name on Broadway" by "keeping her mad." In his estimation, Eva will work harder just to prove him wrong. The subsequent story has Eva appearing in *The Chaperons,* jousting with a rival actress named Lotta Fox—not unlike her real-life enemy Lotta Faust—and eventually losing her vision and falling offstage into an orchestra pit. At the screenplay's end, Eva's eyes are unbandaged in a hospital room. By her side is her now-beloved Oliver Crane, just back from reporting on the Russo-Japanese War—which in reality ended in 1905, before Eva became a big vaudeville star. "It's never going to be dark any more, darling," Eva tells Crane. She opens the blinds, and there, across the street, is the lit-up marquee of Hammerstein's Victoria Theater: "Coming Soon—Eva Tanguay." As never happened in her own life, Eva returns from conflict and ailment back to vaudeville's big time with the man she loved standing by her side.[6]

To George Jessel, Santley's screenplay contained a little too much museum-like fact for the modern moviegoer. At the same time, something about it also made Eva a passive puppet of the men in the story. This did not bother Jessel for feminist reasons; rather, to him it smacked of poor character motivation. Taking pen to paper, Jessel reflected on his own vaudeville days and composed an authoritative-sounding foreword that he attached to the next draft of "I Don't Care," this one turned in by the screenwriter Joseph Fields on September 16, 1948. Wrote Jessel:

> This is a story based on the songs and times of one of the most colorful girls that ever walked on the American stage. She reigned as the queen of vaudeville in a period from 1905 to 1920. Gifted with a radiant personality given to so few, she has become a joy to every audience and a temperamental terror to her managers. She had a style completely her own and had more imitators than Jolson. Critics used words like these about her—cyclonic, unique, impish, unsubmissive to conventions on or off the stage, turbulent and unpredictable. She was show business's problem child and its most devoted slave. This is not hearsay what I am telling you. I was there. I saw her. There was only one Eva Tanguay.

In a sense, Jessel defended the truth of Eva's character; Crane's manipulation, he knew, was unconvincing. But something else struck him as not quite right. At some level, the story threatened to slip away from the narrative confines he sought to impose on it. Ironically, in desiring to keep alive Eva's "unsubmissive spirit" by focusing on her personality, George Jessel was paving the way for a movie that would better serve the needs of the postvaudeville era, an era he was now helping shape. In this context, Eva had to serve Hollywood, not the other way around.[7]

Jessel busied himself with other projects while one writer after another was brought in to take a shot at rewriting the movie. Nothing seemed to gel. The winter of 1948 came and went with the right approach still eluding Jessel and the movie men at Twentieth Century-Fox. The vaudevillian-turned-movie-producer knew what didn't work, but could not articulate what would. Maybe he would know it when he saw it.

The writers Albert and Arthur Lewis, a father and son team, took a shot and turned in their treatment of "I Don't Care" in January 1949. The opening scene has a teenaged Eva enrolled at the Whalom School for Girls in Fitchburg, Massachusetts. She has just returned to her dorm room after sneaking out to catch a performance of "the forbidden play," *Lady Godiva,* starring Francesca Redding. Eva convinces her roommate to get down on all fours and imitate a "white Arabian horse," which she then mounts, letting "her own long hair hang down over her shoulders [and] peeling her clothes down to the bare necessities." Discovered and expelled for her saucy playacting, young Eva moves to New York City to live with her piano-playing uncle, Emil, who is in fact a distant cousin and may have romantic designs on his fetching young houseguest. One could not fault the Lewises for prudery. Not sure what to do with yet another Tanguay biopic screenplay—each one an effort that drifted further and further from the truth but no closer to a satisfying synthesis of past and present—Jessel kicked the matter upstairs to his boss, the daunting overlord of movie production at Twentieth Century-Fox, Darryl Zanuck.[8]

There are few more-storied personages in the history of Hollywood filmmaking than Darryl Francis Zanuck. Of Swiss descent, Zanuck was born in 1902 to a Nebraska hotelier and his wife. After returning from World War I, he began writing film story lines, eventually working for the silent-film slapstick man Mack Sennett and penning *Rin Tin Tin* plots for Warner Bros. in the late 1920s. The Warners made him the head of production in 1931. Two years later, Zanuck cofounded Twentieth Century Films, which later bought out the entertainment mogul William Fox's movie enterprises in 1935, forming the Twentieth Century-Fox studio. Deeply conservative, patriotic, and, most important, a raging micromanager, Zanuck was far from an absentee landlord on the Twentieth Century-Fox lot. Sometimes called "Cinemogul Zanuck," he impressed his tastes, politics, and worldview on the movies his company made. He was a big fan of the biographical picture, or biopic, always looking for ways to present a "sanitized, edited" version of a celebrity's life, according to the film historian George Custen. In Darryl Zanuck's view, the movies he made would reflect a world of temperance, devotion to country and capitalism, and the optimistic belief that the postwar United States was headed toward a glorious future. It was Zanuck's vision, combined with Jessel's, that would ultimately recast the tale of vaudeville and its queen in terms that were meaningful to them and the concerns of their era. As such, Darryl Zanuck took a special interest in Eva Tanguay's story.[9]

Zanuck was unimpressed by the Lewises' fanciful, libidinal rendering. To the production chief, it lacked proper character, motivation, and logic. Reading the screenplay, Zanuck saw Eva's many quarrels resulting only from her "Irish temper" rather than believable character development or an elegance of plot. It was all lame. He wanted the movie to convey *why* Eva had been such a temperamental problem child. Maybe, speculated Zanuck in a flurry of notes and production memos, she was picked on as a kid for having been an immigrant. Or maybe she was a tomboy in a girls' school full of snooty bluebloods. In frustration, Zanuck, too, hauled in a succession of screenwriters, beginning with no less a heavyweight than Herman Mankiewicz, the legendary scribe behind *Citizen Kane*. Others, including Marion Turk and I. A. L. Diamond, pumped out treatments and screenplays. (Diamond was later to co-write Billy Wilder's 1960 classic *The Apartment,* starring Jack Lemmon and Shirley MacLaine.) Poring over them all, Cinemogul Zanuck grumbled. To him the problem was simple. "What is wrong with it is that we have a lousy story," barked the production chief at a meeting in June 1949. It felt stale, predictable. At the center of the movie was a character whose actions appeared improperly motivated. Zanuck still wanted to know: Why did Eva do what she did?

Two screenwriters on the studio lot agreed with Darryl Zanuck. But rather than press harder into the realm of convoluted fiction, Albert E. Lewin and Burt Styler took the unusual step of actually doing some historical research. Looking through archival clipping files, they discovered the real life of Eva Tanguay needed little dressing up to become a gripping, entertaining tale. "As unexciting as the script was to us, the research material on the actual life of Eva Tanguay stimulated our imagination," exulted Lewin and Styler. They urged the movie to focus on the "really wonderful story" of the "real Eva Tanguay," a woman who was "clever, hard-working, glamorous, who defied the social customs of her time…a master of publicity." Their delving also yielded an insight into Eva's core motivation, the very thing Zanuck felt was lacking so far. To Lewin and Styler, Eva felt fundamentally lonely, isolated, and vulnerable. From these psychological wounds sprang her personality and behavior. The way they saw it, Eva's life all but shouted the following plea: "You must understand that I am alone in the world. Who is to protect me if I do not protect myself?" In the writers' estimation, this was the real-life Eva Tanguay's deepest belief (though they did not venture to explain what may have caused her to feel this way). Despite her "admiring throngs," and despite being "the toast of Broadway, the highest-priced and most sought-after performer of her day," Eva felt all alone. "If the story of Eva Tanguay is to be written," argued Lewin and Styler, "we feel that it must maintain the same integrity and fire that was Eva Tanguay." They had been energized by the Tanguay spirit and emboldened by the factual details of her life. It appeared as if something resembling Eva's complex and ultimately sad life story might make its way into the movie. Darryl Zanuck was intrigued.[10]

It was at this crucial moment, when a movie about the life of Eva Tanguay seemed poised to become something other than pure fiction, that George Jessel stepped back in with a vengeance. Possibly he was just trying to reassert his creative control, lest two lowly hacks, with the help of some old newspaper clippings, outshine him. Or maybe he sensed that something bigger was at stake: that the telling of Eva Tanguay's story could serve the greater cause of cementing her world and the world of vaudeville in history. Lewin and Styler, like boy detectives poking around a dusty attic, threatened to unearth, reanimate, and celebrate that past and its leading lady. It was the very time and place that had once given Jessel his start. But for that reason, it was not where he or those around him wanted to be now. Knowing he had first to please Zanuck, George Jessel hatched a remarkable plan.

In a flurry of inspiration, Jessel hammered out a story called "She Went That Way." It told the tale of a group of Twentieth Century-Fox filmmakers attempting to make a movie about the life of Eva Tanguay. In short order, he asked Darryl Zanuck to use it as the basis for the screenplay. Zanuck bit.

It was beautiful—revisionist and conservative all at once. The plot, in Jessel's conceit, would now focus on a group of *contemporary movie producers and writers* laboring to find out the truth, the real story, behind Eva's life. Even the most postmodern of critics, inclined to view all life narratives as artificial constructions, might have been impressed. It was Holmes, Freud, and Melville meeting on the studio back lot. Jessel's plan satisfied Darryl Zanuck's desire for both strong psychological motivation and compelling action. In digging into the mystery of Eva's psyche, the movie would now try to expose her core motivations. By depicting the investigation as the project of his own Twentieth Century-Fox film studio, Jessel made Hollywood and Zanuck, rather than vaudeville and Eva, the film's center of fascination. As George Custen has written, "The very difficulty experienced in finding the best way to frame the life on film became, in the end, the frame used to film the life."[11]

The screenwriter Arthur Caesar was brought in to hammer out a treatment based on "She Went That Way." An early scene has Jessel in his office talking to two of his studio scribes. "Sit down boys," Jessel tells his colleagues, plying them with cigars. "Boys,...you've worked hard on this story and what you've written you've written well—but I'm afraid it is nothing." The "old formula for a musical picture," the one about the "ambitious girl who finally gets her chance when the leading lady runs off with the millionaire," just won't play anymore. It's been done to death. Jessel does not care about the nostalgic genre of the backstage musical. He wants to focus on the *now,* the future even. His character, seated behind his studio-lot desk, demands something "very fresh and different." He says he knew Eva Tanguay only from a distance as an admiring spectator. To make the film, he needs to get closer. One of his underlings asks, "Is there anybody around town that could give us the real McCoy on Eva Tanguay?" A lightbulb goes on in Jessel's head. "Wait a minute," he blurts, recalling the name of a man who had once brought Eva to the studio lot some time ago. "The fellow...had a name like that—Coy...Eddie Coy!" The character Al Lawrence, likely based on Albert Lewin, meets Coy at a bar where the latter recounts how he first met Tanguay when she was a waitress at an after-hours eatery. In a flashback, they form a vaudeville two-act. But when Coy's drinking prevents him from going on one night, Tanguay performs solo and makes a hit. Much of this scripting would make it into the actual movie. Zanuck's men had found their recipe.[12]

The sleuthing writers go on to visit the other men in Tanguay's life: Mike Bennett, head of the Acme Music Corporation (an entirely fictional character), and, later, Larry Woods (also fictional), a singer who somehow talks his way into the *Ziegfeld Follies.* Drama, jealousy, and romantic triangulation follow as each man recalls his experience with Eva Tanguay for the benefit of the studio investigators. They recount the time she hauled off and smacked "somebody like John Barrymore" for imitating "I Don't Care" in public. They also recall how Tanguay's fiery reputation led one journalist to remark that she ought to be "caged," and how she then appeared at Hammerstein's literally in a lion's cage. In the end, she goes overseas to entertain the boys fighting in Europe but gets hurt when she strays too close to the front.[13]

Jessel punched up the new treatment for "I Don't Care" and delivered it to Darryl Zanuck on October 12, 1950. "The producer, of course, doesn't have to be me," he told the production chief, "although it would give it some authenticity." For "the girl," Jessel could see Betty Grable, June Haver, or Mitzi Gaynor.[14]

Zanuck loved the new draft. Reading it, he said he felt "astonishment." He wanted a bit more *Citizen Kane*–like plot though. "All three people who are interviewed about Eva should take credit for her success," he suggested, thus making "a liar of the previous one." In the new version, Jessel's character says, "Of course the present generation of moviegoers probably never heard of her. But when I get through with this picture every little town in the world will know Eva Tanguay! Her name will be known to everyone!" On April 27, 1951, the screenwriter Walter Bullock turned in a screenplay titled *The I Don't Care Girl,* based closely on George Jessel's original story. With some tidying from Darryl Zanuck, this would become the shooting script, finalized two months later. By October 1951, Zanuck was screening dailies and weighing in, struggling over how much brashness and temper to reveal in Tanguay's character. Eva Tanguay may have been the temperamental terror of vaudeville, but Zanuck's audience was mainstream, McCarthy-era America, and that was where his allegiances resided.[15]

Joseph Breen's Production Code office, which had so hampered Mae West in the 1930s, requested several cuts and provided strict advisories, notably that "the intimate parts of the body—specifically, the breasts of women—be fully covered at all times." Some spicy, irreverent dialogue—the sort that the Keith authorities might have pretended to rebuke in vaudeville, only to let it slide—was also ordered out. Specifically, the one-liners "I never get married any place but Greenwich" and "Some of my ex-wives are some of my best friends" were deemed by Breen's people to "contain a very light and flippant attitude towards marriage." The sentiments of course matched Eva's view of marriage. But she was gone, and Breen and Zanuck now reigned. An unspecified "manure gag" also had to go. The studio complied.[16]

BY MID-1951, shooting was ready to commence on *The I Don't Care Girl.* From a short list that also included Betty Grable, Betty Hutton, Doris Day, Shelly Winters, Ava Gardner, Anne Baxter, June Allyson, and Jane Wyman, Mitzi Gaynor emerged with the title role. Born Francesca Marlene von Gerber, Mitzi Gaynor was a Chicago girl of German and Hungarian extraction who was barely twenty years old when *The I Don't Care Girl* started filming. She was born on September 4, 1931. Young Mitzi had learned dancing from her aunt at the age of four, and in her teens took a Carmen Miranda impression on the USO circuit. At fourteen, she appeared in *Song of Norway,* based on the music of Grieg, in Philadelphia, and went on to spend three years honing her musical skills on Broadway. She once remarked that her fundamental rule of living was "always be yourself." She claimed to be naturally impulsive—"all Hungarians are, you know." Her first movie role of any substance was as Betty Grable's teen-age daughter in *My Blue Heaven* (1950). Throughout the 1950s, she was a top draw in Hollywood movie musicals, including *Golden Girl* (1951), in which she played Lotta Crabtree; *Anything Goes* (1956); and, perhaps most famously, *South Pacific* (1958), in which she washed him right out of her hair as Ensign Nellie Forbush. For the Tanguay job, Twentieth Century-Fox paid her $1,000 a week. Not bad, unless you consider that David Wayne was pulling in $2,100 a week as McCoy, and Oscar Levant, a onetime pia-nist in Sophie Tucker's backup band, $5,000 in the role of Bennett.[17]

Lloyd Bacon, who had directed Gaynor in *Golden Girl,* not to mention Sophie Tucker in *Honky Tonk,* was brought in to direct the

Figure 18. Production still from *The I Don't Care Girl* (1952), starring
Mitzi Gaynor as Eva (left) and David Wayne (right).
Hollywood decided to tell a story mainly about itself in its Eva Tanguay biopic.
The film's producer and one of its chief creative forces was George Jessel,
a former vaudevillian.
*(From the Billy Rose Theatre Division, The New York Public Library
for the Performing Arts, Astor, Lenox, and Tilden Foundations.)*

· · · · · · · · ·

Tanguay biopic. Bacon was a big fan of his leading lady. "I love her enthusiasm," he told *Collier's* magazine in 1952. "She's saturated with the bug to act and carry on and make theater." Bacon claimed he liked to glance around the soundstage to see how the grips and tech crew were reacting. "If the electricians are watching a scene from overhead, it's good." When Mitzi did her thing for the camera, their eyes followed her "the way a horse player follows a horse." Bacon believed he had a winner in the making.[18]

THE I DON'T CARE GIRL debuted the day before Christmas in 1952. Although Walter Bullock got credit for the screenplay, despite its derivation from George Jessel's story "She Went That Way," Jessel hardly had reason to fear being overlooked. For starters, he played himself in a number of key scenes. "I don't want alibis or psychoanalysis—I want Eva Tanguay, the woman. Underneath those sequins and feathers and the mop of wild curls was a woman's soul—that's what I want," he tells his studio staff early on in the picture. Though never actually seen, Zanuck himself looms just off camera; at one point Jessel says he's busy—"unless Zanuck wants me."[19]

The plot proceeded through splashy, Bob Fosse–like dance numbers that, as critics were to point out, had nothing whatever to do with vaudeville and everything to do with the jazzy, modernist aesthetics of the 1950s. It rambled, at times entertainingly, toward its predictable end: Tanguay back on top and her love life intact—precisely the opposite of what happened to the dissolute Eva in real life, all in an aesthetic milieu that smacked of the present rather than the past. It was the first and biggest brick in the barrier separating modern entertainment culture from Eva's time and place. Hollywood had worked its magic impressively.[20]

In its huge publicity campaign, the studio played up the picture's strong suits as best it could. Posters trumpeted "The Big Musical about the Bad Girl of Show Business," with Mitzi Gaynor in fishnets and burlesque garb. Newspaper-like articles suggested angles for the press by promoting the film's high production value and the colorful life on which it was supposedly based. "The life of Eva Tanguay, the irrepressible madcap of Broadway in the first part of this century, is recreated in 'The Don't Care Girl' Technicolor musical deriving its title from the famed star's theme song, 'I Don't Care.'" So read a studio press advance. Other gambits for the news media tried to draw parallels between Mitzi and Eva, noting that the former was "gifted with many of the qualities for which Eva

Tanguay was known." The ultimate narrative authority, however, was placed squarely on Jessel's shoulders. Gaynor, it was pointed out, labored under the "guidance of a producer who did know Eva Tanguay and knows intimately the Broadway scene of her era perhaps better than any of his other contemporaries." From script through promotion, the figure of George Jessel stood out prominently. And that of Eva Tanguay fell further into the abyss of muddled storytelling.[21]

Needless to say, the breathlessly cheery publicity materials did not exactly hit their mark—at least as far as the critics were concerned. "Fans of the film musicals will find 'The I Don't Care Girl' a hodgepodge of incidents presumably from the career of Eva Tanguay. It is pretentiously presented but misses." In most critics' eyes, the picture stumbled in two areas: authenticity and narrative focus. The screenplay, for all its endless rewrites and Zanuck-ifications, was deemed "aimless, virtually scriptless,...badly in need of some kind of story line to pull it together." Its big production numbers were assailed for being "very *moderne,* and completely out of keeping with the Tanguay period." Nor was Mitzi Gaynor, legs and all, the proper modern-day embodiment of yesteryear's cyclonic queen of vaudeville. "Miss Gaynor is a good hoofer and sells her songs nicely, but doesn't fit the Tanguay character at all." *Variety,* the publication founded by Sime Silverman to champion vaudevillians, now told it like it was.[22]

Another reviewer rightly called *The I Don't Care Girl* a "confused and inaccurate 'biography'" that "flits from one version to another of the life-story of Eva Tanguay" with "many loose ends flapping in the breeze." The finale, in his estimation, left the filmgoer with an "I-don't-care-either" feeling. Perhaps more important, Eva Tanguay, the "rowdy performer," had acquired a "gentler personality" in the hands of Mitzi Gaynor, Lloyd Bacon, Darryl Zanuck, and George Jessel. Each had partially sanitized vaudeville's cyclonic comedienne almost beyond recognition.[23]

In the end, *The I Don't Care Girl* failed to impress the film-going public as well. A week after it bowed, it was last among the top twenty box-office-grossing films. (Ironically, the leader that week was *Million Dollar Mermaid,* a biopic about Annette Kellerman, whose attempt to become the first woman to swim the English Channel had landed her a successful vaudeville run in Eva's day.) Compared to all films in 1953, the year in which it earned most of its revenues, *The I Don't Care Girl,* at $1.25 million, placed 105th. In the top spot was *The Robe,* a biblical-era drama starring Richard Burton, which pulled in $25 million. Other high earners that year included *From Here to Eternity* ($12.5 million), *Shane* ($8 million), and *Gentlemen Prefer Blondes* ($5.1 million). Few would remember 1953 as the year of *The I Don't Care Girl*.[24]

The I Don't Care Girl failed both as a source of biographical representation and as a backstage musical. The gimmick—Hollywood letting the moviegoer in on its behind-the-scenes movie-making activities—failed to amuse. As far as the actual life of Eva Tanguay was concerned, it was the first and last time public culture concerned itself on such a scale with the onetime superstar of vaudeville. Barely five years after her death, those who once intended to conjure Eva's story had instead misremembered her. Others would attempt to devise stage plays of Eva's life. In 1983, the writers Geraldine Fitzgerald and Donald Laventhall devised a treatment for a one-woman show about Eva's life, called *The I Don't Care Girl: Memories of Eva Tanguay*. This *I Don't Care Girl,* like its Hollywood, big-budget predecessor, was mostly fable, a "fictionalized outline, combining factual events with artistic license." Fitzgerald and Laventhall's eleven-page outline suggested a "format for the presentation of a project to be based on the life of Eva Tanguay that could utilize songs of the period as well as new original material." It ended up in the possession of Tom Eyen, the lyricist of the Broadway musical *Dreamgirls*. Beyond that, the work never saw the light of day. To the writers' credit, they never pitched it as anything but fiction. Its cover page read, "Fictionalized by Geraldine Fitzgerald." Had George Jessel and Darryl Zanuck done that, they might at least have neutralized expectations of the biographical mistreatment that was to follow.

Two weeks after *The I Don't Care Girl* debuted, *Variety* ran an article on the unsuccessful efforts of some show businessmen to resurrect vaudeville. But, noted the publication, "the vaudeville field has become the dust bowl of American show business."[25]

IN THE YEARS SINCE *The I Don't Care Girl,* the life and cultural contributions of Eva Tanguay have become almost entirely lost. If the movie misremembered Eva's story, few individuals or institutions have shown much interest in redressing that fact. While other stars of Eva's era are better included in our cultural memory, such as Sophie Tucker and Harry Houdini, Eva, arguably the last great performer of the live-only era, has slipped from view in a way that leads most people to ask, "Eva *who?*" when her name is mentioned.

Yet much as the curious-minded screenwriters Albert Lewin and Burt Styler had discovered, those who peek over the divide that seems to separate Eva and her time from our current moment glimpse someone fascinating. The online magazine *Slate* dubbed Eva "the biggest rock star in the United States" in her day, and observed a "line across the decades connecting Eva Tanguay and [the Sex Pistols guitarist] Johnny Rotten." And in March 2010 the Quebec-based *Le Devoir.com* ran an article titled "Eva Tanguay, première superstar américaine."[26]

There are some obvious reasons why we don't see Eva in the culture of today. Of course, if she had starred in a string of successful movies we might have greater cause to remember her. (Interestingly, Eva's fame may be increasing thanks to some videos of her on YouTube.) Many great nineteenth-century U.S. actors have suffered the same fate. Edwin Booth and Charlotte Cushman were megastars of the stage in their day. But long before movies, their images faded when the curtain fell.[27]

There is also the fact that Eva left little in the way of a written legacy, something to which actresses before and after her paid close attention. Prominent theatrical women, including Fanny Kemble, Charlotte Cushman, Anna Cora Mowatt, Adah Isaacs Menken, and Sarah Bernhardt, published memoirs, autobiographical fiction, poetry, essays, and short stories that shaped their image and fixed it in popular memory.[28]

By contrast, Eva was never comfortable with the written word (down to her byzantine penmanship and penchant for misspelling, evidenced in her private letters and documents). Though much was written about Eva in the theatrical and sensational press of the 1900s and 1910s, she herself wrote only one piece: a five-part, serialized autobiographical sketch that appeared in the Hearst newspaper supplement *The American Weekly*. It ran from the last week in December 1946 through late January 1947, and Eva died in relative obscurity before the serialized run ended. She had at various times in her life promised book-length autobiographies, but nothing ever seemed to come of it.[29]

In the early 1940s, Eva gave to the radio and print journalist Elza Schallert, wife of the *Los Angeles Times* drama editor Edwin Schallert, "manuscripts and other written data and materials containing information concerning [herself] suitable for adaptation for a stage, screen or radio story of [her] life, or for use in preparing a story of [her] life for publication in book or magazine form," according to court documents. Elza Schallert had written articles about Eva, and sympathetic ones at that. Eva, in a scribbled note to Florence Tanguay Dufresne, wrote of her excitement that "they are considering my life storie [*sic*] on the screen." But as with so many others in her life, Eva grew restive. She accused Schallert of not producing enough, or not producing it fast enough, or not showing enough interest. In September 1943, eight months after she had given Elza

Schallert a trunk full of source materials, Eva demanded it back. Schallert, who was busy working on a biography of the French composer Cécile Chaminade, asked Eva to be patient. Predictably, Eva would be no such thing, and she sued for, and won, the return of her possessions. Despite the feud, Elza Schallert looked with favor on vaudeville's onetime cyclonic marvel, if now from afar. According to Schallert's son William, "My mom admired Eva Tanguay for being a bawdy, raucous entertainer. She didn't hold her tongue and my mom admired that, like Tallulah Bankhead. She had a lot of guts." No one else offered to take Eva's trove of personal memorabilia and memorialize it into a book.[30]

And yet despite her failed attempts to have a meaningful artifact about her life produced for posterity, Eva is nonetheless very much with us. At a time when so much in the world of popular entertainment, and the society that it both shaped and reflected, were in breathtaking transition, Eva drew on the inspiration of the past to forge a living, energizing link with her audiences in a way that no one before her had ever quite done. She defined and swelled the popularity of vaudeville, the first form of truly mass-scale corporate entertainment, by never losing sight of the fact that it relied on an intimate link between human beings.

Eva showed a generation of entertainers such as Mae West and Sophie Tucker that you could push the limits of acceptability by shocking prudish sensibilities while keeping your public enthralled rather than repelled. To those showmen and women of future eras, she demonstrated that conventional notions of talent, having to do with virtuosic skill or expertise, were not only secondary to a magnetic charisma but could be dispensed with altogether if charisma was in abundant enough supply. As such, Eva played a crucial role in inaugurating the era of public fascination with a performer's personality, its charm and traction, above all else. As our current celebrity magazines and gawker websites indicate, we are still very much under that spell.

Eva's openness and personal appeal demonstrated to the early throngs of urban amusement-seekers that a dose of pluck and a winning line could help you navigate the bustling, seemingly ever-changing world around you. If Eva could do it, so could you. Or so she made it seem.

Finally, Eva Tanguay, without the classical training of Sarah Bernhardt or the beauty of Mary Pickford, took on the businessmen who helped invent the modern entertainment industry and made them pay her what she was worth. She never shied from conflict (even when perhaps she should have) and never let herself become a mere commodity in a corporate system. In so doing, she provided a devilish role model for the coming generations of women (and some men) who have sought to triumph onstage, onscreen, and on-air.

Rumor has it that Eva Tanguay's ghost haunts the recesses of the Cohoes Musical Hall, not far north of Albany, in upstate New York. It is unclear why Eva's spectral self would choose to inhabit the innards of a theater that was never particularly important to her in a town she never lived in. But if you cannot make it up to Cohoes, simply deepen your awareness the next time you take in a Lady Gaga concert, watch a Madonna video, listen to a Cher single, spin a Janis Joplin record, or enjoy an old Mae West movie. If you do, you are almost certain to detect the spirit of vaudeville's onetime cyclonic wonder.

Figure 19. A marquee from the Seattle Pantages Theater:
"Eternal Eva Tanguay."
Eva starred on the Pantages vaudeville circuit (and many others) in her heyday.
The marquee called her "eternal." For a time it almost seemed so.
(Private collection, courtesy Dan Johansson.)

. . . .

Eva Tanguay Chronology

1662   Jean Tanguy, the first of Eva's ancestors to arrive in North America, is baptized in Ploudiry, France, near Brest in Brittany. He arrives in New France (Quebec) as a young man, and because of a strong regional accent it is thought his name is Tanguay.

1692   Jean Tanguy marries Marie Brochu. He is known as *La Navette,* or "The Shuttle."

1694   Jean Baptiste Tanguay, eldest son of Jean and Marie is born.

1722   Jean Baptiste Tanguay marries Françoise Geneviève Blais at Contrat Michon.

1749   Jean Baptiste Tanguay marries Angélique Montminy at Saint Vallier. They have a son, Jean François.

1778   Jean François Tanguay, son of Jean Baptiste and Angélique, marries Catherine Blanchard Raynault (or Rayneau). He is Eva Tanguay's great-great-grandfather.

1806   Jean François' son, Michel Tanguay, marries Louise Létourneau at Saint-Marc sur Richelieu.

1837   Michel and Louise's son, Joseph Tanguay, marries Eulalie Dion.

1838   Joseph Octave is born to Joseph and Eulalie. He is Eva's father.

1860   Joseph Octave Tanguay begins practicing medicine, though he is not formally recognized as a physician until 1877.

1860   Joseph Octave Tanguay marries Adèle Pajeau. Born in Keeseville, New York, in 1842, Adèle is later known as Marie.

1861   Joseph Octave and Adèle "Marie" have their first child, a son, named Joseph.

1868   Joseph Octave and Adèle have their second child, also a son, named Adolphe Étienne. He will later be known as Mark McPherson Tanguay.

1874   Joseph Octave and Adèle have their third child, a daughter, named Blanche.

1878   Hélène Eva Tanguay is born on August 1 in Harding Corner, just
        down the road from the village of Marbleton, Quebec. Because she
        weighs only five pounds, she becomes known as "Dr. Tanguay's
        freak baby."

1883   Amid what is then known as the Great Depression of Canada, the
        Tanguays move to Holyoke, Massachusetts, a bustling mill town
        with a population of about 22,000, of whom some 6,500 are French-
        Canadian or of French-Canadian descent. Dr. Tanguay sets up an
        office and a home on Main Street in Holyoke's so-called French Ward.
        A year later, he moves his family to nearby Race Street.

1886   Joseph Octave Tanguay dies, leaving his family near impoverishment.
        Eva makes her stage debut, appearing in an amateur-night amusement
        at Parsons Hall in Holyoke. She wears a dress fashioned from an old
        umbrella and some doilies and napkins. After the laughter dies down,
        she explains that she and her family are poor and she made it herself.
        She dances a hornpipe and sings "The Fisherman and His Child Are
        Drowned." She walks away with first prize: one dollar.

1888   Eva is hired to play the lead in *Little Lord Fauntleroy* when the child lead
        in a local stock troupe, the Redding-Stanton Company, takes ill. She
        spends the next five years on the road, playing children's roles with
        Redding-Stanton.

1897   Eva's "niece," Florence Tanguay, is born. Her birth name is Eva Adela,
        but she is forever known as Florence, or sometimes Flossie. Though
        supposedly the offspring of Eva's brother Adolphe Étienne "Mark"
        Tanguay, she is believed by some to have in fact been Eva's illegitimate
        child with an unknown father.

1899   Adèle "Marie" Tanguay, Eva's mother, dies.

1901   Eva appears in the small but noticeable role of Gabrielle Du Chalus in
        My Lady, a *Three Musketeers* parody, with book by R. A. Barnet and
        music by H. L. Heartz, that had originated in Boston as *Miladi and the
        Musketeers.*

1902   Eva draws raves in the role of Phrosia in the New York production
        of *The Chaperons,* book by Frederic Ranken and music by Isidore
        Witmark. Her song "My Sambo" becomes a hit.

1903   Eva stars as Claire De Lune in *The Office Boy,* book Harry B. Smith
        and music by Ludwig Englander.

1904   Eva stars in *The Sambo Girl,* originally called *The Blonde in Black,* with
        book by Harry B. Smith and music by Gustave Kerker. The play is
        refashioned to accommodate her popular "Sambo" number. But it is
        another song in *The Sambo Girl* that earns Eva lasting fame, "I Don't
        Care." The song was not written by Smith, but was a contribution of
        lyricist Jean Lenox and composer Harry Sutton.

1905–1906 Eva begins devoting much of her stage time to vaudeville, garnering a
        large following and impressive earnings.

1906	Eva stars in the musical comedy *A Good Fellow,* book by Mark Swan and music by Melville Collins. It has been said that Melville Collins was the only man Eva Tanguay ever truly loved, but there is no direct evidence that they were romantically linked. Eva is taken in for police questioning in Iowa City after her male traveling companion, known as "Mr. Leach," brandishes a gun on a Chicago Burlington & Quincy railroad car following an altercation with a brakeman.
1907	Eva is caught shacked up in a hotel room with the theatrical journalist C. F. Zittel by detectives his wife had hired. Eva becomes engaged to the vaudeville industry executive Edward V. Darling. He plays an active role in managing her business affairs but the two are never married.
1908	Julian Eltinge, an actor famous for playing women's parts onstage, proposes publicly to Eva Tanguay. She accepts. The two are never married. Eva suffers the first of what will become several nervous and physical breakdowns in her life. This time, she fully recovers. Eva introduces her act "A Vision of Salome" amid a massive fad of "Salome dancers" in vaudeville and elsewhere. Its racy appeal helps Eva's "Salome" leap to the head of a very large pack. She is paid upwards of $3,500 a week, making her the highest-paid woman in vaudeville, and the highest-paid performer after (allegedly) Harry Houdini. Though the Salome craze dies down by about 1911, Eva continues to perform it sporadically through at least 1913.
1908–1909	Imitating Eva Tanguay becomes a robust subspecialty among vaudeville performers.
1909	Eva is arrested in New York for dancing indecently on Sundays, thus violating the "Sunday Law." Eva headlines *F. Ziegfeld, Jr.'s Revue on the Follies of 1909,* replacing Nora Bayes and Jack Norworth.
1912	Eva plays Praline Nutleigh in *The Sun Dodgers,* book by Edgar Smith and music by E. Ray Goetz. It is her first musical in six years, though the show is really a vaudeville-style patchwork of song and dance.
1913	The *New York Clipper* recognizes Eva as the "greatest 'drawing card' in present day vaudeville." Eva marries her fellow vaudeville trouper Johnny Ford (1881–1963) on a whim. Within days, she is seeking a way out.
1914	Blanche's daughter Lillian Skelding marries the pianist and songwriter Melville Collins.
1915	Johnny Ford and Eva split up, though they will not officially divorce for several more years. The *New York Dramatic Mirror* writes that only two other actresses have followings as big as Eva's: Sarah Bernhardt and Mary Pickford. Eva blocks film producers from releasing the movie *Success,* an assemblage of substandard footage of her filmed about 1908. Eva publicly declares her adherence to Christian Science, though she never officially joins the church.

1915–1918	Eva headlines at vaudeville's most famous venue, the Palace, in New York City, no fewer than ten times.
1916	Eva self-produces a promotional movie called *Energetic Eva*. No prints have survived.
1917	Eva stars in *The Young Mrs. Sanford,* a stage melodrama designed to look like a motion picture. It fails. Eva stars in *The Wild Girl,* a silent movie directed by Howard Estabrook and produced by Selznick Pictures. It is her only real screen effort. A judge grants a divorce to Eva Tanguay. She is no longer married to Johnny Ford.
1919	Eva starts a romantic relationship with fellow vaudevillian Roscoe Ails; he becomes physically abusive.
1919–1921	Eva headlines at the Palace at least eight times.
1923	Melville Collins dies.
1924	By this time, Eva owns significant real estate holdings in Los Angeles.
1927	Eva marries Al Parado, her accompanist. He is less than half her age. Having done it largely for the publicity, Parado later claims, she has the union annulled in short order.
1930	Adolphe Étienne "Mark McPherson" Tanguay dies.
1932	Eva is said to be near death due to a variety of ailments including kidney disease. To everyone's surprise, she pulls through.
1933	Eva's eyesight is restored after operations for severe cataracts; she soon vows to make a stage comeback.
1936	Eva moves into a tiny bungalow in eastern Hollywood; it will be her final residence.
1938	Eva Tanguay is again on the verge of death; her doctors all but give up hope.
1947	Eva Tanguay dies. Her estate totals $584.
1952	*The I Don't Care Girl,* starring Mitzi Gaynor as Eva Tanguay, opens to tepid reviews and unimpressive box-office receipts.

Notes

❦

INTRODUCTION

1. Richmond (Indiana) *Morning Telegraph,* January 23, 1905, New York Public Library for the Performing Arts Theater Collection, Robinson Locke Collection of Dramatic Scrapbooks, vol. 450 (henceforth abbreviated NYPL, Robinson Locke Collection); Vincennes.org, "History," http://www.vincennes.org/category/about-vincennes/history; A Brief History of Vincennes, http://rking.vinu.edu/vinbrief.htm.

2. Richard L. Forstall, "Indiana: Population of Counties by Decennial Censuses; 1900 to 1990," Population Division, U.S. Bureau of the Census, http://www.census.gov/population/cencounts/in190090.txt; Smith, *Historical Sketches,* 273–75.

3. Otherwise unattributed article date-stamped 1905, NYPL, Robinson Locke Col. v. 450.

4. "Lion Tamer" monologue fragment, in Eva Tanguay Collection, acc. 2006.9, Benson Ford Research Center.

5. Ibid.

6. "Not in the Big Time," *Time,* April 20, 1931, in Time-Life Archives, New York; Leider, *Becoming Mae West,* 41–42.

7. Slide, *Encyclopedia of Vaudeville,* 488; Gilbert, *American Vaudeville,* 328.

8. "Urban and Rural Population: 1900 to 1990," www.census.gov/population/censusdata/urpop0090.txt, and "Population: 1790 to 1990," www.census.gov/population/www/censusdata/files/table-4.pdf, both from Population Division, U.S. Bureau of the Census; Nasaw, *Going Out,* 1–9; Banner, *American Beauty,* 175.

9. Sentilles, *Performing Menken,* 66; Ponce de Leon, *Self-Exposure,* 40.

10. For more on Barnum, see Trav S. D., *No Applause,* 57–67, and Glenn, *Female Spectacle,* 26. On nickelodeons, see Gomery, *Shared Pleasures,* 18–33. On "concert saloons," see Gilfoyle, "Policing of Sexuality," 303.

11. Nasaw, *Going Out,* 23.

12. This and previous paragraph: Keith/Albee Vaudeville Theater Collection, MsC 356, scrapbook 8, 244, scrapbook 7, 193, 230, and scrapbook 10, 58; *New York Clipper,* February 20, 1909, 39; Marks, *They All Sang,* 178.

13. This and previous paragraphs: Caffin, *Vaudeville,* 35–36; Gilbert, *American Vaudeville,* 329; Eichenwald, "Americans." Susan A. Glenn argues that Eva "made a virtue of her negative qualities" (*Female Spectacle,* 63). This is a worthy analysis, but cannot fully account for Eva's impact and popularity.

14. This and previous paragraphs: Trav S. D., *No Applause,* 132; *New York Clipper,* January 11, 1913, 7; *Chicago Inter-Ocean,* March 21, 1907; unattributed newspaper clipping, article date-stamped

April 18, 1909, NYPL, Robinson Locke Collection, v. 450; Peiss, *Hope in a Jar*, 3–4, 107; Banner, *American Beauty*, 148.

15. This and previous paragraphs: Caffin, *Vaudeville*, 36; Frederick James Smith, "'I Do Care!' Says Eva Tanguay," *New York Dramatic Mirror*, January 27, 1915, 30; Rosen, "Vanishing Act"; Wes Eichenwald, e-mail message to author, August 26, 2004; deCordova, *Picture Personalities*, 72.

16. Banner, *American Beauty*, 165, 171, 201.

17. Dudden, *Women in American Theatre*, 27–28, 50.

18. Ibid., 75, 77, 85–86, 94, 99; Titone, *My Thoughts Be Bloody*, 314.

19. Dudden, *Women in American Theatre*, 115; Piepmeier, *Out in Public*, 20, 24, 27, 38; Westerfield, "Investigation," 28; Marks, *They All Sang*, 178.

20. Downer, *Eminent Tragedian*, 75–77.

21. Ibid., 257, 283.

22. Brockett, *History of the Theatre*, 418–19, 290–310; For more on Edwin's temperament and John Wilkes's motivations, see Titone, *Thoughts Be Bloody*, 26, 40, 77, 169, 173, 180–81, 225. Edwin Booth was subsequently challenged by the British actor Henry Irving, who nonetheless remained a great admirer of Booth's and always acknowledged the U.S. actor's influence on him. See Holyroyd, *Strange Eventful History*, 133; Shaw, *Titans*, 73.

23. This and previous paragraph: Braudy, *Frenzy of Renown*, 498–99; Harris, *Humbug*, 43–49, 207; Kalush and Sloman, *Secret Life of Houdini*, 11, 39, 42, 77, 81.

24. This and previous paragraph: Sentilles, *Performing Menken*, 6, 8–11, 49–50. Sentilles offers an excellent definition of celebrity. Celebrities, she writes, are those famous individuals who provide "illusory personal relationships in an increasingly impersonal world…distant and close, everywhere to be seen and yet rarely spotted in person" (6).

25. Dudden, *Women in American Theatre*, 149–50, 164; Banner, *American Beauty*, 120–27. Banner also cites the actress Lotta Crabtree (1847–1924) as an important precursor to Eva Tanguay (125).

26. Gänzl, *Lydia Thompson*, 2; Brockett, *History of the Theatre*, 461–62.

27. Dudden, *Women in American Theatre*, 4.

28. Glenn, *Female Spectacle*, 25, 82; Gold and Fizdale, *Divine Sarah*, 112; Woods, "Sarah Bernhardt and the Refining of American Vaudeville," 16–24.

29. See Ponce de Leon, *Self-Exposure*, 42–75; Keith/Albee Collection, University of Iowa, MsC 356, scrapbook 7, 11.

30. Some have claimed that Eva became such a hit by playing the raw-sex card in a show of shocking anti-Victorianism. "She cared no whit for anyone and under the very nose of [vaudeville impresario E. F.] Albee got more sex into her shouted numbers than could be found in a crib street in a mining town," wrote Douglas Gilbert. While sexuality played an important part in Eva's stage efforts (not to mention her offstage shenanigans), it was hardly her raison d'être. She balanced brazen eros and a seemingly coy innocence. In the autobiographical series she wrote for *American Weekly*, Eva claimed that she had never wanted to reveal her shapely form and that her high-speed choreography was invented by way of modesty. When portraying "Coloma, the Hoo-doo, a bare-footed Fiji Islander with a flimsy voile slit skirt, rhinestone ankle bracelets, and scarcely any bodice at all" early in her career, Eva declared that she was determined to "move so fast and whirl so madly that no one would be able to see my bare legs." While Eva probably did not expect the public to have believed such a myth, it nonetheless reflects what she wanted them to believe. It also highlighted a cultural double standard requiring women to be sexually alluring and chaste at the same time. PR efforts like these let Eva take control of her sexual image both in performance and in the press. She appeared, instead of simply a passive victim of powerful male sexual demands, more a sculptor of her own image, ever astride the limits of convention. In a sense, Eva was more a psychological exhibitionist than a physical one. She made her sexuality a useful plaything, just one part of a mercurial, complex personality that rarely failed to amuse. See Westerfield, "Investigation"; Gilbert, *American Vaudeville*, 327–28; Tanguay, "I Don't Care," December 29, 1946, 12.

31. The display is titled "Memories of 23rd Street," by Keith Godard.

1. FREAK BABY AND THE PAPER CITY

1. Charles Darnton, "Eva Tanguay Says She's Not What She Seems on the Stage: She Does Care—My, Yes!" *Evening World,* article date-stamped March 13, 1909, NYPL, Robinson Locke Collection, v. 450; Sentilles, *Performing Menken,* 34–35; Mordden, *Ziegfeld,* 35.

2. Robert, *Eva Tanguay,* 2; supplemental research provided by Jacques Robert; Dickinson, *Short History,* 173.

3. Marriage certificate of Joseph Octave Tanguay and Adèle Pajeau, trans. Jacques Robert.

4. Robert, *Eva Tanguay,* 2; Price, "Noted Vaudeville Star."

5. Birth certificate of Joseph Octave Tanguay, the son, November 1, 1861; birth certificate of Adolphe Étienne Tanguay, July 6, 1868; genealogy of the Tanguay family; all provided/trans. by Jacques Robert.

6. This and prior paragraph: *Baltimore Star,* article date-stamped April 23, 1909, NYPL, Robinson Locke Collection, v. 450; Tanguay, "I Care at Last." Some feminist scholars have noted that donning the mantle of freakishness can liberate the female performer from conventional notions of restrained, socially approved womanly beauty. For more on freakishness and female entertainers, see Rowe, *Unruly Woman,* 33.

7. *Recensement de 1863 pour le Canton de Dudswell,* provided/trans. by Jacques Robert; genealogy of the Tanguay Family.

8. Robert, *Eva Tanguay,* 2; Price, "Noted Vaudeville Star."

9. "Truant Officer Tanguay Disappears," *Holyoke Daily Transcript,* February 12, 1884, 4; "Death of Mrs. Tanguay," *Holyoke Daily Transcript,* February 20, 1884, 4.

10. Association des familles Tanguay inc., *Tanguay;* Tanguay, *Jean Tanguy,* 6; Régent Tanguay, *Que trouve-t-on dans mes 25 éditions du journal* Le Tanguay *de 1998 à 2006* (document compiled and bound by Régent Tanguay), 6. For genealogical information on the Tanguay family, I am deeply indebted to Jacques Robert, local historian, writer, and genealogist in Quebec, who provided me with invaluable information and research. See also French-Canadian Genealogical Society of Connecticut, *Connecticut Maple Leaf.* Because of the added *a,* Jean Tanguy's "Tanguay" heirs are also related, however distantly, to a number of other Tanguys in Europe, including the surrealist painter Yves Tanguy (1900–1955) and Henri Tanguy (1908–2002), a Resistance fighter in World War II and one of the liberators of Paris along with his better-known colleague, Charles de Gaulle.

11. Dickinson, *Short History,* 67–68, 75–76; Linteau, Durocher, and Robert, *Québec,* 44.

12. *Tanguay,* 3rd quarter 2005; Tanguay, *Jean Tanguy,* 16; Linteau, Durocher, and Robert, *Québec,* 13; Dickinson, *Short History,* 31, 34.

13. Dickinson, *Short History,* 54–55.

14. Ibid., 72; Linteau, Durocher, and Robert, *Québec,* 40; Handelman, "Where the Lake Is Deep."

15. Green, *Holyoke,* 99.

16. Ibid., 37, 82–83; Harper, *Story of Holyoke,* 60–61; DiCarlo, *Holyoke-Chicopee,* 206.

17. Bilodeau, "French in Holyoke," 1–5; Green, *Holyoke,* 23, 31. See also Petrin, *French Canadians,* 30, 18–19, 21; Harper, *Story of Holyoke,* 48; Franco-American Centennial Committee. *Souvenir Program,* 19.

18. Michael Cleary, "Brief Review of Holyoke: Past and Present," prepared for Holyoke's sixty-fourth anniversary, March 14, 1914, ms. found in Holyoke History Room, 1; Franco-American Centennial Committee. *Souvenir Program,* 19; "City News," *Holyoke Daily Transcript,* October 3, 1885, 8; DiCarlo, *Holyoke-Chicopee,* 243; Green, *Holyoke,* 367.

19. *Holyoke City Directory 1883* (Holyoke: W. S. Loomis), 403.

20. Bilodeau, "French in Holyoke," 5; Green, *Holyoke,* 113; "City News," *Holyoke Daily Transcript,* October 3, 1885, 8; Daniel Pidgeon, "French-Canadian People in Holyoke" (1885): This is a typewritten, photocopied document I found in the Holyoke History Room and includes a reference to "v. 3, 109–113, Copeland. History of Hampden County." There is a book, Alfred Minot Copeland, ed., *A History of Hampden County, Massachusetts,* Century Memorial Publishing, 1902, but a search in an online archive for phrases in the source document yielded no matches. More curious, the end of this document reads, "Taken from Old

World Questions and New World Answers by Daniel Pidgeon, London, 1885." There is a book, Daniel Pidgeon, *Old World Questions and New World Answers,* 2nd ed., London: Kegan Paul, Trench, 1885, but a search in this book also yields no matches.

21. The Oracle, *Holyoke Daily Transcript,* January 29, 1981, clipping found in Holyoke Public Library.

22. Green, *Holyoke,* 29, 51; "A Select Private Musicale," *Holyoke Daily Transcript,* January 11, 1887, 4; "To-Night's Masquerade Ball," *Holyoke Daily Transcript,* February 5, 1892, 4; "Masks and Faces," *Holyoke Daily Transcript,* February 6, 1892, 4; Hartford, *Working People,* 65, 81.

23. DiCarlo, *Holyoke-Chicopee,* 190; Hartford, *Working People,* 65; Green, *Holyoke,* 109; "City News: Drama and Farce," *Holyoke Daily Transcript,* March 18, 1884, 4; "The Drama of St. Patrick's Night," *Holyoke Daily Transcript,* March 18, 1887, 4; "An Oriental Drama," *Holyoke Daily Transcript,* September 11, 1890, 4; "Program of Prize Speaking," *Holyoke Daily Transcript,* January 13, 1892, 4.

24. Green, *Holyoke,* 374; Holyoke Opera House programs, courtesy of Holyoke Public Library; Susan Laramee, "Opera House Brought Stars, Status to Holyoke after Its 1878 Opening," *Holyoke Transcript-Telegram,* April 1, 1978, 3; "At the Opera House: Dockstader's Minstrels," *Holyoke Daily Transcript,* September 27, 1891, 4; "At the Opera House: The Henry Burlesque Company This Evening," *Holyoke Daily Transcript,* January 29, 1893, 4.

25. *Holyoke Daily Transcript,* January 1, 1890, 8; "Macbeth," *Holyoke Daily Transcript,* January 14, 1890, 7; "Modjeska at Springfield," *Holyoke Daily Transcript,* January 26, 1887, 4; "A New Shakespearian Star," *Holyoke Daily Transcript,* January 14, 1892, 4; "The Holyoke Variety," *Holyoke Daily Transcript,* January 8, 1890, 8.

26. "Theatre Tidbits," *Holyoke Daily Transcript,* November 20, 1893, 2; "Mme. Rhea Married," *Holyoke Daily Transcript,* July 28, 1893, 4; "Stageland Gossip," *Holyoke Daily Transcript,* March 21, 1899, 2; "Both Sides of the Footlights," *Holyoke Daily Transcript,* April 6, 1899, 1; Green, *Holyoke,* 374.

27. DiCarlo, *Holyoke-Chicopee,* 223; "Staged Shows at Mt. Park," ms. found in Holyoke Public Library; "Opening of Pavilion Theatre," ms. found in Holyoke Public Library; "A New Theatrical Venture," *Holyoke Daily Transcript,* February 13, 1893, 4; "Pavilion Theatre," *Holyoke Daily Transcript,* May 21, 1894, 4; "Specialty and Vaudeville," *Holyoke Daily Transcript,* February 20, 1894, 4; "At the Pavilion Theatre," *Holyoke Daily Transcript,* May 24, 1894, 4; "Colored Sports at the Pavilion," *Holyoke Daily Transcript,* June 13, 1894, 4; "Gaiety Burlesque Company," *Holyoke Daily Transcript,* July 27, 1894, 4.

28. "Hospital and Public Library," *Holyoke Daily Transcript,* January 4, 1892, 4; "A Valuable Addition," *Holyoke Daily Transcript,* February 19, 1892, 4; "Full-Fledged Teachers," February 4, 1893, 4; "How Do Holyoke Women Kill Time?" *Holyoke Daily Transcript,* December 9, 1890, 4; "Why Women Marry," *Holyoke Daily Transcript,* March 10, 1899, 5.

29. This and prior paragraphs: Robert, *Eva Tanguay,* 2-3; "Holyoke's I Don't Care Girl Reported Improved," unattributed newspaper clipping, probably from the *Holyoke Transcript* or *Telegram,* in the Holyoke History Room of the Holyoke Public Library, Massachusetts; genealogical and biographical notes, ms. found in Holyoke History Room; Eva Tanguay, "Success," *Variety,* December 12, 1908, 121; Laurel O'Donnell, "History of Holyoke's Churches," http://www.holyokemass.com/transcript/church/ch12.html (accessed April 28, 2006).

30. "Eva Tanguay Dies; Rose to Stage Fame from Amateur Act Here," unattributed newspaper clipping found in Holyoke Public Library; *Holyoke City Directory 1886,* 219; *1887,* 236; *1888,* 266; *1889,* 289 (Holyoke: W. S. Loomis). According to the feminist critic Kathleen Rowe, many actresses have pleaded that they took to the stage in order to help their families in hard economic times, thus keeping their stories within "the familiar terrain of melodrama" (*Unruly Woman,* 5).

31. Ullie Akerstrom, "A Glimpse of the Real Eva Tanguay," ca. 1903, ms. found in Eva Tanguay Collection, acc. 2006.9, Benson Ford Research Center.

32. Commonwealth of Massachusetts, certificate of death, City of Holyoke, Joseph O. Tanguay, September 6, 1886, copy issued and stamped August 10, 2004; Brault, *French-Canadian Heritage,* 84; *Holyoke City Directory 1886,* 219; *1887,* 236; *1888,* 266; *1889,* 289 (Holyoke:

W. S. Loomis); "City Paupers Aided in Holyoke," *Municipal Register of the City of Holyoke for 1889* (Holyoke: Transcript Publishing, 1890), 294–95; Franco-American Centennial Committee. *Souvenir Program,* 18; Petrin, *French Canadians,* 39.

33. Johnson and Morse, *M-O-T-H-E-R,* 3; Wes Eichenwald, "Americans: 'The I Don't Care' Girl: Eva Tanguay (1878–1947)" (unpublished article draft, 2001), 1; Charles Darnton, "Eva Tanguay Says She's Not What She Seems on the Stage: She Does Care—My, Yes!" *Evening World,* article date-stamped March 13, 1909, NYPL, Robinson Locke Collection, v. 450.

34. Walters, *Household Dictionary,* 121; Steadman, *Medical Dictionary,* 154, 522, 544. I am also deeply indebted to Hugh Bases, MD, of New York University Medical Center, and Judith Taylor, MD, physician, author, and medical historian, for their input and expertise.

35. Forbes, Tweedie, and Conolly, *Cyclopaedia,* 1:706; Murchison, *Clinical Lectures,* 246–47; Oliver, *Abdominal Tumours,* 236.

36. Hickman, "Tanguay Tells."

37. Green, *Holyoke,* 54, 123. "By a wide margin, the most recognized evil in Holyoke was drunkenness," notes Hartford (*Working People,* 15). DiCarlo, *Holyoke-Chicopee,*189; City-Data.com, "Holyoke, Massachusetts (MA): Accommodation, Waste Management, Arts, Entertainment & Recreation, etc.—Economy and Business Data & Market Research, http://www.city-data.com/business/econ-Holyoke-Massachusetts.html (accessed April 29, 2006); "The Chief-of-Police's Report," *Holyoke Daily Transcript,* December 19, 1884, 8; Burritt, "Drunkenness in Massachusetts."

38. Pidgeon, "French-Canadian People in Holyoke" (see note 20, above); Green, *Holyoke,* 52; Petrin, *French Canadians,* 132.

39. Carol M. Booker, "Descendents of Blanche Agnes Tanguay," November 19, 2004, supplied to author courtesy of Ashfield Historical Society, Ashfield, Massachusetts.

40. Kunhardt, "Little Lord Fauntleroy."

41. The author of a 2004 article in the London *Observer* had in fact referred to *Fauntleroy* as the "Harry Potter of its day"; see Kellaway, "Up the Garden Path." Kunhardt, "Little Lord Fauntleroy," 71, 74; souvenir program, *Little Lord Fauntleroy,* Broadway Theatre, December 3, 1888, New York Public Library for the Performing Arts Theater Collection; "Niblo's—Little Lord Fauntleroy," *New York Dramatic Mirror,* March 22, 1890, 4; Brockett, *History,* 446; *Vanity Fair,* article date-stamped April 20, 1912, and "Arthur Klein, 79, Discoverer of Jolson," *New York World Telegram & Sun,* article date-stamped November 3, 1964, both in New York Public Library for the Performing Arts Theater Collection.

42. Kunhardt, "Little Lord Fauntleroy," 71–72; "Vivian Burnett, Son of Frances Hodgson Burnett," *Herald Tribune,* July 26, 1937; "Original Fauntleroy Dies in Boat after Helping Rescue 4 in Sound," newspaper clipping, New York Public Library for the Performing Arts Theater Collection.

43. Kunhardt, "Little Lord Fauntleroy," 72; advertisement, *Saratoga Daily Register,* May 4, 1889, 1; James, *Notable American Women,* 3:425.

44. Westerfield, "Investigation," 5–6; "Holyoke's I Don't Care Girl Reported Improved"; Tanguay, "I Don't Care," December 29, 1946, 12; Banner, *American Beauty,* 125.

45. "Miss Redding a Vaudeville Evangelist," *Grand Rapids Press,* article date-stamped April 21, 1903, and "A Successful Comedienne," *New York Dramatic Mirror,* article date-stamped November 6, 1897, both in New York Public Library for the Performing Arts Theater Collection, Locke Envelope Collection, 1854.

46. Dudden, *Women in American Theatre,* 39.

47. NYPL, Robinson Locke Collection, v. 327; "Successful Comedienne" (see note 45, above); Bryan, "Vaudeville to the Silver Screen"; "Hugh Stanton Dead."

48. "At the Opera House," *Holyoke Daily Transcript,* January 4, 1892, 4; "At the Opera House," *Holyoke Daily Transcript,* February 9, 1892, 4; "At the Opera House," *Holyoke Daily Transcript,* February 10, 1892, 4; "At the Opera House," *Holyoke Daily Transcript,* February 11, 1892, 4; "At the Opera House," *Holyoke Daily Transcript,* February 12, 1892, 4; "At the Opera House," *Holyoke Daily Transcript,* February 13, 1892, 4.

49. "The Pavilion Theatre," *Holyoke Daily Transcript,* July 31, 1893, 4; "Theater Tidbits," *Holyoke Daily Transcript,* April 28, 1894, 4.

50. "Sambo Girl Denies She Ever Appeared with Indian Show," *Pittsburg Leader,* article date-stamped May 6, 1907, NYPL, Robinson Locke Collection, v. 450.

51. Unattributed newspaper clipping, article date-stamped February 2, 1919, NYPL, Robinson Locke Collection, v. 297; see also Piepmeier, *Out in Public,* 30–31. It is worth noting that prominent men of the late nineteenth century often described the towns and cities they grew up in as places where they learned to be clever, energetic, and hardworking so as to overcome rigor and hardship and prepare them for later success. P. T. Barnum in particular emphasized the "hard character of his New England youth" in his 1855 autobiography, according to Neil Harris in *Humbug,* 211.

52. "Births Must Be Reported," *Holyoke Daily Transcript,* February 10, 1910.

53. Ibid.

54. Barbara Johnson, personal letter to author, September 28, 2004; Barbara Johnson, interview with author, August 18, 2004; Elaine Dufresne, interview with author, July 13, 2004; Elaine Dufresne, e-mail message to author, August 30, 2004; Doris Luce, interview ms. found in Holyoke Public Library; Ella Merkel DiCarlo, Holyoke, Massachusetts, letter to Barbara Johnson, Parker, Florida, May 11, 1981; Ella Merkel DiCarlo, genealogical research notes regarding Florence Tanguay Dufresne; Barbara Johnson, Sterling, Alaska, letter to Ella Merkel DiCarlo, Holyoke, Massachusetts, April 14, 1981; Ella Merkel DiCarlo, Holyoke, Massachusetts, letter to Barbara Johnson (no address), March 30, 1981; The Oracle, *Holyoke Daily Transcript,* January 29, 1981; Elaine Dufresne, interview with author, July 13, 2004.

55. Oberdeck, *Evangelist,* 206; Gold and Fizdale, *Divine Sarah,* 59.

56. All genealogical speculation and information regarding Mark McPherson Tanguay and "Mark M." in prior paragraphs from the following sources: Barbara Johnson, personal letter to author, September 28, 2004; Ella Merkel DiCarlo, Holyoke, Massachusetts, letter to Barbara Johnson, Parker, Florida, May 11, 1981; Ella Merkel DiCarlo, genealogical research notes regarding Florence Tanguay Dufresne; Barbara Johnson, Sterling, Alaska, letter to Ella Merkel DiCarlo, Holyoke, Massachusetts, April 14, 1981; Ella Merkel DiCarlo, Holyoke, Massachusetts, letter to Barbara Johnson (no address), March 30, 1981; The Oracle, *Holyoke Daily Transcript,* January 29, 1981; Elaine Dufresne, interview with author, July 13, 2004.

57. Ruth Sears, diary, January 27, 1909, ms. courtesy of Ashfield Historical Society.

58. *Connecticut Maple Leaf* 10 (Summer 2001): 28; Wes Eichenwald, e-mail message to author, August 26, 2004; *Holyoke City Directory 1890; 1892; 1897,* 377; *1898,* 374; *1899,* 371; *1900,* 372; *1901,* 386; *1902; 1903,* 399, (Holyoke: W. S. Loomis); Art Corbeil, Newington, Connecticut, letter to author, November 2004; Nancy Garvin, e-mail message to author, October 23, 2004. Eva also became a naturalized American citizen in 1890.

59. Robert A. Howes, Lt. Col. U.S. Army (Ret.), "Genealogy of The Howes Family in America, Descendants of Thomas Howes, Yarmouth, Mass., 1637–1966, with Some Account of the English Ancestry and Early Documents and History," Las Cruces, NM; Nancy Garvin, e-mail message to author, October 21, 2004; Booker, "Descendents of Blanche Agnes Tanguay" (see note 39, above).

60. Roger Howes, interview with author, November 26, 2004.

2. THE SAMBO GIRL IN NEW YORK

1. Banner, *American Beauty,* 134.

2. Gänzl, *Lydia Thompson,* 86, 121, 154, 179; Dudden, *Women in American Theatre,* 138.

3. "'My Lady,' a Showy Burlesque."

4. "Victoria—My Lady"; "My Lady," February 12, 1901; "My Lady," February 13, 1901.

5. "Victoria—My Lady." Dudden notes that since the rise of the leg show in the 1860s, popular theater relied increasingly on "the reduction of woman to her physical appearance" (*Women in American Theatre,* 170).

6. "My Lady" February 13, 1901; "Victoria—My Lady"; "The Stage," *Munsey's Magazine,* September 1898, 933; Ross, "Building and Repairing"; "Ross 'Invented' Travesty," *Minneapolis News,* September 30, 1914.

7. Lydia Thompson's 1868 burlesque, *The Field of the Cloth of Gold,* featured a similarly humorously named trio, Von Schlascher, Von Krasher, and Von Smasher, as "members of a German band," while her *Forty Thieves; or, Striking Oil in Family Jars* counted "The Donkey, from Fifth Avenue, expressly engaged for the piece" in its ranks.

8. "Victoria—My Lady"; "The Columbia Theatre and Promenade De Luxe, Week of January 28, 1901" (program); "Hammerstein's Victoria, Week Commencing Monday February 18, 1901" (program); Slide, *Encyclopedia of Vaudeville,* 489.

9. Various articles from "My Lady" clipping file, New York Public Library for the Performing Arts Theater Collection; Dale, "'My Lady.'"

10. Banner, *American Beauty,* 175–76; Glenn, *Female Spectacle,* 155, 178; Leider, *Becoming Mae West,* 37; MeasuringWorth, http://www.measuringworth.com/uscompare/.

11. Faust: Lotta clipping file, New York Public Library for the Performing Arts Theater Collection; "Lotta Faust, The Laughing Girl."

12. Tanguay, "I Don't Care," December 29, 1946, 12.

13. Ibid.

14. Salsinger, "Miss Eva Tanguay"; clipping: *The Chaperons* by Frederic Ranken and Isidore Witmark, New York Public Library for the Performing Arts Theater Collection.

15. Miriam Michelson, "'The Chaperons' a Nondescript Affair but Chock Full of Good Vaudeville," article date-stamped November 28, 1901, NYPL, Robinson Locke Collection, v. 450.

16. Various articles, New York Public Library for the Performing Arts Theater Collection, Locke Collection, envelope 1829; "Well-Known Managers," *New York Dramatic Mirror,* September 5, 1896. Ranken's wife, Cora Gabrielle Ranken, is said to have worked "side by side with her husband on every opera," though she was, predictably, not credited (*New York Telegraph,* August 5, 1906.)

17. Michelson (see note 15, above); various articles, New York Public Library for the Performing Arts Theater Collection, Locke Collection, envelope 1829; "Well-Known Managers," *New York Dramatic Mirror,* September 5, 1896.

18. New Park Opera House, Erie, Pennsylvania, September 30, Season 1902–03 (program), and The Grand, Kansas City, Missouri, March 15, 1903 (program), Eva Tanguay Collection, acc. 2006.9, Benson Ford Research Center; "Wit in the Chaperons," *Wieting Lobby Chatter of Plays and Players,* Syracuse, January 18, 1902, 3; "Plays and Players," *The Theatre,* July 1902, 6; Banner, *American Beauty,* 190.

19. "Plays and Players"; Tanguay, "I Don't Care," December 29, 1946, 13; Michelson (see note 15, above).

20. "The Day of the Lady Comedian" and "Makes Many Quick Changes," both in NYPL, Robinson Locke Collection, v. 450; Sentilles, *Performing Menken,* 8, 32; Leider, *Becoming Mae West,* 69–70.

21. Glenn, *Female Spectacle,* 50; Kibler, *Rank Ladies,* 13, 50; Fields, *Sophie Tucker,* 14.

22. Oberdeck, *Evangelist,* 204; Rodger, *Champagne Charlie,* 106.

23. The Grand, Kansas City, Missouri, March 15, 1903 (program), Eva Tanguay Collection, acc. 2006.9, Benson Ford Research Center; Tanguay, "I Don't Care," December 29, 1946, 13; "New York—The Chaperons"; "Eva Tanguay, The New Character Actress," *Kansas City World,* April 13, 1902; "The Day of the Lady Comedian" and "Eva Tanguay, the 'Jiggly' Soubrette," both in NYPL, Robinson Locke Collection, v. 450; Witmark and Goldberg, *Ragtime to Swingtime,* 245–46; Sentilles, *Performing Menken,* 27.

24. "Columbia Theatre: 'The Chaperons,'" article date-stamped December 21, 1901, and "Cast for 'The Chaperons,'" in NYPL, Robinson Locke Collection, v. 255 and v. 450; Witmark and Goldberg, *Ragtime to Swingtime,* 242.

25. "Columbia Theatre: 'The Chaperons'" (see note 24, above); Witmark and Goldberg, *Ragtime to Swingtime,* 243–44; "Plays and Players"; various clippings, NYPL, Robinson Locke Collection, v. 93 and v. 255; "New York—The Chaperons"; "At Brooklyn Theaters," *Brooklyn Eagle,* November 23, 1902, 40; Glenn, *Female Spectacle,* 59; "Plays and Players," 5–6.

26. Clipping, The Chaperons by Frederic Ranken and Isidore Witmark, New York Public Library for the Performing Arts Theater Collection.

27. "Andrew Mack in 'Tom Moore', Stock Companies and Vaudeville Houses Offer Bills Running through Comedy, Melodrama and Variety," *Brooklyn Eagle,* November 4, 1902, 14; "Eva Tanguay, the New Character Actress"; various articles "The Chaperons" clipping file, and "'Comedian' Girls Jump to the Front," in NYPL, Robinson Locke Collection, v. 450; "The Day of the Lady Comedian" (see note 23, above); "The grotesque body," writes Kathleen Rowe in *Unruly Woman,* "breaks down the boundaries between itself and the world around it, while the classical body, consistent with the ideology of the bourgeois individual, shores them up" (33). She was "making a spectacle out of herself," to borrow a catchphrase commonly employed by feminist scholars such as Mary Russo, celebrating rather than apologizing for an "inadvertency and loss of boundaries," all of which made her a cultural rebel and object of both negative and positive fascination (Russo, "Female Grotesques," 213).

28. Latchaw, "Eva Tanguay Cared"; Piepmeier, *Out in Public,* 29.

29. Westerfield, "Investigation," 8; Rowe, *Unruly Woman,* 7; Ponce de Leon, *Self-Exposure,* 13.

30. "Must Look Out for Eva Tanguays," *Des Moines Register,* article date-stamped December 6, 1906, NYPL, Robinson Locke Collection, v. 450; Nasaw, *Going Out,* 20.

31. "Mary Beard Wed in Tuxedo Church," *New York Times,* October 23, 1932, 34; "Havemeyer Estate Divided"; Economic History Association, *EH.net,* http://eh.net/hmit/ppowerusd/dollar_answer.php (accessed June 4, 2006, page no longer active).

32. This and previous paragraph: Eva Tanguay, "I Don't Care," December 29, 1946; "Aged Frederick C. Havemeyer Gives $2,500 Sealskin Coat to Eva Tanguay," article date-stamped October 21, 1903, NYPL, Robinson Locke Collection, v. 450; McConnell, "Eva Tanguay," 6; Sentilles, *Performing Menken,* 5–6.

33. Piepmeier, *Out in Public,* 31–32.

34. "Pretty Girls and Tuneful Airs Bring a Warm Broadway Welcome for 'The Chaperons,'" *New York World,* June 6, 1902.

35. "Trixie Friganza Is Dead at 84"; various articles in the NYPL, Robinson Locke Collection, ser. 3, v. 503.

36. Glenn, *Female Spectacle,* 59–62; Rowe, *Unruly Woman,* 63.

37. "Actress Punished Man Who Provoked Her Anger," *Cincinnati Times Star,* undated article, NYPL, Robinson Locke Collection, v. 450.

38. "Frank Daniels Appears in a New Comic Opera," article date-stamped November 3, 1903, New York Public Library for the Performing Arts Theater Collection, Robinson Locke Collection of Dramatic Scrapbooks, v. 145; *The Office Boy,* Colonial Theatre, week of October 26, 1903 (program), Eva Tanguay Collection, acc. 2006.9, Benson Ford Research Center.

39. Clipping dated 1903, New York Public Library for the Performing Arts Theater Collection.

40. "Office Boy."

41. "Frank Daniels in The Office Boy"; "Daniels, Bright 'Office Boy'"; "The Office Boy Scores a Hit," November 3, 1903; "Charles Frohman to Take 'The Office Boy' to London," December 12, 1903; all in New York Public Library for the Performing Arts Theater Collection, Robinson Locke Collection of Dramatic Scrapbooks, v. 145 and v. 450; Fields, *Sophie Tucker,* 45.

42. "Frank Daniels in The Office Boy"; Frank Daniels, "Little Stories of the Stage"; and other unattributed clippings, in New York Public Library for the Performing Arts Theater Collection, Robinson Locke Collection of Dramatic Scrapbooks, v. 145.

43. New York Public Library for the Performing Arts Theater Collection, Robinson Locke Collection of Dramatic Scrapbooks, ser. 2, v. 20, 103.

3. I DON'T CARE

1. *The Blonde in Black,* Knickerbocker Theatre, June 22, 1903 (program).

2. This and previous paragraph: "Harry B. Smith Dies; Librettist for 50 Years," *Herald Tribune,* January 2, 1936; "Harry Smith Dies; Librettist Was 75," *New York Times,* January 2,

1936; unattributed article date-stamped December 1, 1903, NYPL, Robinson Locke Collection, v. 145; Sidney Munden, "Comic Opera or What?" article date-stamped March 10, 1904, and "Among the Musicians," ca. 1889, both in New York Public Library for the Performing Arts Theater Collection; Gänzl, *Lydia Thompson*, 154.

3. "At the Theatres," *New York Dramatic Mirror*, June 20, 1903, 13; "Miss Ring Makes Her Stellar Debut," June 9, 1903, otherwise unattributed article, New York Public Library for the Performing Arts Theater Collection.

4. Glenn, *Female Spectacle*, 25.

5. Eichenwald, "Americans."

6. References to the script of *The Sambo Girl* are based on a manuscript in the Eva Tanguay Collection, acc. 2006.9, Benson Ford Research Center; "West End—The Sambo Girl," in NYPL, Robinson Locke Collection, v. 450.

7. *Toledo Blade*, December 16, 1905, and "Eva Tanguay to Introduce 'Sambo Girl' to the Public at Wilkesbarre To-Night," ca. September 1904, both in NYPL, Robinson Locke Collection, v. 450; Rowe, *Unruly Women*, 3.

8. The only commercially available recording of Eva singing "I Don't Care" may be found on *Music from the New York Stage, 1890–1920*, vol. 2, *1908–1913* (E. Sussex: Pavilion Records, 1993).

9. *Pittsburg Post*, article date-stamped March 27, 1906; unattributed article date-stamped April 23, 1906; *Toledo Blade*, December 16, 1905; "Alvin—'The Sambo Girl,'" *Pittsburg Dispatch*, article date-stamped March 27, 1906; "West End—The Sambo Girl," unattributed article date-stamped 1905; "Staley Helped Eva Out of Difficulty," *Pittsburg Leader*, article date-stamped March 23, 1907; all in NYPL, Robinson Locke Collection, v. 450.

10. "Song Writer in Vaudeville," *New York Telegraph*, April 10, 1908; Dash, "Jean Lenox Sings," *Variety*, May 2, 1908; in Lenox, Jean, Locke Collection, 1156, New York Public Library for the Performing Arts Theater Collection.

11. Kitchen, "Undone by a Song"; "I Really Do Care After All," Eva Tanguay Collection, acc. 2006.9, Benson Ford Research Center; Keith/Albee Collection, University of Iowa, MsC 356, scrapbook 9, 224.

12. Letter to Edward J. Ader, Chicago, February 27, 1918, Eva Tanguay Collection, acc. 2006.9, Benson Ford Research Center.

13. Kitchen, "Undone by a Song"; "Staley Helped Eva Out of Difficulty" (see note 9, above); "Eva Tanguay Creates a Scene," unattributed article date-stamped January 17, 1905; "Eva Tanguay Cancelled Her Engagement," unattributed article date-stamped February 19, 1905; "The Sambo Girl" (advertisement); all in NYPL, Robinson Locke Collection, v. 450; The Casino Season 1904–1905, Philadelphia, week beginning April 17, 1905 (program); and "'Sambo Girl' an Old Man's Darling," *World*, December 1, 1905, Eva Tanguay Collection, acc. 2006.9, Benson Ford Research Center.

14. Cleveland's New Theatre, week beginning May 1, 1905 (program); The Cherry Blossom Grove Atop of the New York Theatre, week commencing July 28, 1902; both in Eva Tanguay Collection, acc. 2006.9, Benson Ford Research Center.

15. "Staley Helped Eva Out of Difficulty" (see note 9, above); "Eva Tanguay Creates a Scene," unattributed article date-stamped January 17, 1905; "Eva Tanguay Cancelled Her Engagement," unattributed article date-stamped February 19, 1905; "The Sambo Girl" (advertisement); all in NYPL, Robinson Locke Collection, v. 450; The Casino Season 1904–1905, Philadelphia, week beginning April 17, 1905 (program); and "'Sambo Girl' an Old Man's Darling," *World*, December 1, 1905, Eva Tanguay Collection, acc. 2006.9, Benson Ford Research Center.

16. Allen, *Horrible Prettiness*, 185–86; Nasaw, *Going Out*, 23–24; Lewis, *From Traveling Show*, 316; Albee, "Albee on Vaudeville." See also Allen, "Vaudeville and Film," 2; Hamilton, *When I'm Bad*, 72–73.

17. This and previous paragraphs from Keith/Albee Collection, University of Iowa, MsC 356, scrapbook 3, 20. On "chasers," see Allen, "Movies in Vaudeville," 71–75.

18. "Eva Tanguay, 69, Dies on Coast"; Keith/Albee Collection, University of Iowa, MsC 356, scrapbook 9, 35. For a good description of the ways in which conventional filmmakers developed the tools to render narrative films "seamless" and "fluid," see Bordwell, Staiger, and Thompson, *Classical Hollywood Cinema,* 24–25.

19. "'Tony' Pastor"; "Dean of Vaudeville Celebrities," *Variety,* March 4, 1906; Pastor, "Tony Pastor Recounts the Origin of American 'Vaudeville,'" 17; Allen, *Horrible Prettiness,* 178; For an excellent description and investigation of variety theater in the nineteenth century, see Rodger, *Champagne Charlie.*

20. Gilbert, *American Vaudeville,* 113–14; Pastor, "Tony Pastor Recounts the Origin of American 'Vaudeville,'" 17, 49; Laurie, *Vaudeville,* 334; "'Tony' Pastor."

21. Snyder, *Voice of the City,* 21; Pastor, "Tony Pastor Recounts the Origin of 'American Vaudeville.'"

22. Snyder, *Voice of the City,* 21, 54; "Vaudeville's Clearing House"; Laurie, *Vaudeville,* 53.

23. Laurie, *Vaudeville,* 53; "B. F. Keith Dead"; "Vaudeville Founded by Keith Thirty Years Ago This Week," *Philadelphia Telegraph,* December 1, 1913.

24. "B. F. Keith Dead"; "B. F. Keith: The Man Who Dared and Won," *New York Star,* October 24, 1903; Allen, *Horrible Prettiness,* 180; "Keith Anniversary," *New York Clipper,* November 29, 1913, 6.

25. "B. F. Keith Dead"; "Keith Anniversary"; Nasaw, *Going Out,* 20; Gilbert, *American Vaudeville,* 200–201. Both "Keith Anniversary" and "B. F. Keith Dead," the latter clearly having drawn much of its "research" from the former, cite the date of Keith's first continuous performance as July 6, 1883, which is incorrect. The correct date may be found in Gilbert's *American Vaudeville,* 200–201. Also, in *The Voice of the City,* Snyder contends that "continuous" was not a big success for Keith.

26. "E. F. Albee Dies"; "E. F. Albee, Co-Founder"; Laurie, *Vaudeville,* 340; "Vaudeville's Clearing House." Neil Harris points out that since the 1820s, cultural leaders in the United States had been searching for "a type to represent the ordinary American." Though several stereotypes emerged in popular literature and political rhetoric, one stuck, that of the "Yankee," who was understood to be "clever, energetic, and flexible." P. T. Barnum stressed this element of his background in his 1855 autobiography. It is likely that impresarios who followed in his footsteps, such as Keith and Albee, chose to trumpet their heritage similarly when given the chance. See Harris, *Humbug,* 207–11.

27. "E. F. Albee, Co-Founder."

28. "E. F. Albee, Co-Founder"; "E. F. Albee Dies."

29. "E. F. Albee, Co-Founder."

30. Samuels and Samuels, *Once upon a Stage,* 38; "E. F. Albee, Co-Founder"; Snyder, *Voice of the City,* 27.

31. Davis, "In Vaudeville"; "B. F. Keith Dead"; Gilbert, *American Vaudeville,* 205; E. F. Albee, "Keith Vaudeville," *New York Clipper,* February 15, 1913, viii; Snyder, *Voice of the City,* 26–27.

32. Allen, *Horrible Prettiness,* 184–85; E. F. Albee, "Keith Vaudeville."

33. "Future of Show Business"; Albee, "Albee on Vaudeville"; Erenberg, "Impresarios of Broadway," 161; B. F. Keith Corporation, *Keith's New Theatre Boston Brochure,* NYPL, Robinson Locke Collection, n.d.; Laurie, *Vaudeville,* 343; Albee, "Twenty Years of Vaudeville"; Higgins, "Origin of Vaudeville"; Allen, *Horrible Prettiness,* 184.

34. Samuels and Samuels, *Once upon a Stage,* 39; Slide, *Selected Vaudeville Criticism,* 206; E. F. Albee, "Future of Show Business," *Billboard,* December 19, 1914, 38.

35. Snyder, *Voice of the City,* 28; B. F. Keith, "What Pleases in Vaudeville," *Criterion,* September 1900, 24; Higgins, "Origin of Vaudeville"; Laurie, *Vaudeville,* 342–43; Hamilton, *When I'm Bad,* 182.

36. Laurie, 342–43; Hamilton, 37; "Business of Vaudeville," in Stein, *American Vaudeville,* 177, 255; Fred Allen, "Two Jugglers Turned Comedians," in Stein, *American Vaudeville,* 177, 255.

37. Stein, *American Vaudeville,* 255.

38. Memoirs of Edward V. Darling, in Edward V. and Alfred T. Darling papers, 1899–1952, ★T-mss. 1986–005, New York Public Library for the Performing Arts Theater Collection; "Tanguay Tantrums Make a Big Mess and Fuss at Hammerstein's," ibid.

39. Memoirs of Edward V. Darling (see note 38, above); for more on the United Booking Offices, see "Vaudeville's Clearing House"; "United Booking Offices"; Snyder, "Vaudeville," 37.

40. Memoirs of Edward V. Darling (see note 39, above).

41. Memoirs of Edward V. Darling.

42. Unattributed article date-stamped August 18, 1905, NYPL, Robinson Locke Collection, v. 450. Compare what Gold and Fizdale write about Sarah Bernhardt: "Her rages were now considered magisterial, her arrogance regal, her promiscuity the divine right of queens. In a word, Sarah had grown larger than life" (*Divine Sarah,* 133).

43. "Eva Tanguay and Her Husband Arrested," otherwise unattributed article datelined December 27, 1905, NYPL, Robinson Locke Collection, v. 450; "Eva Tanguay Sues Railroad"; "Eva Tanguay Finds Trouble Coming and Going," article from the Creston, Iowa, *Capital,* excerpted in *Vanity Fair,* article date-stamped January 26, 1906, NYPL, Robinson Locke Collection, v. 450.

44. "Eva Tanguay Finds Trouble Coming and Going" (see note 43, above).

45. Ibid.

46. Ibid.

47. Ibid.

48. Eva was among the first actresses to use a ploy that would become popular with her peers: claiming to be under the near-constant threat of jewelry theft while traveling. In 1906, Florenz Ziegfeld's leading starlet, Anna Held, got a great deal of PR out of a possibly fake story involving a "satchel" of stolen jewels and money, purloined on a train journey from Chicago to Baltimore. Such tales made actresses seem like adventuring nobles, laden with gemstones, protected by armed suitors, and ever on the way to a new regal opening. It is a narrative that helped further define the modern-day celebrity as somehow familiar—beset with worries—and yet ultimately on a different plane of existence, one in which a primary burden was the potential loss of sparkling diamonds at the hands of ruffians and bandits. See Mordden, *Ziegfeld,* 87. "Eva Tanguay Finds Trouble Coming and Going" (see note 44, above).

49. "Eva Tanguay Is to Marry," unattributed newspaper clipping, article date-stamped May 7, 1909, Memoirs of Edward V. Darling (see note 38, above).

50. "Eva Tanguay Becomes 'Gracious,'" *Vanity Fair,* article date-stamped March 16, 1906, NYPL, Robinson Locke Collection, v. 450.

4. THE CYCLONIC COMEDIENNE; OR, GENIUS PROPERLY ADVERTISED

1. This and previous paragraph: Barbara Johnson, personal letter to author, September 28, 2004; "At the Theatres; Brooklyn Bijou—A Good Fellow," *New York Dramatic Mirror,* April 30, 1904, 14.; "National Theater: 'A Good Fellow,'" *Rochester Post,* article date-stamped November 20, 1906, NYPL, Robinson Locke Collection, v. 450.

2. "National Theater: 'A Good Fellow'" (see note 1, above); "Zzes Around Like Busy Bee," *Syracuse Post-Standard,* article date-stamped November 23, 1906, NYPL, Robinson Locke Collection, v. 450.

3. *Holyoke Transcript-Telegram,* January 18, 1957; McConnell, "Eva Tanguay," 5; "How She Doubles," *Toledo Blade,* September 15, 1906; Ullie Akerstrom, "A Glimpse of the Real Eva Tanguay," ca. 1903, ms. found in Eva Tanguay Collection, acc. 2006.9, Benson Ford Research Center.

4. Robert Speare, "Eva Tanguay at Twenty-Third St.," *New York Telegraph,* July 6, 1907, NYPL, Robinson Locke Collection, v. 450.

5. "Eva Tanguay, 69, Dies on Coast"; Keith/Albee Collection, University of Iowa, MsC 356, scrapbook 9, 35.

6. Keith/Albee Collection, University of Iowa, MsC 356, scrapbook 7, 193. "The Weather," *New York Times,* August 5, 1907, 13.

7. Otherwise unattributed article date-stamped February 19, 1905, NYPL, Robinson Locke Collection, v. 450; Keith/Albee Collection, University of Iowa, MsC 356, scrapbook 8, 5.

8. Keith/Albee Collection, University of Iowa, MsC 356, scrapbook 8, 5, 144.

9. Ibid., scrapbook 7, 251; Keith's Philadelphia, week of September 2, 1907 (program), and Keith's Theatre Cleveland (program), Eva Tanguay Collection, Acc. 2006.9, Benson Ford Research Center.

10. "Academy of Music," *Brooklyn Daily Eagle,* February 6, 1890, 5.

11. Advertisement, *Brooklyn Daily Eagle,* January 3, 1886, 5; advertisement, *Brooklyn Daily Eagle,* January 4, 1896, 6; advertisement, *Brooklyn Daily Eagle,* November 2, 1896, 6; "Vaudeville Houses," *Brooklyn Daily Eagle,* April 2, 1901, 6.

12. "The Wife Relented," *New York Times,* April 27, 1887, 8; "Shaw's Revenge on the Critics," *New York Times,* May 10, 1908, C1.

13. "C. F. Zittel, 66, Dies"; Tanguay, "I Don't Care," January 19, 1947.

14. "This Is 'Zit,'" *New York Telegraph,* article date-stamped September 27, 1907, New York Public Library for the Performing Arts Theater Collection, Carl Florian Zittel file.

15. Ibid; "Eva Tanguay Is Co-Respondent," *New York Telegraph,* newspaper clipping, article date-stamped September 27, 1907, NYPL, Robinson Locke Collection, v. 450; "Eva Tanguay Is Named by Wife as Corespondent [*sic*]," *Cleveland News,* September 29, 1907.

16. "Eva Tanguay Breaks Down," *New York Telegraph,* article date-stamped June 16, 1908, NYPL, Robinson Locke Collection, v. 450.

17. Ibid.

18. Ibid.; "Eva Tanguay Resting," *New York Dramatic Mirror,* June 27, 1908.

19. Will of Ruth H. Weekes, Harry A. Olivar, attorney, June 26, 1975; Akerstrom, "Glimpse of the Real Eva Tanguay" (see note 3, above).

20. Roger Howes, interview with author, November 26, 2004; Booker, "Descendents of Blanche Agnes Tanguay," November 19, 2004, supplied to author courtesy of Ashfield Historical Society, Ashfield, Massachusetts; "Groom 21, Bride 45," *Holyoke Daily Transcript,* April 26, 1909.

21. Sam M'Kee, "Eva Tanguay Is Back and Better," *New York Telegraph,* article date-stamped July 5, 1908, NYPL, Robinson Locke Collection, v. 450.

22. "Eva Tanguay at the Brighton Beach Music Hall," unattributed article, n.d.; Sam M'Kee, article from *New York Telegraph,* date-stamped July 13, 1908; both in NYPL, Robinson Locke Collection, v. 450.

23. "50 Now in Race for Mardi Gras Royal Honors," *New York Evening World,* n.d.; "Irene Franklin's Remarkable Run," unattributed article date-stamped May 2, 1905; "Fifth Avenue," *Variety,* article date-stamped August 1, 1908; *New York Telegraph,* unattributed article date-stamped May 16, 1909; all in NYPL, Robinson Locke Collection, v. 450.

24. *New York Telegraph,* unattributed article date-stamped May 16, 1909, NYPL, Robinson Locke Collection, v. 450.

25. "The Five Best Reasons Why You Should Smoke Eva Tanguay," Eva Tanguay Collection, acc. 2006.9, Benson Ford Research Center.

26. "Victoria—My Lady"; Mark Berger, The Julian Eltinge Project, http://www.thejulianeltingeproject.com/bio.html (accessed October 14, 2004); Charles Darnton, "Eva Tanguay Says She's Not What She Seems on the Stage: She Does Care—My, Yes!" *Evening World,* article date-stamped March 13, 1909, and "Eva Tanguay Will Not Marry There," *New York Telegraph* article date-stamped August 30, 1908, both in NYPL, Robinson Locke Collection, v. 450; Peters, "Gay Deceiver," 87; "Eva Tanguay Fills Colonial at Its Opening," *New York Evening Journal,* September 1, 1908; "Eva Tanguay's Coming Wedding Talk of the Stage," *Evening World,* August 7, 1908, Eva Tanguay Collection, acc. 2006.9, Benson Ford Research Center; Garber, *Vested Interests,* 141.

27. Mark Berger, The Julian Eltinge Project, http://www.thejulianeltingeproject.com/bio.html (accessed October 14, 2004); "Julian Eltinge, Impersonator"; Gänzl, *Lydia Thompson,* 118.

28. Mark Berger, The Julian Eltinge Project, http://www.thejulianeltingeproject.com/bio.html (accessed 14 October 2004); "Julian Eltinge, Impersonator."

29. This and previous paragraphs: Peters, "Gay Deceiver"; Mark Berger, The Julian Eltinge Project, http://www.thejulianeltingeproject.com/bio.html (accessed October 14, 2004); "Julian Eltinge, Impersonator"; article fragment, *Denver Times,* December 22, 1912; Wolf, "Sort of Fellow Julian Eltinge Really Is"; Golden, "Julian Eltinge"; "He Wears a Corset," article dated 1917, NYPL, Robinson Locke Collection, ser. 2, Eli-Yet; Keith/Albee Collection, University of Iowa, MsC 356, scrapbook 5, 140; William E. Sage, "Eltinge Really a Manly Chap, in Fact His Name's Bill Dalton," *Boston Traveler,* May 18, 1912; "Julian Eltinge Latest," *New York Dramatic Mirror,* August 7, 1909, 19; "The Fascinating Widow," article dated August 1912, NYPL, Robinson Locke Collection, ser. 2, Eli-Yet; Granville Sewell, "Julian Eltinge Says His Great Boyhood Ambition Was to Be a Blackface Comedian," *New Orleans Item,* December 4, 1921; Wolf, 794; "Secret of Julian Eltinge's Grace," *Cleveland Leader,* March 23, 1913; "He Wears a Corset"; *Julian Eltinge Magazine* and *Julian Eltinge Magazine and Beauty Hints,* NAFR + ser. 3 v. 432, New York Public Library for the Performing Arts; "Lets Audience Guess," article date-stamped December 8, 1910, New York Public Library for the Performing Arts; "Eltinge Breaks Records," *New York Star,* February 6, 1918; "Star's Weekly Vaudeville Laugh Bulletin," *New York Star,* April 20, 1921; "Who Would You Rather Be," February 21, 1912, ms. found in New York Public Library for the Performing Arts; Holusha, "Theater's Muses"; Mark Berger, e-mail message to author, October 13, 2004; Louella Parsons, "Is Julian Eltinge Going to Wed?" article dated December 16, 1917, NYPL, Robinson Locke Collection, ser. 2; Eli-Yet; "300 at Eltinge Funeral," *New York Times,* March 10, 1941; Hamilton, *When I'm Bad,* 39, 145; Peiss, *Hope in a Jar,* 49.

30. "New Acts of the Week," *Variety,* May 30 1908, 13; Snyder, *Voice of the City,* 153. For jokes about marriage in vaudeville, see Lowry, *Vaudeville Humor,* 171–84.

31. "Victoria—My Lady"; Mark Berger, The Julian Eltinge Project, http://www.thejulianeltingeproject.com/bio.html (accessed October 14, 2004); Charles Darnton, "Eva Tanguay Says She's Not What She Seems on the Stage: She Does Care—My, Yes!" *Evening World,* article date-stamped March 13, 1909, and "Eva Tanguay Will Not Marry There," *New York Telegraph* article date-stamped August 30, 1908, both in NYPL, Robinson Locke Collection, v. 450; Peters, "Gay Deceiver," 87; "Eva Tanguay Fills Colonial at Its Opening," *New York Evening Journal,* September 1, 1908; "Eva Tanguay's Coming Wedding Talk of the Stage," *Evening World,* August 7, 1908, Eva Tanguay Collection, acc. 2006.9, Benson Ford Research Center; Garber, *Vested Interests,* 141.

32. "Eva Tanguay Will Not Marry There" (see note 31, above).

33. Keith's Philadelphia, September 2, 1907 (program), Keith's Theatre Cleveland (program), both in Eva Tanguay Collection, acc. 2006.9, Benson Ford Research Center; "Eva Tanguay the Madcap Genius, a Keith Sensation," *Keith's Theatre News,* November 16, 1908, 2, in Keith/Albee Collection, University of Iowa, MsC 356, scrapbook 8, 244.

5. RIDING SALOME TO THE TOP

1. Southworth, *English Medieval Minstrel,* 6; Bizot, "Salome Era," 72; Cherniavsky, *Salome Dancer,* 142; Glenn, *Female Spectacle,* 96; Hamilton, *When I'm Bad,* 4.

2. Bizot, "Salome Era," 73.

3. Cherniavsky, *Salome Dancer,* 143; "'Salome' Dances the Worst Ever," *Spokane Review,* article date-stamped October 25, 1908, NYPL, Robinson Locke Collection, v. 450.

4. Bizot, "Salome Era," 75–76.

5. Paris, *Louise Brooks,* 35; Fleischer, "Collaborative Projects," 15–17.

6. "New Acts of the Week," *Variety,* July 18, 1908, 12; "New Vaudeville Acts," *New York Dramatic Mirror,* July 25, 1908, 14; "Hammerstein's Biggest Week," *Variety,* July 25, 1908, 10; "Gertrude Hoffman Arrested"; "Gertrude Hoffman in 'Radha,'" *New York Clipper,* August 28, 1909, 731.

7. "Who Is It?" *New York Clipper,* August 29, 1908, 701.

8. Advertisement, *New York Clipper,* February 9, 1907, 1360.

9. Tanguay, "I Don't Care," December 29, 1946, 12; Glenn, *Female Spectacle,* 98.

10. Tanguay, "I Don't Care," January 19, 1947, 7.

11. Memoirs of Edward V. Darling, in Edward V. and Alfred T. Darling papers, 1899–1952, ★T-mss. 1986–005, New York Public Library for the Performing Arts Theater Collection; Tanguay, "I Don't Care," January 19, 1947, 7; Economic History Association, Eh.net, http://eh.net/hmit/ppowerusd/dollar_answer.php (accessed January 16, 2006, page no longer active); "United Booking Offices"; "Williams Goes with Keith," *Variety,* February 16, 1907, 2; "Williams and Albee Talk," February 16, 1907, 4; "Williams Sells Theaters," *New York Clipper,* May 4, 1912, 10; "Percy Williams Houses Sold; About $5,000,000," *Variety,* April 6, 1912, 3.

12. Memoirs of Edward V. Darling (see note 11, above); "All about Salome," *Variety,* August 1, 1908, 7.

13. Tanguay, "I Don't Care," January 19, 1947, 7; Glenn, *Female Spectacle,* 109.

14. "Eva Tanguay as 'Salome'"; Ashton Stevens, "Tanguay Swings, Sings, Sways and Swoons in Salome Dance," newspaper clipping, article date-stamped August 6, 1908, NYPL, Robinson Locke Collection, v. 450; Robert Speare, "Sheath Tights for Little Eva," newspaper clipping, article date-stamped September 10, 1908, NYPL, Robinson Locke Collection, v. 450; Sam M'Kee, "Eva Tanguay Is a Great Salome," *New York Telegraph,* article date-stamped August 4, 1908, NYPL, Robinson Locke Collection, v. 450; letter to Lee Shubert, December 17, 1913, Shubert Archive, New York.

15. "'The Optimists' a Unique Revue," unattributed newspaper article, Mary Baker Eddy Library.

16. Hamilton, *When I'm Bad,* 40.

17. Speare, "Sheath Tights for Little Eva" (see note 14, above); "Eva Tanguay's 'Salome,'" advertisement in *Variety,* October 3, 1908, 2; Tanguay, "I Don't Care," January 19, 1947, 7; Coffin, "All Sorts and Kinds." As the film historians David Bordwell, Janet Staiger, and Kristin Thompson have written about the "classical" Hollywood studios of a past era, to make it big in the realm of popular entertainment, performers and producers had to walk a fine line "between standardization and differentiation." Eva's raucous and well-publicized undress as Salome permitted her to masterfully navigate just such a boundary. Bordwell, Staiger, and Thompson, *Classical Hollywood Cinema,* 110.

18. Sam M'Kee, "Police Called for Eva Tanguay," *New York Telegraph,* article date-stamped June 1, 1909, NYPL, Robinson Locke Collection, v. 450; Stevens, "Tanguay Swings" (see note 14, above); M'Kee, August 4, 1908. The Salome fad died out around 1913, but enjoyed an effervescent revival in 1918, spurred in part by an eponymously titled feature film staring silent-screen beauty Theda Bara (Glenn, *Female Spectacle,* 120–23.)

19. Advertisement, *New York Clipper,* September 12, 1908, 763.

20. "Eva Tanguay Makes Broad Claim"; "Eva Tanguay's 'Salome'" (see note 17, above); Glenn, *Female Spectacle,* 106.

21. "Another Salome Heralded"; Rush, "New Acts of the Week," *Variety,* December 12, 1908, 14; Glenn, *Female Spectacle,* 112.

22. Glenn, *Female Spectacle,* 118; Grossman, *Funny Woman,* 27–31.

23. Glenn, *Female Spectacle,* 112–15.

24. "New Vaudeville Acts," *New York Clipper,* August 10, 1912, 14; Sime [Silverman], "New Acts of the Week," *Variety,* August 9, 1912, 20; Krasner, *Resistance,* 94–95.

25. Jessel, *Elegy in Manhattan,* x, 44–47.

26. Frank Cullen, e-mail message to author, August 27, 2004; David Krasner, e-mail message to author, August 30, 2004.

27. John Graziano, e-mail message to the author, August 31, 2004.

28. Hamilton, *When I'm Bad,* 156; Hodes, *White Women, Black Men,* 1, 176, 201, 210.

29. "Salome Barred in New Jersey," *New York Dramatic Mirror,* August 26, 1908, 17; "Salomes under Observation," *New York Dramatic Mirror,* September 5, 1908, 19; "No 'Salomes' on Orpheum Circuit," *Variety,* September 12, 1908, 1; "No Salomes for Brooklyn," *New York*

Dramatic Mirror, October 24, 1908, 17. For more on the ability of vaudevillians to reconfigure their acts at a moment's notice, see Jenkins, *What Made Pistachio Nuts,* 74.

30. "The Vaudeville Mirror," *New York Dramatic Mirror,* November 27, 1909, 17.

31. Thomas J. Flynn, Brooklyn, letter to Eva Tanguay, March 14, 1911; Hilton Thomas, New York, letter to Eva Tanguay, December 15, 1910; both in Eva Tanguay Collection, acc. 2006.9, Benson Ford Research Center.

32. Keith/Albee Collection, University of Iowa, MsC 356, box 8, records, and scrapbook 10, 58.

33. Ibid., scrapbook 14, 183; Sillman, *Here Lies Leonard Sillman,* 99; Dorothy Gailer, "Leonard Sillman, Producer, Dies; Noted for His 'New Faces' Revues," *New York Times,* January 24, 1982, 32; "Eva Tanguay Big 'Hit' in Topline Act at Pantages," *Los Angeles Times,* August 7, 1928. The songwriter and composer Mary Brett Lorson, currently writing a musical about Eva Tanguay, avers that her great-grandmother, Helena Price, had not only been Eva's dresser for a time, but also her lover. It is true that Price left her husband, the noted architect William Price, to follow Eva on the road; but there is no other evidence that Eva had been sexually involved with her—or any other women.

34. Slide, *Encyclopedia of Vaudeville,* 288; "Next Week Cyclonic Eva Tanguay," B. F. Keith's Theatre, Dayton, OH, February 4, 1918 (program), Eva Tanguay Collection, acc. 2006.9, Benson Ford Research Center; "Eva Tanguay to Appear in Dress Made of $1 Bills," unattributed newspaper clipping date-stamped October 17, 1930, courtesy University of Southern California Regional History Office; "Eva Tanguay—Songs," *Variety,* November 14, 1914, 18; "Keith & Proctor's Fifth Avenue," *New York Clipper,* January 9, 1909, 1179; "Still Another Salome"; "Keith & Proctor's Fifth Avenue," *New York Clipper,* May 13, 1911, 6.

6. RIVALS, IMMITATORS, AND CENSORS

1. Sam M'Kee, "Record for Willa Holt Wakefield," *New York Telegraph,* November 9, 1908; M'Kee, "Now Let Wall Street Beware, for Willa Is in 'the Game,'" *Chicago Tribune,* October 17, 1909; "Blames Eva Tanguay."

2. "Willa Holt Wakefield: The Lady and the Piano" (advertisement); "Willa Holt Wakefield Scores Big Success at the Forsyth," *Atlanta Constitution,* May 28, 1912; Shirley Burns, "Afternoons with Actresses," *Green Book Album,* October 1910, 828; Locke envelope 2545, New York Public Library for the Performing Arts Theater Collection; Keith/Albee Collection, University of Iowa, MsC 356, scrapbook 5, 245.

3. "Act Closed at Hammerstein's without Notice 'Flops' Over," *Variety,* March 13, 1909; "Miss Wakefield on Deck," *New York Star,* March 13, 1909.

4. "Act Closed at Hammerstein's without Notice 'Flops' Over"; "Miss Wakefield on Deck" (for both, see note 3, above); "Miss Wakefield Collects Crowd," *New York Telegraph,* March 9, 1909.

5. "Blames Eva Tanguay"; "Miss Wakefield on Deck" (see note 3, above); "Tanguay Tantrums Make a Big Mess and Fuss at Hammerstein's," unattributed article in scrapbook of Edward Darling, 1909–52, in Edward V. and Alfred T. Darling papers, 1899–1952, *T-Mss. 1986–005, New York Public Library for the Performing Arts Theater Collection; Banner, *American Beauty,* 187.

6. Keith/Albee Collection, University of Iowa, MsC 356, scrapbook 11, 112; "The Keith and Proctor Theatres," *New York Dramatic Mirror,* July 4, 1908, 14; Glenn, *Female Spectacle,* 77.

7. The Alhambra, "Important Engagement of the Cyclonic Comedienne Eva Tanguay Introducing a Selection of New and Original Songs," January 30, 1911 (program), and B. F. Keith's Hippodrome, "Vaudeville's Greatest Star," October 9, 1911 (program), both in Eva Tanguay Collection, acc. 2006.9, Benson Ford Research Center; "Bessie Browning," *New York Clipper,* June 12, 1909; "Keith & Proctor's Fifth Avenue Theatre," *New York Dramatic Mirror,* July 16, 1910; "Amusement Notes," *Duluth Herald;* "Harry Breen's Fol-de-rol," *New York Telegraph,* unattributed article date-stamped June 20, 1914, all in clipping files, New York Public Library for the Performing Arts Theater Collection; Hamilton, *When I'm Bad,* 39; Leider, *Becoming Mae West,* 70.

8. Various clippings, New York Public Library for the Performing Arts Theater Collection, Locke Envelope Collection, 2634.

9. "Maurice Wood in Her Imitation of Eva Tanguay," *New York Star,* July 31, 1909; various clippings, New York Public Library for the Performing Arts Theater Collection, Locke Envelope Collection, 2045; "Admits 'Copping an Act,'" *Variety,* March 6, 1909, 5.

10. Grossman, *Funny Woman,* 85.

11. Glenn, *Female Spectacle,* 79–80.

12. Tanguay, "Eva Tanguay on 'Imitators'"; Glenn, *Female Spectacle,* 80.

13. Advertisement, date-stamped February 26, 1908, NYPL, Robinson Locke Collection, v. 450.

14. "Eva Tanguay Adds to Imitations," *New York Telegraph,* article date-stamped February 25, 1909, NYPL, Robinson Locke Collection, v. 450.

15. "White Rats Urge Protection"; "Irene Franklin Wins!" *New York Clipper,* January 8, 1910, 1217; Silverman, "Vaudeville Artists of America."

16. Memoirs of Edward V. Darling, in Edward V. and Alfred T. Darling papers, 1899–1952, ★T-Mss. 1986–005, New York Public Library for the Performing Arts Theater Collection.

17. "Police Officers Defied by Stars in Vaudeville," *New York Telegraph,* article date-stamped February 8, 1909, NYPL, Robinson Locke Collection, v. 450.

18. Leider, *Becoming Mae West,* 40.

19. Preceding paragraphs from "Police Officers Defied by Stars in Vaudeville"; "Eva Tanguay Suffers Arrest," *New York Telegraph,* article date-stamped July 5, 1909, NYPL, Robinson Locke Collection, v. 450; Hamilton, *When I'm Bad,* 72.

20. "Note and Comment," *New York Dramatic Mirror,* December 11, 1909, 19.

21. Samuels and Samuels, *Once upon a Stage,* 40; Gilbert, *American Vaudeville,* 363; "The Vaudeville Mirror," *New York Dramatic Mirror,* November 27, 1909, 17.

22. Dan Johansson, interview with author, September 10, 2004; Ruth Sears, diary, September 6, 1909, September 18, 1909, and July 31, 1910, ms. courtesy of Ashfield Historical Society; Barbara Johnson, personal letter to author, September 28, 2004.

23. Dan Johansson, interview with author, September 10, 2004; Ruth Sears, diary, December 4, 1909, December 5, 1909, January 1, 1910, January 22, 1910, and March 19, 1910, ms. courtesy of Ashfield Historical Society.

24. Ruth Sears, diary, January 23, 1908, May 12, 1908, April 27, 1909, October 2, 1909, and October 16, 1909, ms. courtesy of Ashfield Historical Society.

25. Ibid.

26. Barbara Johnson, Sterling, Alaska, letter to Ella Merkel DiCarlo, Holyoke, Massachusetts, April 14, 1981; Nancy Garvin, e-mail message to author, October 17, 2004; "Eva Tanguay, Actress, Buys Ashfield Place; Eva Seeks Home for Her Niece," *Greenfield Gazette and Courier,* June 18, 1910, 7; Barbara Johnson, letter to Ella Merkel DiCarlo, Holyoke, Massachusetts, April 27, 1981; Ullie Akerstrom, "A Glimpse of the Real Eva Tanguay," ca. 1903, ms. found in Eva Tanguay Collection, acc. 2006.9, Benson Ford Research Center.

27. Dan Johansson, interview with author, September 10, 2004; Florence Tanguay Dufresne, obituary, *Plainfield Post,* January 7, 1977; Ruth Sears, diary, January 29, 1909 and September 8, 1911, ms. courtesy of Ashfield Historical Society.

28. "About Eva Tanguay," telegram, in Edward V. and Alfred T. Darling papers, 1899–1952, ★T-mss. 1986–005, New York Public Library for the Performing Arts Theater Collection.

29. Ibid.

7. *FOLLIES* AND FORTUNES

1. Grossman, *Funny Woman,* 28; Farnsworth, *Ziegfeld Follies,* chapters 1 and 2; Wilson, "'Way Up Where Breezes Blow,'" 2–3, 5–8; Trav S. D., *No Applause,* 135; Mordden, *Ziegfeld,* 96.

2. Trav S. D., *No Applause,* 135; Allen, *Horrible Prettiness,* 184–85.

3. Henry Jenkins points out: "The Broadway revue...was often dominated by the personality of its producer, be it Ziegfeld, Earl Carroll, George White, or the Shubert Brothers" (*What Made Pistachio Nuts,* 89).

4. Farnsworth, *Ziegfeld Follies,* chapter 1; Mordden, *Ziegfeld,* 9.

5. Farnsworth, *Ziegfeld Follies,* chapter 1.

6. Ibid.

7. Ibid.; Peiss, *Hope in a Jar,* 98.

8. Farnsworth, *Ziegfeld Follies,* chapter 1; "Jardin de Paris: 'Follies of 1909,'" *Theatre Magazine,* August 1909, 37 "Jardin de Paris: 'Follies of 1909,'" *Theatre Magazine,* August 1909, 37; Mordden, *Ziegfeld,* 39, 55, 58.

9. Farnsworth, *Ziegfeld Follies,* chapters 1 and 2; Wilson, "'Way Up Where Breezes Blow,'" 2–3.

10. Fields, *Sophie Tucker,* 32.

11. "Nora Bayes Dies after Operation," *New York Times,* March 20, 1928; "Laughing Nora Bayes Dies by Sudden Turn on Road to Recovery," otherwise unattributed newspaper clipping, New York Public Library for the Performing Arts Theater Collection.

12. "Nora Bayes Dies After Operation"; "Laughing Nora Bayes Dies by Sudden Turn on Road to Recovery."

13. "Reviews of New Plays," *New York Dramatic Mirror,* otherwise unattributed newspaper clipping, "Ziegfeld Follies of 1909" file, New York Public Library for the Performing Arts Theater Collection.

14. "Eva Tanguay a Legitimate Star," *New York Dramatic News,* article date-stamped October 25, 1908, NYPL, Robinson Locke Collection, v. 450; Glenn, *Female Spectacle,* 170.

15. This and previous paragraph: "How Mr. Ziegfeld Won His Point," *New York Telegraph,* article date-stamped October 25, 1908, NYPL, Robinson Locke Collection, v. 450.

16. Ibid.

17. This and previous paragraphs: "She Will Appear Next Monday Evening in 'The Follies of 1909,'" *New York Times,* July 7, 1909, 9:2; unattributed clipping, date-stamped July 8, 1909, Mary Baker Eddy Library for the Betterment of Humanity; *Follies of* 1909 program, Harry Ransom Humanities Research Center, University of Texas at Austin; "Eva Tanguay's Latest Triumph," *New York Star,* undated, unattributed article, NYPL, Robinson Locke Collection, v. 450.

18. This and previous paragraph: Fields, *Sophie Tucker,* 7–31, 35; Tucker, *Some of These Days,* 2–3, 104; Dimeglio, *Vaudeville U.S.A.,* 146.

19. Tucker, *Some of These Days,* 79. Ethan Mordden has argued that Nora Bayes felt threatened by Sophie Tucker's popularity in the *Follies* and insisted Tucker be cut down from several songs to just one, "Moving Day in Jungle Town." But "resenting Tucker's success in that one number, Bayes took both husband and songs out of the show after only a month, leaving Ziegfeld to bring in Eva Tanguay." Mordden thus absolves Eva Tanguay (and Florenz Ziegfeld, for that matter) of any blame in Sophie's mishandling, placing it squarely on Nora Bayes (*Ziegfeld,* 107–9). It does seem that Nora Bayes harbored ill feelings toward Sophie Tucker for years to come, threatening to quit an Albee-produced vaudeville show in 1926 when she discovered she had to share billing with the famous singer (Fields, *Sophie Tucker,* 127).

20. Tucker, *Some of These Days,* 78–79; Fields, *Sophie Tucker,* 35.

21. Farnsworth, *Ziegfeld Follies,* chapter 1.

22. Kibler, *Rank Ladies,* 13.

23. This and previous paragraphs: Tanguay, "I Don't Care," January 19, 1947; "Eva Tanguay Arrested."

24. MeasuringWorth, http://www.eh.net/hmit/ppowerusd/ (accessed February 20, 2006).

25. Detail about Eva's purse from Reminiscences of Al Parado, fall 1957, on page 10 in the Columbia University Oral History Research Office Collection (hereafter CUOHROC).

26. This and previous paragraphs: Tanguay, "I Don't Care," January 19, 1947, 7; "Eva Tanguay Arrested."

27. Reminiscences of Al Parado, fall 1957, on pages 8 and 11, CUOHROC.

28. Ibid., 11–12; Trav S. D., *No Applause,* 160.

29. Reminiscences of Al Parado, fall 1957, 11–12, CUOHROC; memoirs of Edward V. Darling, in Edward V. and Alfred T. Darling papers, 1899–1952, ★T-mss. 1986–005, New York Public Library for the Performing Arts Theater Collection.

30. "Shot in Hotel Bar," *New York Times,* May 26, 1911; Tanguay, "I Don't Care," January 5, 1947; Glenn, *Female Spectacle,* 16; Dick Kreck, "Murder at the Brown Palace: A True Story of Seduction and Betrayal," In Cold Blog, http://incoldblog.wordpress.com/2006/08/04/murder-at-the-brown-palace-a-true-story-of-seduction-betrayal-by-dick-kreck/ (accessed January 12, 2011).

31. Tanguay, "I Don't Care," January 5, 1947; "Eva Tanguay Says—'Did You Ever Do This?'" *Morning Telegraph,* May 15, 1910, 2.

32. Tanguay, "I Don't Care," January 5, 1947.

33. Kreck, "Murder at the Brown Palace" (see note 30, above).

34. Rush, "Fifth Avenue," *Variety,* September 11, 1909, 11; "Holyoke's I Don't Care Girl Reported Improved," unattributed newspaper clipping, probably from the *Holyoke Transcript* or *Telegram,* in the Holyoke History Room of the Holyoke Public Library, Massachusetts; Springfield *Sunday Republican,* October 18, 1936.

35. Caffin, *Vaudeville,* 37.

36. Slide, *Encyclopedia of Vaudeville,* 488; Marks, *They All Sang,* 179–80; Barbara Johnson, personal letter to author, September 28, 2004; Daniel Johansson, interview with author, September 10, 2004.

37. Tanguay, "I Don't Care," January 19, 1947, 6; David Robinson, business manager, Dudley Clements, treasurer, notarized statement, February 14, 1911, Eva Tanguay Collection, acc. 2006.9, Benson Ford Research Center.

38. Tucker, *Some of These Days,* 80; "Eva Tanguay Eager to Help"; United Booking Offices, contract, August 17, 1911, Eva Tanguay Collection, acc. 2006.9, Benson Ford Research Center; Sime Silverman, "New Acts Next Week," *Variety,* December 12, 1913, 18; MeasuringWorth, http://eh.net/hmit/ppowerusd/ (accessed July 2, 2006); Keith/Albee Collection, University of Iowa, MsC 356, scrapbook 14, 183.

39. Mark Barron, "The Associated Press Biographical Service," no. 2977, August 15, 1942; Walter Monfried, "I Don't Care Girl," *New York Journal,* otherwise unattributed clipping, 1945; "Eva Tanguay at Home," *Stage Pictorial,* May 1912; unattributed clipping, possibly from *Variety,* date-stamped February 13, 1909.

40. *Eva Tanguay Souvenir Album,* NYPL, Robinson Locke Collection, v. 450; Ponce de Leon, *Self-Exposure,* 28.

41. "Milo M. Belding Dead," *New York Times,* May 24, 1917, 12; Tanguay, "I Don't Care," January 26, 1947, 6.

42. Albany's Leading Theatre Harmanus Bleecker Hall, Comstock's Amusement Co., "Eva Tanguay in 'The Sun Dodgers,'" October 14, 1913 (program), in Eva Tanguay Collection, acc. 2006.9, Benson Ford Research Center; Tanguay, "I Don't Care," January 19, 1947, 7.

43. Tanguay, "I Don't Care," *American Weekly,* January 5, 1947; "Roosevelt Aid to Cupid: Political Twist to the Latest of Lillian Russell's Weddings, *New York Times,* June 14, 1912, 1; "A. P. Moore Dies; Envoy to Poland," *New York Times,* February 18, 1930, 1, 17; Banner, *American Beauty,* 135.

8. MEN AND OTHER TRAVAILS

1. Tanguay, "I Don't Care," January 5, 1947.

2. This and previous paragraphs: ibid.

3. This and previous paragraphs: Tanguay, "I Don't Care," January 12, 1947.

4. This and previous paragraphs, ibid.

5. Tanguay, "I Don't Care," January 12, 1947, 7.

6. Ibid.

7. Ibid.

8. "Eva Tanguay to the Rescue," apparently *Rochester Telegraph,* incomplete clipping date-stamped December 18, 1907, NYPL, Robinson Locke Collection, v. 450.

9. This and previous paragraph: ibid.; and "Eva Tanguay to Walk's Rescue," *New York Telegraph,* article date-stamped December 26, 1907, NYPL, Robinson Locke Collection, v. 450. For more on Weinberg, see McKelway, "Big Little Man," 524–619.

10. This and previous paragraphs: "Ethel Barrymore Dies in Sleep, 79," *Herald Tribune,* June 19, 1957; Barrymore, *Memories,* 176; Slide, *Encyclopedia of Vaudeville,* 489; "Ethel Barrymore Likes Vaudeville," *New York Dramatic Mirror,* article date-stamped January 29, 1913, NYPL, Robinson Locke Collection, v. 4.

11. Barrymore, *Memories,* 177.

12. "Ethel Barrymore Likes Vaudeville"; "Colonial"; both in NYPL, Robinson Locke Collection, v. 4; Peters, *House of Barrymore,* 140; Oberdeck, *Evangelist,* 299–300.

13. This and previous paragraph: Barrymore, "My Reminiscences"; Leigh Woods, "Suffer the Women" (unpublished manuscript, 2004), 152–53; "Ethel Barrymore Plays Farewell in Vaudeville at Palace," *New York Star,* article date-stamped August 22, 1914, NYPL, Robinson Locke Collection, v. 4; "Ethel Barrymore Brutally Beaten by Her Husband," *Boston Post,* July 6, 1923, 1+; Ethel Barrymore, "At Thirty Every Woman Faces the Crossroads," *McCall's Magazine,* June 1923, 16.

14. Hamilton, *When I'm Bad,* 7; Leider, *Becoming Mae West,* 22–27.

15. Hamilton, *When I'm Bad,* 9; Leider, *Becoming Mae West,* 42.

16. Hamilton, *When I'm Bad,* 44; Leider, *Becoming Mae West,* 41, 70.

17. Trav S. D., *No Applause,* 110. For more on "coon songs," see Furia, "Irving Berlin," 195; Leider, *Becoming Mae West,* 41, 64–67.

18. This and previous paragraph: Keith/Albee Collection, University of Iowa, MsC 356, scrapbook 16, 251; Leider, *Becoming Mae West,* 75, 80, 88.

19. Hamilton, *When I'm Bad,* 43, 47–48, 69.

20. See ibid., chapters 3 and 4.

21. Hamilton, *When I'm Bad,* 240.

22. Rosen, "Vanishing Act"; Wes Eichenwald, e-mail message to author, August 26, 2004.

23. Hamilton, *When I'm Bad,* 249–50.

24. For more on West's writing assistance, see Leider, *Becoming Mae West,* 140.

25. Douglas, *Feminization of American Culture,* 51–52.

26. U.S. Bureau of the Census, *Historical Statistics of the United States, Colonial Times to 1970, Bicentennial Edition,* part 2 (Washington, DC, 1975); Leach, *Land of Desire,* 64–66; "Eva Tanguay—Songs," *Variety,* November 14, 1914, 18.

27. Jack Edwards, letter to Lee Shubert, December 9, 1913, New York, Shubert Archive.

28. Eva Tanguay, Hotel Woodward, New York, letter to Lee Shubert, New York, undated but probably early 1914, Shubert Archive.

29. Tarbell, "Business of Being a Woman"; Peiss, *Hope in a Jar,* 50.

9. MRS. JOHN FORD

1. "Four Dancing Fords," *Pittsburg Gazette,* December 22, 1907; "Four Fords, Cincinnati's Dancers, at Columbia," *Cincinnati Commercial,* March 16, 1910; *Cincinnati Times,* February 29, 1908.

2. "B. F. Keith's," *Indianapolis Star,* December 20, 1910; "Clever Dancer Returns to Crystal Next Week," *Milwaukee News,* July 11, 1913.

3. Keith/Albee Collection, University of Iowa, MsC 356, scrapbook 1, 59, 265, 269, 284.

4. Ibid., scrapbook 5, 57, scrapbook 7, 230, scrapbook 8, 150; "Keith's Overflows with Holiday Crowd," *Philadelphia North American,* article date-stamped September 3, 1907, NYPL, Robinson Locke Collection, v. 450.

5. This and previous paragraph: Keith/Albee Collection, University of Iowa, MsC 356, scrapbook 5, 57, scrapbook 7, 230, scrapbook 15, 96.

6. "Johnny Ford Teams Up Again with Mayme Gehrue," *New York Review,* February 6, 1915; "Southern Vaudeville," *Columbus Journal,* November 4, 1913.

7. Tanguay, "I Don't Care," January 19, 1947, 7.

8. Various articles, "Ford, Johnny" clipping file, New York Public Library for the Performing Arts Theater Collection; marriage certificate, Ann Arbor, November 24, 1913, Eva Tanguay Collection, acc. 2006.9, Benson Ford Research Center.

9. Tanguay, "I Don't Care," January 19, 1947, 7, and "I Don't Care," January 26, 1947, 6. Interestingly, just two years earlier seventeen-year-old Mae West had also rashly gotten married, to a jazz dancer named Frank Wallace while on tour in the same part of the country, in nearby Milwaukee. And it was just as unclear in Mae West's case, since she too seemed opposed by nature to marriage, what could have driven her to tie the knot. "Within a matter of days," wrote Marybeth Hamilton, "she violently recoiled from what she had done" (*When I'm Bad,* 16).

10. This and previous paragraphs: Tanguay, "I Don't Care," January 26, 1947, 6; *Eva Ford v. John W. Ford,* bill for divorce, B-36959, Circuit Court of Cook County, IL, December 19, 1917; "Drunkenness and Heredity," *Current Literature* 31 (September 1901): 341; "Science and Discovery: The Controversy over Alcoholism and Success in Life," *Current Literature* 49 (November 1910): 513–14; "Distinguished Physicians on the Drink Question," *Arena* 41, no. 233 (August 1909): 586–88; Leslie E. Keeley, "Inebriety and Insanity," *Arena* August 1893, 328–37.

11. Tanguay, "I Don't Care," January 26, 1947, 6; MeasuringWorth, *http://www.measuringworth.com/uscompare/relativevalue.php* (accessed January 16, 2012).

12. "Here's Some Scandal," *New York Telegraph,* May 31, 1914.

13. "Eva Tanguay Wakes Up 44th Street Music Hall," *Variety,* December 12, 1913; John Ford, "I Was Built for Speed and Not for Comfort," Eva Tanguay Collection, acc. 2006.9, Benson Ford Research Center.

14. *Eva Ford v. John W. Ford,* bill for divorce, B-36959, Circuit Court of Cook County, IL, December 19, 1917.

15. Nat Sahr, "Eva Tanguay's Husband Arrested," *New York Dramatic Mirror,* article date-stamped April 29, 1914, "Ford, Johnny" clipping file, New York Public Library for the Performing Arts Theater Collection.

16. Unattributed article, *Toledo Times,* May 17, 1914, "Ford, Johnny" clipping file, New York Public Library for the Performing Arts Theater Collection; *Eva Ford v. John W. Ford,* bill for divorce, B-36959, Circuit Court of Cook County, IL, December 19, 1917.

17. Ullie Akerstrom, "A Glimpse of the Real Eva Tanguay," ca. 1903, ms. found in Eva Tanguay Collection, acc. 2006.9, Benson Ford Research Center; Eva Tanguay, Hollywood, CA, to Florence Tanguay Dufresne, March 3, [1945], letter in author's personal collection.

18. "Tanguay at the Nixon," *Pittsburg Leader,* article date-stamped October 20. 1914, "Ford, Johnny" clipping file, New York Public Library for the Performing Arts Theater Collection.

19. *Eva Ford v. John W. Ford,* bill for divorce, B-36959, Circuit Court of Cook County, IL, December 19, 1917; "Tanguay and Ford Let Love Languish," *Decatur Daily Herald,* January 5, 1915, "Ford, Johnny" clipping file, New York Public Library for the Performing Arts Theater Collection.

20. Keith/Albee Collection, University of Iowa, MsC 356, scrapbook 8, 244; Memoirs of Edward V. Darling, in Edward V. and Alfred T. Darling papers, 1899–1952, ★T-mss. 1986–005, New York Public Library for the Performing Arts Theater Collection.

21. Harry L. Tighe, New York, to Eva Tanguay, March 27, 1916; "Harry Tighe," *Variety,* February 27, 1935.

22. MeasuringWorth, *http://www.measuringworth.com/uscompare/relativevalue.php* (accessed January 16, 2012).

23. "Joseph W. Smiley," *New York Times,* December 4, 1945; "Tanguay Would Stop Film," *New York Dramatic Mirror,* July 7, 1915, 32; "Harry Weber," *Variety,* March 15, 1939.

24. Unattributed newspaper article, date-stamped October 27, 1906, NYPL, Robinson Locke Collection, v.450; "Eva Tanguay Turns 'Scientist,'" *New York City Press,* May 9, 1915, Mary Baker Eddy Library for the Betterment of Humanity.

25. "Eva Tanguay Turns 'Scientist'" (see note 24, above); unattributed newspaper article (undated) "Laughing Nora Bayes Dies by Sudden Turn on Road to Recovery," "Bayes, Nora" clipping file, New York Public Library for the Performing Arts Theater Collection; unattributed *New York Times* article date-stamped July 30, 1946, "Nora Bayes, Dead 18 Years, Is Buried Here Simultaneously with Her Fifth Husband."

26. "On the White Way," *Harford Courant*, February 13, 1915, Mary Baker Eddy Library for the Betterment of Humanity.

27. "Eva Tanguay Turns 'Scientist'" (see note 24, above); Eichenwald, "Americans," (unpublished draft, 2001); memoirs of Edward V. Darling (see note 20, above).

28. Smith, "'I Do Care!'"

29. Eva Tanguay, article date-stamped February 2, 1919, NYPL, Robinson Locke Collection, ser. 2, v. 297; Westerfield, "Investigation," 7.

30. Knee, *Christian Science*, 2; Satter, *Each Mind a Kingdom*, 25.

31. Satter, *Each Mind a Kingdom*, 1; Piepmeier, *Out in Public*, 89.

32. Piepmeier, *Out in Public*, 65.

33. Williams, "Founder of Christian Science"; Knee, *Christian Science*, 2.

34. Williams, "Founder of Christian Science," 291, 293; Eddy, *Science and Health*, x.

35. Knee, *Christian Science*, 2; Williams, "Founder of Christian Science," 298.

36. Knee, *Christian Science*, 7, 75, 99.

37. Ibid., 3, 7, 24, 54.

38. Ibid., 7–8; Williams, "Founder of Christian Science," 298–99.

39. Milmine, "Mary Baker G. Eddy," May 1907, 99, 101.

40. Ibid., 115; Williams, "Founder of Christian Science," 298; Satter, *Each Mind a Kingdom*, 5. The Christian Science Church's official website reports that *Science and Health* is in print today "in multiple editions and formats, as well as in 17 languages and English Braille." Readers can also access Eddy's book in electronic formats. See Christian Science Board of Directors, Christian Science, http://christianscience.com/publications/science-and-health/ and The Mary Baker Eddy Library for the Betterment of Humanity, http://www.marybakereddylibrary.org/mary-baker-eddy/writings/science-and-health.

41. Eddy, *Science and Health*, viii, 108, 114, 472.

42. Christian Science, "What Is Christian Science?" http://christianscience.com/what-is-christian-science (accessed March 11, 2012); Eddy, *Science and Health*, viii, 175, 44; Milmine, "Mary Baker G. Eddy," July 1907, 333.

43. Eddy, *Science and Health*, 176, 422; Satter, *Each Mind a Kingdom*, 66.

44. "Eva Tanguay Saves Eye," *New York Times*, May 20, 1933, 11:3; "Eva Tanguay Taking Cure," *New York Times*, December 24, 1932, 10:3; "Eva Tanguay Suffers Relapse," *New York Times*, September 8, 1932, 17:5; "Eva Tanguay Won't Retire Until She Is 140 Years Old," *Pittsburgh Post*, March 14, 1931; all in the Mary Baker Eddy Library for the Betterment of Humanity.

45. Fields, *Sophie Tucker*, 52; Grossman, *Funny Woman*, 168.

46. *Eva Ford v. John W. Ford*, Circuit Court of Cook County, IL, October 22, 1917; *Eva Ford v. John Ford*, B-36969, Circuit Court of Cook County, IL, July 3, 1918, and B-36959, July 7, 1918; Fields, *Sophie Tucker*, 132.

47. *Eva Ford v. John W. Ford*, bill for divorce, B-36959, Circuit Court of Cook County, IL, December 19, 1917; "Eva Tanguay Divorces J. W. Ford," *New York Times*, December 20, 1917, 9:2.

48. "Johnny Ford Teams Up Again with Mayme Gehrue" (see note 6, above); "Johnny Ford Denies It," *Variety*, February 12, 1915; "Johnny Ford," *Variety*, February 26, 1915; "Snappy Acts in Colonial's Bill," *New York Telegraph*, October 10, 1917; all in "Ford, Johnny" clipping file, New York Public Library for the Performing Arts Theater Collection.

49. *Eva Ford v. John W. Ford*, B-36959, Circuit Court of Cook County, IL, June 17, 1918.

50. *Eva Ford v. John W. Ford*, B-36969, Circuit Court of Cook County, IL, July 3, 1918; *Eva Ford v. John W. Ford*, B-36959, order, Circuit Court of Cook County, IL, October 8, 1918.

51. Eva Tanguay, will dated November 21, 1924, New York City; various clippings, New York Public Library for the Performing Arts Theater Collection.

10. THE WILD GIRL

1. Robert C. Allen has argued that movies were not simply used as "chasers" in vaudeville, though the pejorative name certainly stuck. See Allen, "Contra the Chaser Theory."

2. "Acts at the Palace Theatre from March 24 1913 to August 29 1921," in Edward V. and Alfred T. Darling papers, 1899–1952, ★T-Mss 1986–005, New York Public Library for the Performing Arts Theater Collection; contracts, Eva Tanguay Collection, acc. 2006.9, Benson Ford Research Center; A. Herbst, "The Week's Vaudeville Bills in New York: Weekly Laugh Bulletin," B. F. Keith's Palace Theatre, *Star*, week ending March 10, 1918.

3. The German 42-centimeter artillery piece was popularly known as Big Bertha.

4. Marks, *They All Sang*, 179; letter to Edward J. Ader.

5. Hendricks, "History of the Kinetoscope," 43–48.

6. Balio, "Novelty Spawns a Small Business," 5.

7. Allen, "Movies in Vaudeville," 75–76; Balio, "Novelty Spawns a Small Business," 21.

8. Allen, "Movies in Vaudeville," 77. For more on music in nickelodeon theaters, see Abel, "That Most American of Attractions"; "Morals and Moving Pictures," *Harper's Weekly*, 12.

9. Balio, "Novelty Spawns a Small Business," 20.

10. "Morals and Moving Pictures"; Merritt, "Nickelodeon Theaters," 86, 96–97; Balio, "Struggles for Control," 113; Gomery, *Shared Pleasures*, 31.

11. Harrison, *American Film Institute Catalog*, 1038; "Joseph W. Smiley," *New York Times*, December 4, 1945.

12. See Gunning, "Cinema of Attractions."

13. "Screen Shows a New Eva Tanguay."

14. Vazzana, *Silent Film Necrology*, 159; "Howard Estabrook in 'Search Me' at Gaiety Theatre"; "Howard Estabrook"; "Well Known Actor Begins Engagement with Whartons"; and other articles, clipping book, and files, all in New York Public Library for the Performing Arts Theater Collection.

15. Eric Pace, "Howard Estabrook, Won Oscar for 'Cimarron' Screenplay, at 94," *New York Times*, July 26, 1978, B2; "Says Howard Estabrook in Very Interesting Statement," *Hollywood Filmograph*, February 15, 1930.

16. "Tanguay Picture Makes Vaudeville Jealous," *Motion Picture World*, October 6, 1917; Slide, *Encyclopedia of Vaudeville*, 488–89; Glenn, *Female Spectacle*, 218.

17. "Young Mrs. Sanford: The Flash Drama Arrives," *New York Times*, January 30, 1917, 7:2.

18. Benjamin, *Work of Art*, 5, 16; Glenn, *Female Spectacle*, 66. Note the sense of Eva disappearing with a lost world in her *Variety* obituary's sentimental headline: Barry, "Eva Tanguay—'I Don't Care' Girl—Slips Away, Taking an Era with Her."

19. Dan Johansson, interview with author, September 10, 2004; "Eva Tanguay Makes Home Town a Visit," *Holyoke Daily Transcript*, June 17, 1919; Florence Tanguay Dufresne, obituary, *Plainfield Post*, January 7, 1977.

20. Eva Tanguay, Grand Rapids, MI, letter to Lee Shubert, February 15, 1919, Shubert Archive, New York.

21. Eva Tanguay, Cleveland, OH, letter to J. J. Shubert, February 26, 1919, Shubert Archive, New York.

22. Davis, "Syndicate/Shubert War."

23. "Acts at the Palace Theatre from March 24, 1913 to August 29, 1921," in Edward V. and Alfred T. Darling papers, 1899–1952, ★T-mss 1986–005, New York Public Library for the Performing Arts Theater Collection; contracts in Eva Tanguay Collection, acc. 2006.9, Benson Ford Research Center; "Evolution of Cheap Vaudeville"; "Merger in the Far West," *New York Dramatic Mirror*, March 30, 1907, 17; "Pantages Absorbs Western States Vaudeville List," *Variety*, November 14, 1908, 1.

11. KNOCKDOWNS AND COMEBACKS...AND KNOCKDOWNS

1. Jules Tygiel, "The 1920s Economy: A Statistical Portrait," http://bss.sfsu.edu/tygiel/hist427/texts/1920seconomy.htm; Gomery, *Shared Pleasures,* 34.

2. Eva Tanguay, will dated November 21, 1924, New York City.

3. "Eva Tanguay of Vaudeville Fame Is Dead," *Boston Herald,* January 12, 1947.

4. This and previous paragraph: Eva Tanguay, will dated November 21, 1924, New York City.

5. Keith/Albee Collection, University of Iowa, MsC 356, scrapbook 13, 78, and scrapbook 16, 156.

6. Fields, *Sophie Tucker,* 60, 75.

7. Ibid., 71–72, 79–82.

8. Ibid., 48, 69, 83.

9. Tucker, *Some of These Days,* 22, 104; Dimeglio, *Vaudeville U.S.A.,* 146; Fields, *Sophie Tucker,* 83, 91–92.

10. This and previous paragraph: Tucker, *Some of These Days,* 80.

11. Marcus, *Between Women,* 4.

12. Eva Tanguay Collection, acc. 2006.9, Benson Ford Research Center.

13. Ibid.; Tanguay, "I Don't Care," January 26, 1947; *New York Dramatic Mirror,* May 29, 1920, 1109.

14. *New York Dramatic Mirror,* May 29, 1920, 1109; *Morning Telegraph,* January 9, 1919; "Orpheum," *Variety,* February 6, 1920; "Seeing the Show at the Riverside," *New York Star,* February 25, 1920; "Roscoe Ails," *Variety,* February 13, 1920.

15. This and previous paragraphs: Tanguay, "I Don't Care," January 26, 1947, 7; Barry, "Eva Tanguay—'I Don't Care' Girl—Slips Away," 48; Eva Tanguay, Hollywood, CA, letter to Florence Tanguay Dufresne, no address, March 3, [1945]; *New York Dramatic Mirror,* May 29, 1920, 1109.

16. "Roscoe Ails, Eugenic Dad, Flops as Hubby," ca. 1933, undated, unattributed clipping, New York Public Library for the Performing Arts; "Battle in Bath of Roscoe Ails Ends in Court," *Daily Mirror,* September 30, 1935; "Roscoe Ails and Kate Pullman," *Toledo Blade,* undated, unattributed clipping, New York Public Library for the Performing Arts; "The 7-Years' Bad Luck of the Eugenic Papa," *New York Evening Journal,* November 2, 1935, 6.

17. "Eva Tanguay Has the Grip," *New York Times,* December 24, 1924, 10:1; "Eva Tanguay Convalescing," *New York Times,* December 26, 1924, 15:4; "Eva Tanguay Very Ill," *New York Times,* May 30, 1925, 5:3; "Eva Tanguay Not Seriously Ill," *New York Times,* May 31, 1925, 24:3.

18. Grossman, *Funny Woman,* 147–48.

19. Piepmeier, *Out in Public,* 67; "Eva Tanguay Goes Big in Boston: 'Queen of Jazz' Draws Capacity House," 1923, unattributed clipping, Eva Tanguay file, Holyoke History Room, Holyoke Public Library; Smith, "'I Do Care!'"

20. Cocks, "What about Plastic Surgery?" *Good Housekeeping,* June 1930, 152–56; Banner, *American Beauty,* 213–14.

21. Samuel Iglauer, "Correction of Outstanding and Cauliflower Ears," *Hygeia,* April 1926, 196; Cocks, "What about Plastic Surgery?"

22. Peiss, *Hope in a Jar,* 48, 97, 130.

23. Nasaw, *Going Out,* 249; Douglas, *Listening In,* 104.

24. Reminiscences of Al Parado, fall 1957, pp. 1, 2, CUOHROC.

25. Ibid., 2–6.

26. Ibid., 6, 7.

27. Ibid., 12, 13.

28. Ibid., 13–17.

29. Ibid., 18–21.

30. "Eva Tanguay of 'I Don't Care' Fame, to Wed Pianist," *New York Daily Mirror,* January 20, 1927; "Eva Tanguay Seeks Marriage Annulment," *New York Times,* October 9, 1927, 13; "Eva Tanguay Gets Divorce," *New York Times,* October 22, 1927, 2:5; James, *Notable American Women,* 426.

31. Eva Tanguay Collection, acc. 2006.9, Benson Ford Research Center.

32. The Ansonia, described as "popular with theater people and musicians because of its heavy walls, which encouraged late-night partying or practice sessions," had for a time been the home of Florenz Ziegfeld Jr. and his family (Mordden, *Ziegfeld,* 100). "W. E. D. Stokes Saves His Son's Pig," *New York Times,* November 12, 1907, 5; "W. E. D. Stokes Shot by Women," *New York Times,* June 8, 1911, 1; "Life with Stokes Unhappy, Says Wife," *New York Times,* November 3, 1923, 1; "W. E. D. Stokes Dies of Pneumonia at 73," *New York Times,* May 20, 1926; Christopher Gray, "A West Side Developer's Other Side," *New York Times,* August 28, 2005, real estate sec., 10; reminiscences of Al Parado, fall 1957, page 8, CUOHROC.

33. Reminiscences of Al Parado, fall 1957, pages 8–10, CUOHROC.

34. Gomery, "Coming of Sound," 248.

35. *New York Clipper,* June 9, 1900, 348; June 30, 1900, 403; and July 7, 1900, 424; Allen, *Horrible Prettiness,* 190.

36. "B. F. Keith Dead"; http://www.eh.net/hmit/ppowerusd (accessed March 18, 2006); *New York Clipper,* April 13, 1907, 227; *New York Clipper,* February 23, 1907, 30; "United Managers in One Big Corporation," *Variety,* June 22, 1907, 6; "Belasco to Write Sketches," *New York Dramatic Mirror,* March 23, 1907, 19.

37. Samuels and Samuels, *Once upon a Stage,* 23.

38. McLean, 16–17.

39. Robert Snyder described the UBO as a "switching house that linked managers and performers and directed acts around the circuits" (Snyder, "Vaudeville," 137). "Vaudeville's Clearing House."

40. Memoirs of Edward V. Darling, in Edward V. and Alfred T. Darling papers, 1899–1952, ★T-mss 1986–005, New York Public Library for the Performing Arts Theater Collection.

41. Ibid.

42. Ibid.

12. DEATH AND OTHER ENDINGS

1. Harold Bierman Jr., "The 1929 Stock Market Crash," EH.net, http://eh.net/ency clopedia/article/bierman.crash, (posted February 5, 2010, accessed January 16, 2012); "Dow Jones Industrial Average (1900–Present Monthly)," StockCharts.com, http://stockcharts.com/ freecharts/historical/djia1900.html (accessed January 16, 2011).

2. Tanguay, "I Don't Care," January 26, 1947, 7.

3. "Eva Tanguay Sells Home Furnishings," unattributed article date-stamped February 26, 1930, Time-Life Archives; "Eva Tanguay Out of Danger," *New York Times,* September 2, 1932, 18:5; "Eva Tanguay Going Blind," *New York Times,* August 27, 1932.

4. This and prior paragraph: Tanguay, "I Don't Care," January 26, 1947, 7; article fragment, *Time,* date-stamped April 20, 1931, Time-Life Archives; "Eva Tanguay Gets Fine Reception at Mt. Park Casino," *Holyoke Transcript,* June 30, 1931, 6; "Once Periled by Blindness, Eva Tanguay Back on Stage," *Wisconsin Sentinel,* May 11, 1931.

5. Tanguay, "I Don't Care," January 26, 1947, 7; "Eva Tanguay Won't Retire Until She Is 140 Years Old," *Pittsburgh Post,* March 14, 1931; "Eva Tanguay Saves Eye," *New York Times,* May 20, 1933, 11:3.

6. "Eva Tanguay, 50, Says Faith Helped Eyesight," *Boston Traveler,* October 4, 1928, in Mary Baker Eddy Library for the Betterment of Humanity; Friedman, "Girlesk in New York," 15; Tanguay, "I Care at Last," 43; Milmine, "Mary Baker G. Eddy," 99; Knee, *Christian Science,* 13.

7. "Eva Tanguay Taking Cure," *New York Times,* date-stamped July 24, 1932, Time-Life Archives; "Added Attraction," *Time,* date-stamped January 25, 1932, Time-Life Archives; "Eva Tanguay Suffers Relapse," *New York Times,* September 8, 1932, 17:5; "Old Comrades Flock to Aid Eva Tanguay," unattributed article date-stamped August 28, 1932, Time-Life Archives; "Eva Tanguay Going Blind," *New York Times,* August 27, 1932.

8. Eva Tanguay, Hollywood, letter to Florence Tanguay Dufresne, Massachusetts, March 3 (probably 1945, though no year is given on the letter), provided to author by Daniel Johansson.

9. "Sid Grauman, Famed Showman and Prankster, Dies in L.A. at 71," *Variety,* March 8, 1950, 26; John Rosenfield, "Passing Show," *Dallas Morning News,* March 7, 1950, 10, part 2.

10. "Lucy Cotton, 56, Dies in Florida; Pills Suspected," *New York Herald Tribune,* December 18, 1948; *San Antonio Light,* article date-stamped December 28, 1913, NYPL, Robinson Locke Collection, v. 85, ser. 2; Lucy Cotton, "What Do Men Like Best in Women," *Toledo News Bee,* July 7, 1919; "Southern—'Miracle of Love,'" *Columbus Dispatch,* January 26, 1920.

11. Eva Tanguay, Hollywood, letter to Walter Winchell, New York, October 31, 1933, author's private collection; Ernest Cuneo, "Walter Winchell: The Greatest of the Great Gossips," *Saturday Evening Post,* September 1976, 32; "The Last Word on Winchell," *New Yorker,* January 30, 1995, 69–78; "Newspaperman," *Time,* July 11, 1938, 33; Gabler, *Winchell,* xii–xvi, 15, 36–38, 45.

12. Tanguay letter to Winchell, 1933 (see note 11, above); Tucker, *Some of These Days,* 81, 112, 141; "Sophie Tucker an Ageless Star," *New York World-Telegraph & Sun,* February 10, 1966.

13. "Eva Tanguay, Better, Plans Big Comeback," unattributed newspaper clipping, date-stamped October 23, 1932, New York Public Library for the Performing Arts; Leider, *Becoming Mae West,* 346.

14. "Eva Tanguay, Better, Plans Big Comeback" (see note 13, above); "Eva Tanguay to Return to Stage," *New York Times,* February 2, 1933, 21:4; "Eva Tanguay Recovers," *New York Times,* May 12, 1934, 12:6; "Eva Tanguay Saves Eye," *New York Times,* May 20, 1933, 11:3; "Singer Eva Tanguay Looks Herself Over," *Los Angeles Herald Express,* September 6, 1934, 9.

15. "Eva Tanguay Plans Return to Aid Blind," article date-stamped April 9, 1934, Regional History Center, University of Southern California.

16. Eva Tanguay, New York, letter to Florence Tanguay Dufresne, Massachusetts, undated, author's private collection. The letter, on stationery from the Hotel Woodward, designed as a "high-class family hotel" by the architect Nathan E. Clark about 1905, bears the names of both the president and the general manger, T. D. Green and L. H. Bingham, respectively. Thomas D. Green owned the Woodward until 1934, after which time it fell into financial misfortune and had to be taken over by the Bowery Savings Bank. Eva's letter to Florence Tanguay Dufresne is undated but probably written in late 1932 or early 1933, since she encouraged her niece to write her back at the Woodward, but to do so soon since she intended to depart "as it is too high priced for me through summer." Eva also had heard that Florence was to "have a little angel baby," probably meaning she was pregnant with her son, Doug, who was born in 1932. Frank W. Crane, "Hotel Woodward Undergoes Change," *New York Times,* July 18, 1937, real estate section, 1; "Noteworthy Addition for Hotel Woodward on Broadway in Ford Motor Company's New Sixteen-Story Building," *New York Times,* October 1, 1916.

17. "Eva Tanguay Decides She Cares; Seeks Songs Here," *Providence Journal,* January 1, 1933.

18. Calvin, "Big Idea."

19. Eva Tanguay, "How It Feels to Masquerade in Men's Clothes," ms. found in the NYPL, Robinson Locke Collection, v. 450; "Eva Tanguay Opens a Shop," *New York Times,* March 10, 1935, sec. 2, 8:3; "Eva Tanguay Opens Store," *Los Angeles Times,* March 10, 1935.

20. This and previous paragraphs: Eva Tanguay, Hollywood, letter to Florence Tanguay Dufresne, Massachusetts, March 3, [1945], author's private collection.

21. "Eva Tanguay 'Coming Back,'" unattributed article date-stamped October 19, 1936, *People* Magazine Clipping Archive.

22. "Eva Tanguay Failing," *New York Times,* December 11, 1938, 4:2; "Eva Tanguay's Condition Grave," *New York Times,* December 14, 1938, L 33.

23. Eva Tanguay, Hollywood, to Florence Tanguay Dufresne, Massachusetts, March 3, [1945], author's private collection.

24. This and previous paragraph: "NBC Personalities: Ed Wynn," *NBC Advance Program Service,* no. 27, July 5, 1936, 1; Eva Tanguay, letter to the editor of *Stage* magazine, date-stamped October 1938, clipping file, New York Public Library for the Performing Arts Theater Collection; Douglas, *Listening In,* 112.

25. "Eva Tanguay, 64, Refuses to Be Sad," unattributed newspaper article, August 1, 1942, New York Public Library for the Performing Arts.

26. "Topics of the Times," *New York Times,* August 7, 1942, 16:4; *New York Times,* January 10, 1939, from *People* Magazine Clipping Archive.

27. "Eva Tanguay Improving," *New York Herald Tribune,* March 30, 1945; Ed Rees, "Regarding Tanguay," Los Angeles, August 2, 1946, unpublished wire report to Seaver Buck, *Time,* New York, August 15, 1946.

28. "Eva Tanguay, of 'I Don't Care' Fame, Dies at 68."

29. "Eva Tanguay Rites Tomorrow," *New York Times,* article date-stamped January 13, 1947, *People* Magazine Archive; "Eva Tanguay's Funeral Draws Stage Star 'S.R.O.,'" Regional History Center, University of Southern California, Los Angeles; "Harry Leonhardt," *Moving Picture World,* July 10, 1915; Joseph Santley Jr., "300 at Funeral of Eva Tanguay," *Los Angeles Examiner,* January 15, 1947; "Cowboy Cooper Revives the Role He Played in 1907," *New York Herald Tribune,* March 13, 1932; "Eva Tanguay's Funeral," *New York Times,* January 15, 1947, 25:1; Miller, *Plain Speaking,* 84; Joseph Santley Jr., interview with author, June 2, 2004; Satter, *Each Mind a Kingdom,* 249; United Church of Religious Science [now United Centers for Spiritual Living], "One the Path of the Global Heart," http://www.religiousscience.org/ucrs_site/our_founder/first_religious.html (accessed October 25, 2004, website no longer available).

30. Eichenwald, "Americans."

31. Superior Court of the State of California in and for the County of Los Angeles, no. 264927, and related documents; "Eva Tanguay Left $500," *New York Times,* January 24, 1947, 16:2.

EPILOGUE

1. This and previous paragraphs: memo from George Wasson to Lew Schreiber and George Jessel, Twentieth Century-Fox, June 18, 1948, UCLA Film & Television Archive, boxes LR 378 and LR 1387.

2. Custen, *Bio/Pics,* 22; "Mendel B. Silberberg, 78, Dies; Film Lawyer and G.O.P. Adviser," *New York Times,* June 30, 1965, 37.

3. Custen, *Bio/Pics,* 22; Jessel, *Elegy in Manhattan,* 44; memo from George Jessel to Lew Schreiber, Twentieth Century-Fox, August 18, 1948, and memo from George Jessel to George Wasson, Twentieth Century-Fox, August 31, 1948, UCLA Film & Television Archive, boxes LR 378 and LR 1387. For more on Santley, see "Santley Started Stage Career at Three," *Boston Transcript,* article date-stamped May 24, ca. 1917, and "Yes, Sir, Santley Once Played Little Eva," both clippings from New York Public Library for the Performing Arts Theater Collection; "New York Critics Enthuse over 'Vaudeville's Most Artistic Achievement,'" *Stage,* April 17, 1920, 743; Joseph Santley (son), interview with author, June 3, 2004.

4. Memo from Lew Schreiber to George Wasson, Twentieth Century-Fox, June 16, 1948; telegram from George Wasson to E. P. Kilroe, Twentieth Century-Fox, New York, NY; memo from Fulton Brylawski, Washington, DC, June 28, 1948; assignment document from Twentieth Century-Fox to Joseph Santley, July 6, 1948; all in UCLA Film & Television Archive, boxes LR 378 and LR 1387.

5. Joseph Santley, "Treatment: The I Don't Care Girl," July 12, 1948, 1, Cinematic Arts Library, University of Southern California.

6. Ibid. Fought over dueling imperialist aspirations in Manchuria and Korea, the Russo-Japanese War raged from February 10, 1904, to September 5, 1905. At the time, Eva was taking a shortened version of *The Sambo Girl* around the vaudeville circuits. It should be noted that Santley's "I Don't Care" screenplay is structured not unlike a nineteenth-century "well-made play," in which all is revealed in an "aha" moment, called by some literary historians the *scène à faire* ("obligatory scene"). No doubt Santley himself appeared in many such dramas during his time as a stock trouper. On well-made plays, see Stanton's introduction in *Camille and Other Plays,* vii–xxxix.

7. George Jessel, foreword to Joseph Fields, "I Don't Care," first draft continuity, September 16, 1948, Cinematic Arts Library, University of Southern California. As George Custen

has noted, biopics of the era "created a view of history that was based on the cosmology of the movie industry." They "cultivate[d] the interests of their producers, presenting a world view that naturalize[d] certain lives and specific values over alternative ones" (Custen, *Bio/Pics*, 4).

8. Albert Lewis and Arthur Lewis, "I Don't Care," treatment, January 25, 1949; memo from Darryl Zanuck to George Jessel, Twentieth Century-Fox, February 8, 1949, Cinematic Arts Library, University of Southern California.

9. Custen, *Twentieth Century's Fox*, 1, 15, 13.

10. This and previous paragraphs: Albert Lewis and Arthur Lewis, "I Don't Care," treatment; memo from Darryl Zanuck to George Jessel, Twentieth Century-Fox, February 8, 1949; memo from Darryl Zanuck to George Jessel, Twentieth Century-Fox, March 17, 1949; conference notes, meeting of Darryl Zanuck and George Jessel, June 13, 1949; Marian Turk, "The I Don't Care Girl," story line, November 5, 1949; I. A. L. Diamond, "The I Don't Care Girl," treatment, November 10, 1949; memo from Albert E. Lewin and Burt Styler to Darryl Zanuck and F. D. Langlen, Twentieth Century-Fox, April 25, 1950; memo from Darryl Zanuck to George Jessel, Albert Lewin, and Burt Styler, Twentieth Century-Fox, April 26, 1950; all in Cinematic Arts Library, University of Southern California.

11. Custen, *Bio/Pics*, 173.

12. Arthur Caesar, treatment, based on George Jessel, "She Went That Way," original story, Cinematic Arts Library, University of Southern California.

13. Ibid.

14. Memo from George Jessel to Darryl Zanuck, Twentieth Century-Fox, October 12, 1950, Cinematic Arts Library, University of Southern California.

15. George Jessel, "I Don't Care," revisions; Walter Bullock, *The I Don't Care Girl*, screenplay based on an original story by George Jessel, April 27, 1950; Darryl Zanuck, comments on screening of scenes from *The I Don't Care Girl*, with George Jessel, Lloyd Bacon, and Louis Loeffler, October 19, 1951, Cinematic Arts Library, University of Southern California.

16. For further reading, see Inglis, "Self-Regulation in Operation." Memo from Joseph I. Breen, Motion Picture Association of America, to Col. Jason S. Joy, director of public relations, Twentieth Century-Fox, July 8, 1949, Margaret Herrick Library, Academy of Motion Picture Arts and Sciences.

17. Jack Leahy, "Gaynor's a Weight Gainor," *New York Sunday News*, January 18, 1964, 8, and various clippings, New York Public Library for the Performing Arts Theater Collection; casting file, June 9, 1951, William Gordon Collection, folder 139, Margaret Herrick Library, Academy of Motion Picture Arts and Sciences; Fields, *Sophie Tucker*, 133.

18. Goodman, "Merry Madcap"; Fields, *Sophie Tucker*, 144.

19. Memos from Joseph I. Breen, Motion Picture Association of America, to Col. Jason S. Joy, director of public relations, Twentieth Century-Fox, October 25, 1951, December 27, 1951, and July 1949; memo from Joseph I. Breen to Col. Jason S. Joy, January 23, 1952; memo for the files, January 18, 1952; notes of conference with Mr. Van Schmus and Mr. Vizzard of the Motion Picture Association of America and George Jessel, Twentieth Century-Fox, January 16, 1952; all in Margaret Herrick Library, Academy of Motion Picture Arts and Sciences; Custen, *Bio/Pics*, 1, 13, 15, 173.

20. Casting file, June 9, 1951, and July 17, 1951, William Gordon Collection, folder 139, Margaret Herrick Library, Academy of Motion Picture Arts and Sciences.

21. Custen, *Bio/Pics*, 47, 84.

22. "I Don't Care Girl."

23. "The I Don't Care Girl," otherwise unattributed clipping, New York Public Library for the Performing Arts Theater Collection.

24. "National Box Office Survey," *Variety*, December 31, 1952, 3; "Top Grossers of 1953," *Variety*, January 13, 1954, 10–11.

25. Cohen, "Blame High-Pressure Selling."

26. Gilbert, *American Vaudeville*, 327; Rosen, *Vanishing Act*"; Isabelle Paré, "Eva Tanguay, première superstar américaine," *Le Devoir.com*, http://www.ledevoir.com/culture/actualites-culturelles/284419/eva-tanguay-premiere-superstar-americaine (accessed March 11, 2010).

27. Titone, *My Thoughts Be Bloody,* 2, 6; Dudden, *Women in American Theatre,* 85, 101.

28. Dudden, *Women in American Theatre,* 44–48, 83–84; Piepmeier, *Out in Public,* 20; Gold and Fizdale, *Divine Sarah,* 9.

29. Wes Eichenwald, the author of a short profile on Eva for the magazine *American History* in 2001, claims to be in possession of Eva Tanguay's unpublished "autobio." I have made several requests to see the alleged autobiography, but without success.

30. *Tanguay v. Schallert,* 488459, Superior Court, Los Angeles County, CA, September 30, 1943; Eva Tanguay, Hollywood, CA, letter to Florence Tanguay Dufresne, March 3, [1945], author's personal collection; William Schallert, interview with author, May 26, 2004.

Sources and Select Bibliography

ARCHIVES

Ashfield Historical Society, Ashfield, MA.

Cinematic Arts Library, University of Southern California, Los Angeles.

Columbia University Oral History Research Office Collection. Columbia University Libraries, New York. (Abbreviated in the notes as CUOHROC.)

Eva Tanguay Collection. Benson Ford Research Center at The Henry Ford, Dearborn, MI.

Film & Television Archive, University of California at Los Angeles.

Harry Ransom Humanities Research Center, University of Texas at Austin.

Holyoke Public Library History Room, Holyoke, MA.

Keith/Albee Vaudeville Theater Collection. University of Iowa, Iowa City.

Margaret Herrick Library, Academy of Motion Picture Arts and Sciences, Beverly Hills.

Mary Baker Eddy Library for the Betterment of Humanity, Boston.

New York Public Library for the Performing Arts Theater Collection, Robinson Locke Collection of Dramatic Scrapbooks. New York. (Abbreviated in the notes as NYPL, Robinson Locke Collection.)

People Magazine Clipping Archive, New York.

Regional History Center, University of Southern California, Los Angeles.

Shubert Archive, New York.

Time-Life Archives, New York.

SELECT BIBLIOGRAPHY

Abel, Richard. "That Most American of Attractions, the Illustrated Song." In *The Sound of Early Cinema,* edited by Richard Abel and Rick Altman, 143–55. Bloomington: Indiana University Press, 2001.

"Afternoons with Actresses." *Green Book Album,* October 1910, 828.

Albee, E. F. "Albee on Vaudeville in 1912–13." *New York Clipper,* October 5, 1912, 10.

——. "The Future of Show Business." *Billboard,* December 19, 1914, 38.

——. "Keith Vaudeville." *New York Clipper,* February 15, 1913, 8.

——. "Twenty Years of Vaudeville." *Theatre Magazine,* May 1920, 408.

Allen, Robert C. "Contra the Chaser Theory." In *Film before Griffith,* edited by John L. Fell, 105–15. Berkeley: University of California Press, 1983.

——. *Horrible Prettiness: Burlesque and American Culture.* Chapel Hill: University of North Carolina Press, 1991.

——. "The Movies in Vaudeville: Historical Context of the Movies as Popular Entertainment." In Balio, *American Film Industry,* 57–82.

——. "Vaudeville and Film 1895–1915: A Study in Media Interaction." PhD diss., University of Iowa, 1977.

"Another Salome Heralded." *New York Dramatic Mirror,* August 1, 1908, 14.

"A. P. Moore Dies; Envoy to Poland," *New York Times,* February 18, 1930, 1, 17.

Association des familles Tanguay inc. *Tanguay, Tanguer et Durer.* Sillery: Quebec, 3rd quarter 2005.

"At the Theatres: Brooklyn Bijou—A Good Fellow." *New York Dramatic Mirror,* April 30, 1904, 14.

"B. F. Keith Dead." *New York Clipper,* April 4, 1914, 1.

Balio, Tino, ed. *The American Film Industry.* Madison: University of Wisconsin Press, 1985.

——. "A Novelty Spawns a Small Business, 1894–1908." In Balio, *American Film Industry,* 3–26.

——. "Struggles for Control, 1908–1930." In Balio, *American Film Industry,* 103–32.

Banner, Lois. *American Beauty.* Chicago: University of Chicago Press, 1983.

Barry, Ed. "Eva Tanguay—'I Don't Care' Girl—Slips Away, Taking an Era with Her." *Variety,* January 15, 1947, 46+.

Barrymore, Ethel. *Memories: An Autobiography.* New York: Harper & Brothers, 1955.

——. "My Reminiscences." *Delineator,* September 1923, 6–7+.

Benjamin, Walter. *The Work of Art in the Age of Mechanical Reproduction.* 1936. Reprint, New York: Classic Books America, 2009.

Bilodeau, Therese. "The French in Holyoke (1850–1900)." *Historical Journal of Massachusetts* 3, no.1 (1974): 1–12.

Bizot, Richard. "The Turn-of-the-Century Salome Era: High- and Pop-Culture Variations on the Dance of the Seven Veils." *Choreography and Dance* 2, no. 3 (1992): 71–87.

"Blames Eva Tanguay." *New York Times,* March 9, 1909, 2:6.

Bordwell, David, Janet Staiger, and Kristin Thompson. *The Classical Hollywood Cinema: Film Style and Mode of Production to 1960.* New York: Columbia University Press, 1985.

Braudy, Leo. *The Frenzy of Renown: Fame and Its History.* New York: Vintage Books, 1986.

Brault, Gerard J. *The French-Canadian Heritage in New England.* Hanover, NH: University Press of New England, 1986.

Brockett, Oscar G. *History of the Theatre.* 6th ed. Boston: Ally and Bacon, 1991.

Bryan, Jodelle L. "From Vaudeville to the Silver Screen: Popular Entertainment in Lancaster, 1900–1930." *Journal of the Lancaster County Historical Society* 95 (1993): 112.

Burritt, Bailey B. "Drunkenness in Massachusetts." *Survey,* May 7, 1910, 202–3.

"The Business of Vaudeville." *Saturday Evening Post,* May 24, 1924, 196.

Caffin, Caroline. *Vaudeville: The Book.* New York: Mitchell Kennerley, 1914.

Calvin, Kenneth W. "The Big Idea of Fanchon and Marco." *Dance Magazine,* March 1929, 14–16, 63.

"C. F. Zittel, 66, Dies; Publisher of Zit's." *New York Times,* January 31, 1943, 44.

Cherniavsky, Felix. *The Salome Dancer: The Life and Times of Maud Allan.* Toronto: McClelland & Stewart, 1991.

Cocks, Dorothy. "What about Plastic Surgery?" *Good Housekeeping,* June 1930, 152–56.

Coffin, Harriet. "All Sorts and Kinds of Salomes." *Theatre,* April 1909, 132–33.

Cohen, Joe. "Blame High-Pressure Selling of Talent for Vaudeville's Latter-Day Setback." *Variety,* January 7, 1953, 249.

"Colonial: Eva Tanguay a Big Hit." *New York Dramatic Mirror,* April 20, 1907, 17.

Custen, George F. *Bio/Pics: How Hollywood Constructed Public History.* New Brunswick, NJ: Rutgers University Press, 1992.

——. *Twentieth Century's Fox: Darryl F. Zanuck and the Culture of Hollywood.* New York: Basic Books, 1997.

Dale, Alan. "'My Lady' Distinctly Fishy." *New York Journal,* February 12, 1901, 8.

Davis, Hartley. "In Vaudeville." *Everybody's Magazine,* August 1905, 232.

Davis, Peter A. "The Syndicate/Shubert War." In Taylor, *Inventing Times Square,* 147–57.

deCordova, Richard. *Picture Personalities: The Emergence of the Star System in America.* Urbana: University of Illinois Press, 1990.

DiCarlo, Ella Merkel. *Holyoke-Chicopee: A Perspective.* Brattleboro, VT: Book Press, 1982.

Dickinson, John Alexander. *A Short History of Quebec.* Montreal: McGill-Queen's University Press, 2000.

Dimeglio, John. *Vaudeville U.S.A.* Bowling Green, OH: Bowling Green University Popular Press, 1973.

Douglas, Ann. *The Feminization of American Culture.* New York: Farrar, Straus and Giroux, 1977.

Douglas, Susan J. *Listening In: Radio and the American Imagination.* New York: Times Books, 1999.

Downer, Alan S. *The Eminent Tragedian: William Charles Macready.* Cambridge, MA: Harvard University Press, 1966.

Dudden, Faye E. *Women in the American Theatre: Actresses and Audiences, 1790–1870.* New Haven, CT: Yale University Press, 1994.

Eddy, Mary Baker. *Science and Health with Key to the Scriptures.* Boston: First Church of Christ, Scientist, 1971.

"E. F. Albee, Co-Founder of Vaudeville," *New York Times,* March 23, 1930, 4:6.

"E. F. Albee Dies at Palm Beach." *New York Times,* March 12, 1930, 32:2.

Eichenwald, Wes. "Americans: Eva Tanguay." *American History,* December 2001, 26.

Erenberg, Lewis. "Impresarios of Broadway Nightlife," In Taylor, *Inventing Times Square,* 158–77.

"Eva Tanguay Arrested." *New York Times,* March 2, 1910, 18:4.

"Eva Tanguay as 'Salome.'" *New York Clipper,* August 15, 1908, 653.

"Eva Tanguay Eager to Help." *Los Angeles Times,* August 1, 1942, 2:3.

"Eva Tanguay Gets Fine Reception at Mt. Park Casino." *Holyoke Transcript,* June 30, 1931, 6.

"Eva Tanguay Left $500." *New York Times,* January 24, 1947, 16:2.

"Eva Tanguay Makes Broad Claim." *New York Dramatic Mirror,* September 26, 1908, 17.

"Eva Tanguay, of 'I Don't Care' Fame, Dies at 68." *Los Angeles Times,* January 12, 1947, 1:3.

"Eva Tanguay Opens a Shop." *New York Times,* March 10, 1935, 8:3.

"Eva Tanguay, 69, Dies on Coast; Vaudeville's 'I Don't Care' Girl." *New York Herald Tribune,* January 12, 1947, v.

"Eva Tanguay Sues Railroad." *Holyoke Daily Transcript,* February 25, 1906, 6:2.

"Evolution of Cheap Vaudeville." *Variety,* December 14, 1907, 10.

Farnsworth, Marjorie. *The Ziegfeld Follies.* New York: Bonanza Books, 1956.

Fields, Armond. *Sophie Tucker: First Lady of Show Business.* Jefferson, NC: McFarland, 2003.

Fleischer, Mary Rita. "Collaborative Projects of Symbolist Playwrights and Early Modern Dancers." PhD diss., City University of New York, 1998.

Forbes, John, Alexander Tweedie, and John Conolly, eds. *The Cyclopaedia of Practical Medicine.* Vol. 1. Philadelphia: Lea and Blanchard, 1845.

Franco-American Centennial Committee. *Souvenir Program: The Franco-Americans Honor Holyoke's Historic Hundredth.* Holyoke, MA: Franco-American Centennial Committee. June, 1973.

French-Canadian Genealogical Society of Connecticut. *Connecticut Maple Leaf* 10 (Summer 2001): 28.

Friedman, Sam. "Girlesk in New York." *New York Inquirer,* May 17, 1931, 15.

Furia, Philip. "Irving Berlin: Troubadour of Tin Pan Alley." In Taylor, *Inventing Times Square,* 191–211.

"The Future of Show Business." *Billboard,* December 19, 1914, 38.

Gabler, Neil. *Winchell: Gossip, Power, and the Culture of Celebrity.* New York: Alfred A. Knopf, 1994.

Gänzl, Kurt. *Lydia Thompson: Queen of Burlesque.* New York: Routledge, 2002.

Garber, Marjorie. *Vested Interests: Cross-Dressing and Cultural Anxiety.* New York: Routledge, 1992.

"Gertrude Hoffman Arrested." *New York Clipper,* July 31, 1909, 629.

Gilbert, Douglas. *American Vaudeville: Its Life and Times.* New York: Dover, 1940.

Gilfoyle, Timothy J. "Policing of Sexuality." In Taylor, *Inventing Times Square,* 297–314.

Glenn, Susan A. *Female Spectacle: The Theatrical Roots of Modern Feminism.* Cambridge, MA: Harvard University Press, 2000.

Gold, Arthur, and Robert Fizdale. *The Divine Sarah.* New York: Alfred A. Knopf, 1991.

Golden, Eve. "Julian Eltinge: The Queen of Old Broadway." *TheaterWeek,* July 31–August 6, 1995, 21.

Gomery, Douglas. "The Coming of Sound: Technological Change in the American Film Industry." In Balio, *American Film Industry,* 229–52.

——. *Shared Pleasures: A History of Movie Presentation in the United States.* Madison: University of Wisconsin Press, 1992.

Goodman, Ezra. "A Merry Madcap." *Collier's,* February 16, 1952, 15.

Green, Constance McLaughlin. *Holyoke Massachusetts: A Case History of the Industrial Revolution in America.* New Haven, CT: Yale University Press, 1939.

Grossman, Barbara W. *Funny Woman: The Life and Times of Fanny Brice.* Bloomington: Indiana University Press, 1991.

Gunning, Tom. "The Cinema of Attractions: Early Film, Its Spectator and the Avant-Garde." In *Early Cinema: Space, Frame, Narrative,* edited by Thomas Elsaesser, 56–62. London: BFI, 1990.

Hamilton, Marybeth. *When I'm Bad, I'm Better: Mae West, Sex, and American Entertainment.* Berkeley: University of California Press, 1997.

Handelman, David. "Where the Lake Is Deep and the Accent French." *New York Times,* September 4, 2005, travel sec., 7.

Harper, Wyatt. *The Story of Holyoke.* Holyoke, MA: Centennial Committee,1973.

Harris, Neil. *Humbug: The Art of P. T. Barnum.* Chicago: University of Chicago Press, 1973.

Harrison, Patricia King, ed. *The American Film Institute Catalog of Motion Pictures Produced in the United States: Feature Films, 1911–1920.* Berkeley: University of California Press, 1988.

Hartford, William F. *Working People of Holyoke: Class and Ethnicity in a Massachusetts Mill Town, 1850–1960.* New Brunswick, NJ: Rutgers University Press, 1990.

"Havemeyer Estate Divided." *New York Times,* July 2, 1899, 1.

Hendricks, Gordon. "The History of the Kinetoscope." In Balio, *American Film Industry,* 43–56.

Hickman, Walter D. "Tanguay Tells Her Real Age to World." *Indianapolis Times,* November 10, 1927.

Higgins, Harvey Alexander, Jr. "The Origin of Vaudeville." *New York Dramatic Mirror,* May 13, 1919, 719–20.

Hodes, Martha. *White Women, Black Men: Illicit Sex in the 19th Century South.* New Haven, CT: Yale University Press, 1997.

Holusha, John. "A Theater's Muses, Rescued." *New York Times,* March 24, 2000, B1, B6.

Holyroyd, Michael. *A Strange Eventful History: The Dramatic Lives of Ellen Terry, Henry Irving, and Their Remarkable Families.* New York: Picador, 2008.

"Hugh Stanton Dead." *New York Dramatic Mirror,* August 31, 1907, 14.

"I Don't Care." Sung by Eva Tanguay. *Music from the New York Stage, 1890–1920.* Volume 2, *1908–1913.* E. Sussex: Pavilion Records, 1993.

"The I Don't Care Girl." *Variety,* December 24, 1952, 14.

Inglis, Ruth A. "Self-Regulation in Operation." In Balio, *American Film Industry,* 377–400.

Inglis, William. "Morals and Moving Pictures." *Harper's Weekly,* July 30, 1910, 12–13.

"Irene Franklin Wins!" *New York Clipper,* January 8, 1910, 1217.

James, Edward T., ed. *Notable American Women 1607–1950.* Vol. 3, P–Z. Cambridge, MA: Belknap Press of Harvard University Press, 1971.

"Jardin de Paris: 'Follies of 1909.'" *Theatre Magazine,* August 1909, 37.

Jenkins, Henry. *What Made Pistachio Nuts: Early Sound Comedy and the Vaudeville Aesthetic.* New York: Columbia University Press, 1992.

Jessel, George. *Elegy in Manhattan.* New York: Holt, Rinehart and Winston, 1961.

Johnson, Howard, and Theodore Morse. *M-O-T-H-E-R: A Word That Means the World to Me.* New York: Leo Feist, 1915.

"Julian Eltinge, Impersonator, 67." *New York Times,* March 8, 1941.

Kalush, William, and Larry Sloman. *The Secret Life of Houdini: The Making of America's First Superhero.* New York: Atria Books, 2007.

"The Keith Anniversary." *New York Clipper,* November 29, 1913, 6.

Kellaway, Kate. "Up the Garden Path." Review of *Frances Hodgson Burnett: The Unpredictable Life of the Author of "The Secret Garden,"* by Gretchen Gerzina. *Observer,* April 4, 2004, 15.

Kibler, M. Alison. *Rank Ladies: Gender and Cultural Hierarchy in American Vaudeville.* Chapel Hill: University of North Carolina Press, 1999.

Kitchen, Karl K. "Undone by a Song." *Theatre,* May 1913, 143.

Knee, Stuart E. *Christian Science in the Age of Mary Baker Eddy.* Westport, CT: Greenwood Press, 1994.

Krasner, David. *Resistance, Parody, and Double Consciousness in African American Theatre, 1895–1910.* New York: St. Martin's Press, 1997.

Kunhardt, Dorothy. "Little Lord Fauntleroy: This Is the Centennial of His Creator's Birth." *Life,* December 5, 1949, 71–74, 79.

Latchaw, Austin. "Eva Tanguay Cared a Lot, Kansas City Writer Says." *Kansas City Star,* December 19, 1938.

Laurie, Joe, Jr. *Vaudeville: From the Honky-Tonks to the Palace.* New York: Henry Holt, 1953.

Leach, William. *Land of Desire: Merchants, Power, and the Rise of a New American Culture.* New York: Pantheon Books, 1993.

Leider, Emily Wortis. *Becoming Mae West.* New York: Da Capo Press, 2000.

Lewis, Robert M., ed. *From Traveling Show to Vaudeville: Theatrical Spectacle in America, 1830–1910.* Baltimore: Johns Hopkins University Press, 2003.

Linteau, Paul-André, René Durocher, and Jean-Claude Robert. *Québec: A History, 1867–1929.* Toronto: James Lorimer, 1983.

"Lotta Faust, The Laughing Girl in 'The Liberty Belles.'" *Standard.* September 1901, 9.

Lowry, Ed. *Vaudeville Humor: The Collected Jokes, Routines, and Skits of Ed Lowry.* Carbondale: Southern Illinois University Press, 2002.

Marcus, Sharon. *Between Women: Friendship, Desire, and Marriage in Victorian England.* Princeton, NJ: Princeton University Press, 2007.

Marks, Edward B. *They All Sang: From Tony Pastor to Rudy Vallée.* New York: Viking Press, 1934.

McConnell, Sharon. "Eva Tanguay Part II: Holyoke's 'I Don't Care Girl.'" *Chickuppy and Friends,* June 1985.

McKelway, St. Clair. "The Big Little Man from Brooklyn," In *Reporting at Wit's End: Tales from "The New Yorker,"* 524–619. New York: Bloomsbury, 2010.

McLean, Albert F., Jr. *American Vaudeville as Ritual.* University of Kentucky Press, 1965.

McNamara, Brooks. "The Entertainment District at the End of the 1930s." In Taylor, *Inventing Times Square,* 178–90.

Merritt, Russell. "Nickelodeon Theaters, 1905–1914: Building an Audience for the Movies." In Balio, *American Film Industry,* 83–102.

Miller, Merle. *Plain Speaking: An Oral Biography of Harry S. Truman.* New York: Berkeley Medallion Books, 1974.

Milmine, Georgine. "Mary Baker G. Eddy: The Story of Her Life and the History of Christian Science; Mrs. Eddy and Her First Disciples." *McClure's,* May 1907, 97–116.

——. "Mary Baker G. Eddy: The Story of Her Life and the History of Christian Science; Mrs. Eddy and Her First Disciples." *McClure's,* July 1907, 333–48.

Mordden, Ethan. *Ziegfeld: The Man Who Invented Show Business.* New York: St. Martin's Press, 2008.

Murchison, Charles. *Clinical Lectures on Diseases of the Liver, Jaundice and Abdominal Dropsy.* New York: William Wood, 1868.

"My Lady." *New York Times,* February 12, 1901, 9:2.

"My Lady." *New York Times,* February 13, 1901, 6:6.

"'My Lady,' a Showy Burlesque." *Brooklyn Eagle,* May 7, 1901, 6.

Nasaw, David. *Going Out: The Rise and Fall of Public Amusements.* New York: Basic Books, 1993.

"New York—The Chaperons." *New York Dramatic Mirror,* June 14, 1902, 14.

Oberdeck, Kathryn J. *The Evangelist and the Impresario: Religion, Entertainment, and Cultural Politics in America, 1884–1914.* Baltimore: Johns Hopkins University Press, 1999.

"The Office Boy." *New York Times,* November 3, 1903, 5:2.

Oliver, James. *Abdominal Tumours and Abdominal Dropsy in Women.* London: J & A Churchill, 1895.

Paris, Barry. *Louise Brooks: A Biography.* Minneapolis: University of Minnesota Press, 2000.

Pastor, Tony. "Tony Pastor Recounts the Origin of American 'Vaudeville.'" *Variety,* December 15, 1906, 17, 49.

"The Pavilion Theatre." *Holyoke Daily Transcript,* July 31, 1893, 4.

Peiss, Kathy. *Hope in a Jar: The Making of America's Beauty Culture.* New York: Metropolitan Books, 1998.

"Percy Williams Houses Sold; About $5,000,000," *Variety,* April 6, 1912, 3.

Peters, Brooks. "Gay Deceiver." *Out,* December 1998, 85–87.

Peters, Margot. *The House of Barrymore.* New York: Alfred A. Knopf, 1990.

Petrin, Ronald A. *French Canadians in Massachusetts Politics, 1885–1915.* Philadelphia: Balch Institute Press, 1990.

Piepmeier, Alison. *Out in Public: Configurations of Women's Bodies in Nineteenth-Century America.* Chapel Hill: University of North Carolina Press, 2004.

"Plays and Players." *Theatre* 2, no. 17 (July 1902): 2–8.

Ponce de Leon, Charles, L. *Self-Exposure: Human-Interest Journalism and the Emergence of Celebrity in America, 1890–1940*. Chapel Hill: University of North Carolina Press, 2002.

"Pot Pilot Apparently Ran Out of Fuel." *Washington Post,* April 21, 1998, A10.

Price, Bertha Weston. "Noted Vaudeville Star of Many Years Ago Was Native of the Eastern Townships." *Sherbrooke Daily Record,* March 1, 1947.

Robert, Jacques. *Eva Tanguay, la "vamp" de Broadway*. Dudswell, QC: Société d'histoire de Dudswell, 2000."

Rodger, Gillian M. *Champagne Charlie & Pretty Jemima: Variety Theater in the Nineteenth Century*. Urbana: University of Illinois Press, 2010.

"Roosevelt Aid to Cupid: Political Twist to the Latest of Lillian Russell's Weddings. *New York Times,* June 14, 1912, 1.

Rosen, Jody. "Vanishing Act: In Search of Eva Tanguay, the First Rock Star." *Slate,* Dec. 1, 2009. http://www.slate.com/id/2236658/.

Ross, Charles J. "The Building and Repairing of Vaudeville Sketches." *New York Dramatic Mirror,* July 5, 1911, 5.

Rowe, Kathleen. *The Unruly Woman: Gender and the Genres of Laughter*. Austin: University of Texas Press, 1995.

Russo, Mary. "Female Grotesques: Carnival and Theory." In *Feminist Studies, Critical Studies,* edited by Teresa de Lauretis, 213–29. Bloomington: Indiana University Press, 1986.

Salsinger, Harry G. "Miss Eva Tanguay," *Dayton Herald,* October 8, 1904.

Samuels, Charles, and Louise Samuels. *Once upon a Stage: The Merry World of Vaudeville*. New York: Dodd, Mead, 1974.

Satter, Beryl. *Each Mind a Kingdom: American Women, Sexual Purity, and the New Thought Movement, 1875–1920*. Berkeley: University of California Press, 1999.

"The Screen Shows a New Eva Tanguay." *Moving Picture World,* September 22, 1917, 1872.

Sentilles, Renée M. *Performing Menken: Adah Isaacs Menken and the Birth of American Celebrity*. Cambridge: Cambridge University Press, 2003.

Shaw, Dale. *Titans of the American Stage: Edwin Forrest, the Booths, the O'Neills*. Philadelphia: Westminster Press, 1971.

Sillman, Leonard. *Here Lies Leonard Sillman: Straightened Out at Last*. New York: Citadel Press, 1959.

Silverman, Sime. "Why the Vaudeville Artists of America Should Organize." *Variety,* March 17, 1906, 4.

Slide, Anthony. *The Encyclopedia of Vaudeville*. Westport, CT: Greenwood Press, 1994.

———, ed. *Selected Vaudeville Criticism*. Metuchen, NJ: Scarecrow Press, 1988.

Smith, Frederick James. "'I Do Care!' Says Eva Tanguay." *New York Dramatic Mirror,* January 27, 1915, 30.

Smith, Hubbard Madison. *Historical Sketches of Old Vincennes, Founded 1732: Its Institutions and Churches, Embracing Collateral Incidents and Biographical Sketches of Many Persons and Events Connected Therewith*. Vincennes, IN, 1902.

Snyder, Robert W. "Vaudeville and the Transformation of Popular Culture." In Taylor, *Inventing Times Square,* 133–46.

———. *The Voice of the City.* New York: Oxford University Press, 1989.

Southworth, John. *The English Medieval Minstrel.* Suffolk: Boydell Press, 1989.

Stanton, Stephen S. Introduction. *"Camille" and Other Plays,* edited by Stephen S. Stanton. New York: Hill and Wang, 1957.

Steadman, Thomas Lathrop. *Steadman's Medical Dictionary.* Baltimore: Williams & Wilkins, 1976.

Stein, Charles W., ed. *American Vaudeville as Seen by Its Contemporaries.* New York: Knopf, 1984.

"Still Another Salome." *New York Dramatic Mirror,* August 15, 1908, 14.

Tanguay, Dany. *Jean Tanguy et Marie Brochu, pionners de Saint-Vallier de Bellechasse 1694.* Sillery, Quebec: l'Association des familles Tanguay inc., 2000.

Tanguay, Eva. "Eva Tanguay on 'Imitators.'" *Variety,* March 6, 1909, 5.

———. "I Care at Last." *Liberty,* February 11, 1933, 43–44.

———. "I Don't Care." *American Weekly,* December 29, 1946, 12–13.

———. "I Don't Care." *American Weekly,* January 5, 1947, 17.

———. "I Don't Care." *American Weekly,* January 12, 1947, 6–7.

———. "I Don't Care." *American Weekly,* January 19, 1947, 6–7.

———. "I Don't Care." *American Weekly,* January 26, 1947, 6–7.

———. "Success." *Variety,* December 12, 1908, 121.

"Tanguay Would Stop Film." *New York Dramatic Mirror,* July 7, 1915, 32.

Tarbell, Ida. "The Business of Being a Woman." *American Magazine,* March 1912, 565–67.

Taylor, William R., ed. *Inventing Times Square: Culture and Commerce at the Crossroads of the World.* Baltimore: Johns Hopkins University Press, 1991.

Titone, Nora. *My Thoughts Be Bloody: The Bitter Rivalry between Edwin and John Wilkes Booth That Led to an American Tragedy.* New York: Free Press, 2010.

"'Tony' Pastor." *New York Clipper,* September 5, 1908, 722.

Trav S. D. *No Applause—Just Throw Money.* New York: Faber and Faber, 2005.

"Trixie Friganza Is Dead at 84; Starred in Musical Comedies." *New York Times,* February 29, 1955.

Tucker, Sophie. *Some of These Days: The Autobiography of Sophie Tucker.* Garden City, NY: Garden City, 1945.

"United Booking Offices Cleans Up All 'Big Time.'" *Variety,* May 4, 1912, 5.

"Vaudeville's Clearing House." *New York Clipper,* November 29, 1913, 1.

Vazzana, Eugene Michael. *Silent Film Necrology.* Jefferson, NC: McFarland, 2001.

"Victoria—My Lady." *New York Dramatic Mirror,* February 23, 1901, 16.

Walters, Frederick Rufenacht. *A Household Dictionary of Medicine, Preventative and Curative.* London: Sonnenschein, 1890.

Westerfield, Jane. "An Investigation of the Life Styles and Performance of Three Singer-Comediennes of American Vaudeville: Eva Tanguay, Nora Bayes and Sophie Tucker." PhD diss., Ball State University, 1987.

"What Pleases in Vaudeville." *Criterion,* September 1900, 24.

"The White Rats Urge Protection of Originality." *Variety,* May 2, 1908, 8.

Williams, Henrietta. "The Founder of Christian Science." *New England Magazine,* November 1899, 291–304.

Wilson, Marion. "'Way Up Where Breezes Blow on Broadway's Greatest Show:' Establishing the Ziegfeld Brand, 1907–1911." Unpublished manuscript, City University of New York Graduate Center, 2003.

Witmark, Isidore, and Isaac Goldberg. *From Ragtime to Swingtime: The Story of the House of Witmark*. New York: Da Capo Press, 1976.

Wolf, Rennold. "The Sort of Fellow Julian Eltinge Really Is." *Green Book Magazine,* November 1913, 793–803.

Woods, Leigh. "Sarah Bernhardt and the Refining of American Vaudeville." *Theatre Research International* 18 (Spring 1993): 16–24.

Index

Note: Page numbers in *italics* indicate illustrations.